REORDERING CARIBBEAN FUTURES IN THE FIRES OF GLOBAL CHANGE

REORDERING CARIBBEAN FUTURES IN THE FIRES OF GLOBAL CHANGE

EDITED BY

Patricia Northover, Richard L. Bernal, Hamid A. Ghany and Natalie Dietrich Jones

The University of the West Indies Press
Mona • St Augustine • Cave Hill • Global • Five Islands

The University of the West Indies Press
7A Gibraltar Hall Road, Mona
Kingston 7, Jamaica
www.uwipress.com

A catalogue record of this book is available from the
National Library of Jamaica.

ISBN: 978-976-640-982-1 (paper)
978-976-640-983-8 (ePub)

Cover image *Red Bark, Black Wings* by Stefanie Thomas Gilbert-Roberts.
Red Bark. Black Wings weaves a story of resilience, transformation, and deep-root-edness. The steadfast gumbo limbo, native to the region, is a historically significant tree especially with respect to its healing properties and its lightweight yet resilient wood. An endangered swallowtail butterfly, predominantly black, represents one of the largest butterfly species found in the Caribbean. It is symbolic of fragility, adaptation, defiance, and underlines the need for the restoration and protection of natural habitats. The sun is an eternal force guiding the balance of nature and human existence. The variations of blues evoke challenges and possibilities with the ever-changing currents of Caribbean life. The interplay of these elements speaks to fragile ecosystems – where roots, wings, and waves speak to evolution and survival in tumultuous times.

Cover and book design by Robert Harris
Set in Minion Pro 11.2/15 x 24.

Printed in the United States of America

Contents

Part 1. Global Power Shifts and Visions of New World Orderings

Part 4. People on the Move – Mobility Justice for Changing Worlds

Appendices

List of Figures

List of Tables

Preface

NOWHERE IS THE NOTION THAT GLOBALIZATION IS A double-edged sword better understood than in the Caribbean. The conception, and comprehension of everyday life, find clarity, with stark definition, in all aspects of civil society, systems of production, and relations with the world beyond. The academic content gathered here under the theme *Reordering Caribbean Futures in the Fires of Global Change* takes these considerations as a vehicle for rethinking sustainable development paths.

The gladiators of globalization insisted that a level playing field and economic freedom for all would follow, while their discursive adversaries pointed to the visible truth that the role of micro-nation state was diminished and marginalized by market forces controlled by large nations and their super corporate conglomerates. The Caribbean became the classic community where these seemingly contradictory forces contended. Indeed, the impact of globalization on the nation-building process was so profound that, for the state system, it was akin to driving a vehicle on thin ice. With weakened control and the inevitability of implosion, the Caribbean's economic exposure and vulnerability was complete. Sustainability, as a result, became the substance of development discourse in a region derailed by the globalization juggernaut.

Then came the 2007/2008 global finance crisis, quickly followed by compelling evidence of a chronic non-communicable disease pandemic, and more destructive earthquakes, hurricanes and rising sea levels. Behind these latter events is the power of climate change, which poses an existential threat to the region and other small island states. The Caribbean, still grappling with the negative effects of financing its post-colonial development with debt, could not have experienced a more devastating series of circumstances, all linked to the umbilical cord of centuries of extractive colonialism.

The arrival of the COVID-19 pandemic in March 2020 served as a can opener, revealing the concealed persistence of colonialism in general, and its specific legacies. Ranked as the most (if not the only) colonized region in the global economy, the Caribbean has attracted doomsday scenarios from pessimistic quarters. After detailed self-assessments, however, the region seems more prepared for a positive response to new and emerging economic possibilities. The search is on, then, for more sustainable development paths.

The digital development direction, nonetheless, has exposed for all to see the divide that defines the polarity in competitive performance between rich and powerful, and small, weak nations. The cyber chasm within which the Caribbean falls serves as a metaphor for the development decline as well as the galvanization necessary to rekindle transformation and sustainable efforts.

This volume shows that a considerable amount of work is necessary in order to build out a competitive knowledge economy that is consistent with the services economy development model, the kind of contribution the university sector is best prepared and positioned to provide and lead. Economic competitiveness is linked directly to alignment with campuses and their research output. Without an aligned research and development strategy, sustainability cannot be secured. This is an assertion of a fundamental truth, one that is already well known and respected in those parts of the developing world where considerable economic strides are daily reported. The Caribbean is well positioned to respond to the methods of these nations, while indigenizing their excellences as learning societies. This approach will serve to pave the way for the region to emerge and excel.

PROFESSOR SIR HILARY BECKLES
VICE-CHANCELLOR, THE UNIVERSITY OF THE WEST INDIES

Acknowledgements

THIS PUBLICATION PROJECT HAS HAD A LONG HISTORY and gestation process. The original idea for our intervention was sparked in 2018 by the nineteenth annual conference hosted by the Sir Arthur Lewis Institute of Social and Economic Studies (SALISES) in Jamaica, which spoke to "Sustainable Futures for the Caribbean: Critical Interventions and the 2030 Agenda". It was a special moment of looking ahead, yet in the context of celebrating the seventieth anniversary of the University of the West Indies and its signal contributions to regional and national development, spurred on by the desires of Caribbean peoples' intent to escape the yoke of colonial tutelage and exploitation.

Having those achievements in mind, and nestled in the home of cultural, intellectual, political and social heroes such as Claude McKay, Robert Nesta Marley and Louise Bennett-Coverley (Ms Lou), Sylvia Wynter, George Beckford, Norman Girvan, Una Marson, Erna Brodber, Rex Nettleford, Marcus Garvey and the legendary Nanny of the Maroons, to name but a few, we challenged ourselves to think critically about our futures in the context of the freshly minted global sustainable development goals (the SDGs). These goals were already under pressure from catastrophic climate change in the Caribbean region, following the dreadful double impact of category five Hurricanes Maria and Irma in 2017, which caused devastating damage and loss of life, especially within the Leeward Islands, Lesser Antilles, Puerto Rico and the United States. In this context we called upon friends and partners to help us execute our bold hopes for sustainable futures through this conference. We are grateful to those who joined us in Montego Bay, even in the midst of a state of emergency, and enabled us to assemble a rich and diverse community of international and regional scholars, graduate students, local residents, government officials, members of the private sector and non-governmental agencies. We were deliberate in choosing Montego Bay, Jamaica's second capital city, as our host community as we wished to consider afresh the meaning of independence, and the possibilities of a closer Caribbean. A gathering in September 1947 in MoBay was convened to reflect on a closer regional association, mooted then within the emerging imaginary of a Federation of the West Indies. Since then, our dreams of a stronger and closer Caribbean have been carried by the indomitable energies of the everyday strugglers against oppression, drawn from every cultural stripe and sexual orientation, beginning with our formerly enslaved Afro-descendant black workers and indentured labourers, preachers, indigenous resisters and a myriad of cunning Creole aspirants for a better life. Drawing on these rich streams of overlapping histories, we mulled on the contradictions of our development process, contextualized by the wicked problems of social crises, climate change, environmental vulnerability and colonial legacies, but also shaped by a rich history of protest, change, heroism and community activism.

Given our book's conceptual origin through this conference, we are sincerely grateful for the vital conference support we received from the Government of Jamaica, through Minister of Tourism, the Honourable Edmund Bartlett, and his special advisor, Professor Lloyd Waller, and the Bureau of Gender Affairs, represented then by Mrs Siddier Chambers. We are also thankful for the generous support of corporate Jamaica, through the sponsorship of the Jamaica National Group, as well as from the local arm of the international non-governmental organization, National Integrity Action, and from the Fe We Jamaica project, led by Professor Rosalea Hamilton. Our conference intervention also received support from the Caribbean Development Bank; the UN Economic Commission for Latin America and the Caribbean (ECLAC), Subregional Headquarters for the Caribbean; the United Nations Development Programme (UNDP); the Office of the Pro Vice Chancellor for Graduate Studies and Research at the University of the West Indies; the Office of the Vice Chancellor at UWI; and the Institute of Caribbean Studies, Washington, DC. With their support we mobilized a powerful cross-section of community actors and youths, through complementary youth and community forums, who helped us speak to the issues of equity and intersectional youth and gender justice as the *sine qua non* for any possible sustainable development future.

From then to now has been a long journey of twists and turns, as we planned how we wanted to lead in rethinking development, and as we pivoted in light of the unique historical conjunctures we faced through global changes, social inequalities and environmental turbulence. Betwixt and between initial plans for a book series and the solicitation of original papers, a special issue was collated from a selection of the 2018 conference papers that was published in our flagship Caribbean journal, *Social and Economic Studies,* in 2020; a global health pandemic; and radical shifts in the global landscape that pushed us to engage with pivotal voices on Caribbean futures, and provoked us to shift our scope for engagement. Timelines also had to shift as publishers changed and then in the midst of the final stretch home, we were rattled to the bone with the sudden and untimely death in the spring of 2023 of our collaborator and co-editor, Ambassador Richard Bernal, whose dedication to the project of rethinking Caribbean realities and futures was profound. We wish to thank his amazing wife, Margaret, and his estate, for allowing us to publish his paper (with Professor Don Marshall) on China in the Caribbean. We are also deeply indebted to all the authors who lent us their patience as we sought to move ahead in the context of the unpredictable setbacks and challenges we encountered. Special thanks to Ms Shar-Lee Amori, who helped at an important moment in formatting chapters to prepare the manuscript for the review process at the University of the West Indies Press. We also wish to express our deep appreciation to the commissioning editor, Mrs Christine Randle, for her guidance, and to the anonymous reviewers who provoked us to further sharpen our interventions. Thanks as well to the first set of reviewers whom we called upon to help us pursue a rigorous assessment of the ideas assembled here, even before heading to the publisher. The remaining errors and limitations of this work rest fully on our shoulders as editors.

Finally, we would also like to thank the Pro Vice-Chancellor for Graduate Studies and Research, Professor Aldrie Henry Lee, (former University Director of SALISES), for her encouragement to complete this publication project, and The University of the West Indies for providing us with a research and publications grant to complete this work. Despite its long gestation from concept to realization, this collection of critical interventions on the challenges facing us in the region remains salient to our time of climate and geopolitical disorder, and relevant to underpinning demands for just transitions and alternative futures. As we seek to reorder our futures in the context of multiplying climate shocks and chronic indebtedness, we acknowledge that we are at this moment still a Caribbean in turmoil – from the anglophone region to the Hispanic, Dutch and francophone creole spaces. We are still beset by controversial foreign interventions, multiple insecurities and a deep questioning as to who we are and what we believe our communities to be. From this turbulent present, what do we want to inherit as a sustainable future? We wish to dedicate this volume to all those who have struggled for a different Caribbean, including our dear colleague and mentor, Ambassador Bernal. To our friends and family who gave us words of encouragement as we worked to complete this publication, we thank you for your support.

Abbreviations and Acronyms

ACP	African, Caribbean and Pacific countries
ACS	Association of Caribbean States
ADF	Augmented Dickey-Fuller
AML/CFT	Anti-Money Laundering/Combating the Financing of Terrorism
ARDL	Auto-Regressive Distributed Lag
BRI	Belt and Road Initiative
CAF	Development Bank of Latin America and the Caribbean
CARICOM	Caribbean Community
CARIFORUM	Caribbean Forum
CARPHA	Caribbean Public Health Agency
CBERA	Caribbean Basin Economic Recovery Act
CBI	Caribbean Basin Initiative
CBO	community-based organization
CCECC	China Civil Engineering Construction Corporation
CCSA	Caribbean Climate-Smart Accelerator
CCRIF-SPC	Caribbean Catastrophe Risk Insurance Facility – Segregated Portfolio Company
CDEMA	Caribbean Disaster and Emergency Management Agency
CEPEP	Community-Based Environmental Protection and Enhancement Programme
CELAC	Community of Latin American and Caribbean States
CFR	case fatality rate
CLAC Fund	China-LAC Cooperation Fund

CRT	critical race theory
COVAX	COVID-19 Vaccines Global Access
COVID-19	novel coronavirus 2019
CSGM	Climate Studies Group Mona
CSME	Caribbean Single Market and Economy
CSPS	Community, Social and Personal Services
DRR	disaster risk reduction
ECLAC	Economic Commission for Latin America and the Caribbean
ECM	error correction model
EDD	enhanced due diligence
EDF	European Development Fund
EPA	Economic Partnership Agreement
EPHF	Essential Public Health Function
ESDC	Employment and Social Development Canada
EU-CARIFORUM	Economic Partnership Agreement between the European Union and CARIFORUM countries
EVI	Economic Vulnerability Index
FATF	Financial Action Task Force
FAO	Food and Agriculture Organization
FDI	foreign direct investment
FFD	financing for development
FTA	free trade agreement
GCF	Green Climate Fund
GCM	Global Climate Model
GDP	gross domestic product
GNI	gross national income
HSF	Heritage and Stabilisation Fund
ICT	information and communications technology
IDA	International Development Association
IDB	Inter-American Development Bank
IFI	international financial institution
IHR	international health regulations

IMF	International Monetary Fund
IOM	International Organization for Migration
IPCC	Intergovernmental Panel on Climate Change
IR	international relations
IUCN/SSC	International Union for Conservation of Nature/ Species Survival Commission
KPSS	Kwiatkowski–Phillips–Schmidt–Shin
KYC	Know Your Customer
LAC	Latin American and the Caribbean
LDIFF	Log of Productivity Differential
LNG	liquefied natural gas
LROP	Log of Real Oil Price
MW	megawatt
MDGs	Millennium Development Goals
MFN	most favoured nation
NAFTA	North American Free Trade Agreement
NCD	non-communicable disease
NGO	non-governmental organization
NOTL	Niagara-on-the-Lake
NPIS	National Public Investment Systems
OACPS	Organisation of African, Caribbean and Pacific States
OAS	Organization of American States
ODA	official development assistance
OECS	Organisation of Eastern Caribbean States
PAHO	Pan American Health Organization
PAYE	Pay-As-You-Earn
PCR	polymerase chain reaction (test)
PP	Phillips-Perron
PPPs	public-private partnerships
RCM	regional climate model
RCP	Representative Concentration Pathway
REER	real effective exchange rate

ROP	real oil price
SAMOA	SIDS Accelerated Modalities of Action (SAMOA Pathway)
SAWP	Seasonal Agricultural Worker Program
SARS-CoV-2	Severe Acute Respiratory Syndrome Coronavirus version 2
SDGs	Sustainable Development Goals
SDR	Special Drawing Rights
SIDS	small island developing states
SITC	Standard International Trade Classification
SLR	sea level rise
SOEs	state-owned enterprises
SPS	sanitary and phytosanitary measures
SST	sea surface temperature
SRT	social representations theory
SWF	sovereign wealth fund
TECA	Trade and Economic Cooperation Agreement between the European Union and the United Kingdom
TTIP	Transatlantic Trade and Investment Partnership
UHC	universal health coverage
UK-CARIFORUM	Economic Partnership Agreement between the United Kingdom and CARIFORUM countries
UNEP	United Nations Environment Programme
UNESCO	United Nations Educational, Scientific and Cultural Organization
UNFCCC	United Nations Framework Convention on Climate Change
UNHCR	United Nations High Commissioner for Refugees
UNICEF	United Nations Children's Fund
UWI	The University of the West Indies
WHO	World Health Organization
WITS	World integrated Trade Solution

Introduction

PATRICIA NORTHOVER, RICHARD L. BERNAL,[1] HAMID A. GHANY,
AND NATALIE DIETRICH JONES

The special enigma of Caribbean peoples may well lie in their never having
settled for a vision of history as something that must or should repeat itself.
(Mintz 1974, 46)

It is in the nature of crises that problems crying out for solution go unresolved.
And it is also in the nature of crises that the solution, that which the future
holds in store, is not predictable. The uncertainty of a critical situation contains
one certainty only – its end. The only unknown quantity is when and how. The
eventual solution is uncertain, but the end of the crisis, a change in the existing
situation – threatening, feared and eagerly anticipated – is not. The question of
the historical future is inherent in the crises. (Koselleck 1988, 127)

WE LIVE IN TIMES OF UNPRECEDENTED AND EXTRAORDINARY CRISIS as the cascading and
interlocking effects of wars, climate change, technological revolutions and
the COVID-19 pandemic impel us to question the forces underpinning the
architecture of our world of work, education, sociality, governance, well-
being and economic globalization processes in the twenty-first century.
Framed by this daunting context as we approach the 2030s, and motivated
by the ideals of the Global Partnership for the Sustainable Development
Agenda, the Sir Arthur Lewis Institute of Social and Economic Studies
(SALISES) at The University of the West Indies (UWI) invites us to discuss,
explore and reflect upon the conflicts, tensions and contradictions that
abound in this contemporary moment. We believe that it is only upon
a platform of broad and deep critical reflection that one may reimagine
Caribbean futures and reorder our economic, social, political and
environmental practices and policies to meet with the well-being of all,

in what Haitian anthropologist Michel-Rolph Trouillot (1992, 21) called our "awkwardly, but definitely 'complex'" Caribbean societies marked by their heterogeneity, historicity and complex articulation with global and colonial regimes of power.

The Caribbean region, as Puerto Rican historian Gaztambide-Géigel (2004) reminds us, is largely an invention created at the turn of the twentieth century, signalling the transition from European hegemony to US imperialism. The idea of a 'Caribbean region' thus emerged as the US *sought to define itself*, vis-à-vis its former masters, in the context of a geopolitical rivalry for spheres of influence and power – as reflected in the United States' ongoing efforts to operationalize its Munroe doctrine of 1823. Yet this projection of hegemony over 'the Caribbean' did not result in a uniform definition or interpretation of the Caribbean, which as Norman Girvan aptly observed, is "often a matter of perspective and of context" (Girvan 2005, 304). While the Jamaican political economist usefully outlined distinctions between an insular or island Caribbean (composed of the islands, the Three Guianas and Belize) and the Greater Caribbean,[2] or entire basin, he also highlighted the limits of treating the Caribbean as a master signifier, or universal trope, simplistically used to cover different linguistic, political and social groups. He further warned against treating with only the English-speaking Caribbean islands, or reducing the Caribbean to the Caribbean Community (CARICOM),[3] – a regional integration grouping formed in 1973 currently comprising fifteen member states and six associate states – thus overshadowing a regional demographic space where the dominant languages spoken are first Spanish and then French as well as Dutch (inclusive of their Creole variants). 'The Caribbean', then, is more than a geographical referent, as it also speaks to a sociocultural, historical and political reality, as reflected in the varying perspectives held of "the Caribbean",[4] as richly discussed by Gaztambide-Géigel (2004) and as innovatively explored in the Caribbean Atlas project, led by Romain Cruz and Kevon Rhiney.[5]

For our intervention, we draw upon a socio-historical conception of the Greater Caribbean, to include its diasporic communities from those mainland (as well as island) territories that have been shaped by modern culture histories rooted in racialized extraction, exploitation and colonialism, and framed by contact zones mediated by the Atlantic Ocean and Caribbean Sea, genocidal violence, the transatlantic slave trade, plantation-scapes and decolonial struggles. We will thus take our departure from Trouillot, who defined the Caribbean as an "open frontier" with regional boundaries that are "notoriously fuzzy" (Trouillot 1992, 19). Moreover, we share Girvan's views that: "The Caribbean of tomorrow will not be an exclusively Anglophone or Hispanic conception; and it will not be tied exclusively to geographical space or definition. If it survives at all it will be a community of shared economic, social and political interests and strategies that encompasses different languages and cultures and the Caribbean Diaspora. It might well include inter-state co-operation, but if so, this will be only one of a number of spheres of interaction" (Girvan 2005, 315).

Our goal in this publication is to facilitate an engagement and exchange among students and academics, development and policy professionals, the media, public servants, civil society groups, diaspora and youth geared towards reimagining Caribbean development futures. We envision that through this text, and future publications to be promoted by SALISES under the theme of "Reimagining Caribbean Futures: Rethinking Sustainable Development Paths", we will extend the effort to challenge the social and institutional powers that sustain untenable development models and ways of thinking.

Certainly, even though the Global South had been seeking to fashion new kinds of 'development' in response to economic globalization and austerity pressures, the novel corona virus pandemic called for a radical rethink of the rules of policy governance in order to meet the multidimensional economic, social and political impacts of the health crises that shook neoliberal globalization mantras at their core. Furthermore, while many island states in the Caribbean may have weathered the COVID-19 storm well, in terms of limiting the loss of life, the global lockdown and the failures to control the spread of the virus in the Americas meant that the Caribbean region – with its high rates of dependency on food imports, remittances and the tourist dollar – is still grappling with protracted processes of economic adjustment and complex social dislocation mediated by age, class, indigeneity, race and gender dynamics (UNDP 2023;

Henry-Lee 2022; Bobb and Worrell 2022; Henry 2022; Obermuller 2022; ECLAC 2020, 2021; Thame 2021; Alleyne et al. 2021; Mooney and Zegarra 2020; UNCTAD 2020a, 2020b, 2021; CAPRI 2021). One also expects that the effects of increasingly destructive environmental and climate change, accelerated global inequalities as well as unstable and shifting international power relations, as reflected in the Ukraine-Russian and Israel-Gaza war, plus the resurgence of far right politics, will only compound this deep state of Caribbean vulnerability.

Sadly, across the world, the global pandemic has also brought forth the ugly face of racial inequalities and vulnerabilities to the frontlines. And, as Latin America and the Caribbean is identified as one of the most unequal regions of the world (UNDP 2021; CAF 2022), the seed of this racial virus, carried by racial capitalism, has been both deadly and devastating in its effects in the Americas (ECLAC 2021; Edwards 2021; Thame 2021). Globally, this legacy of racial ordering has also led to the re-emergence and popularity of authoritarian or strong nationalisms – the face of new patterns of racialization and racism (Thame 2021). Accordingly, in light of our contemporary global geopolitical environment, characterized by pressures of dissolution, fragmentation and transformation in the post-Brexit, post-COVID rising China and "Make America Great Again" moment, regional mainland and island economies are faced with radical opportunities to either sink separately or swim together. Yet many Caribbean states continue to wrestle with high debt service commitments, growth sclerosis, fiscal deficits, a policy implementation deficit disorder, and increasing crime and violence, which altogether undermine their attempts to pivot in response to the new conjunctures of global instability in pursuit of an increasingly suspect sustainable development global agenda (Brisset 2017; UNDP 2021; ECLAC 2023; UNODC 2023). Indeed, in the 2024 *Sustainable Development Report*, Sachs et al. reported that: "On average, only 16 percent of the SDG targets are on track to be met globally by 2030, with the remaining 84 percent showing limited progress or a reversal of progress" (Sachs et al. 2004, viii).

Moreover, while crises abound, the very idea of 'development' itself – often an expression of a neoliberal cosmology and vision – is subject to deep contestation (Corbridge 2007). But, given the persistence of a "will to improve", as Tania Li (2007) has described governmental strategies for 'progress', our development conundrums are likely to throw up increasing confrontations with existing power hierarchies and calls for different modes of governing for planetary survival and human well-being. This is reflected, for example, in the recent call for a 'decolonial ecology' rooted in Caribbean critical thought and practice for undoing modernity's interlocking colonial and environmental fractures (Ferdinand 2022). Relatedly, many global social justice movements have emerged to contest the moral authority of global architectures of power, insisting on the advancement of human dignity and justice, as well as a *decolonial turn for decolonial futures* (Stein et al 2020; Maldonado-Torres 2011). Thus, we have witnessed the rise of global movements such as the #Rhodesmustfall, #MeToo and #BlackLivesMatter campaigns against gendered and racial violence; as well as appeals for diversity and inclusion led by LGBTQI activism, food sovereignty movements led by the peasants of the world, plus global demands for climate as well as decolonial justice to bring an end to racial genocide and ecocide.

Alongside these claims against violence and dispossession that challenge us to consider what it means to be 'human' and to discredit binary and exclusionary modes of thinking that engender nature-human, gender and racial divides, demands have also been made for deeper inclusion in global governance bodies. This time, however, inclusion has been predicated on a reshaping of global rules, norms, standards and regulations, as well as global calls for reparatory justice for the crimes committed against humanity during the colonial era (Beckles 2021). In the mix, there are also appeals for a real recognition of small island states' inherent conditions of vulnerability and a re-imagining of the global architecture of developmental finance. This is a call that resonates well in the Caribbean region, which contains one of the world's largest concentrations of vulnerable small island and mini-states. These small states must individually – and to different degrees, collectively – face the challenge of sustaining their development processes in the context of the increasingly chaotic liberal world order, declining aid resources, economic uncertainties and increasing environmental challenges, especially that of climate change (Maharaj and Lewis-Bynoe 2016; Sheller 2018; Northover 2020). These dangerous conjunctures of contemporary globalization have placed lives, settlements, property, infrastructure and growth in a tailspin of risk and heavy losses (Trotz and Lindo 2013; IMF 2016;

IPCC 2014, 2018; Rhiney 2020). With respect to the above circumstances, the most vulnerable population subgroups will be racialized communities and indigenous populations, women, children, the elderly, youth and coastal communities. As tragically epitomized in the histories of Hispaniola (Haiti and the Dominican Republic) and Guyana, these social group vulnerabilities will be expressed not only in a deepening insecurity (painfully explosive in the case of Haiti),[6] but also in an increasing refugee crises, challenging territorial borders and professed regional solidarities, as well as sovereign state and local capacities for recognition and respect for the 'other'. In the context of this massive unsettling of the Caribbean, the colonial 'backyard' of American archipelagic space, our region finds itself again in revolutionary times, nurtured by a new multipolar world order (Canterbury 2022).

Inevitably then, Caribbean states are increasingly being called on by their populations, through protest movements and insurgent violence, to urgently address the complexity of these evolving pressures – ranging from entangled colonial and liberalization projects to global economic crises, unsustainable debts, as well as climate change and technological revolutions. These trends threaten to deepen already sharp development deficits in Caribbean spaces, as gauged by the presence of high rates of crime and violence, persistent patterns of poverty and vulnerability, as well as inequity and structural inequality, which coalesce to create precarious lives (UNDP 2021; CAF 2022; UNODC 2023; Walker and Clauzel 2023).

As such, even as we draw closer to the 2030s, provoked by the ideals of the Global Sustainable Development Agenda for a world that values people, planet, peace, prosperity and partnership, the deep, growing gaps between vision and reality are palpable (Sachs et al. 2021, 2024; World Bank 2021; Walker and Clauzel 2023). Whether or not the UN Summit of the Future, or the Antigua and Barbuda Agenda for SIDS, the "Renewed Declaration for Resilient Prosperity", endorsed at the 4th United Nations Conference for Small Island Developing States (SIDS) in May 2024, will make a tangible difference to this growing gap, remains to be seen. We hope, however, that this first edited book, in our broader SALISES publication efforts, will act as a thought catalyst for critical and decolonial imaginaries, and for advancing pathways to just and sustainable Caribbean futures. This publication, while an important intervention, does not address other core issues vital to this task, such as decolonizing education for refashioning futures; exploring the form of digital transformations needed for reconfiguring economy and society; stemming the deepening insecurity from crime and violence; or addressing the environmental and social conflicts embedded in the petro-power pursuits in the Caribbean.[7] It would be infeasible for us to do all of this in one work. The vision we hold at SALISES is for a continuation of this critical engagement on topics relevant to Caribbean spaces, which are hotspots for multi-dimensional violence and inequality, as well as for biodiversity, climate change, geohazards and geopolitical shifts. In this collection, organized into four sections, we address contemporary power shifts and new world orderings; highlight the complex dynamics and drivers of resilience in the areas of health, climate change and debt; tackle the legacy of and redirection needed for the oldest integration movement in the Caribbean, CARICOM; and finally, explore the unsettling power of Caribbean migrant bodies and mobilities in contexts of racialized and unprecedented social, political, economic and environmental change, taking place within what Francois Verges (2017) has described as the "Racial Capitalocene". We now turn to an elaboration of these sections.

GLOBAL POWER SHIFTS AND VISIONS OF NEW WORLD ORDERINGS

The opening section examines some aspects of the future international relations of the Caribbean. It consists of three chapters, which discuss relations of the Caribbean with the United States and China, post-Brexit relations with the European Union and the United Kingdom, vulnerabilities of the Caribbean region and possible moves toward a reconstruction of Caribbean economies with greater social justice, strengthened mutual aid and collective sustainability.

The small developing countries of the Caribbean are seriously impacted by international events and the policies of superpowers. Of particular importance are the policies of the United States and China at present and in the foreseeable future. The nature and intensity of their multi-dimensional rivalry has created turbulence in the Caribbean and indeed, throughout the world. The US perceives China as a rival superpower, challenging it across a range of economic, diplomatic and security issues. The United States is especially sensitive to the Chinese growing presence in the Caribbean, an incursion into the traditional American dominance in the region. The implications of the diplomatic jousting are two-fold: first, those emanating from direct policies in the Caribbean, and second, those resulting from US-China relations across the globe. During the first Trump presidency, US-China relations were characterized by escalating turbulence. Subsequent to the election of Joe Biden as president, the United Sates has sought to reduce tensions between Washington and Beijing. This is a work in progress, in which dialogue has been reestablished, but suspicion of China remains particularly strong among the majority of Americans. It is a situation that governments in the region will have to navigate with skill. Richard Bernal and Don Marshall discuss the issues facing the Caribbean with regard to the situation and trends in US-China relations.

Our Caribbean history of engagement with global trans-territorial flows and their ever-changing cultural, social, economic and political forces have conditioned diverse responses to the current neoliberal phase of transnational capitalism. New global forces have been unleashed by changes related to shifts in production and investment functions to the Global South. This, combined with the "relative decline" of the Euro-American industrial powers, can open up spaces for genuine development, democracy and freedom in the Global South.

The United Kingdom's formal departure from the European Union on 1 January 2021 required a systematic rethinking and reorienting of CARIFORUM countries' trading relationships with two of their most important trading partners – the European Union and the United Kingdom. A critical issue for CARIFORUM countries is how can the region's relationship with these long-standing partners, originally within a colonial framework, be transformed in response to contemporary reality and thereby more effectively promote the region's economic development in the future. Alicia Nicholls examines the challenges and opportunities which confront the Caribbean as it seeks to craft strategies for a future of sustainable development.

Nicholls argues that CARIFORUM's relationship with both partners must take full account of arrangements and the evolving dynamics impacting these relationships, in particular, the post-Brexit UK-EU deal and the new trade policy directions it portends. Any reorientation must also be grounded in a comprehensive trade and development strategy, inclusive of government, private sector, civil society and the diaspora. As a pre-requisite to such a policy exercise, the chapter begins with a succinct overview of the phases of EU/UK-CARIFORUM trade from the Lomé agreements to the respective Economic Partnership Agreements between the European Union and CARIFORUM, and the United Kingdom and CARIFORUM. Consideration is given to the implications of the UK-EU Trade and Cooperation Agreement for CARIFORUM countries' relationships with the United Kingdom and the European Union. The challenges and opportunities for reorienting CARIFORUM's relationships with the European Union and the United Kingdom are analysed.

In her chapter, "Against Caribbean Vulnerabilities in the time of COVID-19: Precarious Futures or Visions for Social Justice?", Mimi Sheller outlines some of the vulnerabilities of the region and the fears for its precarious future, as well as more positive considerations of possible moves toward reconstruction of Caribbean economies with greater social justice, strengthened mutual aid and collective sustainability. She argues that alternative development strategies can help Caribbean nations and non-independent territories to become less reliant on extractive industries and tourism – which ultimately will make them more sustainable, more equitable and less vulnerable to climate emergencies in the future. This vision will take concerted effort to shift both internal development policies within the region, and the policies of influential external actors. As such, it is crucial that the Caribbean region lobbies for its own interests at this pivotal moment.

REIMAGINING CARIBBEAN RESILIENCE AND DEBT DYNAMICS
IN THE ANTHROPOCENE

Section two of the text examines the issues of the Caribbean's health vulnerability in the context of the COVID-19 pandemic, debt and development finance and climate resilience in the Anthropocene. These three papers critically explore the multi-dimensional features of vulnerability in Caribbean small island states and pose questions in relation to the suitability of the existing models for securing social, economic and climate resilience in the region.

Faced with the social and economic fallout from the global pandemic in the Caribbean, in the essay "COVID-19: Health Impact and Resilience Dynamics in the Caribbean", Landis, Lalta, La Foucade and Theodore examine the manifestations and implications of the pandemic in terms of its spread (epidemiology) and impact (consequences) as well as the actions taken nationally and regionally (interventions) to mitigate the consequences on and threats to lives, livelihoods and developmental goals. Beyond the immediacy of COVID-19, the analysis highlights the need for a more multi-dimensional perspective on the role of health in fostering – or frustrating – national development and outlines four specific measures, namely, policy commitment to universal coverage; investment in public health goods; health system efficiency grounded in integrated primary care and restructured health financing modalities. This, they argue, would ensure resilience and sustainability of the Caribbean's health, economic and social welfare systems.

In "Debt and Development Finance Models for Caribbean Small States in the Context of Crises", Alleyne and Pantin point out that for most Caribbean countries, categorized as middle-income developing countries on the basis on gross national income (GNI), they are expected to source development finance based on their perceived prospects. The financing model advanced for their development, including financing the SDGs, assumes that local capital markets and access to external bond-related sources are adequate. It is for this reason that their access to concessional finance has declined precipitously and they are mostly ineligible for international development assistance. Alleyne and Pantin argue that this is a flawed model, as these countries are highly vulnerable to a variety of negative shocks and subject to high sovereign country risks, due to the accumulation of a large debt overhang, despite multiple attempts at traditional debt restructuring. Their vulnerability arises from climate change impacts, natural disasters and other negative external shocks, including the COVID-19 pandemic. While the debt of the region is only US\$57.2 billion, Caribbean debt-to-GDP ratios are among the highest in the world and debt service costs are significant. Alleyne and Pantin go on to show that the limited access to bond markets – and the lack of fiscal space – poses severe difficulties for these countries to finance their development. They therefore propose several innovative financing strategies to lower the debt burden and provide long-term, low-cost financing to the region for sustainable development.

The final chapter in this section is "(Re)Imagining a Climate Resilient Future: A Caribbean Approach", which is a multi-authored contribution that draws on a collective brought together by Prof Michael Taylor, a leading climate scientist in the region at The University of the West Indies, to assess challenges and position the region for climate-resilient futures. While adaptation (adjustment to moderate or to exploit actual/expected climate change) and mitigation (reducing greenhouse gas emissions to minimize future impact) are the primary responses to climate change and its compounding impacts, the authors ask the vital question of how the framing of these approaches should be re-imagined for the Caribbean. Twenty-three Caribbean practitioners from a range of fields and representing a variety of perspectives take another look at the future Caribbean from the lens of a re-imagination as a climate-resilient zone. The chapter presents consensus findings on some characteristics of a climate-resilient zone – in the context of the region's climate reality, and urban and population landscapes – and presents an approach to achieving it, premised on six pillars. In so doing, sixteen necessary intervention points (derived from regional action plans) are also identified as minimum targets to advance climate change resilience within the region. The discourse concludes with thoughts about the proposed approach, including timelines for actions, and the kind of leadership needed to achieve the goal.

DIS/INTEGRATION MOVEMENTS IN THE CARIBBEAN – PREDICATES FOR A RESET

Section three comprises three papers, which examine the likely future of CARICOM and its development challenges, while simultaneously addressing the initial collapse of the West Indian Federation in 1962. Ghany examines the declassified British government documents associated with the result of the Jamaican referendum in September 1961, and the responses of the British and West Indian governments to the prospect of continuing the federation without Jamaica, while negotiating with Eric Williams in Trinidad and Tobago about revising its contribution. Ghany is able to tease out the role played by Arthur Lewis in straddling the political minefields of Williams' desire to leave the federation and Grantley Adams' desire to forge a new federation without Jamaica. Through the declassified documents the reader is able to observe the change in the views of Lewis, who was initially keen on having Trinidad and Tobago included in a revised federation without Jamaica, but he eventually advised the Colonial Office to let Trinidad and Tobago go its own way based on his observation of Williams' shift in attitude between October 1961 and January 1962.

Perhaps the final nail in the federation's coffin was the contempt shown by Williams for his fellow premiers and chief ministers when they came to Trinidad for a meeting with the Secretary of State for the Colonies, Reginald Maudling, in January 1962. Errol Barrow was particularly adversely affected by Williams' attitude and he never forgave him for it. That soured relationship remained intact for many years and affected the integration movement.

Roger Hosein, Carlton Thomas and Regan Deonanan examine to what extent the economic realities that existed in Trinidad and Tobago during the 1980–2018 period contributed to the presence of Dutch disease. More specifically, they examine whether the real oil price has an impact on the real effective exchange rate (REER) in Trinidad and Tobago, which is one of the features of Dutch disease. Their chapter has relevance for energy-producing countries in the region, based on the tools of analysis used. Using data from 1980 to 2018, and the ARDL framework of Pesaran, Smith, and Shin (2001), the Bounds test was used to evaluate the existence of a long-run, co-integrating relationship among the variables and the REER. Toda-Yamamoto's (1995) causality testing was also used to confirm ARDL findings and sectoral data was assessed to determine whether other symptoms of the phenomenon were present. The results suggest that symptoms of Dutch disease from the recently concluded commodity boom, as well as the Balassa-Samuelson effect, are present in Trinidad and Tobago. Further, causality tests confirmed that there was unidirectional causality from oil prices to the REER over the 1980–2018 period. Lastly, they provide some policy recommendations for countries that may experience a natural resource boom and the associated surge in revenues, such as Guyana, to mitigate Dutch disease symptoms that may arise from their impending oil boom.

Winston Dookeran and Preeya Mohan examine how the COVID-19

pandemic is forcing a rethink in macroeconomics and generating geo-strategic shifts in global diplomacy. The Caribbean region faces complex challenges in the formulation of growth strategies in the loop-type shock cycles. The liberal order upon which global institutions were premised is now in flux. This chapter firstly examines the underlying logic of the Lewis model of growth, and points out some of the policy concepts to which growth models must respond as the region faces the negative growth challenges of COVID-19. It describes the logic and argument of the model, locates it in the literature, and looks at the underlying assumptions. Secondly, the chapter looks at CARICOM states' responses to the pandemic and implications for models of development in a post-COVID multipolar global era. The chapter draws upon Caribbean experiences here to posit a need for geo-strategic shifts on the world stage and the metrics of diplomacy for small states. To this end, they conclude that the pandemic has shaken up the foundations of the world of public policy – in finance, politics, health and elsewhere. They argue that "If it is treated as temporary, small states would have lost forever the opportunities for making public policy changes that are critical to our times." In this sense, notwithstanding its huge "life and livelihood" costs across the globe, the pandemic may well be a catalyst for geopolitical shifts in the world order of things.

PEOPLE ON THE MOVE: MOBILITY JUSTICE FOR CHANGING WORLDS

Section four examines issues of historical and contemporary migration in the anglophone Caribbean and its diaspora. While these four chapters span a variety of disciplines, methodological and theoretical orientations, they are united by concerns relating to the experiences of vulnerable migrants and small states' response to inward and outward migration. They raise questions of mobility justice in an era that has been shaped by simultaneous and complex crises of socio-economic decline, disease, contested identity politics, and acceleration of existential threats.

Walker's chapter, "'I Thought No One Would Care': Identity, (Mis) Recognition, and the Windrush Scandal", opens the section. It is an apt introductory chapter, as it describes the experiences of a diaspora population whose exodus to the United Kingdom quintessentially defined Caribbean migration in the post-World War II period. Applying social representation theory, Walker explores how media coverage of the Windrush scandal has shaped the lived experiences of the Windrush generation in the United Kingdom. He points out that the scandal has highlighted the plight of those who suffered following the introduction of the (now acknowledged) racist measures of the Hostile Environment Policy. However, Walker also contends that while mediated discourse has produced a positive narrative of Black UK citizens, which contrasts with the established trope of the bad migrant, the Windrush generation's positioning as victims has perpetuated their stigmatization. The scandal has thus shed light on the highly contested (identity) politics of being Black in the United Kingdom.

In "The Canada-Caribbean Seasonal Agricultural Worker Program (SAWP) in and beyond COVID-19: Involuntary Mobilities, Liberalized Food Systems and Multiple Inequities", Lozanski, Esnard, and Ferrando also assesses the significance of race for migrants' everyday existence. The chapter draws on critical race theory to integrate analysis of seasonal agricultural workers' stories, with the historical and economic context of the seasonal agricultural workers programme (SAWP) in Canada. Framed by moments following the closing and (re)opening of the Canadian border due to the onset of the COVID-19 pandemic, the chapter explores the desirability of SAWP workers, and reflects on the future of the programme. Lozanski, Esnard, and Ferrando draw attention to SAWP workers' realities of poor living and working conditions and the (potential) politics of change spurred by increased consciousness during the pandemic. They also highlight the importance of SAWP to global food chains and call for a reimagined model of agriculture in Canada, as well as in food import-dependent Caribbean SIDS. From the gaze of the Caribbean, reimagining SAWP is a complicated process, since the programme is a key source of employment for several low-income communities. Reimagining would also require deep critique and deconstruction of a programme, which, in some instances, predates the independence era.

In their discussion of the implications of sovereignty for the management of large-scale migratory flows, Dietrich Jones and Mohan focus on the unit of analysis of the state. Their chapter, "Hauntings of Islands' Sovereignties: An Examination of Curaçao and Trinidad and Tobago's Responses to the

Venezuelan Migration Crisis", examines the responses of these two SIDS in the southern Caribbean to the ongoing Venezuelan migration crisis. Using the conceptualization of "hauntings" Dietrich Jones and Mohan argue that these SIDS posture sovereignty through interdiction, detention and deportation of (suspected) undocumented Venezuelan migrants. However, the ghosts of colonialism continue to shape the exercise of sovereignty in these post-colonial states. This is evidenced by Curaçao's reliance on the government of the Kingdom of the Netherlands in its management of the crisis, and Trinidad and Tobago's seeming retreat from a restrictive policy agenda in the face of criticism from international and regional human rights organizations. "Imperial debris", has, therefore, resulted in the articulation of complex embodiments of sovereignty in these borderized states. For other SIDS also experiencing significant increases in arrivals of Venezuelan migrants (and other nationalities), this chapter raises questions concerning balancing respect for the human rights of vulnerable migrants and those seeking international protection with statecraft and border management.

Thomas-Hope's chapter, "Implications of Environmental Change for Migration and Sustainable Futures of Caribbean States", closes this section. It implicitly foregrounds the emerging discourse concerning mobility justice for environmental migrants from the Caribbean by discussing the heightened vulnerability of Caribbean SIDS to climate change. In the context of extreme vulnerability to climate change, is migration a potential adaptive response? Thomas-Hope argues that the answer to this question is not very straightforward. Immobility is common among poorer households and communities; where migration has occurred, remittances have not always been channelled to communities likely to be most impacted by climate change. Thomas-Hope also highlights issues of governance in her discussion of the lack of integration of migration (management) in policies and plans for adaptation to climate-induced change in the Caribbean. In light of the inherent vulnerability of Caribbean SIDS to climate change, adaptation and mitigation responses in the region must be multi-scalar. These should include consideration of the region's high propensity for intra- and extra-regional migration and the anticipated increase in environmentally induced migration due to climate change.

It is our hope that this opening salvo for "Re-imagining Caribbean

Futures" will help to stimulate fruitful critical discourse and a stronger ideation for Caribbean futures that take us beyond the prevailing calls for a return to the "new normal". The historical context and radical challenges faced in the region on every side – from climate, debt and health emergencies to ever-compounding global catastrophic risks and hapless migrant flows – demand something more than our current neoliberal enchantment with macro-economic stability and micro-efficiency mantras. Indeed, our Caribbean peoples, here and abroad, remain hungry for the release of a deep-seated visioning of the urgent and fundamental tasks of reordering, repositioning and rebuilding that have long been needed for our fragile social, economic, environmental and political spaces. And, while our states and leaders remain in an embattled modality, the current crucibles of change do offer opportunities for a global evaluation of the contradictions destroying the "ethics of relation" envisioned by the World Health Organization's One Health initiative – public health ecologies – that warrant a recalibration of borders of respect and protection. Our current crises also offer fresh chances to the people of the Caribbean region to raise our diminished expectations concerning our rights to just futures. These timely breaks from a stale normativity will require our more fulsome collective escape from curses and soured relationships seeded in racial colonial sensibilities that prompt us to belittle the power of our own communities, fracture regional solidarities and be forgetful of our intrinsic interdependencies. The chapters gathered here, in one way or another, all foreground these political stakes (postures and constraints) at play in the different aspects of our policy approaches, grounded in our environmental, geo-political, regional, racialized and nation-state centric postcolonial existence, that are all in need of sharper rethinking and bolder restrategizing for more wholesome and rich Caribbean futures.

NOTES

1. We, the editorial team, are deeply indebted to the late Ambassador Dr Richard Bernal, professorial Fellow at SALISES, UWI, Mona, for his invaluable contributions in making this edited collection possible. His depth and breadth of knowledge, unstinting commitment and wisdom provided us with confident assurance, at each step of the journey, in realizing the vision of this book project. We were floored by his untimely death on 4 January 2023, which left us with great sorrow. We dedicate this introduction to his memory.

2. The Greater Caribbean consists of the G3 – Mexico, Colombia and Venezuela; the Isthmus states – Costa Rica, El Salvador, Guatemala, Honduras, Nicaragua, Panama; and the Insular Caribbean – Cuba, Dominican Republic, Haiti, Jamaica, Trinidad and Tobago, Barbados, the Bahamas and the Organization of the Eastern Caribbean States (OECS) protocol members – Antigua and Barbuda, the Commonwealth of Dominica, Grenada, Montserrat, St Kitts and Nevis, St Lucia, St Vincent and the Grenadines; mainland states – Suriname, Guyana and Belize; Caribbean island states of the Kingdom of Netherlands – Aruba, Curaçao, Sint Maarten; and the dependent territories: the United States – the Commonwealth of Puerto Rico, US Virgin Islands; France – French Guiana, Guadeloupe, Martinique; the United Kingdom – Anguilla, Montserrat, British Virgin Islands, Cayman Islands, Turks and Caicos.

3. The Caribbean Community (CARICOM) consists of the following member states: Antigua and Barbuda, Bahamas, Barbados, Belize, Dominica, Grenada, Guyana, Haiti, Jamaica, Montserrat, St Lucia, St Kitts and Nevis, St Vincent and the Grenadines, Suriname, Trinidad and Tobago. The associate members are: Anguilla, Bermuda, British Virgin Islands, Cayman Islands, Curaçao and Turks and Caicos.

4. Consider here, for example, the "plantation Caribbean", which is used to express a culture zone shaped by slavery and the plantation economy, and reflects an ethno-historical and counter-hegemonic political perspective strongly tied to the critical Caribbean tradition of the New World Group and linked to the concept of the "Plantation Americas" advanced by American anthropologist Charles Wagley (see Gaztambide-Géigel 2004).

5. http://www.caribbean-atlas.com/en/about/the-caribbean-atlas-project.html

6. For a backgrounder on the Haitian crises, see Jemima Pierre's (2023) "Haiti as Empire's Laboratory: As the United States and Its Allies Push Renewed Foreign Intervention, the Uses and Abuses of the First Black Republic as a Testing Ground of Imperialism Offer Stark Warnings. Haiti Still Struggles to Be Free," *NACLA Report on the Americas* 55 (3): 244–50. doi:10.1080/10714839.

2023.2247749. Also, "Haiti's troubled path to development" by Diana Roy and Rocio Labrador (2024), published by the Council on Foreign Relations. https://www.cfr.org/backgrounder/haitis-troubled-path-development. Accessed 1 August 2024.

7.   For readers interested in these topics, the *Social and Economic Studies* journal has published recent special issues on "Teaching and Learning in the Caribbean" with a focus on higher education, edited by Wendy McLean Cook and Garth Lipps, *Social and Economic Studies* 70 (1&2), as well as a volume on "Oil and Guyana's Sociopolitical Future," guest edited by Duane Edwards and Ralph Premdas, *Social and Economic Studies* 70 (3&4).

REFERENCES

Alleyne, D., S. McLean, M. Hendrickson, H. Tokuda, M. Pantin, N. Skerrette, and K. Victor. 2021. *Economic Survey of the Caribbean 2020: Facing the Challenge of COVID-19.* Studies and Perspectives Series No. 99 ECLACL Subregional Headquarters for the Caribbean (LC/TS.2021/1-LC/CAR/TS.2021/1). Santiago: Economic Commission for Latin America and the Caribbean (ECLAC).

Beckles, Hilary. 2021. *How Britain Underdeveloped the Caribbean: A Reparation Response to Europe's Legacy of Plunder and Poverty.* Kingston: The University of the West Indies Press.

Bobb, Daniele, and Leigh-Ann Worrell. 2022. "Gendered Impacts of COVID-19 in Barbados." *Social and Economic Studies* 71 (3&4): 95–112.

Brisset, Nigel. 2017. "Sustainable Development Goals (SDGs) and the Caribbean: Unrealizable Promises." *Progress in Development Studies* 18 (1): 18–35.

Canterbury, Dennis. 2022. *The Caribbean in the New Multipolar World Order.* London and New York: Routledge Press.

Caribbean Policy Research Institute (CAPRI). 2021. *Insult to Injury: The Impact of COVID-19 on Vulnerable Persons and Business.* Kingston: CAPRI.

Corbridge, Stuart. 2002. "Development as Freedom: The Spaces of Amartya Sen." *Progress in Development Studies* 2 (3):183–217.

De La Mata, D., L. Berniell, E. Schargrodsky, F. Álvarez, A. Arreaza, and G. Alves. 2023. *Inherited inequalities: The role of skills, employment, and wealth in the opportunities of new generations.* RED (Report of Economy and Development) 2022. Caracas: CAF Development Bank of Latin America and the Caribbean. Retrieved from https://scioteca.caf.com/handle/123456789/2072.

Economic Commission for Latin America and the Caribbean. 2020. "Addressing the growing impact of COVID-19 with a view to reactivation with equality: New projections." COVID-19 Special Report No. 15, July 2020.

————. 2021. "The Impact of COVID-19 on Indigenous Peoples in Latin America (Abya Yala): Between Invisibility and Collective Resistance." Project Documents (LC/TS.2020/171). Santiago: ECLAC.

————. 2023. *Public Debt and Development Distress in Latin America and the Caribbean*. (LC/TS.2023/20). Santiago: ECLAC.

Edwards, Zophia. 2021. "Racial Capitalism and COVID-19." *Monthly Review* Vol. 72 No. 10 (March). https://monthlyreview.org/2021/03/01/racial-capitalism-and-covid-19/.

Ferdinand, Malcolm. 2022. *Decolonial Ecology: Thinking from the Caribbean World*. Cambridge: Polity.

Girvan, Norman. 2005. "Reinterpreting the Caribbean." In *The Caribbean Economy: A Reader*, edited by Dennis Pantin, 304–18. Kingston: Ian Randle Publishers.

Gaztambide-Géigel, Antonio. 2004. "The Invention of the Caribbean in the 20th Century (The Definitions of the Caribbean as a Historical and Methodological Problem)." *Social and Economic Studies* 53 (3):127–57.

Henry, Clarence. 2022. "COVID-19 and the Repositioning of OECS Economics." *Social and Economic Studies* 71 (3 & 4): 9–36.

Henry-Lee, Aldrie. 2022. "Introduction: The Impact of COVID-19 on Small Island Developing States." *Social and Economic Studies* 71 (3&4):1–8.

International Monetary Fund. 2016. "Small States' Resilience to Natural Disasters and Climate Change – Role for the IMF." IMF Policy Papers. Washington, DC: IMF.

Intergovernmental Panel on Climate Change (IPCC). 2014. "Summary for policymakers." In *Climate Change 2014: Impacts, Adaptation, and Vulnerability. Part A: Global and Sectoral Aspects. Contribution of Working Group II to the Fifth Assessment Report of the Intergovernmental Panel on Climate Change*, edited by C.B. Field et al., 1–32. Cambridge: Cambridge University Press.

————. 2018. "Summary for Policymakers." In *Global Warming of 1.5°C: An IPCC Special Report on the impacts of global warming of 1.5°C above pre-industrial levels and related global greenhouse gas emission pathways, in the context of strengthening the global response to the threat of climate change, sustainable development, and efforts to eradicate poverty*, edited by V. Masson-Delmotte et al., 1–24. Cambridge: Cambridge University Press. doi:10.1017/9781009157940.001.

Koselleck, Reinhart. 1988. *Critique and Crisis: Enlightenment and the Pathogenesis of Modern Society*. Cambridge, MA: MIT Press.

Li, Tania. 2007. *The Will to Improve: Governmentality, Development, and the Practice of Politics*. Durham: Duke University Press. https://doi.org/10.1515/9780822389781.

Maharaj, Deodat, and Denny Lewis-Bynoe. 2016. "A Call to Action." In *Achieving a Resilient Future for Small States: Caribbean 2050*, edited by Denny Lewis-Bynoe. London: Commonwealth Secretariat.

Maldonado-Torres, Nelson. 2011. "Thinking through the Decolonial Turn: Post-continental Interventions in Theory, Philosophy, and Critique An Introduction." *Transmodernity: Journal of Peripheral Cultural Production of the Luso-Hispanic World* 1 (2):1–15.

Mintz, Sidney. 1974. "The Caribbean Region." *Daedalus* (Slavery, Colonialism and Racism) Vol. 103, No. 2 (Spring): 45–71.

Mooney, Henry and Maria Zegarra. 2020. "Extreme Outlier: The Pandemic's unprecedented shock to Tourism in Latin America and the Caribbean." IDB *Policy Brief*, # IDB-PB-339, June 2020, Country Department Caribbean Group. Washington, DC: Inter-American Development Bank.

Northover, Patricia. 2020. "The Quest for Sustainable Caribbean Futures." *Social and Economic Studies* 69 (3/4): 1–25.

Obermuller, Lauraján. 2022. "Double Whammy: Social and Economic Effects of COVID-19 on Young Males in Deprived Communities in Jamaica." *Social and Economic Studies* 71 (3/4):113–39.

Pierre, Jemima. 2023. "Haiti as Empire's Laboratory: As the United States and Its Allies Push Renewed Foreign Intervention, the Uses and Abuses of the First Black Republic as a Testing Ground of Imperialism Offer Stark Warnings. Haiti Still Struggles to Be Free." *NACLA Report on the Americas* 55 (3): 244–50. doi: 10.1080/10714839.2023.2247749.

Rhiney, Kevon. 2020. "Dispossession, Disaster capitalism and the Post-hurricane context in the Caribbean." *Political Geography* 78 (102171): 1–3.

Roy, Diana, and Rocio Labrador. 2024. "Haiti's troubled path to development." New York: Council on Foreign Relations. https://www.cfr.org/backgrounder/ haitis-troubled-path-development. Accessed 1 August 2024.

Sachs, Jeffrey, Christian Kroll, Guillame Lafortune, Grayson Fuller, and Finn Woelm. 2021. *Sustainable Development Report 2021*. Cambridge: Cambridge University Press. doi:10.1017/9781009106559.

Sachs, J.D., G. Lafortune, and G. Fuller. 2024. *The SDGs and the UN Summit of the Future. Sustainable Development Report 2024*. Dublin: Dublin University Press. doi:10.25546/108572.

Sheller, Mimi. 2018. "Caribbean Futures in the Offshore Anthropocene: Debt, Disaster, and Duration." *Environment and Planning D: Society and Space* 36 (6): 971–86.

Stein, Sharon, V. Andreotti, R. Susa, S. Amsler, et al. 2020. "Gesturing Towards Decolonial Futures: Reflections on Our Learnings Thus Far." *Nordic Journal of Comparative and International Education* 4 (1): 43–65.

Thame, Maziki. 2021. "Jamaica, COVID-19 and Black freedom." *Cultural Dynamics* 33 (3): 220–32. https://doi.org/10.1177/09213740211014331.

Trotz, Ulric, and Sharon Lindo. 2013. "Vulnerability and Resilience Building in CARICOM Countries." *Small States Digest* (2): 4–39.

Trouillot, Michel-Rolph. 1992. "The Caribbean Region: An Open Frontier in Anthropology Theory." *Annual Review of Anthropology* 21: 19–42.

United Nations Conference on Trade and Development. 2020a. *COVID-19 and Tourism. Assessing the Economic Consequences*. Geneva: UNCTAD.

———. 2020b. "Impact of COVID-19 on tourism in small island developing states." Available at https://unctad.org/news/impact-covid-19-tourism-small-island-developing-states.

———. 2021. *COVID-19 and Tourism. Assessing the Economic Consequences: An Update*. Geneva: UNCTAD.

United Nations Development Programme. 2021. *Regional Human Development Report 2021 – Trapped: High Inequality and Low Growth in Latin America and the Caribbean*. New York: UNDP.

———. 2023. *Mapping the Socio-Economic consequences of COVID-19 in Latin America and the Caribbean and the adopted responses for recovery*. New York: UNDP.

United Nations Office on Drugs and Crime. 2023. *Global Study on Homicide: Homicide and Organized Crime in Latin America and the Caribbean*. Vienna: UNODC.

Verges, Francoise. 2017. "Racial Capitalocene." In *Futures of Black Radicalism*, edited by Gaye Johnson and Alex Lubin, 72–82. London and New York: Verso.

Walker, Laverne, and Sylvester Clauzel. 2023. *Progress in the Implementation of the Samoa Pathway: Caribbean Regional Synthesis Report*. Studies and Perspective Series No. 121, ECLAC Subregional Headquarters for the Caribbean (LC/TS. 2023/166- LC/CAR/TS. 2023/7). Santiago: ECLAC.

World Bank. 2021. *Global Economic Prospects, June 2021*. Washington, DC: World Bank.

PART ONE

GLOBAL POWER SHIFTS AND VISIONS OF NEW WORLD ORDERINGS

1

The Caribbean in the Escalating US-China Turbulence

RICHARD BERNAL AND DON D. MARSHALL

POLITICAL LEADERS AND DIPLOMATIC REPRESENTATIVES OF THE UNITED STATES and the People's Republic of China have been jousting over trade, security and international influence. This increasingly heated interaction has played out across the world. One of the arenas of febrile rhetoric and diplomatic competition is the Caribbean, a region of small developing countries not otherwise highly considered for their strategic, locational or economic importance. The region, however, is constitutive of an ever-changing landscape of China-Latin American and Caribbean relations. These continue to produce counter opportunities and challenges that open up possibilities for development financing, trade access and market integration, thereby unsettling inter-imperial relations hitherto exclusively Western-centred and dominated.

US-CHINA RELATIONS

Relations between the United States and China deteriorated and became very antagonistic during the course of the first presidency of Donald Trump (2016–2020), ending in a trade war and sanctions on Chinese technology companies. From 2020, his successor, Joseph Biden, had increased dialogue with President Xi Jinping, with commitments to implement mutual understandings at a San Francisco meeting in November 2023. However, the US has continued its containment and suppression of China, leading to rising risks and uncertainty about future bilateral relations under a more determined Trump.

The tensions between the United States and China with respect to the Caribbean became manifest when anxieties attended the growing presence of the latter in the region. It marked a shift from peaceful coexistence in which China's integration into the global economy was encouraged under the administrations of Bill Clinton, George W. Bush and Barack Obama. The underlying rationale was that inducing greater participation in the global economy and international affairs would lead to internal demands and policy pressures for wider private enterprise and democracy across China. It was hoped that the Asian juggernaut would develop a stake in the multilateral trade system by its entry into the World Trade Organization (WTO) and that inclusiveness in international affairs would give it a vested interest in world peace and a cooperative approach to multilateral problem-solving. This was supposed to check China's ambitions and international assertiveness, particularly in Asia. A working alliance with China and Europe would be a bulwark against Russia's unquenched historic thirst for global influence, and assuage its feelings of exclusion and isolation after the implosion of the Soviet Union and its subjugated states in Eastern Europe.

THE US VIEW OF CHINA

China is the largest economy in the world. It a permanent member of the Security Council of the United Nations, and has nuclear weapons, the largest army, and its navy is expanding its presence in the South China Sea. It was felt in US policy circles that as the Chinese became more prosperous and private sector oriented, pressure for more democracy would build, reducing the possibility of a repetition of the Tiananmen Square massacre. However, the response to the 2019–2020 demonstrations in Hong Kong has since cast doubt on the notion of eventual democratization. The belief that the United States must check China's expansionism, evident in its growing role in the global economy, and increasing assertiveness and influence in international affairs soon became widely held, transcending differences between Republicans and Democrats. As John Ratcliffe, Director of National

Intelligence, put it in December 2020: "China poses the greatest threat to America today and the greatest threat to democracy and freedom world-wide since World War II" (*Wall Street Journal* 2020). This dovetailed with concerns across US academic and foreign policy circles about a declining US hegemony and an emerging Asian superpower (Nye 2002; Griffiths and Luciani 2011). Martin Jacques once spoke of when China rules the world (Jacques 2012), and former US Secretary of State Madeleine Albright casually refers to the United States' place in the Chinese century. Others demur. Shambaugh (2013) doubted such a scenario and Fenby (2014), Gurtov (2013) and Kynge (2006) remain convinced that internal contradictions will prevent China's continued rise, much less pre-eminence.

Trump's approach embodied the skeptics' sentiments and was based on pushing back against China, everywhere and all the time, to curtail the incremental erosion of US national security (Fanell 2019). Some argued that this approach was too "confrontational" and of doubtful efficacy (Fravel et al. 2019). A Brookings Institution study concluded that the US-China trade war was more pain than gain for the United States (Hass and Denmark 2020). Yet others appealed for a sort of blended approach of "competitive cooperation" (Grunstein 2019). This was not possible because the Trump transactional approach to foreign policy defined his administration's approach (Beckley 2020).

Under Biden US foreign policy shifted again, but towards the more classical, liberal one, which combined multilateralism with free trade economics and military strength. The US initially sought to promote initiatives that would match China's Belt and Road Initiative (BRI) in appeal and promise, beginning first in Southeast Asia with the Indo-Pacific Economic Framework. This was intended to promote digital free trade. This initiative was buttressed by the establishment of new military alliances, especially with the Philippines, Australia and Japan; and the retention of technology sanctions on China. The COVID-19 pandemic, and the post-lockdown inflation spike occasioned by the outbreak of war in Ukraine and Gaza pre-occupied the attention of the Biden administration and so little was achieved by way of economic gains in Southeast and Central Asia akin to what China's BRI was securing for participant countries in the region.

CHINA'S STRUCTURAL POWER AND INFLUENCE

China's ever-evolving BRI was launched in 2013, striving to improve connectivity through infrastructure, trade, financial integration and people-to-people bonds. By 2024 more than one hundred and twenty countries had signed memoranda of understanding for a number of cross-border, bilateral investment and economic arrangements. Unmatched by any of its core rivals, the BRI's far-reaching commercial and digital dimensions included fibre optic cables, 5G networks, satellites and devices that will enable deeper systemic relations that shall exceed inter-imperial co-formations hitherto fashioned by the United States, the United Kingdom, Canada, France and the European Union. The extent of the reach of China's foreign policy initiatives is captured in how its state-owned enterprises (SOEs), China's development finance institutions, and Beijing are engaged in high-level commercial and diplomatic relations with the governments of countries that otherwise have co-extensive geostrategic and historical relations with other core powers.

China's substantial cross-border lending first to core countries in the 1990s, and later, to developing countries under the BRI; the internationalization of its RMB (renminbi) currency; and the listing of more than one hundred Chinese SOEs in the Fortune 500 list of the world's largest companies are indicators of China's global expansion and pragmatic adaptation of select Western ideals that underpin the neoliberal financial order. As the largest owner of US external debt and the second largest of Britain's external debt, China's structural influence in the international system unsettles attempts to shape the rules of the international political economy on Anglo-American terms only.

CHINA'S GROWING PRESENCE IN THE CARIBBEAN

China's presence has grown in the region over the last fifteen years and so has its potential for influence, as it has increased its development assistance loans for financing construction and infrastructure (Bernal 2010; 2015). Trade relations have been dominated by imports from China, but the most important trade partner of the Caribbean remains the United States. While Chinese migrants and their descendants have been in the region since the late nineteenth century, their numbers remain very small. Recently, Chinese-operated small retail businesses and restaurants have proliferated. Beyond retailing, Chinese foreign direct investment (Bernal 2016a; 2013) has been limited to mining and agriculture in Jamaica, and mining and energy in Guyana (*Starbroek News* Staff Editor 2020).

One of the most discussed issues in recent years has been the question of whether China plans to, or is actually in the process of "taking over the Caribbean" by means of the influence its loans and FDI assumedly offer the governments in the Caribbean. Local concerns have been reinforced by pronouncements by US officials suggesting a pernicious nature to China's engagement in the Latin America and the Caribbean. The fear is often not based on fact, with the most common error being the assumption that every project funded by the Chinese is owned by China. Consequently, the extent of Chinese ownership and indebtedness are significantly overestimated. More on this later.

Given the small trade and investment prospects and the lack of strategic importance of the Caribbean, the question naturally arises as to why would a superpower like China be interested and active here? Other than the offshore energy resources of Guyana and Suriname, what are the motives for China's conduct in the region? Similarly, what explains the receptivity of the Caribbean to economic relations with China?

Contact between China and the Caribbean dates back centuries to the importation of Chinese goods such as tea and small numbers of labourers (Look Lai 2004; Sue-A-Quan 1999), who soon established themselves in the retail trade, in particular, in small groceries (Chen 2004). Today, small communities of Chinese descendants exist across the region (Look Lai 2000; Wilson 2004; Johnson 2006). Formal diplomatic relations between the People's Republic of China and Caribbean states began with the establishment of diplomatic ties with Guyana and Jamaica in the latter half of 1972. Not all Caribbean countries have official diplomatic links with China, as some have chosen instead to have a relationship with Taiwan. Countries recognizing China and Taiwan are shown in Appendix 1.

China has a mix of motives for a growing presence in the Caribbean, but it is driven to extend its novel pathway to globality. One of its objectives is to consolidate the One China policy. China regards Taiwan as an outlaw province, and it is irrecoverably committed to eliminating the diplomatic recognition of Taiwan as a sovereign state. Fewer than fifteen governments recognize Taiwan, with the number giving recognition having declined in recent years as countries switched their allegiance to China. Most of the governments that support Taiwan are small states in Central America, the Caribbean and the Pacific, hence China and Taiwan have concentrated diplomatic attention on them (Bernal 2012). Some Caribbean states have switched their allegiances (sometimes more than once) between the two Asian countries. This has happened as recently as 2007, when St Lucia reversed its recognition in favour of Taiwan. From 1984 until 1996, St Lucia recognized Taiwan, but switched allegiances in 1996 when the government changed. Dominica and Grenada gave up Taiwan for China. Barbados, Guyana, Jamaica, and Trinidad and Tobago have been unwavering in their commitment to the One China policy. Belize, Haiti, St Kitts and Nevis, and St Vincent have resisted the entreaties of China and steadfastly stuck with Taiwan in exchange for increasing aid. Apart from its existence, Taiwan has been an irritant to China: for example, Taiwan's support for protesters in Hong Kong demonstrating against Beijing's actions and its willingness to provide refuge when some of the protesters sought to flee (Chang 2020). In addition, Taiwan maintains two small island outposts in the South China Sea that have strategic importance in spite of their smallness.

China's strategy in the Caribbean consists of:

- First, providing austerity-free development financing and grants, in particular for construction and infrastructure projects executed by Chinese firms;
- Second, cultivating receptivity to Chinese products and expertise and eventually investment via the Belt and Road Initiative, grants, and development loans;
- Third, supporting the establishment of Chinese-owned businesses especially in raw materials and imports from China;
- Fourth, avoiding behaviours of previous superpowers by not demanding public abeyance, building goodwill with Confucius Institutes (in Barbados, Dominica, Guyana, Jamaica Suriname and Trinidad), scholarships and friendship associations, for example, the Jamaica China Business Forum (Pate 2020).

CHINA'S INROADS INTO CENTRAL AMERICA AND THE CARIBBEAN

For more than a decade, China's presence has been increasing in the Caribbean, but this did not arouse concerns in Washington, given how dependent these economies are on the United States. However, when countries in Central America began to switch allegiance from Taiwan to China (Bernal 2017; 2020), the Trump administration reacted. The perceived threat was not the spread of communism, as was the case with perceptions of the Soviet Union in the Cold War era, but a sense of impending economic encroachment as the extension of the global economic rivalry between the world's largest economies. The dominoes started to fall with Costa Rica in 2007 and continued with Panama in 2017, El Salvador in 2018, and Nicaragua in 2021 (Jennings 2019; Ellis 2021), induced by financial aid and export prospects. Rumours persist about the intentions of Belize, Guatemala and Honduras (Graham 2018), which urgently needed economic aid and foreign direct investment. Chinese officials cite US pressure as preventing countries such as Haiti from switching (Huang 2019); more persuasive has been substantially increased aid to retain diplomatic recognition (Tang 2018).

While Venezuela was the main item on the agenda when President Trump met with the leaders of five Caribbean countries – the Bahamas, the Dominican Republic, Haiti, Jamaica and St Lucia – the United States expressed its concern about what it described as China's "predatory economic practices" (Rampton 2019). Previously, the United States regarded as benign the steady escalation in the presence of China in Central America and the Caribbean (Bernal 2018), a region which the United States regards as its third border, traditionally an unchallenged sphere of US influence.

In January 2020, while in Jamaica, US Secretary of State Mike Pompeo advised Caribbean governments to be suspicious of China's loans as it could result in influence which could be used to threaten national security and democracy (Clarke 2020; Saunders 2020). The US ambassador to Jamaica, who had been critical of the government of Jamaica's dealings with Chinese construction companies, alluded to the United States moving to take back its place in its relations with Jamaica (Hall 2020).

A far more valid point which could have been made by the United States is that the Chinese system is not as transparent as that of the Western world.

Projects involving Chinese state enterprises are directly controlled by the government, whereas, in Western capitalism, the state is fully behind their private companies – but at arm's length. This aside, the competitive approach will continue to enjoy the support of Americans, given the antipathy towards socialist countries, the fact that almost a half of US citizens see China as the "most socialist country" in the world, along with Venezuela, and ahead of Russia (STATISTA 2020). They will support a policy of excluding China from the energy resources of Venezuela and Guyana.

The United States has been particularly concerned about Central America since 2018, when Panama, El Salvador, the Dominican Republic and Nicaragua have been open to Chinese aid and FDI (Bernal 2020; Dussel-Peters 2019), and the possibility of increased Chinese influence.

Jamaica, although small, is regarded as an influential country in the region by the United States, as seen in Mike Pompeo's official visit to the island in January 2020, where he reiterated warnings to Caribbean governments about accessing China's loans. These could undermine national security, democracy, the rule of law, destroy the environment, impair the country's debt profile, and encourage corruption without creating jobs (Saunders 2020; *Gleaner* 2020). At the time, US influence had a salutary effect: Prime Minister Andrew Holness, on his return from a state visit to China, announced that Jamaica, as part of its debt management strategy, would no longer borrow from Beijing.

Ultimately, the US response to China in the Caribbean needs to be more robust. In October 2020, legislation extending preferential duty treatment for certain goods produced under the Caribbean Basin Economic Recovery Act (CBERA) was signed into law until 30 September 2030. While this is positive, the Caribbean governments – especially Trinidad and Tobago, where more than two hundred companies benefit from CBERA, representing 36 per cent of total exports (Alvarez 2020) – are still hoping for a package of financial aid and some tangible outcome from the Growth in the Americas Initiative. Meanwhile, the United States is mounting investment missions to Guyana and Jamaica. Guyana has been told that US$200 billion is on offer by a team that includes the Department of Treasury, the Export-Import Bank of the United States, the US International Development Finance Corporation, the Department of State, the Department of National Security, and the Department of Homeland Security (*Guyana Chronicle* 2020). The Biden administration has toned down US public messaging. One indication of a thaw in US-China relations is that the US government is no longer publicly excoriating governments in the Caribbean and Central America for their relations with Beijing; for example, the US embassy in Kingston indicated that Jamaica's relations with China is not a contentious issue between the United States and the island. The embassy spokesman said: "The Government of Jamaica is free to make decisions about whomever they wish to speak with on any matter . . . There is no redline, as far as I'm aware, in terms of our policy on dealing with China" (*Gleaner* 2021b). A major US initiative is still hoped for in the Caribbean.

GUYANA-CHINA ENGAGEMENT

China's involvement in Guyana has taken the form of foreign direct investment in bauxite by the firm Bosai (Bernal 2016a), and infrastructure and construction projects, such as the renovation of the Cheddi Jagan International Airport and the construction of the Skeldon Sugar Factory. Chinese firms have been involved in electricity transmission and fibre optic infrastructure (that is, China National Electronics Import & Export Corporation), telecommunications (Huawei), logging (Bai Shan Lin), the construction of a new Marriott Hotel (Shanghai Construction Group), and the building of the Pegasus Hotel (China Harbour Construction Company). Perhaps more important than what has happened is what could happen, depending on the extent to which there is Chinese involvement in the soon-to-be-cash-rich Guyana, based on the projected revenues from offshore oil (Bryan 2019).

Although the transshipment of cocaine through Guyana is beginning to reach alarming proportions (Ellis 2020a), the attention of the US government may have been piqued by oil in the offshore waters and the participation of China National Offshore Oil Company in the Exxon-led coalition to develop Guyana's offshore oil (Ellis n.d.). ExxonMobil is developing the Stabroek Block of 26,800 square kilometres, with reserves in excess of eight billion barrels. Production started in 2019. Shortly after the Pompeo démarche, ExxonMobil received Guyana's approval for additional development involving an anticipated US$9 billion to tap reserves estimated at six hundred million barrels to produce seven hundred and fifty thousand barrels of oil per day by 2026 (ExxonMobil Newsroom 2020).

Chinese companies, supported by loans from their government, undertook major construction projects, such as the Demerara River Crossing and the US$150 million expansion of the Cheddi Jagan International Airport by China Harbour Engineering Company. The latter project was funded by the EXIM Bank of China. Guyana's digital infrastructure will see a boost from a US$37.6 million deal by the controversial Chinese firm Huawei, aimed at expanding broadband connectivity (*Guyana Chronicle* 2021a). Guyana's government offered no objection to the US$500 million contract for the China Railway First Group to build a hydroelectric plant at Amalia Falls.

Pompeo visited Guyana in September 2020 to sign an MOU to "pave the way for the U.S. private sector to expand their investment portfolio and partner with the Guyanese private sector" (Pompeo 2020). His message was to exhort Guyana to favour US companies in preference to Chinese ones, warning that: "We've watched the Chinese Communist Party invest in countries, and it all seems great at the front end and then it all comes falling down when the political costs connected to that becomes clear" (Leysner 2020). He was no doubt very aware of the enormous oil deposits discovered off the coast of Guyana and China's drive for resources, especially energy (Economy and Levi 2014). Beyond the importance of exploiting the oil deposits, the availability of energy portends well for bauxite smelting and economic activity in general. Guyana's prospective expenditure on imports and public investment presents an opportunity for US firms, with revenue accruing to the government from the oil sector slated to increase from US$300 million in 2020 to an estimated US$5 billion per year by 2025 (Ellis 2020a).

It does appear that the Irfaan Ali administration has its own ideas about sustainable development in the wake of its oil discoveries. In July 2023 President Ali visited China, where he emphasized Guyana's potential as a partner in the areas of food security, climate change cooperation and renewable energy. The two countries also signed an MOU to create an investment and economic creation working group focused on education, agriculture, infrastructure, health and energy. This is an important development, given the absence of any US-led development partnerships or initiatives in the last thirty years, since discussion about a Free Trade Area of the Americas initiative that later led to the establishment of the North American Free Trade Agreement.

SHIFTING RELATIONS WITH THE DOMINICAN REPUBLIC

In a major blow to Taiwan, the Dominican Republic and China signed an agreement in May 2018 to establish diplomatic ties, ending its relationship with Taipei after seventy-seven years. The DR is China's second-largest trading partner in the Caribbean and Central America. In announcing the switch, the DR's foreign minister referred to Taiwan as "an inalienable part of China". Taipei sought to downplay the change and blamed it on China's "dollar diplomacy", specifically mooting a financial package of US\$3.1–\$4.1 billion (Smith and Connor 2018; *Guardian* 2018; A. Wong 2018). The motivation of the Dominican Republic was that the switch would be "extraordinarily positive for the future of our country" and the "needs, potential and future prospects" (Smith and Connor 2018; *Guardian* 2018). In addition to the prospect of a significant increase in development aid loans and FDI, the DR could possibly increase exports to China (Ramzy 2018). In all, eighteen agreements have been signed between China and the DR (Caribbean Council n.d.) encompassing a wide range of projects.

DEVELOPMENT BEYOND THE PRISM OF CHINA'S GOODWILL

China's donations and development loans have generated a lot of goodwill. It has constructed several prominent buildings in Barbados, including an indoor sports complex and a national conference centre. As a measure of its appreciation, Barbados appointed former prime minister Sir Lloyd Erskine Sandiford as its first resident ambassador to China in 2011. China's naval hospital ship *Peace Ark* visited Bridgetown (*Global Times* 2020), and China has contributed funds to the Barbadian military (Willis 2016). In February 2019, Barbados signed on to the Belt and Road Initiative. The government of Antigua described China as an "important development partner" (*Caribbean National Weekly* 2020) – not surprisingly, since it has benefitted materially. China Civil Engineering Construction Corporation (CCECC), formerly the Foreign Aid Bureau of the Ministry of Railways, is a state-owned enterprise, which was established in 1979. It does construction projects all over the world. CCECC has done construction projects in Antigua for more than thirty-five years, including the Creekside Bridge, the multipurpose centre, the Sir Vivian Richards Stadium (a gift from the People's Republic of China), the VC Bird Air Terminal, and is currently engaged in the construction of the Embassy of China building at Marble Hill, and a cargo port at the deepwater harbour. Antigua is also looking to garner FDI in its tourist industry (*Jamaica Observer* 2018). The favourable disposition towards China must be understood against the background of declining US financial aid to Caribbean countries. The region feels neglected and some lingering disappointment is felt. For example, the bitter dispute with the United States over internet gaming. Antigua won the case in the Dispute Settlement Mechanism of the WTO, but was never able to extract the awarded remuneration of US$21 million per annum (Miles 2018). This is the background to Prime Minister Gaston Browne advising the United States that "instead of being concerned with China's growing influence in developing countries, Washington should provide more aid to these nations and not spend billions on useless wars" (*Gleaner* 2018).

The average rate of economic growth for the fifteen CARICOM countries in 2006 was just over 6 per cent, but since the global financial crisis of 2008, it has averaged under 2 per cent per annum, with contractions in 2009 and 2015 and since the advent of COVID-19. The Caribbean region was the worst affected in the entire world, more adversely impacted than other small developing countries (Ruprah 2013; Ruprah, Melgarejo, and Sierra 2014). In an attempt to stimulate economic growth and adjust to adverse external shocks and reconstruction after natural disasters, budgets have been stretched beyond conventional rules of fiscal prudence, and this has led to unsustainable external debt and debt-restructuring exercises. For more than a decade CARICOM member states have been the most indebted countries in the world (King and Tennant 2014; Okwuokei and van Selm 2017). Consequently, over the longer term there has been public under-investment, leaving an enormous infrastructure deficit, a gap which neither local nor foreign direct investment has filled, and an urgent need for development financing. A major contributor to the dearth of financing is that Caribbean countries – other than Haiti and Guyana – have graduated from the most concessional grant and loan facilities because they are classified as middle-income developing countries. While China does not apply this criterion, the United Kingdom has joined the advocacy to remove this impediment on the basis of accepting a vulnerability index as the appropriate benchmark. The United States, however, adheres to this disqualification. The relinquishing of this criterion would enable the United States to be more supportive of the Caribbean. Dr Denzil Douglas, prime minister of St Kitts and Nevis, which has relations with Taiwan, has said bluntly to the United States, "You have to do more than just traditional national security policies . . . we needed money to help the Caribbean" (Wigglesworth 2013).

COVID-19 COMPLICATIONS

The COVID-19 pandemic led to a serious decline in tourist arrivals and expenditure in the Caribbean, resulting in a major contraction in economic growth/activity and a drop in foreign exchange earnings. Additional public health expenditure strained already tight fiscal budgets, aggravating debt management challenges. With the COVID-19 shock, the debt-to-GDP ratio increased in 2020 to more than 80 per cent in Antigua and Barbuda, Belize, Dominica, Suriname and Jamaica (recently down from more than 100 per cent), and 140 per cent in Barbados (IDB 2023; Robinson 2024; IMF 2024a, 2024b). Caribbean governments immediately renewed the perennial call for a Marshall Plan for the region, articulated by Prime Minister Mia Mottley of Barbados in July 2020 (Mell 2020), and back in 2017 by Richard Branson (Nurse 2017) – or, the more recently proposed Caribbean Recovery and Resilient Trust Fund (*Jamaica Observer* 2020). The tourism-dependent Barbadian economy contracted by 27 per cent in the second quarter of 2020 (*The Economist* 2020). Meanwhile, Caribbean governments borrowed heavily from the only source of assistance, the International Monetary Fund (IMF). In May 2020, Jamaica borrowed US$520 million, the equivalent of 3.5 per cent of GDP (IMF 2020). However, the only debt relief that was forthcoming was from the IMF, and only Haiti was eligible and received a mere US$6.5 million (IMF n.d.). Not surprisingly, the prime minister of Dominica, at the annual IMF-World Bank meeting in October 2020, called for more grant and concessional financing for small island developing states (*Caribbean News Service* 2020). Although there has been some post-COVID improvement in debt-to-GDP ratios, the Caribbean remains a highly debt-stressed region. The COVID-19 shock was thus a missed opportunity for US leadership, especially since the Trump administration did not participate in the G-20 Summit in November 2020, which declared their commitment to "implementing the Debt Service Suspension Initiative (DSSI) including its extension through June 2021, allowing DSSI-eligible countries to suspend official bilateral debt service payments" (G20 Leaders' Declaration, Riyadh Summit 2020).

NATIONAL SECURITY – BELOW THE RADAR

China's donations of equipment to Caribbean military and police forces remains small but represent creeping, below-the-radar encroachment in an area dominated by US and UK suppliers. The opportunity may have emerged because, in some instances, assets made available by the United States are assigned, but ownership is not transferred to Caribbean governments. Donations of Chinese military equipment included the donation of construction equipment to the Guyana Defence Force in 2017 and US$1.1 million in non-lethal gear, such as uniforms and tents to the Jamaica Defence Force in 2011. Ironically, some goods sourced from suppliers in the United States were made in China. Donations to Caribbean police forces include US$2.6 million in vehicles to Guyana in 2017 and two hundred motorcycles donated to Trinidad and Tobago in 2019. Perhaps the most noteworthy development was the purchase of an offshore patrol vessel by Trinidad and Tobago in 2014 (Ellis 2020b). Some personnel from the Caribbean have attended military courses in China, but most training continues to be done by the British and the Canadians.

REFRAMING CARIBBEAN POSITIONING AND ITS US/CHINA ENGAGEMENTS

As we stated earlier, the increasing Chinese global presence is being met by a view in Washington that it is necessary to counter China everywhere, all the time. The Caribbean seems an unlikely arena for superpower contestation, but it is, because the increasing Chinese presence, driven primarily by the objective of ousting Taiwan from diplomatic recognition, has aroused US interests and indignation at China's encroachment in the Caribbean and, worryingly so, in Central America. The dilemma for the Caribbean facing the twin crisis of overcoming limited economic diversification and unjust, unsustainable development is how to avoid withdrawal or punitive measures, while mobilizing as much financial assistance and investment from both competing powers. All this, of course, against the backdrop of overcoming the power of coloniality in all of its vestiges and manifestations.

The political divide in the United States is not propitious for either a major aid package or for a new trade pact. The region's need for public sector investment/financing and FDI is urgent. The region has, since the halcyon days of the Caribbean Basin Initiative (CBI), experienced less in terms of economic aid than its concentration of security assistance. Repeated calls have been made for a Marshall Plan for the Caribbean (Dunkley 2020). The United States will have to increase its economic aid if it is to counter the growing influence of China. It has supported the initiatives for more funding from the World Bank, but it is yet to address the ineligibility of Caribbean countries from the most concessional facilities (*CARICOM Today* 2021). Pressure for such a substantial aid package has been growing as illegal migrants from Central America and Haiti continue to seek entry to the United States in increasing numbers. Indeed, a call has been made for a CBI 2 to be launched (Fauriol 2019).

In the absence of a US-led co-prosperity pact, it is necessary to weigh up China-Latin American and Caribbean (LAC) relations, what is trending and what this portends. LAC's exports to China in raw commodities, such as soybeans and crude petroleum oils, have been accelerating in total value since 2002 and increasingly since 2012, outpacing resource-based products with some limited local value-added, such as soybean oil and refined gasoline (IMF 2024). Manufactured exports over the period account for only a quarter of 1 per cent of LAC's Gross Domestic Product. Of the newer, rapidly growing commodity exports between 2019 and 2023, beef and lithium are in the top five LAC exports to China. LAC-China beef exports have quintupled in the last decade and lithium carbonate exports have quintupled in just three years since 2020 (IMF 2024). Chile, Brazil and Peru are the major LAC export suppliers of the top five products to China; Colombia, Mexico and Argentina are the next tier supplier countries; and Suriname and Guyana predominate in the remainder share of total LAC suppliers.

In terms of Chinese outbound FDI to LAC, Ray, Albright, and Peters (2024) referred to varying patterns of investment profiles for different parts of the region. Chinese FDI to South America has been concentrated in energy supply chains "including upstream stages of mining and drilling, as well as downstream stages of power generation and transmission" (Ray, Albright, and Peters 2024, 21). Chinese FDI in Mexico, Central America and the Caribbean has been in manufacturing (particularly the automotive sector, where Mexico predominates), and transport, public works, real estate and infrastructure. By 2023, the largest greenfield investments in LAC were in electric vehicle manufacturing in Mexico, two major lithium projects in Argentina and Peru, and Huawei's US$800 million investment in smartphone manufacturing in Brazil. The character and orientation of Chinese lending and investment are also changing, as Ray, Albright, and Peters report. While public-sector Chinese investors still represent the majority of Chinese FDI, private firms accounted for approximately 40 per cent of all Chinese FDI in LAC between 2019 and 2023. As Chinese SOEs have gained experience operating in the LAC regions, they have relied less on the China Development Bank or the Export-Import Bank of China for direct financing to extend or initiate new activities.

The various ways that LAC governments are accessing Chinese investment are a reflection of the scope of bargaining that the sovereign states have pursued, domestic elite cognition of the transformative dialectic possible in the wake of China's financial and commercial engagement, and the possibilities for building sustainable, autonomous, industrial capacities. The narratives that hold that these countries are caught in debt traps as a result of their sovereign borrowings from China and its related commercial creditors are also overblown.

Ray and Simmons (2024) show that Suriname has the highest public and publicly guaranteed (PPG) debt to China among LAC countries: 14.6 per cent of its GDP. Bolivia, Ecuador, Jamaica, the Dominican Republic and Guyana all owe China between 3 and 4 per cent of their GDPs, and the remainder LAC countries owe China less than 2 per cent of their GDP. In terms of near-term, repayment burdens (2024–2028), Suriname owes China the highest amount, estimated at 2.5 per cent of the value of its projected export revenues for the period 2024–2028. Ecuador is next, with 1.2 per cent of the value of its projected revenues for the same period, and all other LAC countries will pay less than 1 per cent of its export revenue in debt-servicing payments to China over the next five years. China's patient lending therefore serves LAC governments need for development financing at a time of great uncertainty following the end of the pandemic. Moreover, of the four largest classes of creditors worldwide – bondholders, Paris Club, China and multilateral development banks – China plays a relatively minor role as a LAC creditor. Guyana, Jamaica, the Dominican Republic and Suriname's debt stock across all classes of creditors and their debt servicing to same sees China play a relatively minor role in comparison to multilateral development banks, the Paris Club and bondholders (Ray, Albright, and Peters 2024).

From the vantage point of the LAC countries, China's engagements present options for navigating access to newer markets, investments and technology too critical at a time when Anglo-America is bogged down in mitigating wars, escalating domestic upsurges in anti-immigrant sentiments, and unsettling the status quo of market-determined initiatives for building trading and investment alliances. The more experientially immersed China-LAC and China-Caribbean relations become, the greater the tendency for reaction and increased tensions with the USA, especially under a Trump presidency.

REFERENCES

Albright, Madeleine. 2008. *Memo to the President Elect: How We Can Restore America's Reputation and Leadership.* New York: Harper Collins.

Allison, Graham. 2017. *Destined for War: Can America and China Escape Thucydides's Trap?* New York: Houghton Mifflin Harcourt.

Alvarez, Luis M. 2020. "President Trump Signs Extension, to the Benefit of T&T." *Trinidad Express,* 11 October 2020.

Aslund, Anders, and Djoomart Otorbaev. 2020. "China Should Join the Paris Club." Project Syndicate, 14 December 2020. https://www.project-syndicate.org/commentary/china-should-join-paris-club-to-manage-sovereign-debt-by-anders-aslund-and-djoomart-otorbaev-2020-12.

Beckley, Michael. 2020. "Rogue Superpower. Why This Could Be an Illiberal American Century." *Foreign Affairs* 99 (6).

Bernal, Richard L. 2010. "Dragon in the Caribbean: China-CARICOM Economic Relations." *Round Table* 99 (408): 281–302.

———. 2012. "China and Small Island Developing States, Africa-East Asian Affairs." *The China Monitor* no. 1 (August): 3–30.

———. 2013. "China's Rising Investment Profile in the Caribbean." *Economics Brief, Inter-American Dialogue,* October.

———. 2015. "China's Growing Economic Presence in the Caribbean." *The World Economy* 38 (9): 1409–37.

———. 2016a. *Chinese Foreign Direct Investment in the Caribbean. Potential and Prospects.* Inter-American Development Bank.

———. 2016b. *Dragon in the Caribbean – China's Global Re-Positioning: Challenges and Opportunities for the Caribbean,* 2nd ed. Kingston: Ian Randle Publishers.

———. 2017. "Central America and the Caribbean: Relations with China and the United States: Contrasting Experiences! Converging Prospects?" In *China, the U.S. and the Future of Latin America,* edited by David Denoon, 232–67. New York: New York University Press.

———. 2018. "U.S. Shouldn't Ignore China's Influence in the Caribbean." Opinion Editorial, *Miami Herald,* August.

———. 2020. "Increasing Chinese Influence in the Caribbean." In *Handbook of Caribbean Economies,* edited by Robert Looney. New York: Routledge.

Biden, Jr, Joseph R. 2020. "Why America Must Lead Again." *Foreign Affairs* 99 (2).

Brands, Hal. 2020. "Trump Delivered Three Foreign Policy Triumphs." Bloomberg Opinion, October.

Bryan, Anthony T. 2019. "Clear de Way, Guyana Coming Back: Oil, High Expectations, and Cautious Optimism." *Caribbean News Service,* 8 December 2019. https://caribbeannewsservice.com/now/guyana-on-high-oil-expectations/.

Buxbaum, Peter. 2018. "Proposed Steel Tariffs Raise Potential for Retaliation Against US Soybeans." *Global Trade*, February.

Calleo, David P. 1987. *Beyond American Hegemony: The Future of the Western Alliance.* New York: Basic Books.

Caribbean Insight. 2018. "Far Reaching Co-operation Agreements Signed between China and the Dominican Republic." The Caribbean Council, 4 May. https://www.ieyenews.com/far-reaching-co-operation-agreements-signed-between-china-and-the-dominican-republic/.

Caribbean National Weekly. 2020. "Antigua and Barbuda Defends Relationship with China." Published on 5 October 2020. https://www.caribbeannationalweekly.com/caribbean-breaking-news-featured/antigua-and-barbuda-defends-relationship-with-china/#:~:text=Antigua%20and%20Barbuda%20Defends%20Relationship%20with%20China%20October,to%20spread%20paranoia%20with%20the%20relationship%20with%20Beijing.

Caribbean News Service. 2020. "Skerrit Urges IMF to Provide Grant and Concessional Financing for SIDS." 22 October 2020. https://caribbeannewsservice.com/skerrit-urges-imf-to-provide-grant-and-concessional-financing-for-sids/.

CARICOM Today staff writer. 2021. "Caribbean Countries Need Urgent Rethink of Concessional Financing Criteria." Caricom Today, 16 October 2021.

Chang, Felix K. 2020. "China's New Pressure on Taiwan in the South China Sea." Foreign Policy Research Institute16 November 2020.

Chen, Ray. 2004. *The Shopkeepers*. Kingston: Periwinkle.

Clarke, Paul. 2020. "China Fires Back at US – Embassy Calls Trump Troublemaker Starting Fires and Fanning Flames." *The Gleaner*, 23 January 2020.

Crilly, Rob. 2018. "Europe Threatens Tariffs on Levi's Jeans, Bourbon and Harley-Davidson If Trump Sparks Trade War." *The Independent*, 2 March 2018.

Deaux, Joe, Andrew Mayeda, Toluse Okorunnipa, and Jeff Black. 2018. "Trump Says Trade Wars Are 'Good, and Easy to Win'." Bloomberg Politics, 1 March 2018. https://www.bloomberg.com/.../trump-is-said-to-delay-decision-on-steel-and-aluminum-tariffs.

Donilon, Tom. 2020. "Trump's Trade War Is the Wrong Way to Compete with China Focus on Renewal, Not Protectionism." *Foreign Affairs,* 25 June 2019. https://www.foreignaffairs.com/articles/china/2019-06-25/trumps-trade-war-wrong-way-compete-china.

Dunkley, Jascene. 2020. "Caribbean Marshall Plan." CARICOM Today, 4 July 2020. https://today.caricom.org/tag/caribbean-marshall-plan/.

Dussel-Peters, Enrique, ed. 2019. *China's Foreign Direct Investment in Latin America and the Caribbean*. Mexico City: Universidad Nacional Autonoma de Mexico.

Economy, Elizabeth C., and Michael Levi. 2014. *By All Means Necessary. How China's Resource Quest Is Changing the World*. New York: Oxford University Press.

Ellis, Evan. 2020a. "Guyana Opportunities and Challenges for the United States and the Caribbean Basin." Washington, DC: Center for Strategic and International Studies.

———. 2020b. "Chinese Security Engagement in Latin America." Washington, DC: Center for Strategic and International Studies.

———. 2021. "Nicaragua's Flip to China: What Does It Mean for the Region?" Global Americans, 10 December 2021. https://globalamericans.org/nicara-guas-flip-to-china/.

———. n.d. "Security Challenges in Guyana and the Government Response." *Journal of the Americas – Third Edition*, 205–29. https://www.airuniversity.af.edu/Portals/10/JOTA/Journals/Volume%201%20Issue%203/05-Ellis_eng.pdf.

Fanell, James E. 2019. "Stay the Course on China: An Open Letter to President Trump." *Journal of Political Risk*, 18 July 2019. https://www.jpolrisk.com/stay-the-course-on-china-an-open-letter-to-president-trump/.

Fauriol, Georges A. 2019. "Is It Time for a Caribbean Basin Initiative 2.0?" Center for Strategic and International Affairs, 29 January 2019.

Fenby, Jonathan. 2014. *Will China Dominate the 21st Century?* London: Polity Press.

Ferguson, Ellyn. 2021. "Biden Administration Keeps Tariffs as Tai Lays out China Trade Strategy." Roll Call, 4 October 2021. https://rollcall.com/2021/10/04/biden-administration-keeps-tariffs-as-tai-lays-out-china-trade-strategy/.

Fisher, Lucy. 2020. "China Blamed for Barbados Ditching Queen." *The Times*, 23 September 2020. https://www.thetimes.co.uk/edition/news/china-blamed-for-barbados-ditching-queen-h3nx66k5g.

Fravel, M. Taylor, J. Stapleton Roy, Michael D. Swaine, Susan A. Thornton, and Ezra Vogel. 2019. "China Is Not an Enemy." *Washington Post*, 3 July 2019.

G20 Leaders. 2020. "G20 Leaders' Declaration Riyadh Summit." Riyadh: G20 Saudi Arabia Summit.

Global Times. 2020. "UK Politicians Aim to Upset Developing China-Barbados Ties." *Global Times*, 26 September 2020.

Graham, David. 2018. "Honduras President Laments U.S. Aid Cuts, Eyes Role of China." *Reuters*, 24 September 2018. https://www.reuters.com/article/us-hon-duras-politics-idUSKCN1M42R6.

Griffiths, Rudyard, and Patrick Luciani, eds. 2011. *Does the 21st Century Belong to China? Kissinger and Zakaria vs Ferguson and Li: The Munk Debate on China*. Toronto: Anansi.

Gruber, Jonathan, and Simon Johnson. 2019. *Jump-Starting America: How Breakthrough Science Can Revive Economic Growth and the American Dream*. New York: Public Affairs.

Grunstein, Judah. 2019. "The U.S. Should Base Its China Strategy on Competitive Cooperation, Not Containment." *World Politics Review*, 17 April 2019.

Gurtov, Mel. 2013. *Will This Be China's Century? A Skeptic's View*. Boulder: Lynne Rienner.

Guyana Chronicle staff reporter. 2020. "G$42 Trillion Available to Guyana." *Guyana Chronicle*, 14 October 2020.

———. 2021a. "China Railway to Build Amaila Falls Hydro." *Guyana Chronicle*, 2 November 2021.

Jamaica Gleaner staff reporter. 2021b. "US Cools Rhetoric on Ja-China Ties." *The Gleaner*, 17 November 2021.Hall, Arthur. 2020. "Tapia Fires Latest Salvo in Verbal War with China." *Jamaica Observer*, 2 February 2020.

Hass, Ryan, and Abraham Denmark. 2020. "More Pain than Gain: How the US-China Trade War Hurt America." Brookings, 7 August 2020. https://www.brookings.edu/articles/more-pain-than-gain-how-the-us-china-trade-war-hurt-america/.

Huang, Kristin. 2019. "Beijing Targets Haiti as Bid to Isolate Taiwan from Its Diplomatic Allies Heads to the Caribbean." *South China Morning Post*, 14 September 2019.

International Monetary Fund. 2020. "IMF Executive Board Approves a US$520 Million Disbursement to Jamaica to Address the COVID-19 Pandemic." IMF press release No. 20/217, 15 May 2020. https://www.imf.org/en/News/Articles/2020/05/15/pr20217-jamaica-imf-executive-board-approves-disbursement-to-address-the-COVID-19-pandemic#:~:text=IMF%20Executive%20Board%20Approves%20a%20US%24%20520%20Million,urgent%20balance-of-payments%20needs%20stemming%20from%20the%20COVID-19%20pandemic.

———. n.d. "COVID-19 Financial Assistance and Debt Service Relief." IMF. https://www.imf.org/en/Topics/imf-and-COVID-19/COVID-Lending-Tracker.

———. 2024. "World Economic Outlook, April 2024 Edition." https://www.imf.org/en/Publications/WEO/weo database/2024/August.

———. 2024a. "2024 Article IV Consultation with Belize." IMF Country Report No. 24/124. https://www.imf.org/en/Publications/CR/Issues/2024/05/15/Belize-2024-Article-IV-Consultation-Press-Release-and-Staff-Report-549008.

———. 2024b. "2024 Article IV Consultation with Dominica." IMF Country Report No. 24/192. https://www.imf.org/en/Publications/CR/Issues/2024/06/27/Dominica-2024-Article-IV-Consultation-Press-Release-Staff-Report-and-Statement-by-the-551143.

Inter-American Development Bank. 2023. "Dealing with Debt in the Caribbean." *Caribbean Economics Quarterly* 13(3). https://publications.iadb.org/en/caribbean-economics-quarterly-volume-12-issue-3-dealing-debt-caribbean.

Irwin, Douglas A. 2011. *Peddling Protectionism: Smoot-Hawley and the Great Depression*. Princeton: Princeton University Press.

Jacques, Martin. 2012. *When China Rules the World: The End of the Western World and the Birth of a New Global Order,* 2nd ed. New York: Penguin Books.

Jamaica Observer. 2018. "Antigua Wants China to Partner on State-Funded Projects." *Jamaica Observer,* 21 January 2018.

———. 2020. "Barbados PM Calls for Establishment of Caribbean Recovery and Resilient Trust." *Jamaica Observer,* 9 December 2020.

Jennings, Ralph. 2019. "Taiwan Loans Nicaragua $100 Million in Ongoing Bonding between Isolation Nations." *Los Angeles Times,* 23 February 2019.

Joffe, Josef. 2013. *The Myth of America's Decline: Politics, Economics, and a Half Century of False Prophecies.* New York: Liveright Publishing.

Johnson, Kim. 2006. *Descendants of the Dragon: The Chinese in Trinidad.* Kingston: Ian Randle Publishers.

Kennedy, Paul. 1987. *The Rise and Fall of the Great Powers.* New York: Vintage Books.

King, Damien, and David Tennant. 2014. *Debt and Development in Small Island Developing States.* New York: Palgrave-Macmillan.

Kynge, James. 2006. *China Shakes the World: A Titan's Rise and Troubled Future and the Challenge for America.* New York: Houghton Mifflin.

Lee, Yee Nee, and Spencer Kimball. 2020. "Biden Says He Won't Immediately Remove Trump's Tariffs on China." CNBC Politics, 2 December 2020. https://www.cnbc.com/2020/12/02/biden-tells-nyt-columnist-he-wont-immediately-remove-trumps-tariffs-on-china.html.

Leysner, Jason. 2020. "Pompeo Asks Suriname, Guyana to Favour US Business over China." Al Jazeera, 18 September 2020. https://www.aljazeera.com/economy/2020/9/18/pompeo-asks-suriname-guyana-to-favour-us-business-over-china.

Look Lai, Walton. 2000. *The Chinese in the West Indies 1806–1995: A Documentary History.* Kingston: University of the West Indies Press.

———. 2004. *Indentured Labour, Caribbean Sugar: Chinese and Indian Migrants to the British West Indies.* Baltimore: John Hopkins University Press.

Mahbubani, Kishore. 2020. *Has China Won? The Chinese Challenge to American Primacy.* New York: Public Affairs.

Mell, P. 2020. "Mottley Calls for 'Caribbean Marshall Plan'." *New York Caribbean News,* 15 July 2020. https://www.nycaribnews.com/articles/mottley-calls-for-caribbean-marshall-plan/.

Miles, Tom. 2018. "Antigua 'Losing All Hope' of U.S. Payout in Gambling Dispute." Reuters, 22 June 2018. https://www.reuters.com/article/uk-usa-trade-antigua-idUSKBN1JI0VZ.

Mosher, Steven W. 2006. *Hegemon: China's Plan to Dominate Asia and the World.* New York: Encounter Books.

Nau, Henry R. 1990. *The Myth of America's Decline.* Oxford: Oxford University Press.

ExxonMobil Newsroom. 2020. "ExxonMobil to Proceed with Payara Development Offshore Guyana." ExxonMobil, 20 September 2020. https://corporate.exxonmobil.com/News/Newsroom/News-releases/2020/0930_ExxonMobil-to-proceed-with-Payara-development-offshore-Guyana.

Nurse, Michelle. 2017. "Marshall Plan for the Caribbean." CARICOM Today, 13 November 2017. today.caricom.org/tag/marshall-plan-for-the-caribbean/.

Nye, Joseph S. 2002. *The Paradox of American Power: Why the World's Only Superpower Can't Go It Alone*. Oxford: Oxford University Press.

Obama, Barrack. 2020. *A Promised Land*. New York: Crown.

Okwuokei, Joel Chiedu, and Bert van Selm. 2017. "Debt Restructuring in the Caribbean –The Recent Experience." In *Unleashing Growth and Strengthening Resilience in the Caribbean*, edited by Krishna Srinivasan, Inci Otker, Uma Ramakrishnan, and Trevor Alleyne. Washington, DC: International Monetary Fund.

Pate, Durrant. 2020. "Accelerating Trade between Jamaica and China Now Possible Business Forum Receiving Traction in Both Countries." *Jamaica Observer*, 9 October 2020.

Pineda, Jorge. 2019. "China Accuses U.S. of Meddling with Dominican Republic Ties." Reuters, 23 May 2019. https://www.reuters.com/article/world/china-accuses-u-s-of-meddling-with-dominican-republic-ties-idUSKCN1ST2HN/.

Policy Planning Staff, Office of the Secretary of State. 2020. "The Elements of the China Challenge." US Department of State, Washington, DC. https://www.state.gov/wp-content/uploads/2020/11/20-02832-Elements-of-China-Challenge-508.pdf.

Pompeo, Michael R. 2020. "Secretary Michael R. Pompeo and Guyana President Mohamed Irfaan Ali at a Press Availability, Remarks to the Press." US Department of State. 18 September . https://2017-2021.state.gov/secretary-michael-r-pompeo-and-guyana-president-mohamed-irfaan-ali-at-a-press-availability/index.html.

Rampton, Roberta. 2019. "Trump Dangles Investment to Caribbean Leaders Who Back Venezuela's Guaido." Reuters, 22 March . https://www.reuters.com/article/us-venezuela-politics-caribbean-idUSKCN1R313H.

Ramzy, Austin. 2018. "Taiwan's Diplomatic Isolation Increases as Dominican Republic Recognizes China." *New York Times*, 1 May.

Ratcliffe, John. 2020. "China Is National Security Threat No. 1." *Wall Street Journal*, 3 December.

Ray, Rebecca, Zara C. Albright, and Enrique Dussel Peters. 2024. "China-Latin America and the Caribbean Economic Bulletin – 2024 Edition." Boston University Global Policy Development Centre.

Ray, Rebecca, and B. Alexander Simmons. 2024. "Now or Never: Mobilizing Capital for Climate and Conservation in a Debt-Constrained World." Boston University

Global Development Policy Center. https://www.bu.edu/gdp/2024/02/02/now-or-never-mobilizing-capital-for-climate-and conservation-in-a-debt-constrained-world/.

Robinson, Mary. 2024. "Breaking the Cycle of Debt in Small Island Developing States (SIDS): the Antigua and Barbuda experience." ODI working paper, Overseas Development Institute, London. https://media.odi.org/documents/Antigua_and_Barbuda_case_study.pdf.

Ruprah, Inder. 2013. *Does Size Matter? Yes, If You Are Caribbean!* Washington, DC: Inter-American Development Bank.

Ruprah, Inder, Karl Melgarejo, and Ricardo Sierra. 2014. *Is There a Caribbean Sclerosis? Stagnating Economic Growth in the Caribbean.* Washington, DC: Inter-American Development Bank.

Saunders, Alphea. 2020. "China Says, US Criticisms of Investments in Jamaica Groundless." *Jamaica Observer,* 23 January.

Schwab, Klaus. 2017. *The Fourth Industrial Revolution.* New York: Crown Business Books.

Scott, Kennedy. 2020. "Mapping the Future of U.S. China Policy: Views of U.S. Thought Leaders, the U.S. Public, and U.S. Allies and Partners." Washington, DC: Center for Strategic and International Studies.

Sevastopulo, Demetri, and William Langley. 2021. "US to Blacklist Eight More Chinese Companies Including Dronemaker DJI." *Financial Times,* 14 December.

Shambaugh, David. 2013. *China Going Global.* Oxford: Oxford University Press.

Smith, Nicola, and Neil Connor. 2018. "Dominican Republic Cuts Diplomatic Ties with Taiwan in Victory for China." *The Telegraph,* 1 May.

Starbroek News Staff Editor. 2020. "Chinese Company Completes Acquisition of Guyana Goldfields." *Starbroek News,* 25 August.

STATISTA. 2020. "The Most Socialist Countries According to Americans." Statista, 6 October. https://www.statista.com/chart/23116/share-of-americans-considering-countries-socialist/.

Sue-A-Quan, Trevelyan. 1999. *Cane Reapers: Chinese Indentured Immigrants in Guyana.* Parksville, BC: Riftswood Publishing.

Tang, Didi. 2018. "Taiwan Stumps up $150m after Haiti Threat to Withdraw Support." *The Times,* 31 May. https://www.thetimes.co.uk/article/give-us-aid-or-lose-another-ally-haiti-tells-taiwan-cwlhodjpf.

Tankersley, Jim. 2018. "Trump's Steel Tariffs Raise Fears of a Damaging Trade War." *New York Times,* 2 March.

The Economist. 2020. "The Pandemic's Indirect Hit on the Caribbean." *The Economist,* 20 August.

The Gleaner. 2018. "Antigua PM Says US Should Invest In Developing Countries and Not Focus on China's Influence." *The Gleaner,* 22 October.

———. 2020. "China's Caribbean Presence Among Issues Discussed at JA, US Bilateral Talks." *The Gleaner*, 7 December.

The Guardian. 2018. "Taiwan Dumped by Dominican Republic amid Pressure from China." *The Guardian*, 1 May.

Thoenig, Mathias, and Thierry Verdier. 2003. "A Theory of Skill-Biased Innovation and Globalization." *American Economic Review* 93 (3): 709–28.

Trading Economics. 2021. "Credit Rating: Countries." https://tradingeconomics. com/country-list/rating.

Wall Street Journal Editorial Board. 2018. "Trump's Tariff Folly." *Wall Street Journal*, 1 March. https://www.wsj.com/articles/trumps-tariff-folly-1519950205.

Wallerstein, Immanuel. 2002a. "The Incredible Shrinking Eagle: The End of Pax Americana." *Foreign Policy* no. 131: 60–69.

———. 2002b. "The Eagle Has Crash Landed." *Foreign Policy* no. 131 (July): 60–68.

Whaples, Robert. 1995. "Where Is There Consensus Among American Economic Historians? The Results of a Survey on Forty Propositions." *Journal of Economic History* 55 (1): 139–54.

Wigglesworth, Robin. 2013. "Caribbean in Crisis: Chequebook Diplomacy." *Financial Times*, 17 December.

Willis, Kiersten. 2016. "Barbados Receives Largest Military Donation from Chinese." Atlanta Black Star, 23 December. https://atlantablackstar.com/2016/12/23/china-provides-6m-military-aid-barbados/.

Wilson, Andrew R. 2004. *The Chinese in the Caribbean*. Princeton: Marcus Weiner.

Wise, Carol. 2020. *Dragonomics: How Latin America Is Maximizing (or Missing Out On) China's International Development Strategy*. New Haven: Yale University Press.

Wong, Andy. 2018. "China Forges Ties with Dominican Republic Offering $4.1 Billion Package in a Blow to Taiwan." ABC News, 2 May. https://www.abc.net. au/news/2018-05-02/taiwan-dumped-by-dominican-republic-in-a-blow-to-taiwan/9718578.

Wong, Edward. 2018. "Mike Pompeo Warns Panama Against Doing Business with China." *New York Times*, 19 October.

Zakaria, Fareed. 2008. *The Post-American World*. New York: W.W. Norton.

2

Caribbean Futures and the Post-Brexit Deal
Challenges and Opportunities

ALICIA NICHOLLS

THE UNITED KINGDOM'S FORMAL DEPARTURE FROM THE EUROPEAN Union,[1] referred to here as the post-Brexit moment, demands a systematic reorienting of the CARIFORUM[2] region's trading relationships with two of its longest trading partners. For nearly half a century, CARIFORUM's trading relationships with the United Kingdom and the European Union were the same. While EU-CARIFORUM trading relations, under the wider EU-ACP relationship, have undergone several tectonic shifts over the years, there have been some constants. Structurally, CARIFORUM exports to the European Union remain concentrated predominantly in low value-added commodities, with some exceptions. Pattern-wise, even after the United Kingdom joined the European Communities (the forerunner to the European Union) in 1973, it remained CARIFORUM countries' most significant economic and diplomatic partner within the European Union. This was generally to the exclusion of developing strong ties with newer EU member states.

One tectonic shift which neither the European Union nor CARIFORUM countries could have anticipated was the UK referendum vote in 2016 to leave the European Union, and its actual withdrawal five years later. The post-Brexit EU-UK trading relationship is coupled with a constellation of other factors that impact EU/UK-CARIFORUM trading relations, including the new trade policy directions announced by the European Union and the United Kingdom, and their growing prioritization of trade with non-traditional partners. It also occurs against the backdrop of a global landscape that is fundamentally different from when the EU-ACP relationship was first conceived. A critical question CARIFORUM countries must consider is how can the region's relationship with two of its longest trading partners, initially born out of the colonial experience, be better oriented to adequately serve the region's strategic development imperatives for the creation of better Caribbean futures?

This chapter critically considers this question and presents the challenges and opportunities for CARIFORUM's evolving post-Brexit relationships with the European Union and the United Kingdom. It argues that CARIFORUM's relationship with both partners must account for the evolving dynamics impacting these relationships. Any reorientation must be grounded in a wider trade strategy guided by a sound sustainable development policy, marshalling, among others, the diaspora, the private sector and economic diplomacy in reorienting both relationships for mutual benefit. The remainder of the chapter is organized as follows: Section one sets the context by providing a brief overview of the phases of EU/UK-CARIFORUM structured trade from the Lomé agreements to the present-day EU/UK-CARIFORUM EPAs. Section two considers the implications of the UK-EU Trade and Cooperation Agreement (TECA) for CARIFORUM countries' relationships with the United Kingdom and the European Union. Section three discusses the challenges and opportunities to reorient CARIFORUM's relationships with the European Union and the United Kingdom, respectively, for better sustainable development outcomes. Section four is the conclusion.

PHASES OF THE EU/UK-CARIFORUM STRUCTURED TRADING RELATIONSHIP

The colonial history which forged the EU/UK-CARIFORUM relationship is relevant for understanding CARIFORUM countries' position in the global political economy and the forces that shaped their contemporary relationships with both the European Union and the United Kingdom respectively. Perhaps Demas (2005, 89) put it best when he argued that the mercantilist system left "a set of institutional features which profoundly affected the economies of the countries".[3] Although some of the features

Demas identified have changed, such as the switch from mono-crop to largely tourism-based economies, others remain evident when analysing CARIFORUM's internal and external trading relations. Although CARICOM and the Dominican Republic had already possessed a free trade agreement prior to the EPA, trade between the two remains limited.[4] It is these and other birth marks, emanating from the colonial process, which must be addressed if the CARIFORUM countries are to reorient their relations with both parties for better sustainable development outcomes.

PRE-EPA TRADING ARRANGEMENTS

From the 1800s, the Imperial Preference governed trade between the United Kingdom and its colonies (Glickman 1947). When the United Kingdom acceded to the European Communities with effect from 1 January 1973, many of its former colonies had already achieved self-government, were politically independent or on their way to becoming so. In joining the European Communities, the United Kingdom ceded responsibility for its foreign trade policy to that bloc. This development started the English-speaking Caribbean's structured trading relationship with continental Europe, and was institutionalized with the formation of what was then called the African, Caribbean and Pacific Group of States (the ACP Group) in 1975 by the Georgetown Agreement. The ACP encompasses seventy-nine former colonies of the main EU powers. CARIFORUM (the Caribbean Forum of that grouping) comprises fifteen countries. In 2019, the Georgetown Agreement was revised and, inter alia, the organization's name was changed to the Organisation of the African, Caribbean and Pacific Group of States (OACPS).[5]

From 1975 to 2000, the EU-ACP relationship centred on the EU extension of unilateral preferential access to its market and development assistance for ACP countries (Hurt 2003; Gibb 2000). Attached to the Lomé Conventions were specialized commodity protocols for ACP bananas, rum, beef/veal and sugar. As the market access terms for ACP-originating products were more favourable than those provided by the European Union to other developing countries, the Europeans required successive waivers from the World Trade Organization (WTO) from its obligations under Article 1(1)

(General Most Favoured Nation Treatment) of the General Agreement on Tariffs and Trade (GATT).[6] Since 1959, the European Development Fund (EDF) has been the main EU source of development assistance to OACPS and the overseas territories. There have been eleven EDFs, with the twelfth spanning 2021–2027. The fund is separate from the EU budget and directly financed by EU countries.

By the mid-1990s, the European Union had begun to openly rethink the effectiveness of the EU-ACP relationship. The 1996 Green Paper on ACP-EU relations found that the Lomé preferences had not increased ACP exports to the EU bloc, and only in limited cases had there been diversification (Commission of the European Communities 1996). The EU preference for a WTO-compatible replacement was unsurprising, given the WTO challenges brought by the US on behalf of its US-based multilateral corporations.[7]

The 1996 Green Paper further found that although the EU market then accounted on average for more than 40 per cent of ACP sales, ACP exports' share to the European Union dropped from 6.7 per cent in 1976 to 2.8 per cent in 1994, while other less preferred exporters increased their market share (Commission of the European Communities 1996, xiii). The report noted that the value of Lomé trade preferences had dropped and stood to decline further due to several factors (Commission of the European Communities 1996, 16) and "have not been sufficient to enhance export growth and increase diversification" (Commission of the European Communities 1996, 17). The Lomé preferences were also found to "have not been sufficient to enhance export growth and increase diversification". Even after three decades of preferences, the birthmarks of the colonial experience characterized the EU-CARIFORUM relationship. That is, the concentration remained on traditional exports, limited diversification, and patterns of trade generally oriented towards the former colonial power, as opposed to more diversified among the EU member states.

In a subsequent green paper, the European Union proposed a two-pronged approach comprising the negotiation of an overarching framework agreement, followed by region-specific agreements (Commission of the European Communities 1997). The Cotonou Agreement was signed in June 2000 for a twenty-year period, establishing the principles underpinning a new EU-ACP trading relationship based on reciprocity. Article 36.1 mandated the parties "to take all the necessary measures to ensure the conclusion of new WTO-compatible Economic Partnership Agreements".[8] It rolled over the trade provisions of the previous regime until 2007, by which time EPAs between the EU and ACP regions were to have been signed (Vahl 2011, 2).[9]

THE EU-CARIFORUM ECONOMIC PARTNERSHIP AGREEMENT

Negotiations on the EU-CARIFORUM EPA commenced in Jamaica in April 2004. On 15 October 2008, CARIFORUM became the first of the six ACP regions to sign a WTO-compatible EPA with the European Union, as agreed to under Article 36.1 of the Cotonou Agreement. The EU-CARIFORUM EPA, which now governs the trade aspect of the CARIFORUM-EU relationship, has been provisionally applied since 29 December 2008.[10] Although Haiti participated in the EPA negotiations and signed the agreement on 11 December 2009, it has not yet ratified it (European Commission 2020, 26).[11]

The EU-CARIFORUM EPA is a region-to-region agreement that covers trade in goods, services, investments, as well as other disciplines. It provides for the immediate duty-free, quota-free liberalization of all CARIFORUM-originating goods entering the EU market, while allowing for phased, liberalized EU access to the CARIFORUM market over a twenty-year period. The EPA not only replaces the unilateral preferential regime with a WTO-compatible agreement, but is also WTO-plus in some areas (Gonzales 2011).

The EU-CARIFORUM EPA was noteworthy for three reasons. First, the level of development cooperation provisions infused throughout the text was unprecedented. Its approach has three broad aims: to raise the development of partner countries, promote regional integration and integrate these countries into global markets (European Commission 2020). This can be contrasted with the NAFTA-type agreements, the dominant model utilized by the United States and Canada, which generally lack any significant special and differential treatment for developing country partners in the form of differentiated commitments or development assistance. Second, at the time of its conclusion, the EU-CARIFORUM EPA was among the first to contain explicit reference to the concept of sustainable development,[12] and in particular the Millennium Development Goals (MDGs),[13] not just in its preambular text, but throughout the agreement. Third, while WTO-compatible, the EU-CARIFORUM EPA provides for asymmetric reciprocity with differentiated commitments, not just between the European Union and CARIFORUM, but also among CARIFORUM countries (Bernal 2013).

More than a decade after the signing of the EPA and provisional application, the empirical data, as presented in the two monitoring reports, have found little to no impact of the agreement on either increasing EU-CARIFORUM trade or development of the region. This is not due to any flaws in the EPA itself, as chronic under-utilization is a feature of all trade agreements that CARICOM has entered into with third countries. In one of the most comprehensive publicly available studies to date on the utilization of CARICOM's agreements, McLean and Khadan (2014) found no significant improvement in CARICOM's export performance and little movement up the value chain, despite several agreements.

Both reviews of the EPA identified several reasons for the disappointing trade performance, including implementation delays in both the EU and CARIFORUM countries, hindered by the severe fallout that CARIFORUM countries suffered due to the global economic and financial crisis of 2008 (European Commission 2014). CARIFORUM economies also faced several other shocks over the period,[14] including hurricanes and then the COVID-19 pandemic, which negatively impacted the pace of EPA implementation. Moreover, inadequate productive capacity and supply side constraints affecting the region's private sector have made converting EPA market access into market penetration difficult, while greater trade and investment promotions were needed (European Commission 2014). Data shortages on the CARIFORUM side also made objective findings difficult (European Commission 2014).

In a study prepared for Caribbean Export, Chaitoo (2019, 7) identified similar findings adversely impacting CARIFORUM countries' merchandise exports to the European Union, including the high costs of shipping and marketing; difficulty meeting technical regulations and standards; the need for on-the-ground market research; and the lack of capacity to implement food safety regulations and testing facilities to address UK/EU regulatory requirements, in particular dairy, poultry and other meats. Regarding services, Chaitoo (2019, 8) highlighted as constraints the small size of regional service firms, competitiveness issues, market intelligence needs, the need to establish credibility, access to financing, and the traditional focus of Caribbean countries' incentives programmes on traditional manufacturing or agricultural sectors, and not non-tourism services.

The most recent EPA review, which covered the period 2008–2018 found some progress since the 2014 study. Twenty-five out of the then twenty-eight EU countries and ten out of fifteen CARIFORUM countries had ratified the EPA, an improvement over the 2014 figures (European Commission 2020). Technical barriers to trade contact points, which had not been established at the time of the 2014 report, were now present in all CARIFORUM countries except two. CARIFORUM countries also made "significant progress" in customs and trade facilitation, despite "substantial shortcomings" remaining (European Commission 2020).

The report identified several noteworthy trends in EU-CARIFORUM trading relations over the review period. First, total goods trade between the European Union and CARIFORUM had not expanded since 2008. While EU exports to CARIFORUM had increased since 2008, CARIFORUM exports to the EU were lower in 2018 than in 2008 when the agreement was signed. The European Union now has a trade surplus compared to a deficit with CARIFORUM in 2008. Second, it found that the European Union represented a declining share of CARIFORUM imports from the world and that CARIFORUM's trade with the bloc has not increased in importance relative to its trade with other partners. The share of EU-bound CARIFORUM exports was 22 per cent in 2007, but at the time of the review was four percentage points less (European Commission 2020, 75).

Third, the report showed that there was high concentration in the goods traded between CARIFORUM and the European Union, with four countries accounting for more than half of EU-CARIFORUM trade flows: the Dominican Republic (32 per cent), Trinidad and Tobago (25 per cent), the Bahamas (16 per cent) and Jamaica (8 per cent) (European Commission 2020, 66). Fourth, this concentration is not limited to goods trade. The report noted that while there was a five-fold increase in EU foreign direct investment to CARIFORUM countries, the majority went to the Bahamas and Barbados. The increase could not be attributed to the EPA (European Commission 2020).

The fourth trend identified was that CARIFORUM exports to the

European Union remained largely undiversified and concentrated primarily in low value-added goods. They are "composed mainly of chemicals and related products (21 per cent), mineral fuels (21 per cent), and food and live animals (19 per cent)", according to the European Commission (2020).

One area of export promise is cultural services, given growing European interest in Caribbean culture (Chaitoo 2019, 19). There are also carnivals with Caribbean elements in the United Kingdom, Belgium, Germany, the Netherlands, Sweden and Switzerland (Chaitoo 2019, 22). The main European consumers of Caribbean creative products are music festival organizers and carnival promoters or bands (Chaitoo 2019, 21). Even here, however, challenges have to be addressed. The Protocol on Cultural Cooperation has not yet been activated (Burri and Nurse 2019) and most European and Caribbean creatives are unaware of the EPA or its cultural provisions (Chaitoo 2019, 21). However, there appears to be "immense political will to increase efforts towards advocacy and operationalization" (Burri and Nurse 2019, 7) and those few creatives familiar with the protocol expressed interest in seeing its implementation (Chaitoo 2019, 21). Other challenges included obtaining visas and work permits to supply cultural services in some countries; access to finance for joint film projects, the lack of sponsorship experienced by Caribbean carnival operators in the European Union; the lack of collaboration among Caribbean bands; the absence of a mechanism among Caribbean artists/entertainers in the European Union for collecting royalties for their songs/music; and the cost of bringing artists from overseas (Chaitoo 2019).

The EPA has sought to address these structural deficits through its wide-ranging development cooperation and technical assistance provisions found throughout the text, including in each chapter.[15] The European Development Fund finances the EU development assistance to the ACP through (i) national indicative programmes to specific countries; (ii) the Caribbean Regional Indicative Programme; (iii) the Intra-ACP envelope; and (iv) thematic budget lines (European Commission 2020, 43). Since its establishment in 1996, the Caribbean Export Development Agency, the only region-wide trade and investment promotion agency in the OACPS, has operated programmes targeting many of the structural impediments facing Caribbean firms. However, these issues are deep and cannot be solved immediately.

With Brexit then pending, the EPA Monitoring Report also zeroed in on the UK-CARIFORUM trading relationship. It found that in 2018 the United Kingdom ranked third among the EU member states in terms of trade with CARIFORUM, with total imports and exports amounting to €1.6 billion (European Commission 2020). UK trade constituted 11 per cent of EU exports to CARIFORUM and 13 per cent of EU imports from CARIFORUM of total trade. It concluded, therefore, that while the United Kingdom is a significant partner for CARIFORUM, it is "not disproportionally large" (European Commission 2020, 80).

The second trend identified by the EPA Monitoring Report was that despite being the third ranking overall, in 2018 the United Kingdom was the largest EU export destination for Belize and St Lucia, and second or third largest for Barbados, Dominica, the Dominican Republic, Grenada, Guyana and Jamaica (European Commission 2020). It was also the number one EU source of imports for five CARIFORUM countries (Barbados, Dominica, Grenada, St Lucia, and Trinidad and Tobago), and the second largest source for five others (Antigua and Barbuda, Belize, Guyana, St Vincent and the Grenadines, and St Kitts and Nevis (European Commission 2020, 80). Moreover, the report determined that the United Kingdom was crucial for certain sectors of CARIFORUM exports. For example, it accounted for 33 per cent of total CARIFORUM exports to the EU under the food and live animals sector. The most significant products were the traditional exports of bananas, fruits, sugar, fish products, prepared food stuffs and spirits (European Commission 2020, 80).

The third trend identified was that the share of UK-CARIFORUM trade as a total of EU-CARIFORUM trade has been on a decline, fluctuating between 20 per cent and 10 per cent of total EU-CARIFORUM trade (European Commission 2020). Though reaching a high point soon after the financial crisis and as the EPA was implemented, it has been slowly decreasing to below the pre-EPA level (European Commission 2020). This is supported by UK Office of National Statistics data from 2021, which shows that overall, CARIFORUM countries' goods as a percentage of total UK imports has been declining. In 2000, the United Kingdom imported £515 million in goods from the fifteen CARIFORUM countries, representing 0.48 per cent of UK imports from the world. In 2020, it imported £591 million in goods from the fifteen CARIFORUM countries, an increase in total imports, but represented only 0.29 per cent of the UK total (Office of National Statistics 2021). Over the twenty-year period from 2000, UK imports from CARIFORUM countries declined as a percentage of its total imports, except for a spike to 0.53 per cent in 2009, immediately after the signing of the EU-CARIFORUM EPA.

Aside from goods trade, the United Kingdom remains a major tourism source market for many Caribbean countries and for Barbados, in particular, the main source of FDI in the luxury second home sector. This was particularly evident in the period immediately after the Brexit referendum outcome, when the sharp declines in the pound sterling's value relative to the US dollar caused a reduction in real estate sales by British buyers of second homes in Barbados.[16]

UK-CARIFORUM EPA

To prevent a disruption in market access for CARIFORUM exporters to the UK market post-Brexit, CARIFORUM and the United Kingdom immediately engaged in what has been described by CARICOM officials as a "technical dialogue" to roll over the provisions of the EU-CARIFORUM EPA to cover post-Brexit UK-CARIFORUM relations. Some may argue that CARIFORUM should have renegotiated the EPA with the United Kingdom to gain a better deal.[17] But closer examination reveals such a renegotiation was not practical at the time, given the overriding concern of preserving trade continuity and extant preferences between the CARIFORUM and UK markets. Failure to negotiate a roll-over agreement in time would have caused regional exporters to face MFN tariffs in the UK market.[18] The UK-CARIFORUM EPA was, therefore, concluded and signed on 22 March 2020, and is being provisionally applied as of 1 January 2021. Suriname signed the agreement later on 5 March 2021.[19] The UK-CARIFORUM EPA replicates, to the extent possible, the substantive text of the EU-CARIFORUM EPA.

IMPLICATIONS OF THE UK-EU TRADE AND COOPERATION AGREEMENT

After the UK Government invoked Article 50 of the Treaty on European Union on March 29, 2017,[20] there was much uncertainty over whether it would have been able to conclude a post-Brexit trade deal with the EU before the end of the transition period.[21] Against the odds, the parties announced an agreement on 24 December 2020.[22]

As of 1 January 2021, the UK-EU TECA is being provisionally applied, marking a new era in the UK-EU trading relationship. It provides for tariff-free, quota-free trade on originating goods between the UK and EU. While the UK-EU TECA sets out the framework for the parties' post-Brexit trade and wider cooperation, it does not approximate the EU single market or the customs union, and customs controls now apply to UK-EU trade. These include the completion of import and export declarations and subjection to customs checks for regulatory compliance, factors which increase the time and cost of conducting business. A British Chamber of Commerce Survey 2021 found that "half (49%) of the exporters surveyed reported facing difficulties in adapting to the changes in the trade of goods' following 1 January 2021" (British Chamber of Commerce 2021).

Many CARIFORUM producers use the UK as an entry point into the EU market (European Commission 2020; Chaitoo 2019). According to the most recent EPA review, these strategies include establishing "a local presence in the UK, the use of UK warehouses or the partnership with distributors in the UK" (European Commission 2020, 80). It also identified the large Caribbean diaspora in the UK as "a key facilitating factor" (European Commission 2020, 80).

The UK-CARIFORUM EPA allows UK and CARIFORUM exporters to use EU materials or processing in exports to each other and still qualify as 'originating' in the United Kingdom or CARIFORUM countries respectively for the purposes of the agreement.[23] However, the UK-EU TECA could impact the global supply chain strategies of firms that had relied on the United Kingdom as a node in their supply chain with the European Union due to existing logistical routes. The impact will depend on the kind of goods or services that they export. It will also be up to the European Union to decide whether the United Kingdom's sanitary and phytosanitary standards (SPS) merit it being listed as a third country allowed to export food products to the European Union. This would have implications for CARIFORUM countries that use the UK as a base to export those goods subject to SPS standards. UK standards might eventually diverge from those of the European Union, forcing CARIFORUM exporters to comply with two sets of standards, should they continue to use the United Kingdom as the base for export into the EU market.

While there is no official data on the extent to which CARIFORUM's access to the EU or UK markets have been impacted, one change is that CARIFORUM exporters require new customs documentation for the United Kingdom.[24] In light of these new non-tariff barriers to trade between the UK and EU, CARIFORUM firms, which currently utilize the UK as a basis for EU market entry, should reconsider their market entry strategies. These can include establishing a commercial presence in the EU, exporting directly to the EU by establishing links with EU-based intermediaries in ports of entry, such as Rotterdam (the Netherlands). The Dominican Republic and Suriname maintain close ties with Spain and the Netherlands, respectively, due to historic and linguistic ties. However, for the anglophone countries in CARIFORUM, an option may be to deepen relations with the Republic of Ireland, the remaining EU Member State with a majority anglophone population. While Irish-CARIFORUM diplomatic ties and logistical connectivity do not presently proximate UK-CARIFORUM ties, there are historic ties which may make the Republic of Ireland a possible alternative base for firms from anglophone CARIFORUM countries seeking to establish an EU presence.

REORIENTING THE RELATIONSHIP FOR BETTER CARIBBEAN FUTURES

CARIFORUM countries' relationship with the European Union and the United Kingdom show several 'birthmarks' of the colonial process, namely the high concentration of CARIFORUM exports to just a few EU countries; limited export diversification; and the concentration of mainly traditional and generally low-value-added products. The COVID-19 impact on Caribbean economies further reiterated the region's need to expand its exports, and to reduce its heavy reliance on tourism and travel trade for such a significant proportion of GDP, employment and foreign exchange.

The region's trade agreements, not just the EU-CARIFORUM EPA, are under-utilized and the UK-CARIFORUM EPA is likely to face a similar fate, and not achieve the expected development outcomes. Simply put, trade agreements by themselves cannot foment sustainable development. Their negotiation, conclusion and implementation must be moored to a wider trade and development strategy. The region demands a new approach to its trade, one which focuses on solid development outcomes and situates the region's trade policy within a broader sustainable development policy.[25] This is not a novel recommendation. Bernal (2013), for example, spoke of "strategic global repositioning", a concept on which he had elaborated in a previous work in 1996.[26] While it is beyond the scope of this chapter to outline a trade and development policy or strategy for the region, it should include institutional strengthening; improving the ease of doing business; building private sector capacity; leveraging the diaspora; economic diplomacy; and frequent monitoring and evaluation of trade agreements' performance.

Diversification of the region's trade, including engagement with non-traditional trading partners, is necessary for post-COVID-19 sustainable recovery. It is also vital to deepen and diversify existing trading relationships, such as those with the European Union and the United Kingdom. Although the United States is by far the Caribbean's largest trading partner and China has increased its economic footprint within the region,[27] the EPAs with the European Union and the United Kingdom are CARIFORUM's only FTAs with developed country partners.[28] They are also the region's only agreements with development provisions infused throughout, and the European Union remains the Caribbean's largest source of official development assistance. However, since signing the EPA and provisional application in 2008, the European Union has continued, and even accelerated, the pace of its negotiation and conclusion of trade agreements with third parties.[29] The United Kingdom has also quickly intensified its trade agreement negotiation post-Brexit. Therefore, the margin of preference that CARIFORUM goods enjoy in both markets is fast eroding, and further evidences the need for a more strategic approach to deepening its relationship with both parties.

EU-CARIFORUM RELATIONS

Prior to Brexit, CARIFORUM countries had little incentive to deepen diplomatic and economic engagement with non-traditional EU partners, including influential EU member states like France and Germany, and newer member states which have little familiarity or empathy for the region's development circumstances. This is because the United Kingdom was generally regarded as an advocate for the region at the EU table on many issues. In the post-Brexit era, however, CARIFORUM countries must deepen direct links with the remaining EU countries with which they have traditionally had little direct diplomatic engagement beyond representation in Brussels. This is especially so given the growing EU penchant for extra-jurisdictional rule-making in areas which directly impact Caribbean countries. Its arbitrary blacklisting of Caribbean international financial centres has been a sore point in EU-CARIFORUM relations, and poses reputational and commercial risks for affected Caribbean countries (Remy and Nicholls 2020).[30]

EU DEVELOPMENT COOPERATION AND ASSISTANCE

Another major concern for CARIFORUM countries was the possible impact of Brexit on EU development assistance to the region. The United Kingdom contributed about 15 per cent to the EDF budget (Døhlie Saltnes 2018). Humphrey (2016, vi) noted that "the loss of the UK's budget contribution, particularly its key-based portion of the EDF, could lead to reduced funding for the Caribbean's regional and national Indicative Programmes". However, the EDF is being phased out as a special fund and has been incorporated for the first time under the EU Budget for 2021.[31] It is, therefore, too early to objectively assess to what extent the UK departure has had an impact on levels of EU development assistance.

EPA AWARENESS, IMPLEMENTATION AND MONITORING

Limited awareness remains of the EPA's existence by CARIFORUM and EU firms (European Commission 2020; Chaitoo 2019).[32] EPA implementation and awareness raising should be accelerated if the gains of the agreement are to be realized. EPA implementation can be fast-tracked by addressing the challenges and shortcomings identified in the monitoring report (European Commission 2020, 86). For example, strengthening the currently weak trade enquiry points, through greater financial and human resources, is vital as they are among the first points of call for potential exporters when exploring trade opportunities.

The EPA report further lamented the lack of a formal mechanism for EPA reporting, and formal benchmarks or indicators to assess the effectiveness of the EPA (European Commission 2020). Most publicly available analysis on the operation of CARIFORUM countries' trade agreements is conducted by the trading partner. CARIFORUM countries must take a more systematic approach to ensuring its trade agreements are leading to the outcomes desired by commissioning periodic reviews of the performance and operation of their trading agreements. This will require access to data, which remains a perennial problem in the region due to human resource capacity constraints facing statistical offices, among other things.

NEW EU TRADE POLICY DIRECTION

In 2021, the European Union articulated a new trade policy direction that raised several issues, which CARIFORUM countries had to consider as they sought to reorient their relations with that bloc. First, its new "open, sustainable and assertive" trade policy would be based on "open strategic autonomy", which "emphasises the EU's ability to make its own choices and shape the world around it through leadership and engagement, reflecting its strategic interests and values" (European Commission 2021a, 5). CARIFORUM countries could expect the European Union to much more vigorously articulate and defend its interests on trade matters, including potentially on matters germane to the region in the multilateral trading system.

Second, the European Union places greater priority on its relationships with other partners. Reference to the Caribbean was made only once in the communication on the way forward for the new EU trade strategy (European Commission 2021a; 2021b), and it was not among the regions specifically mentioned for deepening EU partnerships. This, however, is not new, as the ACP relationship has been a declining priority for the European Union over the years, particularly with the EU expansion and inclusion of newer members (Bernal 2013; Ravenhill 2004). For their part, CARIFORUM countries have also been more actively courting non-traditional trading partners.

The European Union interacts with CARIFORUM countries on various political levels: through bilateral arrangements, CARIFORUM, the broader OACP and more recently, the European Union-Community of Latin American and Caribbean (EU-CELAC).[33] The thirty-three CELAC countries[34] are the European Union's fifth largest export partner (European Parliament 2019). Two factors explain its increased pivot to Latin America, namely, many are emerging economies, and more recently, the increasing loss of EU market share in LAC to China (European Parliament 2019). Additionally, "the EU strategy has also aimed to balance the dominant US footprint in LAC and to secure EU market access to the region" (European Parliament 2019, 2). While LAC countries have similar interests and development challenges, and deepening CARIFORUM-Latin America trade has advantages, there are also differences. The EU-CELAC relationship is important, but should not be a substitute for the EU-CARIFORUM relationship.

Fourth, the European Union has also noted that it would be "reinforcing the EU's focus on implementing and enforcing trade agreements, and ensuring a level playing field for EU businesses" (European Commission 2021a). This muscular rhetoric was likely aimed at China. However, similar to its treatment of the Caribbean on tax and AML/CFT matters, the European Union may decide to take action against CARIFORUM countries if it feels that EU firms are at a disadvantage in their markets. The EPA Monitoring Report noted that one EU business association pointed out the difficulties encountered by EU companies in entering CARIFORUM countries' markets "because of a lack of transparency on the relevant rules and regulations for the sector" (European Commission 2020, 86). Transparency commitments are among those included throughout the EPA.

LEVERAGING THE DIASPORA

Although the United Kingdom was the largest hub for the Caribbean diaspora in the European Union, smaller pockets of Caribbean expatriates live in Belgium, the Netherlands and France. CARIFORUM countries should consider the role that their EU-based diasporas could play in deepening relations with the European Union, through diaspora-mapping initiatives, for example. Regional business support organizations (BSOs) can better tap into the diaspora and diaspora associations as sources of market intelligence, and business mentoring and coaching for CARIFORUM entrepreneurs interested in trading with EU firms or establishing an EU presence.

LEVERAGING ECONOMIC DIPLOMACY

Diplomatic missions can play a crucial role in providing on-the-ground market intelligence for CARIFORUM traders seeking to access the EU market. To this extent, the designation of trade attachés to diplomatic missions in European capitals would be useful. Given limited resources and the expense of maintaining individual diplomatic missions, the region could consider the feasibility of establishing more joint embassies in key capitals or creating a region-wide system of trade commissioners, similar to the Canadian Trade Commissioner Service, which falls under the purview of Global Affairs Canada and whose remit is trade promotion with key markets of trade interest.[35] An assessment of the feasibility of these suggestions is outside the scope of this chapter, but it is recommended that a study be commissioned by CARICOM to assess the possible pros and cons of either approach.

UK-CARIFORUM RELATIONS

The United Kingdom evinced a greater appetite for meaningful deepening of its commercial relationship with the Caribbean post-Brexit. From 2012, it implemented a trade envoy system in which a network of parliamentarians selected by the prime minister is appointed to regions that it deems to have substantial trade and investment prospects. In 2020, the UK prime minister appointed a trade envoy for the twelve Commonwealth Caribbean countries.[36] Prior to this, the United Kingdom also announced the opening of new Resident High Commissioners' offices in Grenada, Antigua and Barbuda, and St Vincent and the Grenadines as part of its expanded diplomatic network across the Commonwealth (UK Government 2018).

On 18 March 2021, the Tenth UK-Caribbean Ministerial Forum took place. Although due biennially, this high-level forum had not been held since 2016 and was the first since Brexit.[37] The communique issued at the conclusion reaffirmed the parties' commitment to the forum as "an an important vehicle for dialogue, partnership and cooperation, reflecting the special relationship that exists between the United Kingdom, the Caribbean States and the British Overseas Territories".[38] The parties also agreed on a detailed action plan to be implemented from 2021 to 2023 for mutual cooperation.[39] Specifically on trade and commercial relations, those CARIFORUM countries which had not yet done so agreed to ratify the UK-CARIFORUM EPA. A UK-Caribbean business-to-business roundtable will be established, and the parties also agreed to promote and expand UK-Caribbean trade flows, and reduce market access barriers for one another's exporters.

The Commonwealth Secretariat has undertaken some discussion and research of post-Brexit trading opportunities for its members and capitalizing on what has been branded the "Commonwealth Advantage".[40] However, at this stage, the UK government is unlikely to formalize the Commonwealth trading relationship through an FTA, as it seeks to accelerate FTA negotiations with larger partners.

BLACKLISTING OF CARIBBEAN IFCS

Blacklisting is a space to watch in UK-CARIFORUM relations. Since the United Kingdom is no longer an EU member, it has formulated its own list of high-risk third countries for anti-money laundering (AML) purposes. Unlike the EU, the United Kingdom has not created its own listing methodology and its list mirrors the Financial Action Task Force (FATF) lists. However, like the EU list, the UK list unfortunately lumps all the listed jurisdictions, whether on the FATF grey list or blacklist, into one blacklist and requires that transactions involving these listed jurisdictions be subjected to Enhanced Due Diligence (EDD).[41]

GLOBAL BRITAIN IN A COMPETITIVE AGE

Even before its official exit from the EU, the United Kingdom had begun to carve out for itself an independent voice on the world stage under the "Global Britain" concept. The concept was first articulated by then prime minister Theresa May in her Lancaster House Speech in 2017 (Thiboud 2018; May 2017). While her successor, Boris Johnson, adopted this nomenclature in his speeches, the concept remained nebulous until early 2021, when it was elucidated in his House of Commons address, following the release of a report entitled *Global Britain in a Competitive Age: The Integrated Review of Security, Defence, Development and Foreign Policy*.[42] The report noted that the United Kingdom "will continue to play a leading international role in collective security, multilateral governance, tackling climate change and health risks, conflict resolution and poverty reduction" (UK Government 2021). It had already established itself as a leading proponent of free trade through its ambitious trade agreement roll-over programme to preserve market access for its exporters and investors, and pursue more FTAs.[43]

There are at least three ways in which the values espoused under Global Britain align with the Caribbean's interests. First, the United Kingdom has made taking a leading role in climate action, a central goal under its aim to build resilience at home and abroad. In June 2019, it became the world's first major economy to pass a net-zero emissions law, committing to bringing its emissions to net zero by 2050.[44] Climate action is also one of the six areas of cooperation under the UK-Caribbean Action Plan (CARICOM 2021). Second, the United Kingdom reiterated that it "remains deeply committed to multilateralism", which is an important tenet of Caribbean countries' foreign policy (UK Government 2021). A third area for CARIFORUM-UK cooperation is health. The United Kingdom identified bolstering its domestic and international action to address global health risks as part of its wider biosecurity approach (UK Government 2021, 93). Importantly, it remains a top donor to the COVAX Facility, which assists developing countries' access to COVID-19 vaccines.

DEVELOPMENT ASSISTANCE

The United Kingdom has always been and remains a major donor of development assistance internationally. Globally, it is the third largest Development Assistance Committee provider of official development assistance, donating US$19.4 billion (equivalent to 0.7 per cent of gross national income) in 2019 (Organisation for Economic Co-operation and Development 2020). In 2020, the UK GDP contracted by 9.9 per cent, "marking the largest annual fall in UK GDP on record" (Office of National Statistics 2021). Much of this fallout was due to the impact from the COVID-19 pandemic. Economic fallout in the United Kingdom might adversely impact both British travel and investment to CARIFORUM countries, as well as development assistance. The UK government announced its decision to reduce its commitment to spend 0.7 per cent of its gross national income on official development assistance made in 2013 to 0.5 per cent. It further noted that the UK will remain a world leader in international development and will return to its commitment to spend 0.7 per cent of gross national income on development when the fiscal situation allows (UK Government 2021, 5). Not all CARIFORUM countries are eligible for official development assistance (ODA),[45] but many receive non-ODA assistance from the United Kingdom which could be affected by the cuts.

Even while an EU member, the United Kingdom also provided bilateral assistance to the region outside of its contribution under the European Development Dunc (EDF) through, inter alia, scholarships, humanitarian and military aid, and other technical support for disaster relief and fighting drug trafficking. Though acknowledging the importance of UK input to the EDF budget, Humphrey (2016, 9) predicted that "since major parties in the UK seem favourably disposed towards ensuring that Britain maintains a significant external development profile, they might be prepared to increase the UK's development aid to the Caribbean". This appears to be the case, as the United Kingdom pledged to maintain its current aid levels to the region during the Tenth UK-Caribbean Ministerial Forum.[46]

LEVERAGING THE DIASPORA AND PRIVATE SECTOR

The Caribbean diaspora in the UK are valuable *demandeurs* of Caribbean products.[47] Private sector organizations and consultancy firms in the UK, whose role involves the active promotion of UK-Caribbean trade and investment, can be better engaged by individual firms, chambers of commerce and export promotion agencies in the region to identify markets and products of export interest.

UK-CARIFORUM EPA IMPLEMENTATION

The existing EPA implementation units– at the CARICOM Secretariat and in individual CARIFORUM countries – are for the EU-CARIFORUM EPA. It is unlikely that CARIFORUM countries will set up separate EPA implementation units for the UK-CARIFORUM EPA. The more feasible option, given the scarcity of resources, would be to subsume implementation of the UK-CARIFORUM EPA into the functions of the extant EPA units.

The institutions under the EU-CARIFORUM EPA have been replicated in the UK-CARIFORUM EPA. The Joint UK-CARIFORUM Council, responsible for the agreement's implementation, and the UK-CARIFORUM Trade and Development Committee, will need to have persons appointed to them. Additionally, two joint institutions (namely, the Special Committee on Agriculture and Fisheries, and the Technical Sub-Committee on Development Cooperation), which were established after the signing of the EU-CARIFORUM EPA, are directly included through dedicated articles in the UK-CARIFORUM EPA's text.

CONCLUSION

The post-Brexit moment is an important catalyst for CARIFORUM to reorient its relationships with both the United Kingdom and the European Union for better development outcomes, but with the recognition that trade agreements by themselves cannot foment development, and must be linked to a sound trade and development policy and strategy. This is even more critical now that the COVID-19 shock has reiterated the need for

CARIFORUM countries to diversify their economies. Any reorienting of the region's relationships with the United Kingdom and the European Union must seek to address the features inherited from the colonial relationship, such as the need for greater export and export partner diversification within the European Union. This reorientation must also take cognizance of the changing dynamics of the EU-UK trading relationship, as well as their new trade policy directions.

CARIFORUM countries must formulate sound export and investment promotion strategies, moored to a wider trade and development strategy that seeks to build institutional and private sector capacity. Regional and domestic export and investment promotion agencies, the diaspora, private sector bodies and diplomatic missions will all have key roles to play in executing these strategies for reorienting CARIFORUM's EU and UK relations for better futures.

NOTES

1. With the United Kingdom's official departure, the twenty-seven remaining member states of the European Union are Austria, Belgium, Bulgaria, Croatia, Cyprus, Czech Republic, Denmark, Estonia, Finland, France, Germany, Greece, Hungary, Ireland, Italy, Latvia, Lithuania, Luxembourg, Malta, the Netherlands, Poland, Portugal, Romania, Slovakia, Slovenia, Spain and Sweden.

2. For the purposes of the EPAs, the CARIFORUM parties are Antigua and Barbuda, the Bahamas, Barbados, Belize, Dominica, Dominican Republic, Grenada, Guyana, Haiti, Jamaica, St Kitts and Nevis, St Lucia, St Vincent and the Grenadines, Suriname, and Trinidad and Tobago. Although Haiti signed the EU-CARIFORUM EPA on 11 December 2009, it is not yet applying the agreement. Haiti has not signed the UK-CARIFORUM EPA.

3. According to Demas (2005, 89), these features included the export monoculture of sugar in a relatively unprocessed form; foreign ownership and foreign decision-making, basing of the entire productive system on metropolitan preferences; failure to establish linkages between productive units within each island and between different islands of the region; competitive rather than complementary strategies of development taking the force of fierce rivalry between different islands for the retention or gaining of privileged preferential

positions in the British market; the absence of genuine national economies and the existence of regional disintegration rather than integration.

4. The Dominican Republic enjoys a large surplus with CARICOM, but does not represent a major source of exports to the region as a whole. According to ITC Trade Map data, in 2019, CARICOM imported US\$1,000,257,000 in goods from the Dominican Republic, out of US\$40,734,327,000 from the world. CARICOM only exported US\$383,692,000 to the Dominican Republic in 2019.

5. The Georgetown Agreement was revised by Decision No. 1/CX/19 of the 110th session of the ACP Council of Ministers, held in Nairobi, Kenya, on 7 December 2019.The Revised Georgetown Agreement was endorsed by the 9th Summit of the ACP Heads of State and Government, Nairobi, Kenya, 9–10 December 2019. Inter alia, the preamble has been amended and the agreement's objectives expanded to include reference to issues of climate change, the environment, peace and security. A dispute resolution mechanism has also been added.

6. The EU preferences for ACP-originating goods under the Lome Conventions and the Cotonou Agreement did not meet the exceptions for developing countries from the General Agreement on Tariff and Trade's Most Favoured Nation clause under the 1979 Decision on Differential and More Favourable Treatment, Reciprocity and Fuller Participation of Developing Countries, more commonly referred to as "The Enabling Clause". This clause, an exception to the GATT) Most Favoured Nation) clause, allows for developed countries to provide preferences to developing countries that they do not provide to other developed countries. See generally, Roman Grynberg (1998). "The WTO incompatibility of the Lome Convention trade provisions". https://crawford. anu.edu.au/pdf/wp98/sp98-3.pdf.

7. Bernal (2020) shows the history of this conflict, using the case study of Chiquita International to demonstrate how that US multinational company was able to convince the Clinton administration to put its corporate interests over US national interests in challenging the EU preferential regime for ACP bananas before the WTO's dispute settlement system.

8. Article 36 of the Cotonou Agreement

9. Negotiations on a successor to the Cotonou Agreement, the Samoa Agreement, were concluded in December 2020. The Samoa Agreement was endorsed by the OACPS in February 2021, but some EU member states have expressed reservations that it had strayed beyond the mandate. The agreement has subsequently been signed, although some OACPS members have not signed due to various reservations. See https://www.consilium.europa.eu/en/policies/samoa-agreement/.

10. The signing of the EPA was not entirely welcomed as some prominent regional academics called for the Caribbean to reject it (Girvan 2009; Brewster, Girvan, and Lewis 2008).

11. However, as the only Least Developed Country in the Caribbean, Haiti benefits from the EU Everything but Arms (EBA) Initiative.

12. The concept of sustainable development speaks to development that "meets the needs of the present without compromising the ability of future generations to meet their own needs" See World Commission on Environment and Development, *Our Common Future* (Oxford University Press, 1987).

13. The eight MDGs have been succeeded by the seventeen Sustainable Development Goals, part of the 2030 Agenda for Development that UN member states agreed to in 2015.

14. For example, Dominica faced severe damage from Tropical Storm Erika (2015) and Hurricane Maria (2017) and the Bahamas' Abacos and Grand Bahama Islands suffered severe devastation from Hurricane Dorian (2019). More recently, the La Soufriere volcanic eruption in St Vincent and the Grenadines was another natural shock at the same time as the COVID-19 pandemic, affecting not just St Vincent but neighbouring islands like Barbados with severe ashfall.

15. Article 8 of the EC-CARIFORUM EPA outlines seven primary priorities for cooperation, building capacity to comply the commitments, promoting private sector and enterprise development, diversifying CARIFORUM exports, among other things.

16. The author was working in the Barbados real estate sector at the time and witnessed this firsthand.

17. For example, the EU-CARIFORUM EPA's investment chapter only contains investment liberalization commitments, as the European Commission had lacked competency for investment protection and promotion/facilitation.

18. See generally Mohammed Razzaque and Brendan Vickers "Post-Brexit UK-ACP Trading Arrangements: Some Reflections" in *Trade Hot Topics Issue* (London: Commonwealth Secretariat, 2016), which highlighted some of the implications of Brexit for UK-ACP trade.

19. See https://www.gov.uk/government/news/suriname-signs-cariforum-uk-epa#:~:text=Suriname%20becomes%20the%2014th%20CARIFORUM,to%20businesses%2C%20consumers%20and%20investors.

20. Article 50 of the Treaty on European Union (TEU) outlines the procedure under which an EU member may voluntarily withdraw from the bloc. The United Kingdom's triggering of the article formally commenced its process of withdrawal from the European Union and is the first instance of that article being used by an EU member state to withdraw from the union.

21. These included politically sensitive issues, such as fishing rights, which have been covered in the agreement, and some issues on which consensus has not been reached at the time of the agreement's conclusion, such as equivalence for financial services.

22. See generally the press release from the European Union of 24 December 2020, announcing the conclusion of the agreement: https://ec.europa.eu/commission/presscorner/detail/en/ip_20_2531.

23. The parties agree that EU content and processing can be cumulated in the parties' exports to each other. See Protocol I (Rules of Origin Protocol) of the UK-CARIFORUM EPA.

24. This is based on the author's informal discussions with some private exporters to the United Kingdom.

25. Some CARIFORUM countries, for example Belize and Jamaica, have formulated comprehensive national trade policies.

26. Bernal (2013, 186) defines the concept as "a process of repositioning a country in the global economy by implementing a strategic plan". He outlined several elements of what constitutes "strategic global repositioning", namely predictable institutional arrangements for governance; a stable macroeconomics policy framework; global best practice business environment; envisioning new development perspectives; continuous enhancing of international competitiveness; fluidity in resource allocation/mobilization; improving productivity, connectivity, corporate re-dimensioning and renewal; modernization of international marketing; recalibrated strategic planning; and a seamless regional economic space (Bernal 2013, 186–98).

27. Bernal (2014) provides a comprehensive examination of China's growing economic impact in the region, which is largely in the form of providing concessional loans for infrastructure projects.

28. This is with the exception of the Dominican Republic, which is part of the CAFTA-DR FTA with the United States.

29. See https://ec.europa.eu/trade/policy/countries-and-regions/negotiations-and-agreements/.

30. The EU-CARIFORUM EPA's Article 226(2) provides that nothing in the EPA or any arrangement pursuant to it is to be construed as preventing the adoption or enforcement of any measure aimed at preventing tax avoidance or evasion under double taxation agreements, other tax agreements or domestic fiscal legislation, which might limit CARIFORUM countries' ability to have the matter settled within the EPA's dispute settlement provisions. However, it would not preclude CARIFORUM from using the institutional arrangements established under the EU-CARIFORUM EPA as mechanisms under which to raise the blacklisting issue (see Remy and Nicholls 2020).

31. See https://www.consilium.europa.eu/en/press/press-releases/2020/12/17/multiannual-financial-framework-for-2021-2027-adopted/.

32. This is despite extensive awareness campaigns conducted by EPA units and BSOs for the private sector, particularly in the immediate years following the EPA's signing. These often took the form of awareness seminars and the publication of special literature on the opportunities under the agreement.

33. Among the CELAC countries, the European Union has trade agreements with CARIFORUM and the Central American Group, a multiparty trade agreement with three countries of the Andean Community (Colombia, Ecuador and Peru), and agreements with Mexico and Chile. It has also signed and not yet ratified an FTA with Mercosur, which has faced opposition from several EU countries over environmental protection concerns. See generally, European Parliament "EU trade with Latin America and the Caribbean" (European Parliamentary Research Service, 2019).

34. Founded on 23 February 2010 at the Rio Group and Summit of Latin America and the Caribbean on Integration and Development in Mexico, CELAC is one of several political groupings within the Americas and comprises thirty-three states in the LAC region. See generally, Montoute et al., *The Caribbean in the European Union-Community of Latin American and Caribbean States Partnership* (Hamburg: EU-LAC Foundation, 2017).

35. See https://www.tradecommissioner.gc.ca/index.aspx?lang=eng.

36. The current UK envoy to the twelve Commonwealth Caribbean countries is Darren Henry, MP. The twelve Commonwealth countries are: Antigua and Barbuda, the Bahamas, Barbados, Belize, Dominica, Grenada, Guyana, Jamaica, St Lucia, St Kitts and Nevis, St Vincent and the Grenadines, and Trinidad and Tobago.

37. The Ninth UK-Caribbean Ministerial Forum was held on 29 April 2016 in Freeport, Bahamas. The communique from the meeting may be accessed at https://assets.publishing.service.gov.uk/government/uploads/system/uploads/attachment_data/file/521235/Ninth_UK-Caribbean_Ministerial_Forum_Communiqu_.pdf.

38. Communique issued at the conclusion of the Tenth UK-Caribbean Ministerial Forum, para. 1.

39. It outlined the following six substantive areas of joint action: recovery from the COVID-19 pandemic, bilateral and regional cooperation, trade and commercial relations, cooperation against organized crime and economic crime, values and international cooperation, and climate change.

40. Between 2016 and 2017, the Commonwealth Secretariat released several analytical reports looking at the prospects and implications of Brexit for Commonwealth countries and deeper Commonwealth trade. See for example:

https://thecommonwealth.org/sites/default/files/news-items/documents/ BrexitandCommonwealthTrade.pdf.

41. See https://assets.publishing.service.gov.uk/government/uploads/system/ uploads/attachment_data/file/1001026/Advisory_Notice_June__2021.pdf.

42. The report states that "What Global Britain means in practice is best defined by actions rather than words. The fundamentals of this Government's approach to national security and international policy are reflected in the actions we have taken since the 2019 general election. They demonstrate an active approach to delivering in the interests of the British people: sustaining the UK's openness as a society and economy, underpinned by a shift to a more robust position on security and deterrence. This runs alongside a renewed commitment to the UK as a force for good in the world – defending openness, democracy and human rights – and an increased determination to seek multilateral solutions to challenges like climate change and global health crises, as seen in our response to COVID-19" (UK Government 2021, 14).

43. The European Union and the United States had been negotiating the TTIP, but negotiations ended abruptly after the commencement of the first Trump presidency. The European Union and Australia are still in the process of negotiating an FTA since 2018.

44. See https://www.gov.uk/government/news/uk-becomes-first-major-economy-to-pass-net-zero-emissions-law

45. Only those countries and territories listed on the Organisation for Economic Co-operation and Development's Development Assistance Committee's List of Official Development Assistance Recipients are eligible to receive ODA. Barbados, the Bahamas, St Kitts and Nevis, and Trinidad and Tobago have been excluded from the list because of their high-income status. The current list of ODA-eligible countries and territories may be accessed here: https:// www.oecd.org/dac/financing-sustainable-development/development-finance-standards/DAC-List-ODA-Recipients-for-reporting-2021-flows.pdf.

46. Janaury 2021, the United Kingdom committed to maintain its share of funding to the Caribbean Development Bank's Special Development Fund, pledging up to £21m over the next four years (UK Government 2021b). Moreover, under the UK-Caribbean Action Plan, it promised to "work with the Caribbean to support pandemic preparedness in the region" (CARICOM 2021). It also pledged to, among other things, "maintain its recently expanded permanent diplomatic presence in the Caribbean, while delivering on current aid commitments, including for the UK-Caribbean Infrastructure Fund and support on climate resilience and disaster risk reduction; inclusive economic recovery; and governance and security" (CARICOM 2021).

47. According to the most recent UK population census of 2011, "there were

594,825 Black Caribbean people in England and Wales, making up 1.1% of the total population" (UK Government 2019). This excludes non-black Caribbean migrants, such as Indo-Caribbean, and white and mixed Caribbean citizens.

REFERENCES

Bernal, Richard. 1996. *Strategic Global Repositioning and Future Economic Development in Jamaica*. Miami: University of Miami.

———. 2013. *Globalization, Trade and Economic Development: The CARIFORUM-EU Economic Partnership Agreement*. New York: Palgrave Macmillan.

———. 2014. *Dragon in the Caribbean: China's Global Re-Dimensioning – Challenges and Opportunities for the Caribbean*. Kingston: Ian Randle Publishers.

———. 2020. *Corporate versus National Interest in US Trade Policy: Chiquita and Caribbean Bananas*. New York: Palgrave Macmillan.

Brewster, Havelock, Norman Girvan, and Vaughan Lewis. 2008. "Renegotiate the CARIFORUM EPA," *Trade Negotiations Insights* 7 (3) (April) .

British Chamber of Commerce. 2021. BCC Brexit survey: "Half of UK exporters report difficulties adapting to changes relating to EU-UK goods trade", 11 February 2021. https://www.britishchambers.org.uk/news/2021/02/bcc-brexit-survey-half-of-uk-exporters-report-difficulties-adapting-to-changes-relating-to-eu-uk-goods-trade.

Burri, Mira, and Keith Nurse. 2019. *Culture in the CARIFORUM- European Union Economic Partnership Agreement: Rebalancing Trade Flows between Europe and the Caribbean?* UNESCO Report, 2 July 2019. https://ssrn.com/abstract=3413874.

CARICOM. 2021. "Tenth UK-Caribbean Forum: Action Plan." https://www.caricomstats.org/E-CISTAR/2021/03/18/tenth-uk-caribbean-forum-action-plan/, published on 18 March 2021, Georgetown, Guyana.

Chaitoo, Ramesh. 2011. "Investment and Trade in Services." In *The CARIFORUM-EU Economic Partnership Agreement: A Practitioners' Analysis*, edited by Americo Beviglia Zampetti and Junior Lodge, 101–28. Alphen aan den Rijn: Kluwer Law International BV.

———. 2019. *CARIFORUM-EU Economic Partnership Agreement: A Firm-level Review Focused on Trade and Investment*. Report prepared for the Caribbean Export Development Agency, St Michael, Barbados.

Commission of the European Communities. 1996. "Green Paper on relations between the European Union and the ACP countries on the eve of the 21st century: Challenges and options for a new partnership." Brussels: Commission of the European Communities.

———. 1997. "Guidelines for the negotiation of new cooperation agreements with the African, Caribbean and Pacific (ACP) countries." Communication From the Commission to the Council and the European Parliament, Brussels.

De Groot, Olaf, and Miguel Pérez Ludeña. 2014. *Foreign direct investment in the Caribbean: Trends, determinants and policies.* Studies and Perspectives Series (The Caribbean). Port of Spain: Economic Commission for Latin America and the Caribbean (ECLAC). https://repositorio.cepal.org/bitstream/handle/11362/36620/1/S2014046_en.pdf.

Demas, William. 2005. "The Political Economy of the English-speaking Caribbean." In *The Caribbean Economy: A Reader,* edited by Dennis Pantin, 88–110. Kingston: Ian Randle Publishers.

Døhlie Saltnes, Johanne. 2018. "Why the debate over the European Development Fund is a question of politics." LSE Blog. https://blogs.lse.ac.uk/europpblog/2018/06/29/why-the-debate-over-the-european-development-fund-is-a-question-of-politics/#:~:text=The%20UK's%20contribution%20to%20the%20EDF%20currently%20amounts%20to%2015,Nordic%20countries%2C%20and%20the%20Netherlands.

European Commission. 2014. 'Monitoring the implementation and results of the CARIFORUM-EU EPA', http://trade.ec.europa.eu/doclib/docs/2014/october/tradoc_152824.pdf.

———. 2020. "Ex-post evaluation of the Economic Partnership Agreement (EPA) between the European Union and CARIFORUM". https://trade.ec.europa.eu/doclib/docs/2020/february/tradoc_158657.pdf.

———. 2021a. "Communication From the Commission to the European Parliament, the Council, the European Economic and Social Committee and the Committee of the Regions. Trade Policy Review – An Open, Sustainable and Assertive Trade Policy." Brussels, 18 February.https://eur-lex.europa.eu/legal-content/EN/TXT/?uri=CELEX%3A52021DC0066.

Gibb, Richard. 2000. "Post-Lome: The European Union and the South." *Third World Quarterly* 21 (3): 457–81.

Girvan, Norman. 2009. "Implications of the Economic Partnership Agreement (EPA) for the CSME". *Social and Economic Studies* 58 (2), :91–127.

Glickman, David L. 1947. "The British Imperial Preference System". *Quarterly Journal of Economics* 61(3) : 439–70.

Gonzales, Anthony. 2011. "EPA WTO Compatibility: A View from a WTO Perspective." In *The CARIFORUM-EU Economic Partnershp Agreement: A Practitioners' Analysis,* edited by Americo Beviligia and Junior Lodge, 217–37. Alphen aan den Rijn: Kluwer Law International BV.

Government of the United Kingdom. 2018. "Foreign Secretary expands UK Commonwealth diplomatic network." https://www.gov.uk/government/news/

foreign-secretary-expands-uk-commonwealth-diplomatic-network.

———. 2019. "Black Caribbean ethnic group: facts and figures." Published 27 June. https://www.ethnicity-facts-figures.service.gov.uk/summaries/black-caribbe-an-ethnic-group.

———. 2021a. "UK commits to maintain funding share of Caribbean Special Development." Foreign, Commonwealth & Development Office, London, 29 January. https://www.gov.uk/government/news/uk-commits-to-maintain-fund-ing-share-of-caribbean-special-development.

———. 2021b. "With UK aid support, people in Cote d'Ivoire to be first vaccinated through COVAX: Foreign Secretary's statement." Foreign, Commonwealth & Development Office, London, 1 March. https://www.gov.uk/government/news/foreign-secretary-statement-with-uk-aid-support-people-in-ivory-coast-to-be-first-vaccinated-through-covax.

———. 2021c. *Global Britain in a Competitive Age: The Integrated Review of Security, Defence, Development and Foreign Policy.* https://assets.publishing.service.gov.uk/government/uploads/system/uploads/attachment_data/file/975077/Global_Britain_in_a_Competitive_Age-_the_Integrated_Review_of_Security__Defence__Development_and_Foreign_Policy.pdf

Grieger, Gisela. 2019. "EU trade with Latin America and the Caribbean: Overview and figures." Brussels, 16 December. https://www.europarl.europa.eu/thinktank/en/document/EPRS_IDA(2019)644219

Humphrey, Errol. 2016. "How will BREXIT affect the Caribbean? Overview and indicative recommendations." European Centre for Development Policy Management Discussion Paper No. 199. https://ecdpm.org/work/how-will-brex-it-affect-the-caribbean-overview-and-indicative-recommendations

Hurt, Stephen R. 2003. "Co-operation and Coercion? The Cotonou Agreement between the European Union and ACP States and the End of the Lomé Convention." *Third World Quarterly* 24 (1): 161–76.

Inter-American Development Bank (IDB). 2020. *Caribbean Quarterly Bulletin 20209* (4). https://publications.iadb.org/en/caribbean-quarterly-bulletin-2020-vol-ume-9-issue-4-december-2020.

May, Theresa. 2017. "The government's negotiating objectives for exiting the EU." Prime Minister's speech at Foreign, Commonwealth & Development Office, London, 17 January. https://www.gov.uk/government/speeches/the-govern-ments-negotiating-objectives-for-exiting-the-eu-pm-speech.

McLean, Sheldon, and Jeetendra Khadan. 2014. *An assessment of the performance of CARICOM extraregional trade agreements: An initial scoping exercise.* Santiago de Chile: Economic Commission for Latin America and the Caribbean (ECLAC).

Montoute, Annita, Andy Knight, Jacqueline Laguardia Martinez, Debbie Mohammed, and Dave Seerattan. 2017. *The Caribbean in the European-Union-*

Community of Latin American and Caribbean States Partnership. Hamburg: EU-LAC Foundation.

Nicholls, Alicia. 2011. "Investment Provisions in the CARIFORUM-EC Economic Partnership Agreement: What Implications for CARIFORUM-EU Investment Relations?" Social Sciences Research Network (SSRN), 12 May. https://papers. ssrn.com/sol3/papers.cfm?abstract_id=1799426.

Organisation for Economic Co-operation and Development (OECD). 2020. "Aid by DAC members increases in 2019 with more aid to the poorest countries." OECD, Paris, 16 April. https://www.developmentaid.org/api/frontend/cms/ file/2020/11/ODA-2019-detailed-summary.pdf.

Ravenhill, John. 2004. "Back to the nest? Europe's Relations with the African, Caribbean and Pacific Group." In *EU Trade Strategies: Between Regionalism and Globalism*, edited by Vinod Aggarwal and Edward A. Fogarty, 118–47. New York: Palgrave Macmillan.

Remy, Jan Yves, and Alicia Nicholls. 2020. "A WTO Trade Response for CARICOM to Counter EU blacklisting?" Shridath Ramphal Centre Trading Thoughts, 3 December. https://shridathramphalcentre.com/a-wto-trade-response-for-car-icom-to-counter-eu-blacklisting/.

Thibaud Harrois. 2018. "Towards 'Global Britain'? Theresa May and the UK's Role in the World after Brexit." *Observatoire de la Société Britannique* 21: 51–73. https:// doi.org/10.4000/osb.2119.

UN Trade and Development (UNCTAD). 2021. Investment Trends Monitor Issue 38 (January). https://unctad.org/system/files/official-document/diaeiainf2021d1_ en.pdf.

Vahl, Remco. 2011. "From Cotonou to Bridgetown: The Birth of the Caribbean EPA." In *The CARIFORUM-EU Economic Partnership Agreement: A Practitioners' Analysis*, edited by Americo Beviglia Zampetti and Junior Lodge, 1–10. Alphen aan den Rijn: Kluwer Law International BV.

3

Against Caribbean Vulnerabilities in the Time of COVID-19

Precarious Futures or Visions for Social Justice?

MIMI SHELLER

CARIBBEAN ECONOMIES HAVE BEEN SHAKEN IN RECENT YEARS by the global economic recession brought on by the coronavirus pandemic's global mobility disruption, as well as the ongoing ravages of climate change, such as extreme heat, drought, coral bleaching and rising sea levels. Many islands were still trying to rebuild from powerful recent hurricanes (Matthew in 2016, Irma and Maria in 2017, Dorian in 2019, and so on) when the pandemic delivered a further blow. The collapse of tourism due to the closures of borders and the disruption of cruise tourism revealed the underlying social, political and economic vulnerability already experienced by many Caribbean islands. Although Barbados, Dominica and Antigua scrambled to attract digital nomads and give temporary residence to remote workers during the pandemic, these were only temporary panaceas to deeper woes.

The case becomes more compelling with every passing year that the Caribbean region must transition toward more climate-proof and sustainable economies if its people hope to have a future. Yet, often, that is not what is happening. Instead, most Caribbean governments push forward "development" agendas that involve more fossil fuel extraction and use; more extractive industries, such as mining; and more tourism developments that put immense pressure on fragile ecologies. Guyana is under floodwater again, even as it tears out mangroves and threatens the health of communities to build oil-processing facilities. The Jamaican government permits more mining and coastal development for tourism, even as it faces environmental ruination and community protests. Haiti is held hostage to violence and authoritarian politics, while women are confronted with wide-ranging violence and Haitian children face increasing malnutrition. None of this is sustainable. None of this offers a foundation of hope for a Caribbean future.

This is a pathway to self-destruction, like that exercised in the past in St Croix, as David Bond (2021) has described in the dismantling of the VI Corp's community-based agricultural programmes of the New Deal era, in favour of Hess Oil and Harvey Aluminium; like that exercised by the Jamaican government in opening up the protected Cockpit Country to bauxite mining (Figueroa 2019); like the displacement of Haitian small farmers to make way for the Caracol Industrial Park in an alleged effort to "build back better" after the 2010 earthquake (ActionAid USA 2015). With each blow the Caribbean is losing its population, destroying its agricultural base, ruining what is left of healthy ecologies, and weakening its social and cultural fabric.

In this article I seek to outline some of the vulnerabilities of the region and the fears for its precarious future, as well as more positive consideration of possible moves toward reconstruction of Caribbean economies with greater social justice, strengthened mutual aid, and collective sustainability. I argue that alternative development strategies can help Caribbean nations and non-independent territories to become less reliant on extractive industries and tourism – which ultimately will make them more sustainable, more equitable, and less vulnerable to climate emergencies in the future. This will take concerted effort to shift both internal development policies within the region, and the policies of influential external actors. It is crucial that the Caribbean lobbies for its own interests at this pivotal moment. While rivalry between the United States and China opens new foreign relations alignments and investment possibilities, the self-serving security and economic agendas of both superpowers must not be allowed to determine the direction taken by the region (Handy 2019; Semple 2020). Nor should it tempt Caribbean leaders into cutting deals that lock in further extractive industry, ecological destruction or tourism over-exploitation.

However, geopolitics and international relations are not the main foci of this chapter. Instead, I want to draw attention to visions for alternative futures that emerge from Caribbean histories of social critique and political mobilization. The argument proceeds in four steps: first, I describe the vulnerabilities due to a changing climate and increasing pressure from natural disasters across the Caribbean region, arguing for the concept of vulnerability to these *unnatural* disasters as a colonial legacy.

Next, I turn to the vulnerabilities brought about by over-dependence on tourism, over-tourism and extractive forms of it and compare the concept of being "stuck with tourism" (Córdoba Azcárate 2020) to the concept of mobility justice as an alternative path. Third, I turn to the argument for financing of "climate debt" by high-emitters of greenhouse gases through international agreements for climate funding, or the payment of climate loss and damages by corporations.

Finally, this leads to analysis of alternative ways forward that might look beyond extractive industries of tourism, mining and large-scale infrastructure, and towards more sustainable regenerative economies based on agroecology and food sovereignty that would resist the extractive forces that benefit external actors while harming Caribbean ecologies and people. I argue that such visions of alternative Caribbean futures can help build the basis for broader social investments in renewable energy, cultural products, education, digital technology, and connections to diaspora mobilities. This vision for a resilient Caribbean will require stronger intra-regional cooperation, more careful use of resources, and social commoning.

CLIMATE VULNERABILITY AND UNNATURAL DISASTERS

The Central American and Caribbean region has been identified for some time as one of the global "hot spots" that are particularly sensitive to the effects of climate change (Giorgi 2006). Climate models generally predict that various regions of the Caribbean will become drier, with mean annual temperatures increasing by between 1° and 5°C by the 2080s, and the greatest warming and decrease in rainfall occurring around the Greater Antilles (Mimura et al. 2007; Taylor et al. 2018). Climate change also exacerbates other environmental stressors, including the bleaching of coral reefs, loss of seagrass beds, severe beach erosion, saltwater intrusion, and deforestation. Under these conditions, it is crucial that the region protect its natural assets, including forests that support cloud formation and freshwater sources, mangroves and reefs that protect coastlines and replenish beaches, and agricultural land that should be carefully stewarded.

In a paper on the extreme vulnerability of the Caribbean region to climate change, the Global Americans working group (2019, 1) notes that "specific hazards such as rising sea levels, warming temperatures, deforestation, and more frequent and extreme weather events, place the Caribbean at higher risk, to the point of coastal communities and entire islands potentially disappearing if the dangers of global warming are not addressed collectively and urgently today." The projected consequences of climate change have strong implications for the long-term development of the entire Caribbean region, with sectors at higher risk including tourism, fisheries, agriculture, human settlements and infrastructure. The high risk to all these sectors requires connected thinking to plan for greater sustainability on all fronts, but especially demands reducing dependence on fossil fuels, while building soil , forest and ocean conservation through more regenerative practices.

The strength and frequency of hurricanes have increased in recent years, with Matthew striking Haiti in October 2016; Irma barrelling through the northeastern Caribbean in September 2017, devastating Barbuda, French and Dutch St Maarten, Anguilla, Tortola and other parts of the British Virgin Islands, the US Virgin Islands, some of the outer islands of the Bahamas and areas of Puerto Rico, the Dominican Republic and Haiti, before sweeping across Florida; quickly followed by Maria's devastating blows especially to Dominica, Puerto Rico, Cuba, the US Virgin Islands, and Turks and Caicos, in the same month. And the slow-moving Category 5 Dorian in September 2019 razed entire communities in Grand Bahama and the Abacos, becoming the most intense tropical storm ever to hit the Bahamas. Other hurricanes have continued to hit the region since then, repeatedly inflicting damage. But equally damaging are the growing impacts of extreme heat and drought (NASEM 2023).

These recent disruptive events provoke us to ask how Caribbean nations can create more sustainable futures. Many are highly dependent on tourism as one of the main pillars of their economy, which in turn depends heavily on well-functioning infrastructure. Rebuilding tourism and transport infrastructure after natural disasters has often been one of the main quick fix recovery projects undertaken after environmental crises. However, tourism recovery in the current situation poses several problems, echoing previous issues with tourism development more generally, but especially obstacles to post-disaster reconstruction under conditions of climate change.

Many analysts of climate change now refer to seemingly natural hazards such as hurricanes and earthquakes as producing "unnatural disasters" because of the ways in which risk and vulnerability are structured by all-too-human structures of inequality (O'Keefe et al. 1976; Kelman et al. 2016). As Ilan Kelman (2014, 120) has argued, "The rhetoric emphasizing climate change as today's biggest problem might be neglecting the past history of development theory, policy and practice." In doing so, it depoliticizes responses to climate change. Kelman argues that the emphasis on physical hazards, rather than social and economic vulnerabilities "tends to distract from other long-term development challenges" and "to shift focus away from opportunities for reducing vulnerability, including during community reconstruction." Instead, we should be focusing on the ongoing "deep-seated problems such as poor resource access, inequity, exploitation, lack of choices available, marginalization and injustice" (Kelman 2014, 120).

This critique implies a need to think politically about forms of vulnerability and resilience in relation to economic recovery in the future, including after the COVID-19 pandemic, which also connects to recent Caribbean perspectives on climate justice. In an overview of climate justice issues in the Caribbean region, April Baptiste and Kevon Rhiney (2016, 17) argue that "Marginalized groups experience climate change effects differently from the wealthy and privileged, and this vulnerability must be adequately addressed both from a political and an ethical perspective." In 2017, Puerto Rican anthropologist Yarimar Bonilla likewise wrote of that year's hurricanes in the Caribbean, "Vulnerability is not simply a product of natural conditions; it is a political state and a colonial condition." While some governments have been relying on the return of mass tourism to reboot their economies, I want to turn next to the problems of over-tourism and the call to move beyond it.

BEYOND TOURISM: ENVISIONING ALTERNATIVE FUTURES
THROUGH MOBILITY JUSTICE

A large body of work already exists on the relationship between tourism, sustainability and resilience in small island contexts (for example, Kelman 2020; Mowforth and Munt 2015; Mahon et al. 2013; Pelling and Uitto 2001), and on the wider environmental impacts of tourism (Gössling 2002; Gössling and Hall 2006; Gössling et al. 2016). The collapse of Caribbean travel brought on by COVID added a new complicating factor. With the fall in tourism earnings predicted to have devastating effects on dependent economies, some argue that rather than "build back better", there is an urgent need to rebuild more sustainable economies and societies "beyond tourism" (Thompson 2020). There can be no going back to normal under the circumstances (Gössling et al. 2020).

This would appear to be a compelling moment to not simply rebuild existing tourism-dependent economies, but to find new approaches to reduce this over-dependence on tourism, to mitigate the heavy carbon-footprint of tourism, as well as to repair the harmful effects of "over tourism" (Dodds 2019; Dodds and Butler 2019). We need to "reconsider tourism's growth trajectory", argues Gössling, and "accelerate the transformation of sustainable tourism" (Gössling et al. 2020, 13, 15). This also includes the prevention of some of the unintended consequences of ecotourism (Duffy 2002, 2008; Córdoba Azcárate 2020), and adapting to the predicted disruptions that ongoing climate change emergencies will bring to tourism (Reddy and Wilkes 2012; Becken and Hay 2007; Hall and Higham 2005).

There was already a longstanding critique of the problematic reliance on so-called development through tourism, which had many negative impacts on small islands. Campling argued that for "the genuine 'sustainable development' of SIDS, a popular democratic base of island citizens must exist within island societies that in turn cooperate and coordinate – including material, political-social and operational linkages – across the spatially disparate regions of the global oceans" (Campling 2006, 1). More recently, Cave and Dredge (2020) point out that, "rising concerns about climate change, overtourism, declining employment and labour conditions and resource degradation have all highlighted the inadequacy of the current capitalist system in addressing the failures of mass tourism. Now, under COVID-19, there are calls for tourism to move beyond 'business as usual' and to find a pathway to regenerative tourism." They argue that such regenerative tourism would embrace a "diverse economies framework", which "envisages the co-existence of capitalist, alternative capitalist and non-capitalist practices and provides a pathway to more resilient and regenerative tourism practices in tourism".

How then can the Caribbean's tourism-dependent and extractive economies make this transition? It is clear that alternative visions for Caribbean development are needed, both to avoid over-dependence on extractive and ecologically damaging forms of tourism, and to prepare the region for climate change adaptation. Nor can relying on oil extraction or extractive mining be a solution, given the climate emergency, as I shall outline further below. However, many business leaders ask how will already economically weakened governments pay for this transition? Even if a climate fund is created by high-polluter nations, how will its investment be determined? Who will benefit?

Vulnerability to the growing climate emergency is a historical colonial legacy of dependent capitalism and this must inform alternative visions for the future. As I have argued in "Caribbean Futures in the Offshore Anthropocene: Debt, Disaster, and Duration" (Sheller 2018a, 974): "Capitalism changed climate in the past and continues to do so today. Colonialism and slavery then created the gradients of vulnerability to its consequences . . . Debt is a form of extraction, and always has been in the Caribbean. Historical practices of debt exploitation and extraction have contributed to the making of vulnerability to climate change."

We can see this in the unjust indemnity that France demanded of Haiti in 1825, leading to a century of indebtedness; and in the unpaid debt of British slavery reparations that the CARICOM Reparations Commission continues to lobby for (Beckles 2013); and in the unpayable debt imposed on Puerto Rico in the twentieth century and the dismantling of public services under the US Oversight, Management, and Economic Stability Act (PROMESA).

In each case, former slave-holding colonial and imperial powers have continuously extracted capital, and continue to extract it via the modern mechanisms of international finance mechanisms and debt payments that prevent sustainable development (Sheller 2018a). Yet it is possible to flip this script. One new way to think about the connection between climate change and human mobility is through the concept of mobility justice (Sheller 2020). Mobility justice is a way to understand the deep flows of inequality and uneven accessibility in a world in which the mobile commons have been enclosed as private property. It is a call for a new understanding of the politics of movement and a demand for justice for all in terms of how, when and where we move or remain in places, without necessarily owning them as property.

Mobility justice has deep connections to Indigenous Caribbean, African diaspora and Maroon relations to land and ocean as a shared space of relations for sustenance and reproduction, both human and more-than-human. Mobility justice is an overarching concept for thinking about how power and inequality inform the governance and control of all forms of movement. This analytical tool can help us connect personal embodied experiences of injustice (such as those associated with gender-based violence or racist policing) with neighbourhood scale, national scale, and global scale injustices. On each of these levels, the capacity to self-determine one's movements is dependent on intersecting systems of oppression like racism, sexism, classism and ableism. Mobility justice helps us understand, for example, how the experience of someone who is forced to constantly move because of homelessness is related to the experiences of migrant workers or "climate refugees". It allows us to offer a critique of both tourism and humanitarian "voluntourism" as unequal forms of mobility (Sheller 2020).

And it also allows us to recognize how what Adriana Maria Garriga-Lopez (2020, 132) describes as "counternormative or decolonial knowledges about water, farming, food, art, and ecology [can help us] create livable futures for Puerto Ricans and Caribbean people more broadly" through the exercise of "ecological marronage". As she forcefully explains,

> Through their revolutionary praxis of radical autonomy and self-determination (including the capacity to determine what they will eat), Puerto Rico's independent artists, coastal foragers, and small farmers have been at the forefront of resistance to the undemocratic regime imposed by the Puerto Rico Fiscal Oversight and Management Board under PROMESA ... The democratic deficit

that exists in Puerto Rico guarantees the continuing use of debt as the justification for a permanent crisis (Garriga-Lopez 2020, 126–27, 132).

In the aftermath of climate disasters such as hurricanes, we find, in fact, that communities are already working toward more sustainable ways of communal support, care and recovery. It is these experiments in interstitial commoning, I suggest, that point us toward alternative Caribbean futures.

This leads to a critique of current discourses of indebtedness, vulnerability, resilience, and who can offer purported "climate solutions". In the next section I want to make the case for reconsidering who is indebted to whom, based on the historical trajectory of colonialism, energy use, and extractive economies that have shaped the modern Caribbean, as well as the Global North, and our entangled relations with each other.

FROM CLIMATE DEBT TO CLIMATE REPARATIONS

A central tenet of mobility justice is that those of us in the industrialized regions of the Global North, especially the wealthiest 10 per cent, consume more energy and more fossil fuel than most people in the world. Historically, the US economy (and military-industrial complex) has contributed by far the largest share of global greenhouse gases. Daniel Farber (2008) argues that there is a clear moral case that Americans today are most responsible for a disproportionate amount of greenhouse gases because of our energy-intensive lifestyles, and that we have caused harm to the poorest and most vulnerable because we failed to take reasonable measures to limit our emissions. The lifestyles of the well-off "kinetic elite" or "polluting elite" – that is, those with high energy-consumption and high motility (Kaufmann et al. 2004) – are especially responsible for excessive carbon emissions, causing climate displacement around the world.

The notion of "climate debt" refers to the debt owed by the Global North (especially the United States, as the largest contributor to greenhouse gases) to the peoples and places that have been most harmed by climate change. Yet it builds on earlier relations of coloniality, through which "unpayable debt" was imposed on countries in the so-called "Third World", while the actual debt owed back to enslaved peoples by slave-owning profiteers went unacknowledged, along with the claims for justice and reparations by

Indigenous peoples.[1] This underpins the argument for climate reparations as well as for dealing more fairly with climate displacement across Latin America and the Caribbean.

If we understand that industrialization was built upon relations of indigenous genocide, land theft, colonial exploitation and enslavement, that then morphed into ongoing forms of neocolonialism and extraction, then we can see where responsibility for ecological harm and climate displacement rests: with the industrial and post-industrial Global North that benefitted and continues to benefit from these global economies (Sultana 2025). "Rather than explaining [climate migration] as a function of the environment, climate, or nature," argues Andrew Baldwin et al. (2019, 291), "mobility justice is powerful precisely because it positions capitalism, along with its fossil-fueled infrastructures of air travel, automobility, suburbanization and consumerism, at the very centre of the concern about climate change and displacement". A mobility justice and climate debt approach would put the wealthiest countries and people in the world today in the hot seat, as well as the multinational companies that have benefitted from the extractive global economy.

Rather than the exclusionary lockdown of borders around the world, therefore, we should focus on the question of responsibility and reparations in a moral, legal and financial framework under international law. Such an approach can build upon the work of the Caribbean Reparations Commission and others who have powerfully advocated for reparations for slavery. Climate reparations could be a crucial mechanism for extending the call for reparations for slavery into one that benefits all affected regions of the world and peoples who suffered harms from slavery. Slavery and colonialism were based upon complex relational systems of mobility injustices, including settler colonialism as land theft and indigenous displacement and genocide. Enslavement itself was a complex system of racialized (im)mobilities, including ecological destruction for plantation monocultures and the logistical systems for the global circulation of plants as commodities. Mining and energy extraction industries that began with the extraction and circulation of substances such as whale oil, guano, wood, and rubber later grew to include oil drilling, coal mining, bauxite mining, and so on.

Within the broader discussion of climate reparations two pathways can be taken. The first is a case for "corrective justice" negotiated between governments within an international jurisdiction. The collective moral responsibility of high greenhouse gases (GHG) emitters to make financial recompense to climate creditors forms an adequate basis to hold the United States and the European Union morally accountable for some calculable and bearable share of the harms of climate change. This could be paid into an international Green Climate Fund. Climate reparations would also enable "creditor countries" – including every country in the Caribbean region, which have contributed little to overall global GHG – to fund adaptation efforts that would also strengthen their economies and build social and ecological safety nets for "placekeeping" (Gray 2023), rather than displacement. One practical mechanism for this would be an international compensation commission that could receive claims from countries for specific incurred adaptation expenses (Farber 2008).

The second and quite different pathway for making a case for climate compensation is through tort litigation for loss and damage against the major fossil fuel companies. Through class action lawsuits filed under multiple jurisdictions, reparations could be sought for those harmed and corporations could be held responsible for specific injury. "The call for compensation for loss and damage is also supported by well-established rules and principles of international law, including the right to reparations for injury resulting from violations of international law" (Wewerinke-Singh and Hinge Salili 2019). According to key legal arguments on behalf of Vanuatu by Margaretha Wewerinke-Singh and Diana Hinge Salili, the Warsaw International Mechanism for Loss and Damage offers the best opportunity as a facility for loss and damage finance under the auspices of the United Nations Framework Convention on Climate Change. Dozens of lawsuits in multiple jurisdictions against fossil fuel majors are using a range of legal strategies: tort law, product liability, consumer protection, racketeering, and state constitutional rights. The number of cases focused on the climate crisis around the world has doubled since 2015, bringing the total number to more than two thousand (Setzer and Higham 2022).

Lastly, there is also a deeper moral case for climate reparations based on the long-term effects of systems of colonial racial capitalism and racialized exclusion of black, brown and indigenous people from full citizenship. Malini Ranganathan and Eve Bratman argue for moving from a framework of climate resilience to "abolitionist climate justice", which entails centring "historical environmental and housing-related racisms, the intersectional drivers of precarity and trauma experienced by residents beyond those narrowly associated with 'climate'; and an ethics of care and healing practiced by those deemed most at risk to climate change" (Ranganathan and Bratman 2019). Abolitionist climate justice is reparative of racism, coloniality, and climate-induced harm together because it embeds climate debt in longer historical timeframes and claims for reparative humanism. Together, these approaches to climate debt and climate justice open new ways of considering the reconstruction of Caribbean economies, not only after dramatic hurricanes, but also in the face of the chronic and constant impacts of worsening climate change.

JUST RECOVERY

Movements for just recovery offer a very different vision of post-disaster reconstruction and climate resilience than those found in mainstream disaster response discourses and "build back better" ideologies. Community-based grassroots movements in the Caribbean have proposed reconstruction projects based on more sustainable mobilities, low-impact tourism, visions for alternative development, and alternatives to capitalist extraction. Community-based organizations and advocacy networks such as the Platform for Alternative Development in Haiti (PAPDA) and the Boricuá Organization for Ecological Agriculture in Puerto Rico seek to move beyond hegemonic Global North perspectives on resilience by highlighting radical opportunities for sustainable development linked to environmental justice, food justice and climate justice (Sheller 2018b; 2020). Organizations like Para la Naturaleza Solidarity Fund in Puerto Rico "supports nature-based solutions that foster the well-being of natural and human ecosystems".[2] The Caribbean Agroecology Institute has as its mission to "catalyze knowledge exchange, build capacity, and support transitions to resilient agroecological systems that provide for sustainable livelihoods rooted in justice and equality in the Caribbean".[3] It is these kinds of initiatives that activists and advocates should make central to disaster recovery and climate adaptation initiatives, if the region is to have any kind of sustainable future.

In a journal special issue on "not-so-natural disasters" in the Caribbean, the contributors show how alternative community organizations and grassroots movements propose alternative scenarios for resilient recovery. They became "complementary actors to the limited and slow state- or market-relief response" and rejected the "historical prioritization of Caribbean government towards perpetual economic growth in their development agendas". Instead, these organizations sought to develop "space that could be used to grow subsistence crops, which is not only essential to mitigate starvation after a natural disaster but reduces the dependency on food imports" (Cruz-Martinez et al. 2018). In Puerto Rico, post-Hurricane Maria, this vision has involved the formation of people's assemblies and locally organized resilience hubs to offer mutual aid and engage communities in planning. We see the combining of climate justice and food justice strategies by organizations such as Resilient Power Puerto Rico, which distributes solar-powered generators for creating small-scale community-run micro-grids, and Boricuá Organization for Ecological Agriculture, which sends out "agroecology brigades" to deliver traditional seeds and soil, and train people in their cultivation (Pérez-Lizasuain 2018). Garriga-Lopez (2020, 132) further argues that,

> Empowering poor communities to use scientific and technical knowledge through citizen science, valorizing black and indigenous knowledges about land and farming, and buttressing autonomy for women, girls, and gender-nonconforming people through the reclamation of small farming and egalitarian water management practices is more than an important feminist, trans/queer, and decolonial agenda. It might also be Puerto Rico's only real hope of adapting to the environmental and economic changes currently underway.

Rather than rebuilding tourism as it is, or turning to ecologically damaging extractive industries such as mining, we might learn from these agroecological projects how to plant and expand Caribbean food sovereignty through agricultural practices, such as regenerative, low-till and no-till conservation agriculture, multistrata agroforestry, silvopasture, tree intercropping, use of tropical staple trees, and multi-crop gardening systems known as *conuco*, an Arawak term for farming practices that still persist throughout the Caribbean (Sheller 2021). These kinds of visions for recovery are very much in line with visions for more sustainable tourism linked to preserving biodiversity, while drawing on innovative sustainable culinary systems (Hall 2006; Hall and Gössling 2013). Alternative economies of community-based organizations call for the complete reconstruction of economies, labour relations, relations to the natural world, and relations to each other. This demands mobility flexibility, allowing for movement in the hurricane season, so that people in affected localities can find temporary respite. It also calls for protecting water sources, coastal areas and fisheries, mangroves and coral reefs, as well as implementing programmes for soil conservation, replanting forests, and investing in agroecological improvements.

The return of such indigenous knowledge and horticultural practices might make the Caribbean more resilient in the face of climate emergencies (Mercer et al. 2007; Sheller 2021). We might also imagine building backward and forward linkages between such agroecological projects and local food markets within a renewed vision for sustainable tourism that is non-extractive; tourism that supports local farmers; renewable energy micro-grids; and more regenerative circular economies that also reduce waste. The move away from heavy reliance on imported food would also reduce plastic waste, if more fresh food could be marketed locally. This could also include urban gardens and vertical farms that can be placed on roofs in dense urban areas, as well as larger hydroponic farming systems that have been successful in Mandeville, Jamaica, for example. There have also been efforts at spinoffs into higher value-added food products. Beyond agriculture, though, modern, middle-income Caribbean economies need other pillars to stand on. Unfortunately, the expansion of extractive industries has been the primary solution for many governments, desperate for foreign investment, and is promoted by foreign multinational corporations and multilateral investment banks. Guyana is already building massive fossil fuel extraction infrastructure. Suriname is close on its heels, and the Bahamas and Barbados are preparing for licensing oil prospecting in their offshore waters.

CONCLUSION: BEYOND EXTRACTIVISM

In January 2020, I had the honour of being invited to give a keynote speech at the University of the West Indies in Mona, hosted by the Centre for Reparation Research, on the subject of climate justice, which formed the basis for some of the arguments in this chapter. As reported in the *Jamaica Gleaner* after the event, I argued that the "coloniality of climate is not an event that happened in the past. It is an ongoing relation of uneven consumption based on the exploitation and sacrifice of some peoples and lands and ecologies for the benefit of others." I continued:

> Every day we sacrifice the places where mining takes place, drilling, forest-burning industrial agriculture, polluting factory production, water extraction, waste disposal and toxic dumping. Our food system is equally reliant on fossil fuels and distant plantations, and contributes huge amounts in forest clearance, as we have seen in the burning Amazon. And this is crucial for understanding the impact of the hurricanes that have taken place in the Caribbean and the climate death that produces vulnerable populations.[4]

During that visit to Jamaica, I joined my friend, filmmaker Esther Figueroa, on a trip to the western parishes. I had worked with Esther on her film *Fly Me to the Moon*, which tells the story of bauxite mining and aluminium production in Jamaica and around the world. We drove past the Jiuquan Iron and Steel Company (JISCO) Alpart alumina plant in St Elizabeth, which reopened in 2016 after an eight-year closure, but was again temporarily closed. We drove past the massive, toxic red mud lakes left over from bauxite processing. We drove through the lands that were slated for further open-pit bauxite mining, under the lax regulations of the government of Prime Minister Andrew Holness, whose continuing dismissal of environmental impact reviews (or overturning on appeal) has exposed vast swathes of the primary and rare tropical forest of Jamaica's interior, and home of the Trelawny Maroons, to incredibly destructive mining (even if a core homeland is protected).

Esther and I also visited the Windsor Research Station, deep in the forests, where my university also had sent researchers from the Academy of Natural Sciences to study biodiversity and measure indicators of climate change found in the shells of Jamaican land snails. Here, I was both stunned by the beautiful diversity of the forest, and appalled by the inroads being made by slash-and-burn farming. I saw with my own eyes how one man with a machete and fire could cut down half an acre of ancient primary rainforest, right at the source of the Martha Brae River, simply to plant a few small crops. We knew this violated the National Environment and Planning Authority rules, but no one was there to stop it; and once done, it is too late to ever recover such a forest. This was heartbreaking to see, and I longed for a land distribution policy that would give small farmers access to land, capital and tools, so they would not have to destroy forests. What if old plantation land was redistributed, the soil improved, and farmers could grow there?

Yet small farmers are small fry compared to giant transnational mining corporations, who will tear through dozens of acres with bulldozers and heartlessness. The words of Hugh Dixon, head of the South Trelawny Environmental Agency, are still ringing in my ears: "The exploitation of these resources has a direct bearing on the exposure that we subject ourselves to with the impacts of climate change," Dixon said. "If you destroy the landscape to get to an ore and in so doing, you deprive your populace, your indigenous people, your sustainability, to the priority given to external corporate entities, then you are opening yourselves up to the climate change, which is an inevitable destructive agent".[5]

This is what extraction means, whether it is done to mine ore for aluminium production, gravel for building highways, or sand for "replenishing" beaches; or done by bulldozing mangrove forests to build hotels to sit upon those fake beaches served by the extractive labour demanded of docile cheerful workers in "paradise" (Nixon 2015; Córdoba Azcárate 2020). We must resist all these forms of extraction that are destroying the environmental sustainability of the Caribbean region and will leave every island more vulnerable to drought and hurricanes, less food secure, less water secure, and finally, unable to adapt to a new climate.

Ultimately, it is the responsibility of all of us to keep the trees in the forest, to keep the oil in the ground, to keep the bauxite in the mountain, as Arundhati Roy tells us, to keep the mangroves on the shoreline, to keep the fish in the sea, and to keep the Caribbean alive. We must have a vision that moves beyond extractivism, while providing people with livelihoods through shared economies of reproduction, social care and natural health. Communities in Haiti, in Puerto Rico, and elsewhere are showing us how to do this, leading the way.

Building on their example, I have argued that the payment of climate reparations can be a starting point for supporting and expanding such a vision, sustaining societies based on renewable energy and food justice, mutual solidarity and sharing of community-to-community assistance. Once this strong social basis is established, then the Caribbean will be in a better position to develop sustainable tourism, creative economies, social entrepreneurship, educational investment, diaspora travel connections, and many of the other components of a future economy that regional leaders, like Barbados' prime minister, Mia Mottley, powerfully call for. But without a bio-natural-socio-ecological basis for survival, nothing will be sustainable. All of us, whether in the Caribbean or in the Global North, need to stop the destruction that is still unfolding – before it is too late.

ACKNOWLEDGEMENT

This work was supported in its final stages through the Caribbean Climate Adaptation Network (CCAN) a NOAA Climate Adaptation Partnerships team Grant Number NA22OAR4310545.

NOTES

1. See *Caribbean Syllabus: Life and Debt in the Caribbean* (2018), by the Unpayable Debt Working Group, led by Frances Negrón-Muntaner and Mimi Sheller, and the second edition *#NoMoreDebt: Caribbean Syllabus*, available at https://caribbeansyllabus.wordpress.com/caribbean-syllabus/.
2. See their mission at https://www.paralanaturaleza.org/en/solidarity-fund/.
3. See https://www.caribbeanagroecology.org/.
4. http://jamaica-gleaner.com/article/news/20200312/earth-today-cockpit-country-climate-justice-issue.
5. http://jamaica-gleaner.com/article/news/20200312/earth-today-cockpit-country-climate-justice-issue.

REFERENCES

ActionAid USA. 2015. *Building Back Better? The Caracol Industrial Park and Post-earthquake Aid*. Washington, DC: ActionAid USA, January 2015.

Baldwin, Andrew, Christiane Frölich, and Delf Rothe. 2019. "From Climate Migration to Anthropocene Mobilities: Shifting the Debate." *Mobilities* 14 (3): 289–97.

Baptiste, April, and Kevon Rhiney. 2016. "Climate justice and the Caribbean: an introduction." *Geoforum* 73: 17–21.

Becken, Susanne, and John E. Hay. 2007. *Tourism and Climate Change: Risks and Opportunities*. Clevedon, Buffalo and Toronto: Chennel View Publications.

Beckles, Hilary. 2013. *Britain's Black Debt: Reparations for Caribbean Slavery and Native Genocide*. Kingston: University of the West Indies Press.

Bond, David. 2021. "Manufactured Progress: Harvey Aluminum on St. Croix (Part 4)." *The St Thomas Source*, US Virgin Islands, 30 May 2021. Accessed 2 June 2021 at: https://stthomassource.com/content/2021/05/30/manufactured-progress-harvey-aluminum-in-st-croix-part-4/.

Bonilla, Yarimar. 2017. "Why would anyone in Puerto Rico want a hurricane? Because someone will get rich." *Washington Post*, 22 September 2017.

———. 2020. "The coloniality of disaster: Race, empire and the temporal logics of emergency in Puerto Rico, USA." *Political Geography* 78 (April 2020). https://doi.org/10.1016/j.polgeo.2020.102181.

Bonilla, Yarimar, and Marisol Lebron, eds. 2019. *Aftershocks of Disaster: Puerto Rico Before and After the Storm*. New York: Haymarket Books.

Cave, Jenny, and Diane Dredge. 2020. "Regenerative tourism needs diverse economic practices." *Tourism Geographies* 22 (3): 503–13. doi.org/10.1080/146166 88.2020.1768434.

Córdoba Azcárate, Matilde. 2020. *Stuck with Tourism: Development, Space and Power in Contemporary Yucatan*. Oakland: University of California Press.

Cruz-Martinez, Gilbran, Melissa Fernandez-Arrigoitia, Janialy Ortiz Camacho, and Patria Roman-Velazquez,eds. 2018. Special Issue: "The Making of Caribbean Not-so-Natural Disasters." *Alternautas* 5 (2).

Dodds, Rachel, ed. 2019. *Overtourism: Issues, Realities and Solutions*. Boston: DeGruyter.

Dodds, Rachel, and Richard Butler. 2019. *Overtourism: Tourism at Its Breaking Point*. Berlin: Walter de Gruyter GmbH.

Duffy, Rosaleen. 2002. *A Trip Too Far: Ecotourism, Politics and Exploitation*. London and Sterling: Earthscan Publications.

Duffy, Rosaleen. 2008. "Neoliberalising Nature: Global Networks and Ecotourism Development in Madagascar." *Journal of Sustainable Tourism* 16 (3): 327–44.

Farber, Daniel A. 2008. "The Case for Climate Compensation: Justice for Climate Change Victims in a Complex World." *Utah Law Review* 2008 (2): 377–414.

Figueroa, Esther, dir. *Fly Me to the Moon.* 2019. Co-producer Mimi Sheller. Kingston: Vagabond Media.

Garriga-López, Adriana María. 2020. "Debt, Crisis, and Resurgence in Puerto Rico." *small axe* 62 (July): 122–32.

Giorgi, F. 2006. "Climate change hot-spots." *Geophysical Research Letters* 33, L08707.

Global Americans Working Group. 2019. "The Caribbean's Extreme Vulnerability to Climate Change: A Comprehensive Strategy to Build a Resilient, Secure and Prosperous Western Hemisphere." Accessed 9 May 2020 at https://theglobala-mericans.org/reports/the-caribbean-extreme-vulnerability-climate-change/.

Gössling, Stefan. 2002 "Global environmental consequences of tourism." *Global Environmental Change,* 12 (4): 283–302. https://doi.org/10.1016/S0959-3780(02)00044-4.

Gössling, Stefan, and C. Michael Hall, eds. 2006. *Tourism and global environmental change: Ecological, economic, social and political interrelationships.* London and New York: Routledge.

Gössling, Stefan, A. Ring, L. Dwyer, A.C. Andersson, and C.M. Hall. 2016. "Optimizing or maximizing growth? A challenge for sustainable tourism." *Journal of Sustainable Tourism,* 24 (4): 527–48. https://doi.org/10.1080/09669582.2015.1085869.

Gössling, Stefan, Daniel Scott, and C. Michael Hall. 2020. "Pandemics, tourism and global change: A rapid assessment of COVID-19." *Journal of Sustainable Tourism* 29 (1): 1–20. doi: 10.1080/09669582.2020.1758708.

Gray, Summer. 2023. *In the Shadow of the Seawall: Coastal Injustice and the Dilemma of Placekeeping.* Berkeley: University of California Press.

Hall, C. Michael. 2009. "Degrowing tourism: Decroissance, sustainable consumption and steady-state tourism." *Anatolia* 20 (1): 46–61. https://doi.org/10.1080/13032917.2009.10518894.

Hall, C. Michael, and Stefan Gössling, eds. 2013. *Sustainable culinary systems. local foods, innovation, and tourism & hospitality.* London: Routledge.

Hall, C. Michael, and James E. S. Higham, eds. 2005. *Tourism, Recreation and Climate Change.* Clevedon and Buffalo: Channel View Publications.

Handy, Gemma. 2019 "Antigua: sprawling 'Chinese colony' plan across marine reserve ignites opposition." *The Guardian,* 20 June 2019.

Kaufmann, Vincent, Manfred Bergman, and Dominique Joye. 2004. "Motility: Mobility as Capital." *International Journal of Urban and Regional Research* 28 (December): 745–56.

Kelman, Ilan. 2014. "No change from climate change: vulnerability and small island developing states." *Geographic Journal* 180: 120–29.

———. 2020. "Islands of vulnerability and resilience: Manufactured stereotypes?" *Area* 52 (1): 6–13.

Kelman, Ilan, J.C. Gaillard, J. Lewis, and J. Mercer. 2016. "Learning from the history of disaster vulnerability and resilience research and practice for climate change." *Natural Hazards* 82: 129–43.

Lew, Alan A., Joseph M. Cheer, Michael Haywood, Patrick Brouder, and Noel B. Salazar. 2020. "Visions of travel and tourism after the global COVID-19 transformation of 2020." *Tourism Geographies* 22 (3): 455–66.

Mahon, R., S. Becken, and H.G. Rennie. 2013. *Evaluating the business case for investment in the resilience of the tourism sector of small island developing states.* Canterbury and Christchurch: Lincoln University.

Mercer, J., Dominey Howes, Ilan Kelman, and K. Lloyd. 2007. "The potential for combining indigenous and western knowledge in reducing vulnerability to environmental hazards in small island developing states." *Environmental Hazards* 7: 245–56.

Mimura, N., L. Nurse, R.F. McLean, J. Agard, L. Briguglio, P. Lefale, R. Payet, and G. Sem. 2007. "Small islands. Climate Change 2007: Impacts, Adaptation and Vulnerability." *Contribution of Working Group II to the Fourth Assessment Report of the Intergovernmental Panel on Climate Change*, edited by M.L. Parry, O.F. Canziani, J.P. Palutikof, P.J. van der Linden, and C.E. Hanson, 687–716. Cambridge: Cambridge University Press.

Mowforth, Martin, and Ian Munt. 2015. *Tourism and Sustainability: Development, Globalisation and New Tourism in the Third World*, 4th ed. Abingdon and New York: Routledge.

National Academies of Sciences, Engineering, and Medicine. 2023. *Communities, Climate Change, and Health Equity: Lessons Learned in Addressing Inequities in Heat-Related Climate Change Impacts.* Proceedings of a Workshop-in Brief. Washington, DC: The National Academies Press. https://doi.org/10.17226/27204.

Nixon, Angelique V. 2015. *Resisting Paradise: Tourism, Diaspora, and Sexuality in Caribbean Culture.* Jackson: University Press of Mississippi.

O'Keefe, P., K. Westgate, and B. Wisner. 1976. "Taking the naturalness out of natural disasters." *Nature* 260: 566–67.

Pelling, M., and J. Uitto. 2001. "Small island developing states: natural disaster vulnerability and global change." *Global Environmental Change Part B: Environmental Hazards* 3 (2): 49–62.

Pérez-Lizasuain, César. 2018. "Entering the Contact Zone? Between Colonialism, Neoliberal Resilience and the Possibility of Emancipatory Politics in Puerto Rico's Post-Maria." *Alternautas*, 28 September 2018.

Ranganathan, Malini, and Eve Bratman. 2019. "From urban resilience to abolitionist climate justice in Washington, D.C." *Antipode* 28 June 2019. https://doi.org/10.1111/anti.12555.

Reddy, Maharaj Vijay, and Keith Wilkes. 2012. *Tourism, Climate Change and Sustainability.* London: Routledge.

Semple, Kirk. 2020. "China Extends reach in the Caribbean, Unsettling the U.S." *The New York Times,* 9 November 2020. https://www.nytimes.com/2020/11/08/world/americas/china-caribbean.html.

Setzer, Joana, and Catherine Higham. 2022. *Global Trends in Climate Change Litigation: 2022 Snapshot.* London: Grantham Research Institute on Climate Change and the Environment and Centre for Climate Change Economics and Policy, London School of Economics and Political Science, June 2022. Available at: www.lse.ac.uk/granthaminstitute/publications-global-trends-in-climate-changelitigation-2022.

Sheller, Mimi. 2018a. "Caribbean Futures in the Offshore Anthropocene: Debt, Disaster, and Duration." *Environment and Planning D: Society and Space,* 36 (6): 971-86.

———. 2018b. "Caribbean Reconstruction and Climate Justice: Transnational Insurgent Intellectual Networks and Post-Hurricane Transformation." *Journal of Extreme Events* 5 (4): 1–18.

———. 2020. *Island Futures: Caribbean Survival in the Anthropocene.* Durham: Duke University Press.

———. 2021. "Reconstructing Tourism in the Caribbean: Connecting pandemic recovery, climate resilience, and sustainable tourism through mobility justice." *Journal of Sustainable Tourism* 29 (9): 1436–49. doi.org/10.1080/09669582.2020.1791141

Sultana, Farhana (ed.) 2025. *Confronting Climate Coloniality: Decolonizing Pathways for Climate Justice.* London and New York: Routledge.

Taylor, Michael A. 2017. "Climate change in the Caribbean – learning lessons from Irma and Maria." *The Guardian,* 6 October 2017. Accessed at: https://www.theguardian.com/environment/2017/oct/06/climate-change-in-the-caribbean-learning-lessons-from-irma-and-maria.

Taylor, Michael A., T.S. Stephenson, A. Chen, and K.A. Stephenson. 2012. "Climate Change and the Caribbean: Review and Response." *Caribbean Studies* 40: 169–200.

Thompson, Peter. 2020. "Barbados Beyond Tourism." Wunnuh, 28 April 2020. Accessed at http://wunnuh.org/barbados-beyond-tourism/.

Unpayable Debt Working Group. 2018. *Caribbean Syllabus: Life and Debt in the Caribbean.* Led by Frances Negrón-Muntaner and Mimi Sheller. Available at https://caribbeansyllabus.wordpress.com/caribbean-syllabus/.

Wewerinke-Singh, Margaretha, and Diana Hinge Salili. 2020. "Between negotiations and litigation: Vanuatu's perspective on loss and damage from climate change." *Climate Policy* 20 (6): 681–92.

PART 2.

(RE)IMAGINING CARIBBEAN HEALTH, DEBT AND RESILIENCE DYNAMICS IN THE ANTHROPOCENE

4

COVID-19 Health Impact and Resilience Dynamics in the Caribbean

R. CLIVE LANDIS, STANLEY LALTA, ALTHEA LA FOUCADE AND KARL THEODORE

BY 30 JUNE 2022, DAY 911 OF THE COVID-19 PANDEMIC, total cases worldwide had exceeded 543 million, according to the World Health Organization (WHO) COVID-19 Dashboard. The death toll exceeded 6.4 million persons, although the crude Case Fatality Rate (CFR) had fallen compared to the first wave of the disease in China, Europe and the Americas. The distribution of the pandemic revealed that the region of the Americas had the third highest proportion of cases and the highest proportion of deaths (see figures 4.1A and 4.1B).

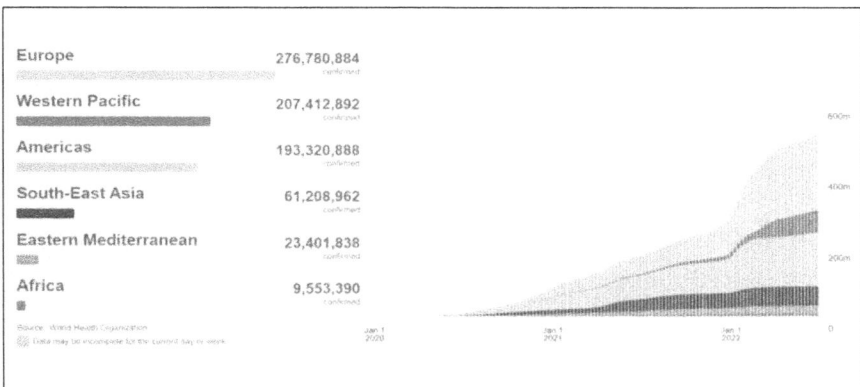

Figure 4.1A: Global distribution of COVID-19 cases by WHO region as at 30 June 2022

Source: WHO Coronavirus (COVID-19) Dashboard (https://covid19.who.int/)

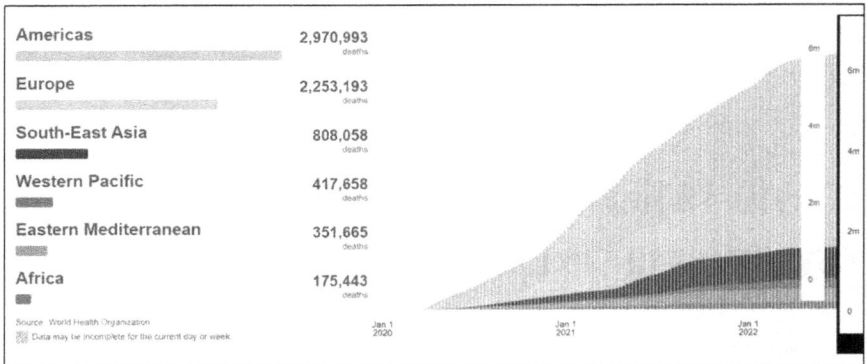

Americas	2,970,993 deaths
Europe	2,253,193 deaths
South-East Asia	808,058 deaths
Western Pacific	417,658 deaths
Eastern Mediterranean	351,665 deaths
Africa	175,443 deaths

Source: World Health Organization
Data may be incomplete for the current day or week

Figure 4.1B: Global distribution of COVID-19 deaths by WHO region as at 30 June 2022
Source: WHO Coronavirus (COVID-19) Dashboard (https://covid19.who.int/)

The Caribbean is grouped by WHO in this worst affected region of the Americas, but does this accurately reflect the COVID-19 experience in these small countries? The Caribbean is often overlooked due to data collection complexities from this constellation of small states with limited resources and a mélange of sovereignty. For example, less than half of Caribbean countries are included individually in the WHO's CFR statistics nor are they reported collectively.

The impact of COVID-19 in the Caribbean – comprising diverse small island developing states – is inextricably linked to their peculiar vulnerabilities:

- Small size – with regard to population, gross domestic product (GDP) and dependence on a limited range of exports, but a vast range of imports, including health inputs, for example, medical supplies, vaccines and investments. These limit their ability to influence international developments as well as their capacity to withstand global shocks (trade, travel, financial and pandemics such as COVID-19);
- Proneness to natural disasters (hurricanes, volcanoes, drought and flooding) and the damaging effects of climate change (global warming and rising sea levels) on infrastructure, lives and livlihoods (Meesen et al. 2024);
- Categorization as middle- and high-income-per-capita countries – this limits access to concessionary financial and technical inflows, with negative spillover effects in high levels of internal and external debt;

- Varying levels of poverty and inequality that affect vulnerable groups through housing, informal sector activities, uptake of education and health services that increase the likelihood of risky health behaviour by these 'contact-intensive' groups and communities.[1]

These socio-economic vulnerabilities constrain the ability of Caribbean SIDS to contain the direct and indirect effects of COVID-19, and highlight the need for systematic investment in the *resilience* of health systems to improve health protection, sustain health gains and enhance national development.

Given the above, the objectives of this paper are to:

i.   analyse the epidemiology of the pandemic as it unfolded across the Caribbean. (Comparative analyses were conducted on cases and deaths inclusive of 30 June 2022 in an effort to cover the main pandemic and period of mandatory reporting among most countries;)

ii. examine the public health and socio-economic impact of COVID-19; and

iii. advance recommendations for building resilience into healthcare systems, both to sustain health progress and contribute to overall socio-economic welfare.

CONTEXT: NEXUS BETWEEN COVID-19, HEALTH AND CARIBBEAN ECONOMIES

COVID-19 highlighted the multi-layered linkages between population health and the functioning of the economic and social protection systems. There are two aspects of this convergence:

i.   At the individual/household level, health status (illness/injury, disability, death) directly influences the quantity and quality of labour, that is, a country's human capital, and consequently, levels of earnings, productivity, savings for capital investment, and public financing activities (tax revenues and subsidies);

ii. At the community level, health serves an enabling function in facilitating the confidence for business operations and public sector investments that help to both improve health and the social determinants of health, such as poverty, inequality and other welfare-inducing programmes as recommended in the United Nations' Sustainable Development Goals (SDGs).

These linkages are summarized in figure 4.2, which tracks the implications of COVID-19 for health and the economy/national income:

• Most enterprises, especially travel and tourism,[2] small and medium-sized firms, and informal sector operatives were negatively affected (by closure or reduced operations) by governments' lockdown measures and declining customer patronage.[3]

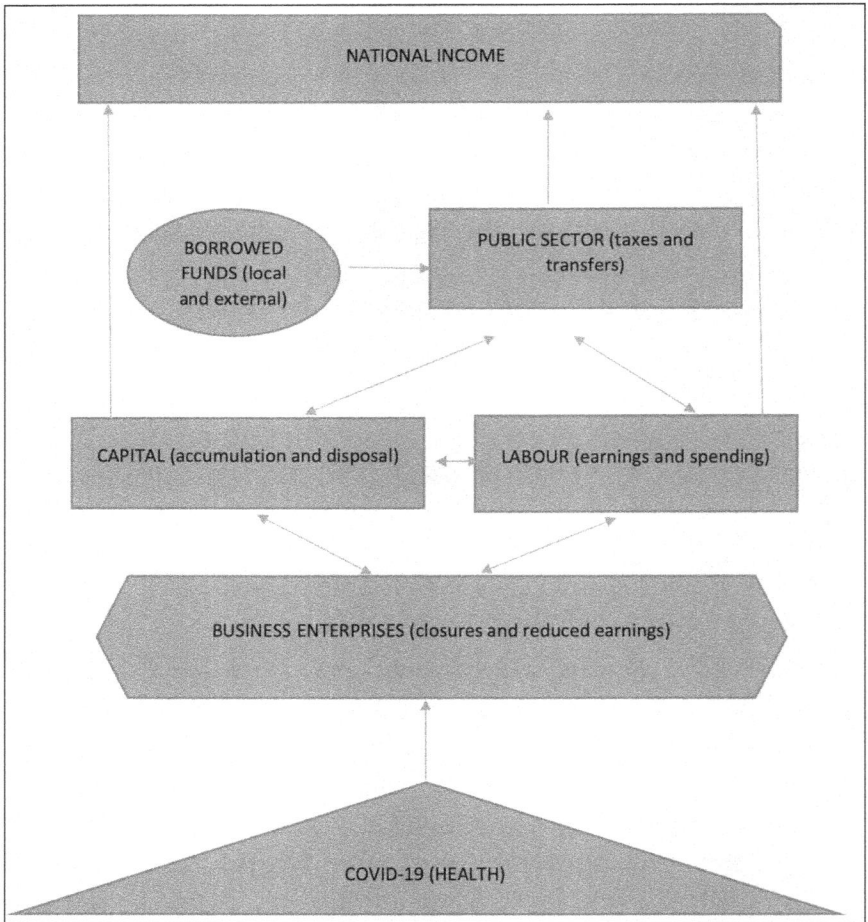

Figure 4.2: Tracking the implications of COVID-19 for the economy
Source: Authors' construct

- Disruptions severely curtailed employment (labour) and earnings by businesses and workers, leading to reduced levels of savings (for further capital investment) and tax payments (for public sector activities).
- With reduced revenue on the one hand and some access to borrowed and grant funds on the other, public-sector agencies sought to continue routine operations and provide stimulus packages to businesses, as well as unemployment and social protection benefits to affected population groups.[4]
- The impact of these three inter-related inputs (labour, capital and public sector activities) is reflected in the aggregate national income.

The clear message from these mutually dependent relationships is that if the health of the population is not properly secured, the economy and overall social welfare will be pointed irreversibly downwards. (This relationship was explicitly recognized by the Caribbean Community (CARICOM) Heads of Government since their 2001 Nassau Declaration, "The health of the Region is the wealth of the Region" (Pan-American Health Organization and CARICOM 2006).

METHODOLOGY

Defining the Caribbean depends on a mix of politics, geography, language and history. The dominant geo-political grouping is CARICOM, with fifteen member states and five associates covering three languages – English, French and Dutch. Another grouping, the Association of Caribbean States (ACS) spans thirty-seven countries with four languages – Spanish, French, Dutch and English. The Dutch, French, UK and US Caribbean dependencies comprise their own political groupings.

Complexities multiply as the Caribbean is sometimes grouped among the Americas, for example, by the Pan-American Health Organization (PAHO), or as Latin America and the Caribbean (LAC), or as the Organisation of African, Caribbean and Pacific States (OACPS). Such a multiplicity of groupings inevitably creates data lacuna regionally and internationally. Hence, a fundamental approach in our methodology has been to combine and integrate data from key international and regional sources with a major focus on CARICOM countries.

The epidemiological aspects of the pandemic (spread, distribution and human toll) in the Caribbean compared to non-Caribbean regions have been sourced from the WHO,[5] Our World in Data[6], the UWI COVID-19 Task Force[7] and the Johns Hopkins Coronavirus Resource Center.[8]

Secondary data on the broader health and development aspects of the pandemic, that is, how COVID-19 exposed and exacerbated Caribbean vulnerabilities with implications for resilient health systems have largely been sourced from international organizations such as the IMF, the World Bank, PAHO and the Caribbean Public Health Agency.

THE EPIDEMIOLOGY OF COVID-19 IN THE CARIBBEAN

An analysis of cases and deaths per capita among selected Caribbean states shows that the region has fared relatively well compared to its North and South American neighbours and tourism source markets in Europe (see Table 4.1).

Cuba (along with Haiti and the Dominican Republic) has the highest population in the Caribbean and accounted for approximately two thirds of the 1.7 million confirmed COVID-19 cases recorded in the Caribbean and CARICOM territories. Cumulative cases per one hundred thousand were lower in Cuba, Haiti and the Dominican Republic compared to the United States, the United Kingdom, the European Union, Canada and South America. Data on cumulative cases, however, is subject to in-country testing capacity and therefore questions may remain, for example, over the low number of confirmed cases reported in Haiti, which had conducted the lowest proportion of PCR tests per capita in the Caribbean.

Another indicator that is less prone to under-reporting is deaths per capita. Using this measure, table 4.2 demonstrates that deaths (per one hundred thousand) in the Caribbean were lower compared to the United States, the United Kingdom, the European Union and South America, although this hides some variation among Caribbean countries. The three most populous countries – Cuba, Haiti and the Dominican Republic – as well as nineteen of the twenty CARICOM states, recorded less cumulative deaths per one hundred thousand compared to the United States, the United Kingdom, the European Union and South America.

Table 4.1: COVID-19 cases per 100,000 — Caribbean vs other regions as at 30 June 2022

Caribbean subregion	Country/Region	Cases/100,000
CARICOM	Cayman Islands	39,538
Non-Caribbean	United Kingdom	33,629
Non-Caribbean	European Union	32,512
CARICOM	Barbados	29,761
Non-Caribbean	United States	25,468
CARICOM	Bermuda	24,852
CARICOM	Montserrat	23,023
CARICOM	British Virgin Islands	22,153
CARICOM	Anguilla	21,763
CARICOM	Dominica	20,413
CARICOM	Belize	5,621
CARICOM	St Lucia	14,994
CARICOM	Grenada	14,463
Non-Caribbean	South America	13,608
CARICOM	Turks and Caicos	13,583
CARICOM	Suriname	13,076
CARICOM	St Kitts and Nevis	12,567
CARICOM	Trinidad and Tobago	10,894
Non-Caribbean	Canada	10,229
Caribbean	Cuba	9,864
CARICOM	Antigua and Barbuda	9,198
CARICOM	Bahamas	8,758
CARICOM	St Vincent and the Grenadines	8,700
CARICOM	Guyana	8,299
CARICOM	Jamaica	5,044
Caribbean	Dominican Republic	5,386
CARICOM	Haiti	273

Source: Our World in Data (https://ourworldindata.org/coronavirus).

To assist Caribbean public and policymakers with actionable data on the epidemiology and broader impact of the pandemic, the University of the West Indies organized a surveillance task force on 29 February 2020.[9] The regional heat-map illustrated in figures 4.3A and 4.3B shows that, with the

Table 4.2: COVID-19 deaths per 100,000 – Caribbean vs other regions as at 30 June 2022

Caribbean subregion	Country/Region	Deaths/100,000
Non-Caribbean	South America	299
Non-Caribbean	United States	298
Non-Caribbean	United Kingdom	297
CARICOM	Trinidad and Tobago	261
Non-Caribbean	European Union	247
CARICOM	Suriname	220
CARICOM	Bermuda	215
CARICOM	St Lucia	211
CARICOM	British Virgin Islands	201
CARICOM	Bahamas	199
CARICOM	Grenada	185
CARICOM	Montserrat	181
CARICOM	Barbados	168
CARICOM	Belize	168
CARICOM	Guyana	155
CARICOM	Antigua and Barbuda	150
CARICOM	Jamaica	110
Non-Caribbean	Canada	107
CARICOM	St Vincent and the Grenadines	107
CARICOM	Dominica	93
CARICOM	St Kitts and Nevis	90
CARICOM	Turks and Caicos	79
Caribbean	Cuba	76
CARICOM	Anguilla	57
CARICOM	Cayman Islands	41
Caribbean	Dominican Republic	39
CARICOM	Haiti	7

Source: Our World in Data (https://ourworldindata.org/coronavirus).

exception of Haiti, the CARICOM countries were able to contain the first wave of the pandemic throughout the summer months of 2020, following synchronous border closures and lockdown measures implemented during the last weeks of March and the beginning of April 2020.

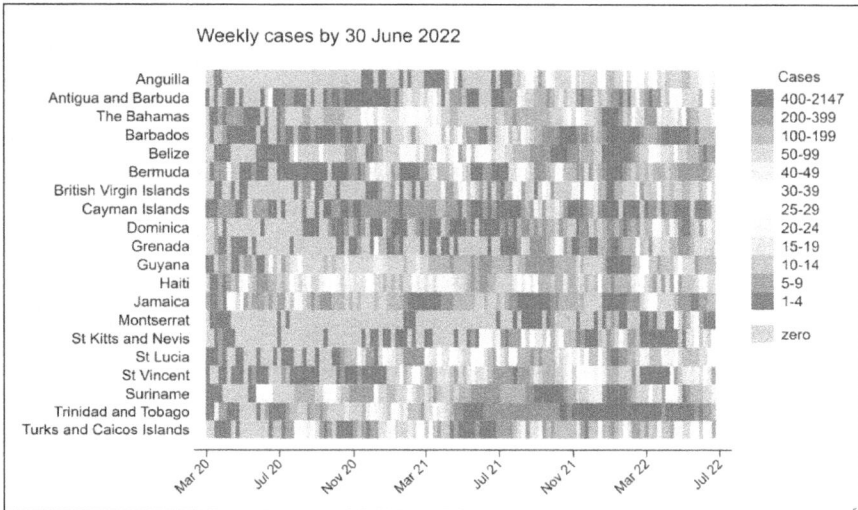

Figure 4.3A: Heat-map of COVID-19 outbreak: Cases among 20 CARICOM members (10 March 2020 to 30 June 2022)

Source: The UWI COVID-19 Task Force (www.uwi.edu/covid19); and COVID-19 Public Health Group, The University of the West Indies, Cave Hill Campus (https://ianhambleton.com/uploads/heatmaps _ CARICOM.pdf)

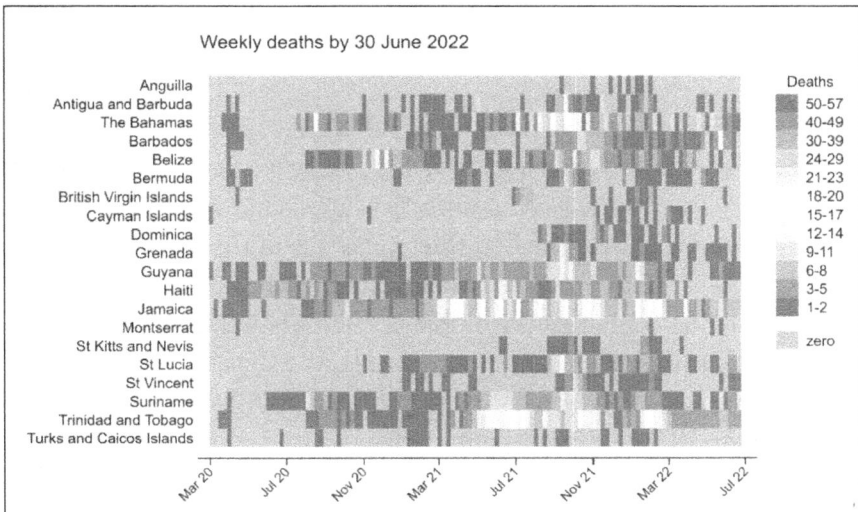

Figure 4.3B: Heat-map of COVID-19 outbreak: Deaths among 20 CARICOM members (10 March 2020 to 30 June 2022)

Source: The UWI COVID-19 Task Force (www.uwi.edu/covid19); and COVID-19 Public Health Group, The University of the West Indies, Cave Hill Campus (https://ianhambleton.com/uploads/heatmaps _ CARICOM.pdf)

Since the partial reopening of most Caribbean countries in June 2020, the outbreak evolved into a 'patchwork' pandemic. Countries with land borders generally struggled to contain outbreaks during this phase, including Suriname, which borders Brazil; Belize, which borders Mexico, and Haiti, which borders the Dominican Republic. Island countries such as Jamaica and the Bahamas also experienced periodic outbreaks as they conditionally reopened to tourists in the summer of 2020.

However, even countries that handled the first wave with minimal cases, such as Barbados, Dominica, Cayman, Bermuda, and Trinidad and Tobago, struggled to contain the epidemic over the long run. Outbreaks in the first six months of 2021 were driven by more contagious variants of SARS-CoV-2, such as the alpha variant in Jamaica and gamma variant in Trinidad and Tobago, and subsequent waves were propagated widely across CARICOM members by the delta variant in 2021 and omicron variants in 2022 (Sahadeo 2023). Despite endemic spread predominantly by omicron variants, it is notable that deaths in CARICOM states abated by June 2022.

PREPAREDNESS, IMPACT AND RESPONSE TO COVID-19

HEALTH AND THE HEALTHCARE SYSTEM

The impact of COVID-19 has played out as opposite extremes in the Caribbean: comparatively benign from a public health perspective, but very severe from a socio-economic perspective. The public health perspective was contextualized over the first fifteen months of the pandemic by the UWI COVID-19 Task Force benchmarking Caribbean countries against nations that had contained the outbreak relatively well at the time, such as New Zealand, Iceland and Singapore (UWI COVID-19 Task Force 2021). Figure 4.4, derived over the first fifteen months of the pandemic for Barbados, illustrates how containment was successfully maintained following suppression of a brief first wave in April 2020, until an outbreak in prisons emerged in January 2021.

The graph for Jamaica shows how the country grappled with multiple outbreaks but nonetheless maintained relative control over the epidemic when viewed in relation to comparator countries.

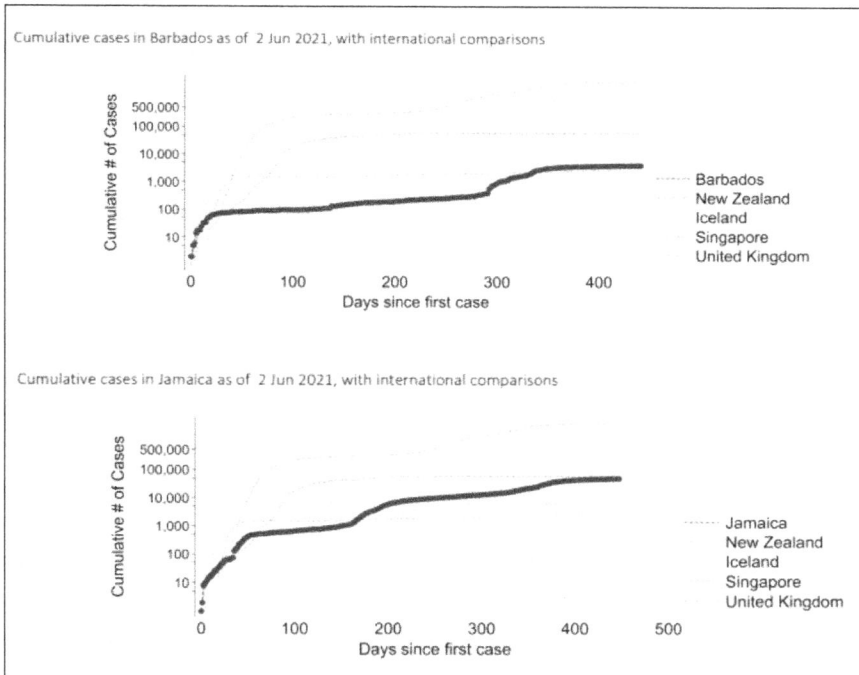

Figure 4.4: Cumulative COVID-19 cases in Barbados and Jamaica
Source: The UWI COVID-19 Task Force (www.uwi.edu/covid19)

The relatively favourable public health outcomes across the Caribbean in terms of containment of the pandemic, lower case numbers and cumulative deaths per capita compared to the neighbouring regions of North and South America is worth commenting on. The Crude Case Fatality Rate across twenty-two Caribbean countries (average of 1.2 per cent) does not explain the difference, since these were broadly similar for North America (1.2 per cent in the United States and 1.1 per cent in Canada).

Research from the UWI has demonstrated that the Caribbean countries were able to implement internal travel/social restrictions and (as island states) border closures relatively quicker than a range of comparative countries (Murphy 2020).[10]

Some commentators have cited lack of international cooperation and solidarity globally as a reason for the relatively fragmented public health response, in which uncontrolled epidemics were concentrated in countries with populist governments (United Nations 2020; UN News 2020; Williams

Table 4.3: COVID-19 CFR, Caribbean vs other regions as at 30 June 2022

Caribbean subregion	Country/Region	CFR
CARICOM	Haiti	2.6
CARICOM	Trinidad and Tobago	2.4
CARICOM	Bahamas	2.3
Non-Caribbean	South America	2.2
CARICOM	Jamaica	2.2
CARICOM	Guyana	1.9
CARICOM	Suriname	1.7
CARICOM	Antigua and Barbuda	1.6
CARICOM	St Lucia	1.4
CARICOM	Grenada	1.3
CARICOM	St Vincent	1.2
Non-Caribbean	United States	1.2
Non-Caribbean	Canada	1.1
CARICOM	Belize	1.1
CARICOM	Bermuda	0.9
CARICOM	British Virgin Islands	0.9
Non-Caribbean	United Kingdom	0.9
Non-Caribbean	European Union	0.8
CARICOM	Montserrat	0.8
Caribbean	Cuba	0.8
Caribbean	Dominican Republic	0.7
CARICOM	St Kitts	0.7
CARICOM	Barbados	0.6
CARICOM	Turks and Caicos	0.6
CARICOM	Dominica	0.5
CARICOM	Anguilla	0.3
CARICOM	Cayman Islands	0.1

Source: Our World in Data (https://ourworldindata.org/coronavirus).

et al. 2020; Wilson et al. 2020). As argued elsewhere, the cohesive political leadership in CARICOM, coupled with technical leadership from public health and disaster management agencies, notably the Caribbean Public Health Agency (CARPHA) and the Caribbean Disaster and Emergency

Management Agency (CDEMA), may have played an important role in initial containment of the epidemic (Landis 2021a; Landis 2021b). These Caribbean emergency and security agencies – experienced in weather-related emergencies –were at the forefront of the pandemic response of CARICOM sustaining inter-island movement of medicines and samples through the Regional Security System, stockpiling strategic supplies and maintaining supply chains.

From a psychological standpoint, Caribbean populations might also have been conditioned to comply to public health proclamations and stay-at-home mandates due to the annual passage of tropical cyclones (Hambleton 2020; Landis 2021b).

Additionally, the relatively proficient handling of the epidemic by lead response agencies in CARICOM countries was supported by the regional UWI that was entrusted with epistemic authority to deliver public goods through timely, policy-oriented health information to CARICOM states (Landis 2021a). Hence, despite having to manage periodic surges in COVID cases, hospitalization and spillover disruptions in other routine health care operations, the outbreak was relatively well handled in the Caribbean from a public health perspective.

ECONOMIES

As a region, the economic impact of COVID-19 in the Caribbean was quite severe, particularly in 2020[11] and early 2021. Select data on Caribbean countries – economic growth rate, public finances and public debt – over the period 2020–2022 as shown in Appendix 2 (IMF 2020, 2023; ECLAC 2020) helps to contextualize these disruptive effects.

In terms of economic growth, except for Guyana, the data showed a moderate increase in real GDP and overall economic performance in pre-pandemic 2019, with most countries still struggling to recover from the 2008–2009 global financial crisis (IMF 2020; ECLAC 2020b). However, in 2020, as shown in Appendix 2, average real growth rates plunged by 14.6 per cent in tourism-dependent countries, ranging from -3.7 per cent in St Vincent to -23.6 per cent in St Lucia (and -24 per cent in Aruba). Similarly, though less extreme, growth rates fell in commodity-exporting countries such as Haiti (-3.3 per cent), Trinidad and Tobago (-9.1 per cent) and Suriname (-15.9 per cent). Only Guyana, with its oil exploitation success, had positive growth of 43.5 per cent (IMF 2023).

Growth rates improved significantly in 2021 and 2022, averaging 9.1 per cent and 9 per cent in tourism-dependent countries, and 4.8 per cent and 25.4 per cent among commodity exporters (including Guyana). Projections suggest continuing moderate increases in growth rates, despite clear variability among CARICOM countries (IMF 2023).

Similar negative figures were also observed from indicators of fiscal performance, that is, fiscal deficits (using government primary balance as a percentage of GDP)[12] and growth of public debt (using gross government debt as a percentage of GDP).

Other relevant data in 2020 showed increased unemployment and under-employment; increasing levels of income inequalities; and increasing provisions for defaulting loan payments – both individual and business – by major financial intermediaries in these countries (IMF 2020; ECLAC 2020b; World Bank 2021).

Overall, the data suggest that the net effect of the COVID-19-induced economic decline in 2020, the improvements in 2021 and 2022 would still find several Caribbean countries 'poorer' than they were in 2015 (IMF 2023).

SOCIAL

COVID-19 highlighted the significance of social determinants for individual and community health. Consistent with global trends, disaggregation of the Caribbean data shows that the pandemic had a disproportionate impact – infection, hospitalization, death – on households with low incomes, deprived communities (urban and rural) and other vulnerable groups such as the elderly and those with co-morbidities (IMF 2020; ECLAC 2020b). These are generally consistent with similar findings from the ongoing epidemic of chronic diseases in the Caribbean (PAHO 2019; CARPHA 2020).

Unskilled blue-collar workers in frontline jobs in hospitality, retail trade services and other contact-intensive (compared to remote amenable) occupations, as well as in the informal sector (the 'precariat') have encountered more job losses, disruption of earnings, and uncertainty about future earnings prospects (Perkins 2021; Perkins and Landis 2020). For them, actions to earn a livelihood and cope with the economic and health fallout from COVID-19 do not always conform to the compliance requirements of public health directives. In real terms, the pandemic and poverty are intertwined, that is, the pandemic fuels inequality and poverty, while poverty and inequality provide fertile grounds for propagating the pandemic.

At the community level, COVID-19 deepened current cultural patterns of household and caring duties predominantly done by women, especially with stay-at-home health directives affecting schoolchildren, the elderly, and other sick relatives (Wedderburn 2021). The data also suggest that COVID-19 may have contributed to increasing levels of domestic abuse, with consequent implications for health and social services (ECLAC 2021).

MITIGATION MEASURES

The major policy responses and mitigation measures – health directives including vaccination, border controls, economic and social restraints,[13] and social protection – implemented by Caribbean countries are shown in table 4.4.

National vaccination campaigns – which began around March 2021 – fell short of targeted 60–70 per cent for herd immunity, and highlighted a range of issues, including global access, availability, diplomacy and efficacy on the one hand, as well as community acceptability, human rights/choice and hesitancy on the other (UNICEF 2022; PAHO 2023). Vaccination rates (complete schedules) averaged 46 per cent in CARICOM states, and (excluding outliers such as Haiti with 3 per cent, Cayman Islands with 96 per cent) ranged from 26 per cent in Jamaica to 63 per cent in Antigua).[14]

Despite these mitigation measures, COVID-19, alongside the ongoing epidemic of non-communicable diseases (NCDs), imposed heavy burdens on the capabilities of Caribbean health systems and may have slowed down health improvements, particularly among vulnerable groups (Seon et al. 2024). In parallel, despite short-term welfare transfers and business stimulus packages, weak economic performance resulting in fiscal, business and household spending constraints curtailed national and household

Table 4.4: Main COVID-19 mitigation measures and actions by Caribbean countries

Health	Border controls	Economic	Social/Social protection
Revised public health laws	Restrictions on entry and exit – air and sea	Reduced work hours	Restricted public gatherings, including court matters, cultural and sporting events
Quarantine and isolation	Testing and quarantine provisions	Work from home provisions	Closure of schools with more distance learning
Parallel health system facilities	Penalties for non-compliance	Restricted businesses to essential services	Curfews and penalties
Screening and testing		Salary grants	Transport restrictions
Laboratory upgrades		Business stimulus plans	Cash transfers
Increased health budget		Debt relief	Food transfers
National COVID task force		Tax reduction relief	Rental assistance
Vaccination (from March 2021)		Increased public borrowing	

Source: ECLAC (2021). "COVID-19 Observatory in Latin America and the Caribbean: Measures and Actions at the National Level" (https://www.cepal.org/en. Accessed on 20 June 2021)

capabilities to invest in health. These constrain the broader development roles of health in human capital formation, poverty reduction, and fostering economic and social investments.

Projections by the WHO Global Preparedness Monitoring Board (2020) suggest that Caribbean countries must be prepared for periodic pandemics, health emergencies and economic disruptions. These underscore the significance of building resilience in health systems – and the wider socio-economic structures – as a priority action in Caribbean countries.

RECOMMENDATIONS FOR BUILDING HEALTH RESILIENCE

Conceptually, healthcare system resilience may be defined as the ability of health institutions and actors to anticipate, prepare for and manage (absorb, adapt and transform) current and projected health and health-induced shocks (WHO 2019; PAHO 2020a; Lal et al. 2020), that is, limit disease spread, loss of life and collapse of basic services. In terms of actionable measures, Thomas et al. (2020) identified three modalities:

- Financial resilience: the protection of national funds for healthcare particularly, resources for the vulnerable in the face of economic contraction;
- Adaptive resilience: the management of the system with fewer resources, through efficiencies, while not sacrificing key priorities, access or entitlements;
- Transformatory resilience: the implementation of desirable and realistic reforms when current organization, structures and strategies are no longer feasible.

For vulnerable Caribbean SIDS, resilience in the face of COVID-19, other health concerns, and broader economic and environmental shocks requires measures for short-term prioritization of health tasks, including preparedness for surges, as well as for medium-term sustainability of the healthcare system. These measures must be aligned with other overarching initiatives to strengthen the economic and social welfare systems, as envisaged in the SDGs.

In this regard, four strategic synergistic responses can be advanced:

a. Universal health care: establishing or re-affirming that equitable access and quality health care for all are policy and sectoral priorities;
b. Public health: increasing investments to strengthen and expand public health goods and services, both at the national and regional levels;
c. Efficiency: focusing at the operational levels on value for money in allocation and utilization of health resources, with primary healthcare as the cornerstone;
d. Financing: reshaping health financing systems to support the above responses in an equitable and accountable manner.

UNIVERSAL HEALTH CARE AS A POLICY PRIORITY

For resilience rather than vacillating, on-off attention in emergencies only, healthcare systems need to be firmly grounded in overall national development plans and priorities. At the policy and operational levels, attention should focus on the SDGs Goal 3, "Ensuring Healthy Lives and Well-being for All" and Target 3.8, "Achieving UHC along with other health-related Goals.[15]

The overall objectives of UHC are summarized in the statements "Leave no one behind" and "Health for all" in terms of access to quality health care. For this, countries are expected to progressively enhance capabilities pertaining to three core aspects as outlined in figure 4.5 below:

- Coverage and entitlements to health benefits for all population groups, regardless of age, gender, income or pre-existing health conditions;
- Barrier-free access to an essential package of quality healthcare services, given the country's burden of disease (mix of infectious diseases like COVID-19, maternal and child health concerns, NCDs, and trauma-related incidents);
- Adequate financing for the above, generated in an equitable manner that does not leave low-income and vulnerable persons financially distressed.

The WHO and World Bank's UHC monitoring report (2021) showed most CARICOM countries (except Haiti) scored between 67 and 74 per cent

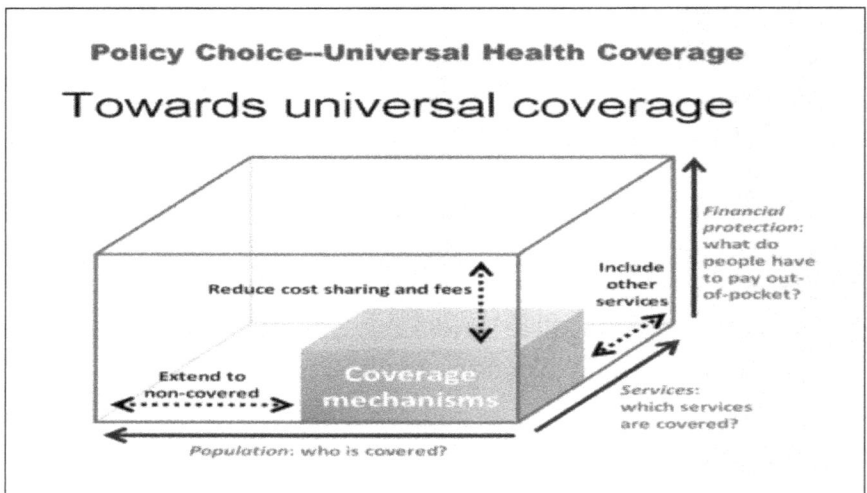

Figure 4.5: Towards universal coverage (adapted from the WHO 2010)
Source: World Health Organization (2010)

(optimal is 100 per cent) in 2019 in terms of their UHC Service Coverage Index (Indicator 3.8.1).[16] Most Caribbean countries also performed reasonably well in terms of Financial Protection (Indicator 3.8.2), with less than 5 per cent of households having 'catastrophic' health expenses (exceeding 10 per cent of total household income/consumption in any single year).

In comparison, the Institute for Health Metrics and Evaluation (2020) analysed data (some actual, some proxy) on 204 countries to prepare an Effective (Health) Coverage Index. Caribbean countries were assessed with average scores around fifty-five, ranging from thirty-six in Haiti to sixty-one in the Bahamas and Barbados (optimal attainable score is one hundred). Despite some methodological and data challenges, their findings showed that the Caribbean has several gaps in progressing towards UHC, especially in managing infectious and chronic diseases, HIV-AIDS and pregnancy-neonatal conditions.[17]

The key point from infusing a UHC approach into national development plans is for all health concerns, progress and implications to be measured and kept on the national agenda, that is, health in all policies, rather than in emergencies only, as with COVID-19. In this way, health issues are not ignored or relegated when investment, disinvestment or other sectoral re-prioritization matters are being considered.

The second critical element for resilience is dedicated budgetary investment to expand competencies for delivering public health goods/ services. These are essential community-oriented health goods (including managing emergencies such as COVID-19) designed to protect, improve, and restore health of individuals and communities, thus enabling progress in other socio-economic investments. These goods/services include a mix of national, regional and international activities with the Ministry of Health as the main implementing and coordinating agency (PAHO 2002).

PAHO specified eleven of these public health goods called essential public health functions (EPHFs), and measured competencies of Caribbean (and Latin American) countries to manage/implement these functions. As shown in table 4.5, the Caribbean scored reasonably well in two functions (public health surveillance and managing emergencies), but only average or rather poorly in the other functions (such as quality of care; research and development; and regulations and enforcement).[18]

Table 4.5: Essential public health functions: Performance scores (1.00 = optimal)

Functions	Average for Latin American countries	Average for Caribbean countries
Monitoring health status and performance	0.57	0.56
Public health surveillance and control	0.63	0.63
Health promotion	0.54	0.55
Social participation and empowerment	0.46	0.46
Planning, policies, and steering role	0.52	0.53
Regulations and enforcement	0.44	0.42
Promotion of equitable access to services	0.56	0.63
Human resource development	0.36	0.45
Quality of care	0.21	0.26
Research and development	0.35	0.38
Managing emergencies and disasters	0.71	0.71
Overall average	0.49	0.51

Source: Compiled from PAHO (2002)

INVESTMENT IN PUBLIC HEALTH GOODS

Specific data on the Caribbean in relation to health emergencies and disasters may be gleaned from reports provided to the WHO (2019) on the state of readiness and competence in implementing the International Health Regulations (2005).[19] Table 4.6 shows that the overall score for CARICOM countries was average (53 per cent), with major gaps in terms of preparedness for radiation emergencies, chemical events, zoonotic events, and legislation and financing.

Recognizing interdependencies as well as the human resource, infrastructure and cost constraints of each island acting alone, Caribbean countries have implemented a series of agreements on regional public health goods.[20] CARPHA (2020) reported that of the thirteen agreed categories – such as health legislation, promotion, training, public-private partnerships, information systems and minimum packages of health services – in the Caribbean Cooperation in Health IV programme, 2016–2025, four were

Table 4.6: Performance on IHR (2005)

Core capacities	Americas average (%)	CARICOM average (%)
Legislation and financing	66	47
IHR coordination and focal point	76	72
Zoonotic events management	66	47
Food safety	69	69
Laboratory systems	75	71
Surveillance	74	59
Human resources	67	56
National health emergency framework	66	59
Health service response capability	57	52
Risk communications and advocacy	63	53
Points of entry	64	50
Chemical events	55	31
Radiation emergencies	54	24
Overall average	66	53

Source: Compiled from scores reported by members to the 72nd World Health Assembly (2019a)

"in place"; two "in process"; five "not in place"; and the remaining two had no data.

In all three assessments above (EPHFs, IHR and Regional Public Health Goods) that were conducted before COVID-19, Caribbean countries showed noticeable progress in implementing some community-oriented public health goods. However, given the experience with COVID-19, more systematic action is urgently needed to address gaps and deficiencies, such as in information systems, human resources, legislation and financing, thereby enhancing health progress and, by implication, the contribution of health to overall development.

FOCUS ON SYSTEMIC EFFICIENCY AND PRIMARY CARE IN HEALTH SERVICES DELIVERY

Operationally, and especially in small, resource-poor countries, like the Caribbean, health system resilience requires efficiency in allocation and use of resources. This assumes greater significance given the expectations of slow and uneven economic recovery globally and in the Caribbean post-COVID-19, thus implying ongoing constraints on spending in health.

Data from the WHO (2010) on health sector operations globally point to significant systemic shortcomings in efficiency levels, with an estimated 20 to 40 per cent of health resources wasted or inefficiently used. The causative factors include:

- too much emphasis on doctor-centred, hospital-based curative services;
- overuse of hospital emergency facilities versus more appropriate lower-level facilities;
- inadequate medical record-keeping, leading to duplicative medical tests at primary and hospital levels in the public and private sectors;
- inappropriate in-patient length of stay, including inadequate intermediate step-down care facilities for recovering patients and 'bed-blockers';
- wastage in procurement, storage, prescribing and dispensing of pharmaceuticals.

Additionally, one can include concerns over excess expenditure on overseas care in the smaller Caribbean countries – selection of patients, choice of referral hospitals, terms of payment and auditing of claims.

Securing efficiencies in the health sector as well as equity in access (UHC) can be optimally advanced through expanding investments focusing on integrated primary care systems.[21] As stipulated by the WHO (2019b), "Primary health care provides the programmatic engine for UHC. It remains the most cost-effective way to address comprehensive health needs close to people's homes and communities", including situations where health emergencies such as COVID-19 dominate national attention and squeeze resources away from the wider health sector. Integrated – as opposed to fragmented – care revolves around primary care, with systematic linkages to include public health goods, secondary and tertiary care services, and other non-health sectors influencing social determinants of health, that is, education, housing, sanitation, nutrition and social welfare (PAHO 2019).[22]

As COVID-19 has highlighted, small Caribbean countries can achieve greater efficiencies and value for money in health spending by expanding regional collaboration in critical activities, such as accessing protective equipment, testing reagents and vaccines, as well as in overseas referrals, movement of health professionals, quality standards, and research. In this regard, existing arrangements for procuring vaccines and medications through the Organisation of Eastern Caribbean States' pooled procurement system, PAHO's Revolving Fund, and public health services through CARPHA can provide platforms for consolidation and expansion.

The key point is that, given their small size, resource constraints, limited room for error and waste, and overall vulnerabilities, Caribbean health sectors must place a premium on value for money in all spending. Consequently, targeting and auditing efficiency becomes imperative for building resilience in and future-proofing financing and delivery of health services.

ROBUST UNIVERSAL HEALTH FINANCING SYSTEMS

The fourth critical element in building resilience is the requirement for a robust, universal and equitable health financing system that facilitates implementation of the above three elements – UHC; public health goods; efficiency and integrated primary care. In analysing health financing in the Caribbean, the HEU, Centre for Health Economics, UWI (2018) estimated that health spending accounted for around six per cent of GDP. With funding from three major sources – taxes, out-of-pocket payments and health insurance – the analysis pinpointed persistent concerns over adequacy of health funds (health financing gap), access to care and cost burden by lower income groups (equity in access and cost sharing gap), and efficiency in utilization of funds (performance accountability gap).

For Caribbean health financing systems to secure universality, efficiency and sustainability, countries may need to shift from the current uncoordinated and inequitable system with dependence on tax funds, to one with a more defined mix or 'guided pluralism' of financing instruments. This is indicated in table 4.7 below with the guided pluralism comprising:

- Dominant, ring-fenced public funds for public health goods provided by well-resourced public sector agencies;
- Dominant, mandatory, pre-paid, pooled health funds (such as Social/ National Health Insurance plans) for *individual* health services – primary and secondary/tertiary care (including specified overseas care), delivered by certified public and private providers;

Table 4.7: Proposed pattern of health provision and financing for the Caribbean

Health services	Health providers	Health financing sources		
		Taxes–Budget	S/NHI	Private payments
Public-community health goods	Public agency	Dominant	Limited	Limited
Ambulatory-outpatient care	Public and private clinics	Limited	Dominant	Limited
Inpatient care	Public and private hospitals	Limited	Dominant	Limited
Drugs, diagnostics, imaging	Public and private facilities	Limited	Dominant	Limited
Overseas care	Public and private facilities	Limited	Dominant	Some
Training and research	Public and private centres	Some	Some	Some

Source: Compiled by authors

- Limited, residual, supplementary private funds – largely private health insurance and limited out-of-pocket payments for care in public and private facilities;
- Mix of programme-driven public and private funds (grants) for training and research.[23]

Supporting this guided pluralism approach to health financing should be a coordinated health information system providing real-time data for tracking and auditing provision, utilization and financing of health services, and overall performance in the public and private health sectors. The driving concern should not be more funds for health, but more value for money in the use of those funds, that is, the extent to which necessary quality care is accessible to all, regardless of socio-economic circumstances.

CONCLUSION

With tsunami-like impact, the COVID-19 pandemic has penetrated and buffeted communities and countries in the Caribbean and globally like no other infectious disease since the Spanish flu of 1918–1920. Beyond its devastation of human lives, disruption of economic progress and deepening of global and national divisions into haves and have-nots, the pandemic has redefined what is 'normal', and reshaped global and local approaches to health security and sustainable human development.[24]

Given the scale, severity and duration of the pandemic, the data suggest that most Caribbean countries managed reasonably well in containing the direct health threats (cases and deaths). However, the pandemic-induced economic and social disruptions were particulary severe, with some analyses suggesting that the Caribbean may have lost a decade of human development.

The health system challenges arising from COVID-19 were layered onto an ongoing NCD epidemic, along with periodic weather and infection emergencies, thus resulting in the creation of 'syndemic' conditions. As suggested above, systematic and well-resourced measures are necessary to build resilience and sustainability platforms into health systems, including priority attention to UHC (health for all) and 'health in all' policies; expanded provision of public health goods; efficiency in use of health resources, led by renewed primary care initiatives and a restructured 'guided pluralism' in health financing.

COVID-19 has also highlighted a number of areas where the health systems of the region, as in other parts of the world, can be strengthened. In this regard, stronger Caribbean-wide action will be needed in:

a. Strengthening laboratories and the laboratory network, with the objective of much better coverage and much quicker response in periods of emergency;

b. Doubling efforts to reduce the incidence of NCDs, given the vulnerability of affected persons to infections and viruses like COVID-19;

c. Bringing the health systems fully into the digital age and expanding digital healthcare solutions (telemedicine, e-health, including e-prescriptions and electronic records);

d. Enhancing global and regional alliances for shared resouces, including robust supply chains, given Caribbean dependence on vaccinations and other essential medical supplies from external sources. For example, better links with Cuba and other countries to ensure that more of the medications required will be produced within the region.

Overall, a more resilient and responsive health system is imperative, not just for protecting and sustaining individual and community health, but also broader socio-economic benefits, given the nexus between health, society and the economy.

NOTES

1. In its analysis of the inadequacy of lockdowns to contain the spread of the virus, the International Monetary Fund (2020) pointed to "the prevalence of poverty, informality of labour markets, and the inability to practice social distancing in densely populated urban areas" as contributing factors.

2. Categorized among the most tourism-dependent regions in the world, Caribbean countries such as Antigua, Aruba, British Virgin Islands, St Kitts and Nevis, the Bahamas, Turks and Caicos, St Lucia, Jamaica and Barbados rely on tourism-related activities for 30–45 per cent of their GDP, and 30–90 per cent of employment, according to the Economic Commission for Latin America and the Caribbean (2020a).

3. On the other hand, business activities that experienced growth during COVID-19 were technology-based services; online sales; food and pharmacy establishments; and sanitation/cleaning services.

4. ECLAC (2020b) estimated these fiscal expenditures ranged from 0.5 per cent of GDP in Guyana to 4.4 per cent in Antigua, and as high as 19.2 per cent in Barbados in 2020.

5. www.who.int/emergencies/diseases/novel-coronavirus-2019

6. https://ourworldindata.org/coronavirus

7. www.uwi.edu/covid19

8. https://coronavirus.jhu.edu/

9. The UWI COVID-19 Task Force was established ten days before the first case of the pandemic in the English-speaking Caribbean. The UWI published *daily* surveillance updates for cases and deaths for the twenty CARICOM member states (fifteen members plus five associates).

10. The tropical climate may also have been protective, although some countries like Puerto Rico and Mexico had relatively larger outbreaks compared to their Caribbean counterparts.

11. This was emphasized by CARICOM Heads of Government in their communique on preparing a Caribbean Economic Recovery and Transformation Plan – "Member States faced a perfect storm of a public health crisis, an economic crisis and a deepening debt crisis" (CARICOM Secretariat 2020).

12. Included in the estimates of fiscal expenditures are the additional transfers and support funds for the health sector to counter the negative repercussions of COVID-19 (prevention, testing, treatment and infrastructure activities) as well as other stimulus and social protection measures.

13. This includes the local challenges of balancing public health imperatives/regulations with curtailment of some rights and freedoms, such as freedom of movement, gathering, expression and earning a living ("No jabs, no jobs").

14. https://www.paho.org/en/covax-americas (updated on 17 November 2023 and accessed on 30 November 2023).

15. Some of the main health-related SDGs are: Goal 1. reducing poverty; 2. ending hunger; 4. quality education; 5. gender equality; 6. clean water and sanitation; 8. decent work and economic growth; 10. reducing inequalities; and 13. climate action.

16. The WHO's UHC Service Coverage Index estimates performance in coverage of and access to essential services based on tracer interventions for reproductive, newborn and child health; infectious diseases; and NCDs.

17. The Institute for Health Metrics and Evaluation (2020) used 23 indicators covering five health services types (promotion, prevention, treatment, rehabilitation, palliation) across life cycle groups (newborn, children under five years, children and adolescents aged five to nineteen, adults twenty to sixty-four years, older adults (sixty-five and over). Countries such as Iceland, Japan and Singapore were ranked in the highest performing decile, while several sub-Saharan countries and Afghanistan, Haiti and Papua New Guinea were placed in the lowest performing decile.

18. Except for one or two countries, Caribbean states have not taken any consistent actions to monitor and update assessments of performance of these public health functions since the first reports in 2001. PAHO (2020b) updated these functional capacities in 2020 and has been engaging countries with new assessments.

19. These are legally binding regulations for WHO members, designed to prevent, protect, control and provide coordinated international responses to the spread of health risks and diseases.

20. These relate largely to PAHO-CARICOM guided plans since the 1980s for Caribbean Cooperation in Health I, II, III and IV.

21. Data from PAHO (2019) suggests that, except for Barbados (33 per cent), all other Caribbean countries are spending less than the recommended 30 per cent of their health budgets on primary health care.

22. PAHO (2019) defines integrated people-centred care as "The management and delivery of health services such that people receive a continuum of health promotion, disease prevention, diagnosis, treatment, disease management,

rehabilitation, and palliative care services through the different levels and sites of care . . . according to their needs throughout the life course."

23. The broader platform should be expanding the role of public-private partnerships in health, given projected fiscal constraints post-COVID-19, and competition for state resources to rebuild all sectors and to manage debt obligations.

24. See the call-to-action priorities recommended by the WHO Global Preparedness Monitoring Board (2020): responsible leadership; engaged citizenship; strong and agile national and global health security systems; sustained investment in prevention and preparedness commensurate with the scale of a pandemic threat; and robust global governance of preparedness for health emergencies.

REFERENCES

Caribbean Public Health Agency. 2020. *The Caribbean Cooperation in Health-IV Report 2020: Regional Public Goods in Focus.* Port of Spain: CARPHA.

CARICOM Secretariat. 2020. "Communique issued at conclusion of the 41st Meeting of the Conference of Heads of Government of the Caribbean Community via videoconference, 29 October 2020." https://caricom.org/communique-issued-at-the-conclusion-of-the-forty-first-meeting-of-the-conference-of-heads-of-government-of-the-caribbean-community-via-videoconference-29-october-2020/.

Economic Commission for Latin America and the Caribbean. 2020a. *COVID-19 Reports: Recovery Measures for the Tourism Sector in LAC Present and Opportunity to Promote Sustainability and Resilience.* Santiago: ECLAC.

———. 2020b. *The Caribbean Outlook: Forging a people-centred approach to sustainable development post COVID-19.* (LC/SES.38/12). Santiago: ECLAC.

———. 2021. *Report on the dialogue on population impacts and policy responses to the COVID-19 pandemic in the Caribbean.* Santiago: ECLAC.

Hambleton, Ian R., Selvi Jeyaseelan, and Madhuvanti M. Murphy. 2020. "COVID-19 in the Caribbean small island developing states: Lessons learnt from extreme weather events." *Lancet Global Health* 8 (9): e1114–15.

HEU, Centre for Health Economics. 2018. "Health Financing in the Caribbean: Current Situation, Challenges and Responses." Presentation at PAHO Sub-regional Dialogue on Health Financing in the Caribbean. 28–29 August, Barbados.

Institute for Health Metrics and Evaluation. 2020. "Measuring UHC Based on and Index of Effective Coverage of Health Services in 204 Countries and Territories,

1990–2019: A Systematic Analysis of the Global Burden of Disease Study 2019." *Lancet* 396: 1250–84.

International Monetary Fund. 2020. *World Economic Outlook: Regional Economic Outlook – Western Hemisphere: Pandemic Persistence Clouds the Recovery.* Washington, DC: IMF.

———. 2023. *Regional Economic Outlook – Western Hemisphere: Securing Low Inflation and Nurturing Potential Growth.* Washington, DC: IMF.

Lal, Arush, N. Erondu, D. Heymann, G. Gitahi, and R. Yates. 2021. "Fragmented health systems and COVID-19: Rectifying the misalignment between global health security and universal health coverage." *Lancet* 397 (10268): 61–67.

Landis, R. Clive. 2021a. "Coronavirus and CARICOM: The Benefit of a Regional University in a Coherent Pandemic Response." In *Coronavirus and Islands: Fracturing the 'Old Normal' in the Caribbean and the Pacific*, edited by Y. Campbell and J. Connell. London: Palgrave McMillan.

———. 2021b. "COVID-19 among Caribbean SIDS: An effective public health response rooted in resilience." United Nations Educational, Scientific and Cultural Organization (UNESCO) Knowledge Series: Inclusive COVID-19 Recovery in the Caribbean. https://unesdoc.unesco.org/ark:/48223/pf0000378067.

Meesen, Bruno, A. Ancia, D. Gill et al. 2024. "When One Size Does Not Fit All: Aid and Health System Strengthening for Small Island Developing Countries". *Health Policy and Planning* 39 (1) i4–i8. https://doi.org/10.1093/heapol/czad089

Murphy, Madhuvanti M., S.M. Jeyaseelan, C. Howitt, N. Greaves, H. Harewood, K.R. Quimby, N. Sobers, R.C. Landis, K.D. Rocke, and I.E. Hambleton. 2020. "COVID-19 containment in the Caribbean: The experience of small island developing states." *Research in Globalization* 2: 100019.

Pan American Health Organization. 2002. Public Health in the Americas: Conceptual Renewal, Performance Assessment and Bases for Action. Washington, DC: PAHO.

———. 2019. *Universal health in the 21st century: 40 years of Alma Ata-Report of High-level Commission.* Washington, DC: PAHO.

———. 2020a. *Resilient health systems: Progress Report (CD8/INF/14).* Washington, DC: PAHO.

———. 2020b. *The Essential Public Health Functions in the Americas: A Renewal for the Twenty-first Century-Conceptual Framework and Description.* Washington, DC: PAHO.

———. 2023. COVID-19 Vaccination in the Americas Dashboard. https://ais.paho. org/imm/IM_DosisAdmin-Vacunacion.asp. Accessed 29 November 2023.

Pan American Health Organization and CARICOM Secretariat. 2006. *Report of the Caribbean Commission on Health and Development.* Washington, DC: PAHO.

Perkins, Anna. 2021. "A closer look at the secondary impacts of COVID-19 on the Caribbean: Why ethics still matter." United Nations Educational, Scientific and Cultural Organization (UNESCO) Knowledge Series, *Inclusive: COVID-19 recovery in Caribbean SIDS*. https://easterncaribbean.un.org/sites/default/files/2021-06/knowledge_series_unesco_3.pdf.

Perkins, Anna, and Clive R. Landis. 2021. *Ethics amidst COVID-19: A brief ethics handbook for Caribbean policymakers and leaders*. Cave Hill: The UWI COVID-19 task Force. https://www.uwi.edu/covid19/resources/resources-policymakers.

Sahadeo, N.S.D., S. Nicholls, F. Moreira, A. O'Toole, V. Ramkissoon, et al. 2023. "Implementation of genomic surveillance of SARS-CoV-2 in the Caribbean: Lessons learned for sustainability in resource-limited settings." *PLOS Global Public Health* 3 (9): e0001455.

Seon, Q., N. Greaves, M. Campbell et al. 2024. "Exploratory Empirical Model of Combined Effects of COVID-19 and Climate Change on Youth Mental Health". *Nature Mental Health* 2, 218–27.

Thomas, Steve, A. Sagan, J. Larkin, J. Cylus, et al. (2020). European Observatory on Health Systems and Policies: *Strengthening health systems resilience: key concepts and strategies*. Regional Office for Europe, World Health Organization. https://apps.who.int/iris/handle/10665/332441.

United Nations Children's Fund. 2020. *EDUCATION ON HOLD: A generation of children in Latin America and the Caribbean are missing out on schooling because of COVID-19*. Panama: UNICEF.

———. 2022. *COVID-19 Vaccine Hesitancy Survey Report 2021*. Christchurch: UN Barbados and the Eastern Caribbean Multi-Country Office and USAID.

United Nations. 2015. "Sustainable Development Goals." https://sdgs.un.org/goals.

———. 2020. "With more than 1.5 million lives lost to COVID-19, world leaders in General Assembly demand urgent action to guarantee equitable distribution of life-saving vaccines." 31st Special Session of the General Assembly, United Nations, 3 December. https://www.un.org/press/en/2020/ga12293.doc.htm.

United Nations News. 2020. "Global cooperation is our only choice against COVID-19, says WHO chief." United Nations News, 6 August. https://news.un.org/en/story/2020/08/1069702.

Wedderburn, Judith. 2021. "The End Game is not to go back to where we were: addressing gender gaps." UNESCO Knowledge Series, *Inclusive: COVID-19 Recovery in the Caribbean*. https://easterncaribbean.un.org/sites/default/files/2021-06/knowledge_series_unesco_3.pdf.

Williams, Caitlin R., Jocelyn G. Kestenbaum, and Benjamin M. Meier. 2020. "Populist Nationalism Threatens Health and Human Rights in the COVID-19 Response." *American Journal of Public Health* 110 (12): 1766–68.

Wilson, Kumanan, Sam Halabi, and Lawrence O. Gostin. 2020. "The International Health Regulations (2005), the threat of populism and the COVID-19 pandemic." *Global Health* 16 (1): 70.

World Bank. 2021. *Global Economic Prospects*. Washington, DC: The World Bank Group.

World Health Organization. 2012: *World Health Report 2010: Health systems financing – The path to universal coverage*. Geneva: WHO.

———. 2019a. *Reports to the World Health Assembly*. Geneva: WHO.

———. 2019b. *Primary Health Care on the Road to Universal Health Coverage: 2019 Monitoring Report*. Geneva: WHO.

WHO Global Preparedness Monitoring Board. 2020. *A World in Disorder – Global Preparedness Monitoring Board Annual Report*. Geneva: WHO.

WHO and World Bank. 2021. *Tracking Universal Health Coverage – 2021 Global Monitoring Report*. Geneva: WHO.

5

Debt and Development Finance Models for Caribbean Small States in the Context of Crises

DILLON ALLEYNE AND **MACHEL PANTIN**[1]

FINANCING SUSTAINABLE DEVELOPMENT IS A MAJOR CHALLENGE FOR small island developing states (SIDS) and this has been articulated since the Barbados Programme of Action for the Sustainable Development of SIDS (United Nations 1994). This challenge is even more urgent in light of the economic and social disruptions that the COVID-19 pandemic has caused. COVID-19 directly impacted the capacity of the subregion to address its sustainable development priorities.

The challenge to accessing affordable development finance has been complicated by the higher sovereign risk arising from significant debt and low economic growth in the region. Policy missteps and fiscal profligacy – a common narrative – have not been the root causes of debt accumulation in the region. Rather, debt was driven by negative external economic shocks, extreme weather events and climate change-attendant challenges (ECLAC 2018). Indebtedness and other macroeconomic problems have been exacerbated by the COVID-19 health crisis, which had a devastating effect on tourism and service sectors in the Caribbean. Likewise, the resulting risk avoidance by the private sector in domestic financial markets and worsening global financial conditions are compounding these effects. The fact is, countries of the region need to build their resilience and in doing so, they need to manoeuvre on two fronts with respect to sourcing financing for development. They must leverage all that is possible domestically, and at the same time strive to secure the resources that they can never generate domestically, and which are crucial to meet the enormous challenges they face as SIDS.

The first section of this chapter examines some conceptual issues in addressing debt and development finance in the Caribbean. Part two examines the low-growth, high-debt nexus and the impact of COVID-19. Part three argues that the middle- and high-income status of countries of the sub-region affects their access to much-needed concessional finance, and urges the use of vulnerability indices to determine such access by Caribbean countries. Part four explores the limits to domestic financing, and part five analyses attempts to access international finance and the challenges faced. The final section suggests a way forward, with a variety of recommendations to address the financing gap.

SOME CONCEPTUAL CONSIDERATIONS

One of the major issues that have dominated the discussion about small states is whether they should receive special and differential treatment in financial and other markets due to inherent vulnerabilities arising from negative economic shocks, disasters and climate-related effects. A popular perspective which argues that SIDS are largely middle-income countries, and quite capable of accessing international finance on graduation, leans heavily on work typified by Easterly and Kraay (2000). They tested whether small states are any different from other states in terms of their income, growth and volatility outcomes. After controlling for location, they concluded that small states have higher per capita gross domestic product (GDP) than other states in their region. This income advantage, they suggest, is largely due to a productivity advantage, constituting evidence against the idea that small states suffer from an inability to exploit increasing returns to scale. They admit to the volatility of the terms of trade, which was a feature of small states, but suggest that their greater openness, on balance, has a positive net payoff for growth. They conclude that one policy measure that might be relevant for small states is to further open up to international capital markets to better diversify risk, but the benefits of even that are still unresolved in the literature. They come to the incredible conclusion that small states are no different from large states, and so should receive the same policy advice.

In a similar vein, Godfrey Baldacchino and Geoffrey Bertram (2009), using the idea of strategic flexibility, argue that small states are nimble and, by and large, have been able to do very well, based on per capita income. They do mention the limitations of this measure, but nonetheless claim that there is evidence that vulnerability overstates the incapacity of small states as they are "strategically securing their place in the world".

Matthew Bishop (2012), in responding to these perspectives, suggests that authors may be drawing misleading conclusions in their (again, admirable) quest to stress the agential capacity of small states and societies. Thus, as he suggests, vulnerability is not weakness and does not preclude the exercise of creative agency.

Another area in which small states are severely challenged is the fact they are not at the international decision-making table on global financial rulemaking. Bustillo and Artecona (2015) have argued that global financial regulations are framed by standard setters in Europe and the United States, and are imposed on developing countries where the characteristics and structure of financial systems are different and cannot meet these standards.

For this reason, in the matter of black and grey listing, with respect to offshore financial centres and the loss of correspondent banking relations – with its potential to disrupt remittance flows and add to the unbanked – small states, like those of the Caribbean, can merely react to these changes. Many of these regulatory changes, such as anti-money laundering and counter-terrorist financing (AML/CFT), and know your customer (KYC) regulations, were enacted after the global financial crisis in which small states had no part to play.

Bustillo and Artecona (2015) suggest that the lack of representation of emerging and developing countries in standard-setting bodies may affect the effectiveness of global financial regulation and run the risk of setting standards that have unintended, harmful consequences on these economies. The implication is that including countries with diverse economic interests in decision making could minimize and even prevent harmful unintended consequences of global financial rulemaking.

Caribbean countries have, on average, sustained high debt burdens, which have helped to increase their sovereign risks and make accessing finance more costly. At the same time, the region has not had robust growth, which can enable countries to grow out of debt. The next section examines the debt and growth nexus in the context of COVID-19.

THE DEBT AND GROWTH NEXUS AND THE COVID-19 CHALLENGE

No discussion about financing for sustainable development in the Caribbean can be meaningful if it does not factor in the current debt crisis facing the subregion in a context of low economic growth. Since the global financial crisis of 2008–2009, growth rates for most countries have not returned to pre-crisis levels. This has been partly due to the difficult international climate for growth as well as the high debt burden that has accumulated over time. Before 2020 many tourism-based economies' growth rates were improving, mostly due to the expansion of the US economy, while goods producers[2] were facing low commodity prices. This is illustrated in figure 5.1 below. The right panel shows the trend decline in growth, while the left shows the significant debt overhang.

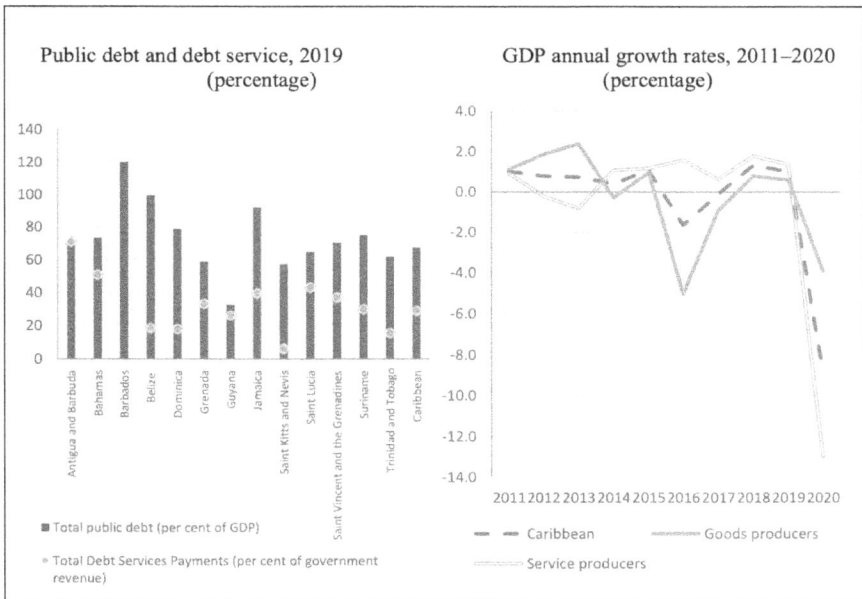

Figure 5.1: Caribbean public debt and growth rates

Source: Authors (on the basis of official data)

According to a study done by ECLAC, the Caribbean economies demonstrate a decidedly negative linear relationship between debt and growth (McLean et al. 2020). In addition, the debt service (interest and amortization) costs are high relative to public revenue (Alleyne et al. 2019).

Over time, several countries in the Caribbean have had to seek International Monetary Fund (IMF) support and multiple restructuring of their debt, but nonetheless, the average has remained high (Hurley 2015). Meanwhile, low growth has been accompanied by increasing public aspirations, especially in light of the sustainable development goals (SDGs). The prospects for robust growth in the near term, especially for countries relying on tourism markets, are not optimistic.

The COVID-19 pandemic has severely impacted economies the world over, mainly through social distancing lockdowns, and travel restrictions. Service industries have borne the brunt of these measures, and in the Caribbean, COVID-19 resulted in a significant loss in revenue and foreign exchange earnings in the tourism sector, upon which most economies are dependent. The loss will result in a dramatic fall in service exports and a fall in tourism's contribution to GDP growth. In early 2020, ECLAC (Abdulkadri et al. 2020) estimated the impact of the pandemic on tourism across the subregion[3] – the total expected loss in visitor expenditure from both stayover and cruise arrivals – to range from US$21 billion to US$27 billion. Contribution to GDP growth was estimated to range from -6.4 percentage points to -8.2 percentage points.

The negative impact on the sector will be manifested in reduced earnings for tourism service providers, hotels, taxi drivers and craft vendors, and lower purchases from the commerce, distribution and agriculture sectors (Abdulkadri et al. 2020). This will severely dampen the earnings and livelihoods of small business owners and workers in these sectors. Job losses in this sector will disproportionately affect women since, on average in the Caribbean, 10.5 per cent of the female labour force works in accommodation and food service, compared to 4.6 per cent of males.

The worldwide travel restrictions also caused an unprecedented fall in the demand for energy and lower fuel prices in 2020. Trinidad and Tobago's oil and gas sector was significantly affected by the pandemic, along with Guyana's nascent oil industry. The reduction in GDP resulting from the fall in energy prices was estimated to range between 3.2 per cent and 4.4 per cent in Trinidad and Tobago, and between 5.8 per cent and 11 per cent in Guyana.

Increasing growth and reducing debt will be critical in the next few years as the COVID-19 pandemic has exposed many areas of inequality in the Caribbean. The most glaring relates to education services, since many households did not have access to adequate ICT infrastructure at the beginning of the pandemic. Novel ways were employed to address this digital gap, as many children were being left behind. As a resilience-building strategy, a broadband infrastructure will have to be deployed across the Caribbean to improve interconnection across all sectors. Such a framework will also be useful for supporting disaster preparedness and risk reduction strategies. But this kind of sustainable infrastructure will require considerable financing – mostly from governments – either utilizing existing Universal Service Funds[4] or increased borrowing.

Much of the financing efforts to reduce the impact of COVID-19 has been sourced through reorienting existing budgetary flows and increased borrowing. For example, of the US$1.2 billion spent in the Caribbean in the first half of the year, more than 50 per cent had been sourced through additional borrowing.

THE MIDDLE-INCOME QUESTION AND VULNERABILITY

At the heart of the argument against special and differential treatment for SIDS is their so-called middle and upper-middle income categorization, despite their inherent vulnerability. The Caribbean is the second most hazard-prone region in the world, due to both its geographical location and the concentration of its population in coastal areas. The evidence is that almost 17 per cent of the 10,271 disasters registered worldwide between 1970 and 2010 occurred in Latin America and the Caribbean. Natural threats in the region range from hurricanes, floods and drought to volcanic eruptions, among others (Bello et al. 2017). In many cases a single hurricane affects not just the immediate area, but often several islands, disrupting supply chains, and causing damage and losses of several orders of magnitude in relation to GDP.

At the same time, most Caribbean SIDS are categorized as upper-middle or high-income countries, based on their gross national income per capita. The subregion, and the SIDS group in general, have long argued that this is an inappropriate categorization as it does not consider the extreme vulnerabilities of these countries to natural disasters, climate change and negative external economic shocks. The vulnerability of the subregion is well-documented. It is estimated that Caribbean SIDS suffer at least US$3 billion every year in damage and losses from hurricane impacts alone. ECLAC estimated that in 2017, hurricanes Irma and Maria caused some US$93 million worth of damages and losses in the Caribbean, and most of the financing for rebuilding had to be sourced from domestic and international sources on commercial terms (ECLAC 2018). More recently, Hurricane Dorian affected many countries, with the most affected being the Bahamas, with estimated damages and losses of US$2.5 billion and US$717.3 million respectively. The total cost[5] of Hurricane Dorian was approximately US$3.4 billion, and it cost the Bahamas economy 1 percentage point of GDP growth.

The Caribbean subregion is also vulnerable to multiple hazards which contribute to its environmental fragility. Exposure to pollution from both land-based sources and transshipment spills of hazardous cargo also have the potential to do significant harm to the subregion's fragile ecosystems. Meanwhile, the persistent influx of sargassum onto beaches of tourism-dependent countries is causing increasing concern.

These challenges notwithstanding, the Caribbean still finds itself in an international climate that uses income per capita as the principal measure of their capacity to overcome them. This classification of the majority of Caribbean countries has deafened the international community to their appeals for special and differential treatment. As a result, they find it difficult to access international concessional finance.

Table 5.1 shows the categorization of SIDS in general and how the Caribbean countries compare in this process. While several are either vulnerable or extremely vulnerable, based on the United Nations Environmental Programme's vulnerability index, few are eligible for the World Bank's International Development Association (IDA) lending and must seek financial assistance on less generous terms. For the purposes of COVID-19, a few were made IDA-eligible but reverted to their original

Table 5.1: SIDS are largely middle income and highly vulnerable

Country	Income group	Lending category	Environmental vulnerability index	GNI per capita, PPP (current international $), 2019
Antigua and Barbuda	High income	IBRD	Vulnerable	21,500
Bahamas	High income		At risk	35,760
Bahrain	High income		Highly vulnerable	44,140
Barbados	High income		Extremely vulnerable	15,730
Belize	Upper middle income	IBRD	At risk	6,630
Cabo Verde	Lower middle income	Blend	Vulnerable	7,310
Comoros	Lower middle income	IDA	Vulnerable	3,220
Cuba	Upper middle income		Highly vulnerable	–
Dominica	Upper middle income	Blend	Extremely vulnerable	12,460
Dominican Republic	Upper middle income	IBRD	Highly vulnerable	18,280
Fiji	Upper middle income	Blend	Highly vulnerable	13,260
Grenada	Upper middle income	Blend	Highly vulnerable	16,250
Guinea-Bissau	Low income	IDA	Vulnerable	2,220
Guyana	Upper middle income	IDA	Resilient	9,900
Haiti	Low income	IDA	Highly vulnerable	1,790
Jamaica	Upper middle income	IBRD	Extremely vulnerable	9,770
Kiribati	Lower middle income	IDA	Extremely vulnerable	4,650
Maldives	Upper middle income	IDA	Extremely vulnerable	17,880
Marshall Islands	Upper middle income	IDA	Highly vulnerable	–
Mauritius	High income	IBRD	Highly vulnerable	26,410
Micronesia, Fed. Sts.	Lower middle income	IDA	Extremely vulnerable	–
Palau	High income	IBRD	Highly vulnerable	–

Table 5.1 continues

Table 5.1: SIDS are largely middle income and highly vulnerable (*cont'd*)

Country	Income group	Lending category	Environmental vulnerability index	GNI per capita, PPP (current international $), 2019
Papua New Guinea	Lower middle income	Blend	At risk	4,470
Samoa	Upper middle income	IDA	Highly vulnerable	6,490
São Tomé and Principe	Lower middle income	IDA	At risk	4,090
Seychelles	High income	IBRD	Highly vulnerable	29,300
Singapore	High income		Extremely vulnerable	92,020
Solomon Islands	Lower middle income	IDA	Vulnerable	2,350
St. Kitts and Nevis	High income	IBRD	Highly vulnerable	25,920
St. Lucia	Upper middle income	Blend	Extremely vulnerable	15,140
St. Vincent and the Grenadines	Upper middle income	Blend	Highly vulnerable	12,880
Suriname	Upper middle income	IBRD	Resilient	15,200
Timor-Leste	Lower middle income	Blend	Not available	4,730
Tonga	Upper middle income	IDA	Extremely vulnerable	–
Trinidad and Tobago	High income	IBRD	Extremely vulnerable	26,950
Tuvalu	Upper middle income	IDA	Extremely vulnerable	6,170
Vanuatu	Lower middle income	IDA	Vulnerable	3,310

Source: World Bank, World Development indicators database; UNEP Environmental Vulnerability Index
Note: Eligibility for IDA support depends on a country's relative poverty, defined as GNI per capita below an established threshold and updated annually ($1,185 in the fiscal year 2021). IDA also supports some countries, including several small island economies, that are above the operational cutoff but lack the creditworthiness needed to borrow from the International Bank for Reconstruction and Development (IBRD). They are referred to as 'blend' countries.

status after the crisis. This process of graduation that moves countries out of concessional eligibility has been a serious challenge to funding sustainable development, which requires long-term, affordable finance.

Building back better after each disaster adds to the debt burden, leading to a significant portion of government revenue being diverted from development projects to debt-service payments. Caribbean governments have argued that an index of vulnerability is a true measure of their country's capacity to access finance and such an index would help the subregion to garner much-needed concessional resources. While a variety of indices exist, the United Nations has developed a credible Economic Vulnerability Index (EVI) which can be used to assess the needs of member states.

LIMITS TO DOMESTIC FINANCING

The search for affordable sources of development finance by SIDS includes drawing on domestic sources. The Addis Ababa FFD Action Agenda recognizes that while not all the financing for development can be sourced from domestic sources, domestic finance, including that from the private sector, is important. That agenda emphasized such innovative approaches as blended finance, in which Official Development Assistance (ODA) can be blended with private capital inflows, including foreign direct investment (FDI). With no access to significant ODA, this is not a realistic option for the Caribbean.

It is to be noted, following Sagasti (2013), that SIDS find it difficult to generate adequate amounts of both domestic and international development finance (see figure 5.2).

Caribbean countries are no different and they are dependent on external financing, given their limited capacity to mobilize and harness domestic financial resources from small and risk-averse private financial sectors. The domestic banking sector in the Caribbean is dominated by the commercial banks. It has also been suggested that development banks might be more appropriate as a vehicle for financing development rather than commercial banks. Recently, however, such banks, where they still exist, tend to only lend to the commercial banks, which employ the same strict evaluation criteria for accessing loans. Thus, even though considerable liquidity exists in domestic banking systems, it has been difficult to incentivize the private sector to support certain areas of sustainable development.

Capital markets are very thin and the private banking sector is very averse to risk, unless returns can be guaranteed. Nevertheless, some progress has

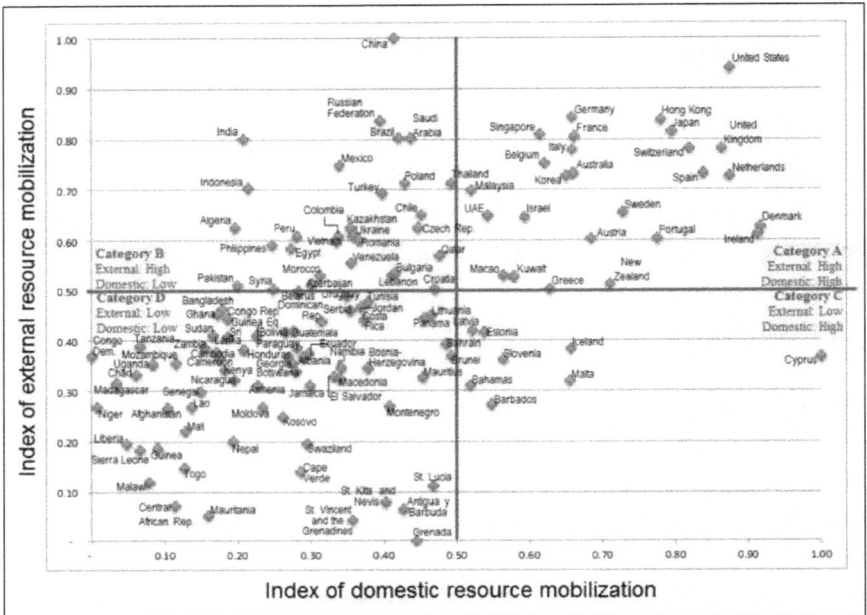

Figure 5.2: SIDS have lower capacities to mobilize domestic and external resources

Source: Francisco Sagasti. 2013. "From 'graduation' to 'gradation' in international development finance." Development Progress

been made in harnessing domestic capacity to address disasters of a certain magnitude. The Caribbean Catastrophe Risk Insurance Facility Segregated Portfolio Company (CCRIF-SPC) is a multi-country, risk pool facility that provides parametric insurance, where predefined conditions guarantee automatic payouts when triggered by a major loss event. It is a regional catastrophe fund designed to limit the financial impact of hurricanes and earthquakes. The packages offered have since been expanded to include policies for excessive rainfall, with guaranteed payments within fourteen days of an event.[6]

Despite their importance, these payouts are generally insufficient for rehabilitation to pre-disaster levels,[7] and some countries have raised concerns that the funds have been inadequate, and the parameters should be reviewed.[8] It is important to note that the CCRIF-SPC products are focused on destruction of physical assets, and none are specifically designed for pandemic-type disasters. Recently, in light of the COVID-19 crisis, CCRIF received a US$11 million grant from the European Union, which provided premium support for CCRIF members, with a discount of 26 per cent on their gross premium for the upcoming policy years (CCRIF 2020). Besides the CCRIF, other avenues for domestic support and innovative approaches must be found to harness domestic capital markets, while reducing their risks. Inclusive micro-finance solutions can empower small businesses and vulnerable communities, which are often the most defenceless to climate change and natural hazards, while alleviating poverty by stimulating economic growth. These products typically include micro-credit, micro-deposit and micro-insurance schemes. In the context of Caribbean SIDS, micro-finance mechanisms must be effectively structured so that groups who cannot access finance through traditional means can have the opportunity to do so.[9]

TAX REVENUE AND DOMESTIC SAVINGS

It has been suggested that public financing for development is challenging for many SIDS due to several factors. For example, the provision of public goods largely falls to the state and tends to be more expensive on a per capita basis compared to countries with larger populations. The liberalization of trade, especially in SIDS, has eroded tax bases, given the heavy dependence on trade taxation for generating tax revenue (Hurley 2015).

Given the relative importance of indirect taxes and the difficulty of managing direct taxes beyond PAYE taxpayers, revenue elasticity tends to be low. The tendency in recent years in the Caribbean has been to expand the tax base and reduce the tax rates while de-emphasizing direct taxes relative to indirect taxes. For countries with large informal sectors arising from continual negative external shocks, revenue buoyancy also tends to be low. Figure 5.3 (below) shows the tax effort from 2010 to 2017, which has been increasing over time. Much of this has been due to the fiscal consolidation programmes consequent on the high debt that have emphasized raising revenue and compressing mostly capital spending. Even though tax reforms can be helpful in trying to reduce tax evasion and avoidance, tax revenues are insufficient to meet the development demands of Caribbean countries.

Not surprisingly, many Caribbean countries carry large current account

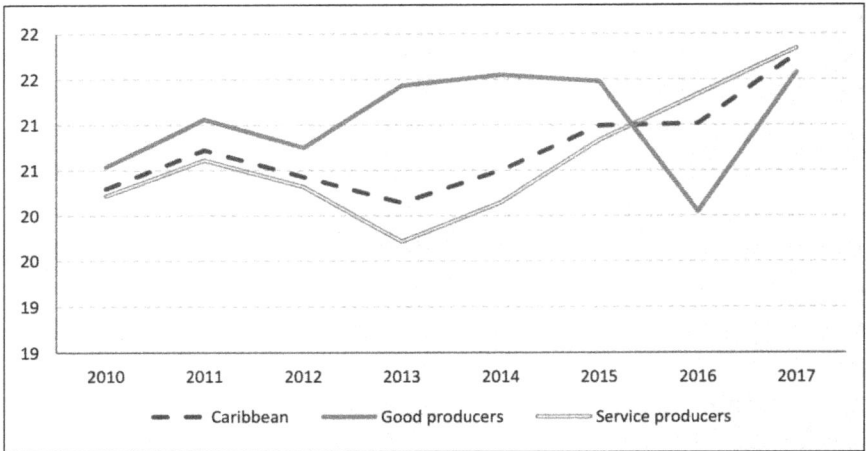

Figure 5.3: Tax revenue (per cent of GDP), 2010–2017

Source: UNU-WIDER Government Revenue Dataset.
Caribbean countries include Antigua and Barbuda, the Bahamas, Barbados, Belize, Dominica, Grenada, Guyana, Jamaica, St Kitts and Nevis, St Lucia, St Vincent and the Grenadines, and Suriname.

deficits as their capacity to export has declined in line with lower growth. Such deficits most likely increased in the aftermath of the COVID-19 pandemic. Figure 5.4 (below) shows the average level of current account balance and fiscal balances over the period 2015–2018. Except for Trinidad and Tobago, all other countries are experiencing fiscal deficits. However, even that country has sustained large deficits over the last two years. The high current account deficit has placed additional pressures on governments to maintain consumption in the face of falling export capacity. Thus, the current account deficit also drives the fiscal deficit, as was found empirically by Alleyne (2018).

Another important source of finance for development can come from public savings. However, in light of the high debt burden and considerable debt service, public savings are likely to be low. Figure 5.5 (below) shows the savings rate for all SIDS, low- and middle-income countries and the Caribbean. While for the low- and middle-income countries the savings rate is about 30 per cent, it is about 10 per cent lower in the Caribbean, which is still higher than all SIDS.

The fiscal deficits, together with high debt, make it difficult for Caribbean

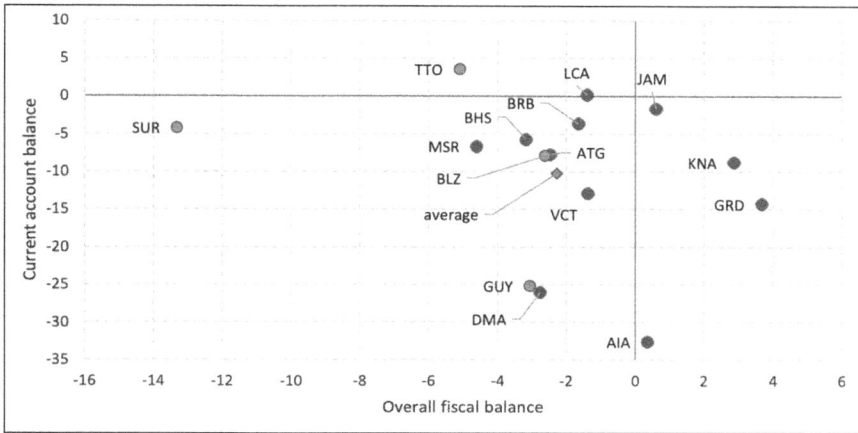

Figure 5.4: Overall fiscal and current account balance (per cent of GDP), 2016–2019 average
Source: Authors (on the basis of official data)

countries to generate fiscal buffers. Public-private partnerships remain a viable option, especially for Caribbean countries with limited access to development finance.[10] More broadly speaking, the private sector, including from philanthropic sources, must be incentivized to participate in financing critical aspects of the 2030 Agenda. This will be possible as governments make their priority areas clear and are able to skilfully negotiate with

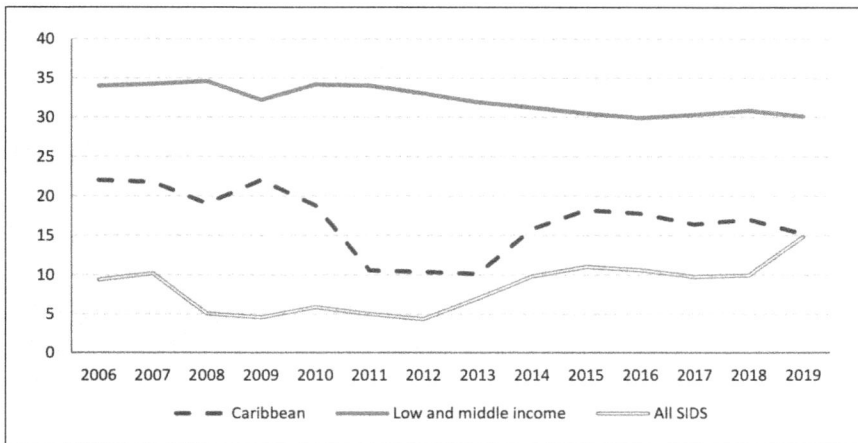

Figure 5.5: Gross domestic savings (per cent of GDP), 2006–2019
Source: World Bank, World Development indicators database

the private sector to bear a balanced portion of the risks and returns. It is important that such partnerships be based on transparency and accountability. Other schemes, such as those suggested by Ram (2020), if they can properly account for risks, could incentivize the domestic private sector to help finance sustainable development. He suggests the floating of bonds that could be attractive to the domestic private sector, including major non-financial institutions. Other schemes, such as the floating of diaspora bonds, given the large Caribbean diaspora, have also been suggested. Such suggestions ought to be taken seriously, given the lack of resources in the public sector and the high level of liquidity in the domestic banking system (Alleyne 2019).

ACCESS TO INTERNATIONAL FINANCE IN THE CARIBBEAN

Due to the middle-income categorization of several of its economies, the Caribbean has seen a declining contribution of Official Development Assistance (ODA) to promote its sustainable development. The implication of this is that most of the development finance must be accessed on commercial terms. In addition, limited opportunities exist to access global financial bond markets, due to their relatively small demand and associated elevated sovereign risks (Bustillo et al. 2018).

In light of the so-called graduation of most Caribbean economies, net ODA has declined over time, falling to a trickle by 2017. Meanwhile, private flows have been on the increase, mostly led by a constant flow of net remittances. Remittances have proven to be quite robust, even in recessions, although very much skewed to some countries more than others. In contrast to the decline in ODA flows, private capital flows have been on the rise.

Besides net remittances, Caribbean economies receive a large flow of foreign direct investment relative to their size. The average ratio of inward FDI to GDP in the 2007–2017 period was 3.4 per cent for the subregion. In terms of absolute amounts, the top five recipients of FDI were Jamaica, Bahamas, Barbados, Trinidad and Tobago, and Guyana. FDI flows to the Caribbean were on an upward trend until 2008, and on a downward trend following the global financial crisis, until 2012. Although there has been a slight recovery since then, these flows have become more volatile. Migrant remittances to the

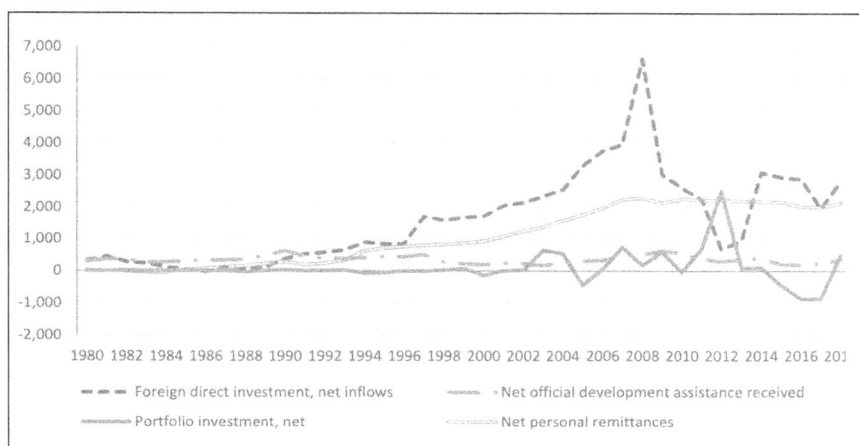

Figure 5.6: The Caribbean (13 countries): Main external financing flows (US$ millions), 1980–2018

Source: World Bank, World Development Indicators.
Caribbean countries are Antigua and Barbuda, the Bahamas, Barbados, Belize, Dominica, Grenada, Guyana, Jamaica, St Kitts and Nevis, St Lucia, St Vincent and the Grenadines, Suriname, and Trinidad and Tobago.

Caribbean have also increased substantially, becoming the most dynamic component of international capital flows, together with FDI, and exceeding 8 per cent of GDP in some countries. Following the 2008 global financial crisis, FDI flows to the Caribbean declined and became more volatile; but flows of net personal remittances remained resilient, and since 2011 have overtaken FDI as the largest source of foreign financing to the Caribbean. Clearly, the dependable flows are FDI and remittances, but preliminary results show that FDI has fallen in light of the COVID-19 pandemic. Table 5.2 lists FDI inflows for thirteen Caribbean states in 2018 and 2019.

In the case of portfolio investment,[11] inflows have increased since 2014, following some critical debt restructuring.[12] However, they represent a much smaller share of the total external inflows and have shown more unpredictability. Due to their volatility and small role in the region, these flows are often overlooked as a source of financing, but through innovative instruments and increased cooperation, they could play a more active role in the mobilization of resources towards development objectives.

Table 5.2: Foreign Direct Investment (US$ millions), 2018 and 2019

Countries	2018	2019
Antigua and Barbuda	135	139
Bahamas	491	265
Barbados	242	215
Belize	122	103
Dominica	13	33
Grenada	154	131
Guyana	1,180	1,695
Jamaica	775	665
St. Kitts and Nevis	94	92
St. Lucia	40	31
St. Vincent and the Grenadines	110	113
Suriname	131	72
Trinidad and Tobago	-700	184

Source: World Bank, World Development Indicators

ACCESSING INTERNATIONAL DEBT MARKETS

Although access to international capital markets and flows of private capital towards Latin America and the Caribbean have increased significantly in the past fifteen years, for the most part, Caribbean countries have not borrowed as frequently or on the same terms as some of the larger economies in the region (Bustillo and Velloso 2014). Access to international capital markets is more limited and costly for some Caribbean countries than for other larger countries in the region, as they face particular constraints in attracting global capital. One area of interest is the trajectory of Caribbean bond issuance and spreads, as well as credit quality. When the amount of bond issuance is examined, the volume of Latin America and the Caribbean international bonds rose considerably in recent years, from US$40 billion in 2000 to a record US$145 billion in 2017. However, Caribbean debt issuance remains a small share of the regional total. In 2011, this share reached its lowest level since 2003, as Caribbean economies struggled to return to pre-global financial crisis levels. This share followed an upward trend from 2011 to 2015, but then headed downwards, probably linked to a number of

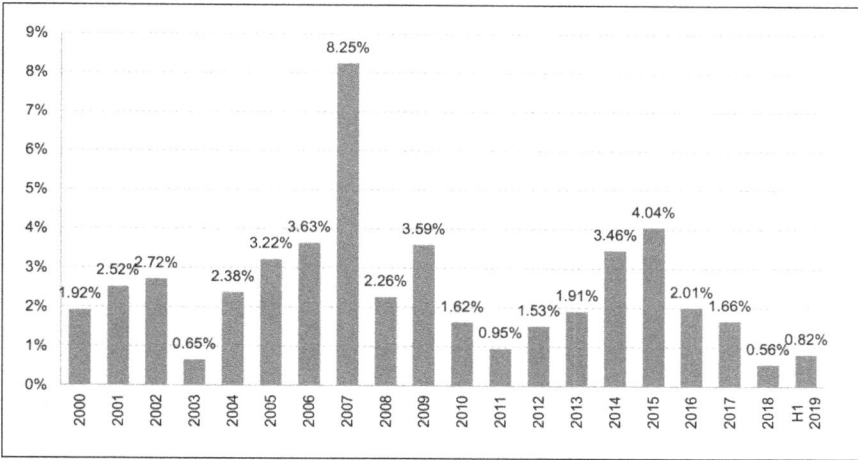

Figure 5.7: The Caribbean (7 countries): Annual debt issuance as a share of the regional total (percentage), 2000–July 2019

Source: Economic Commission for Latin America and the Caribbean (ECLAC), *The Caribbean Outlook: Forging a people-centred approach to sustainable development post-COVID-19* (LC/SES.38/12), Santiago, 2020.
Note: Based on data available for the Bahamas, Barbados, Belize, Grenada, Jamaica, Suriname, and Trinidad and Tobago

factors, including rising debt, limited economies of scale, and the downturn in commodity prices. Bustillo et al. (2018) suggest that the return of volatility to global financial markets in 2018 negatively impacted overall bond sales, and the Caribbean issuance share reached its lowest level of the 2000–2019 (July) period (see figure 5.7).

Caribbean issuance, sovereign and corporate combined, totalled US$33.2 billion in the 2000–2019 (July) period and represented only 2.3 per cent of the Latin America and the Caribbean region's total. Only seven Caribbean countries tapped international debt markets during this period. The top three issuers in the region were Jamaica, Trinidad and Tobago, and the Bahamas (see figure 5.8).

With respect to corporate issuance, only a few Caribbean companies have tapped international markets, and most are either transnational corporations or state-owned, with the latter representing about a third of the total Caribbean corporate issuance in international debt markets in the 2005–2019 (July) period. Bustillo et al. (2018) argue that the fact that only a reduced number of large companies have access to international

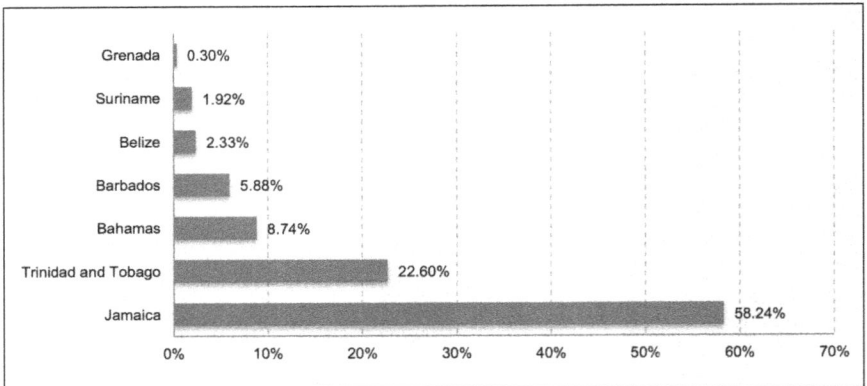

Figure 5.8: The Caribbean (7 countries): Country shares of debt issuance (percentage), 2000–July 2019

Source: Economic Commission for Latin America and the Caribbean (ECLAC), The Caribbean Outlook: Forging a people-centred approach to sustainable development post-COVID-19 (LC/SES.38/12), Santiago, 2020. *Note:* Based on data available for the Bahamas, Barbados, Belize, Grenada, Jamaica, Suriname, and Trinidad and Tobago.

debt markets suggests that the corporate sector, mirroring the sovereign sector, faces the same challenges brought about by limited economies of scale and constrained competitiveness.

The number of sectors in which such issuance took place is also very limited. More than 90 per cent of the Caribbean issuances took place in two sectors – telecommunications and energy, including power, and oil and gas.

CREDIT QUALITY IN THE CARIBBEAN

The debt overhang in the Caribbean has increased sovereign risk, and the fiscal challenges have increased the cost of borrowing abroad, despite the low-interest-rate regime that obtains globally.

Caribbean countries experienced downgrades in their credit risk rating during the global financial crisis, and many of them have yet to regain their previous rating. Due to the small size and underdeveloped capital markets in many of their economies, credit ratings do play an important role in investors' decisions.[13]

It is interesting to note that the credit quality of the Caribbean started from a better position in the mid-1990s than the rest of the wider region.

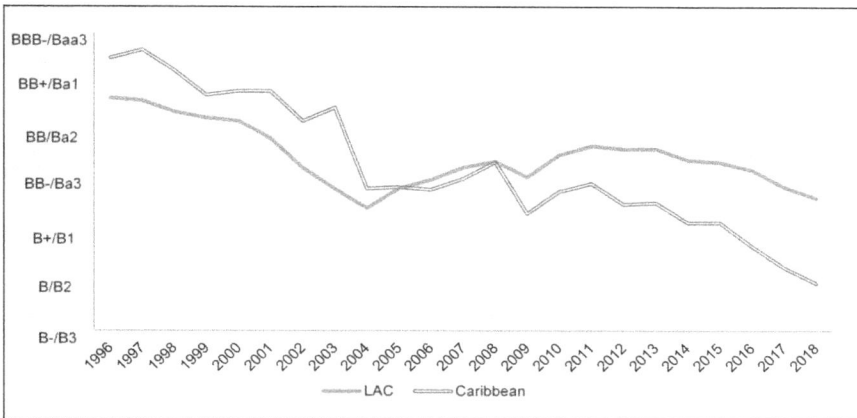

Figure 5.9: The evolution of credit ratings in Latin America and the Caribbean (25 countries – Average credit rating: Fitch, Moody's and Standard & Poor's)

Source: Bustillo et al. (2018), on the basis of data available from Fitch, Moody's and Standard and Poor's.
Note: Based on data for Argentina, the Bahamas, Barbados, Belize, Bolivia, Brazil, Chile, Colombia, Costa Rica, Cuba, Dominican Republic, Ecuador, El Salvador, Guatemala, Honduras, Jamaica, Mexico, Nicaragua, Paraguay, Peru, St Vincent and the Grenadines, Suriname, Trinidad and Tobago, Uruguay and Venezuela. The Caribbean average rating includes seven countries: Barbados, the Bahamas, Belize, Jamaica, Suriname, St Vincent and the Grenadines, and Trinidad and Tobago. Investment grade: BBB–/Baa3 and above.

While Latin America and the Caribbean's overall creditworthiness showed an improvement after 2004, credit quality in the Caribbean continued the downward trend that started in the mid-1990s. This was due to low economic growth, rising debt and fiscal deterioration, plus the fallout from recurrent natural disasters. According to Bustillo and Velloso (2014), most of the credit rating downgrades that took place in the aftermath of the global financial crisis were motivated by worsening fiscal conditions, as financial instability brought about by the global financial crisis weighed heavily on the countries' fiscal accounts.

The discussion suggests that limited access to international financial markets has been available to both government and the private sector, and this means that the regional capital is constrained, due to its small size, high debt burden and the vulnerabilities flowing from natural disasters.

A WAY FORWARD

The issue of sourcing financing for development has always been a challenge for Caribbean member states. In light of the COVID-19 crisis, immediate additional financing is necessary on concessional terms in order to forestall the diminution of resources to existing projects and activities, and to prevent a debt and liquidity crisis. In terms of the immediate vulnerabilities, a number of useful proposals have been offered in the initiative, "Financing for development in the era of COVID-19 and beyond", which was co-convened by Jamaica and Canada, and led by the secretary general of the United Nations (Ellmers 2020).

Among some of those proposed are the following:

Immediate responses:

- Across-the-board debt standstill for all developing countries that have no access to financial markets and cannot service their debt.
- Provide foreign currency liquidity to developing countries through dollar swaps.

Medium-term responses:

- Establish sovereign debt-restructuring mechanisms.
- Increase IMF quota subscriptions or issue additional special drawing rights (SDRs).

A number of recommendations have also been made over time, including some proposed by ECLAC, to address the financing gap.

THE CARIBBEAN RESILIENCE FUND[14]

It has been recognized that to address the sustainable development of the Caribbean, long-term affordable development financing is necessary. ECLAC (2016) has proposed the initiation of a global fund that can be rolled out at the regional level to address Caribbean resilience building, especially with respect to region-wide projects. Such a fund would attract large-scale financing, including concessional financing from the Green Climate Fund (GCF), which can also be used to leverage other financial flows to the region.

While there are a variety of other facilities aimed at climate financing, the GCF remains a major source of concessional finance.

A DEBT-FOR-CLIMATE ADAPTATION SWAP INITIATIVE

Under this initiative, ECLAC proposed the use of funds from various supporting financial sources to reduce the debt at a discount, with the resultant repayment placed in a resilience fund to address green investments aimed at climate change mitigation and adaptation measures, and economic transformation.

CLIMATE CHANGE FINANCING AND THE GCF

Climate change impact is an existential threat to the subregion and being able to address its effects in all sectors is most important. One of the major sources of concessional finance for adaptation purposes is available through the GCF. However, few Caribbean countries have been able to access substantial resources from the GCF, as the processes for accessing such finance are complex and requires capacity building in the public sector at a time when fiscal retrenchment is being pursued. Caribbean member states must join with other SIDS to lobby to make this process more accessible.

STATE CONTINGENT INSTRUMENTS AND LIABILITY MANAGEMENT OPERATIONS

In light of the extreme vulnerability of Caribbean economies, international financial institutions should support the frequent use of state contingent instruments, such as GDP-linked bonds and hurricane clauses, to address debt-service challenges that arise after extreme events, such as natural disasters, and sustained negative external economic shocks. Such instruments would waive debt repayments until a crisis is over. It is important to note that both Barbados and Grenada have been able to secure limited waivers in their hurricane clauses, and it is suggested that this should be the norm in future borrowing among Caribbean SIDS.

The international financial institutions can also provide guarantees for debt reprofiling through liability management operations, which increase fiscal space, lengthen the debt repayment period, and allocate a portion of funds for liquidity enhancement and climate adaptation.

CONCLUSION

Financing for sustainable development continues to be an important issue for Caribbean countries and they must continue to explore every opportunity to raise such finance at an affordable cost, both domestically and internationally. In the short run, the opportunities for significant financial inflows are limited, since growth was negative in 2020 and was not robust in 2021. At the same time, new demands have risen for investment in the health sector to prepare for future pandemics, and in supporting a robust ICT infrastructure for development, to give a few examples. For this reason, a variety of initiatives must be pursued, as has been argued in this chapter, to increase financing to address the sustainable development goals.

NOTES

1. The opinions expressed in this chapter are to be attributed solely to the authors and are not necessarily the views of their respective organizations.
2. Goods producers are Belize, Guyana, Suriname, and Trinidad and Tobago. Service producers are Antigua and Barbuda, the Bahamas, Barbados, Dominica, Grenada, Jamaica, St Kitts and Nevis, St Lucia, and St Vincent and the Grenadines.
3. The sub-region here included all thirty member and associate member countries of ECLAC's Caribbean Development and Cooperation Committee.
4. These are levies by telecommunications providers that are used to facilitate universal internet access.
5. Damages, losses and additional costs
6. For the period June 2007 to October 2018, an estimated 2.5 million persons in the region benefitted from thirty-eight pay-outs totalling US$139 million in thirteen of its twenty member countries. Additionally, the Bahamas received approximately US$12.8 million following the passage of Hurricane Dorian in 2019.
7. A case that illustrates the importance of such an insurance mechanism is the Bahamas in 2015 and 2016. In October 2015, Hurricane Joaquin affected

Acklins, Crooked Island, Long Island, Rum Cay and San Salvador. The parameter of affected population, as percentage of total population, did not trigger the payment of the premium to the country on this occasion. The government made the decision not to renew the CCRIF-SPC insurance policy. In October 2016, the country was affected by Hurricane Matthew, specifically the following islands: New Providence, Grand Bahama, Andros and Berry islands. According to the ECLAC's damage and loss assessment, the effect of Hurricane Matthew was more than five times that of Hurricane Joaquin. Since there was no active insurance policy in 2016, the country did not receive any insurance compensation. As of 2017, the Bahamas again decided to buy the CCRIF-SPC insurance (ECLAC and IDB 2015; 2016).

8.   In attending to these demands, CCRIF-SPC did a revision of their models in 2019. A second memorandum of understanding was signed in October 2017 between CCRIF-SPC and the OECS to establish a cooperation framework until 2023 with the objective of assisting sub-regional governments to adopt DRR policies. Additionally, the organization has introduced new agriculture and fisheries insurance products, including the Caribbean Oceans and Aquaculture Sustainability Facility, which also incorporates a micro-insurance component.

9.   Jamaica has developed an exemplary micro-credit model under its Pilot Project for Climate Resilience, where loans are offered to rural communities at concessionary rates to implement adaptation activities. Approximately US$17.5 million was allocated to an Adaptation Programme and Financing Mechanism Project by Climate Investment Funds (CIF) through the IDB for implementation by the Planning Institute of Jamaica, and the Ministry of Economic Growth and Job Creation. These national entities provide a Climate Change Adaptation Line of Credit to approved financial institutions (that is, mutually owned cooperative banks and credit unions) through the Development Bank of Jamaica. In turn, these approved financial institutions (chosen based on their existing presence in rural communities across Jamaica) provide grants and loans with a ceiling of J$5 million (approximately US$36,700), underwritten by funds from the Pilot Project. While programmes such as this are a meaningful step towards increased financial resilience, their coverage and accessibility need to be greatly expanded to encourage more participation throughout the region.

10. St Lucia, for example, has been using PPPs for the last two decades. Early examples include the building and operation of the Ministry of Communications complex in 1997 and new police stations in 2000. Other examples are road improvement projects using private-sector partners.

11. Note: portfolio investment flows are defined as cross-border transactions

and positions involving equity or debt securities, other than those included in direct investment or reserve assets. Negative values represent increases in financial liabilities and positive values represent increases in net financial assets.

12. Some of these debt restructurings include: Belize (2013, 2017), Jamaica (2010, 2013), Grenada (2013–15), St Kitts and Nevis (2011), Antigua and Barbuda (since 2010).

13. Together, the three main credit rating agencies – Fitch, Moody's and Standard & Poors – provide ratings for about seven Caribbean states, including Barbados, the Bahamas, Belize, Jamaica, Suriname, Trinidad and Tobago, as well as St Vincent and the Grenadines, which is rated only by Moody's and was rated for the first time only in 2016.

14. The European Union has signed two agreements with the World Bank's Global Facility for Disaster Reduction and Recovery (GFDRR) to provide funding totalling €30.7 million to strengthen disaster risk management (DRM) in the Caribbean. The programmes will support plans for long-term resilience and climate-smart growth strategies, and assist with designing and implementing innovative policy and investment initiatives. The two programmes that will benefit are the Caribbean Regional Resilience Building Facility (€27.7 million) and the Technical Assistance Program for Disaster Risk Financing and Insurance in Caribbean Overseas Countries and Territories (€3 million). The Caribbean Regional Resilience Building Facility will support fifteen Caribbean countries by providing technical assistance to mainstream resilience, leveraging investments to reduce vulnerability, and expanding financial protection against disasters.

REFERENCES

Abdulkadri, Abdullahi, Dillon Alleyne, Catarina Camarinhas, Michael Hendrickson, Francis Jones, Sheldon Mc Lean, Machel Pantin, Willard Phillips, Nyasha Skerrette, and Hidenobu Tokuda. 2020. *The Case for Financing: Caribbean Resilience building in the face of the COVID-19 pandemic* (LC/CAR/TS.2020/7). Santiago: Economic Commission for Latin America and the Caribbean (ECLAC).

Alleyne, Dillon. 2018. "Structural Constraints and Macroeconomic Policies to Promote Sustainable Growth in the Caribbean." *Social and Economic Studies* 67 (2&3) (2018): 5–41.

Alleyne, Dillon, Michael Hendrickson, Sheldon McLean, Maharouf Oyolola, Machel Pantin, Nyasha Skerrette, and Hidenobu Tokuda. 2019. *Economic Survey of the Caribbean 2019*, Studies and Perspectives Series, ECLAC Subregional Headquarters for the Caribbean, No. 82 (LC/TS.2019/116-LC/CAR/TS.2019/5). Santiago: Economic Commission for Latin America and the Caribbean (ECLAC).

Baldacchino, Godfrey, and Geoffrey Bertram. 2009. "The beak of the Finch: Insights into the Economic development of Small Economies." *The Round Table* 98 (401): 141–60. https://doi.org/10.1080/00358530902757867.

Bello, Omar, Marion Khamis, Claudio Osorio, and Leda Peralta. 2017. *Mainstreaming disaster risk management strategies in development instruments: policy briefs for selected member countries of the Caribbean Development and Cooperation Committee*. Studies and Perspectives Series, ECLAC Subregional Headquarters for the Caribbean, No. 58 (LC/TS.2017/80). Santiago: Economic Commission for Latin America and the Caribbean (ECLAC).

Bishop, Matthew. 2012. "The political economy of small states: Enduring vulnerability?" *Review of International Political Economy* 19 (5) (December): 942–60.

Bustillo, Inés, and Helvia Velloso. 2014. *Access to international capital markets: recent developments in Central America and the Caribbean* (LC/WAS/L.129). Washington, DC: Economic Commission for Latin America and the Caribbean (ECLAC).

Bustillo, Inés, and Raquel Artecona. 2015. *Global Financial Rulemaking and Small Economies*. Studies and Perspectives Series (LC/ WAS/L.134). Washington, DC: Economic Commission for Latin America and the Caribbean (ECLAC).

Bustillo, Inés, Helvia Velloso, Winston Dookeran, and Daniel Perrotti. 2018. *Resilience and capital flows in the Caribbean* (LC/WAS/TS.2018/2/-*). Washington, DC: Economic Commission for Latin America and the Caribbean (ECLAC).

Caribbean Catastrophe Risk Insurance Facility. 2020. "CCRIF SPC Mmakes payout to Belize for excess rainfall event associated with tropical cyclones Amanda and Cristobal." CCRIF press release, 24 June 2020.

Easterly, William, and Aart Kraay. 2000. "Small states, small problems? Income, growth, and volatility in small states." *World development* 28 (11): 2013–2027.

Economic Commission for Latin America and the Caribbean. 2016. *Report on the Fourth Meeting of the Caribbean Development Roundtable* (LC/CAR/L.490). Santiago: ECLAC.

———. 2018. *The Caribbean Outlook, 2018* (LC/SES.37/14/Rev.1). Santiago: Economic Commission for Latin America and the Caribbean (ECLAC).

———. 2020. *The Caribbean Outlook: Forging a people-centred approach to sustainable development post-COVID-19* (LC/SES.38/12), Santiago: Economic Commission for Latin America and the Caribbean (ECLAC).

Ellmers, Bodo. 2020. *Financing for Development in the Era of COVID-19 and Beyond: A snapshot of the ongoing work at the United Nations in times of crisis*. Aachen/Berlin/Bonn: Global Policy Forum.

Hurley, Gail. 2015. "Financing for Development and Small Island Developing States: A Snapshot and Ways Forward." UNDP and UN-OHRRLS Discussion Paper.

McLean, Sheldon, Hidenobu Tokuda, Nyasha Skerrette, and Machel Pantin. 2020. *Promoting debt sustainability to facilitate financing sustainable development in selected Caribbean countries. A scenario analysis of the ECLAC debt for climate adaptation swap initiative.* Studies and Perspectives Series, ECLAC Subregional Headquarters for the Caribbean, No. 89 (LC/TS.2020/5-LC/CAR/TS.2019/12). Santiago: Economic Commission for Latin America and the Caribbean (ECLAC).

Ram, Christopher. 2020. *Resilience Impact Securities with Equity (RISE): How to Finance and Democratize Resilience-Building in the Post-COVID-19 Era.* Small States Matters No. 2020/02. London: Commonwealth Secretariat. https://doi. org/10.14217/7d652258-en.

Sagasti, Francisco. 2013. "From 'Graduation' to 'Gradation' in International Development Finance." https://franciscosagasti.com/site/wp-content/uploads/2022/02/A-Sagasti-2013-From-graduation-to-gradation-in-development-finance-2013.pdf

United Nations General Assembly. 1994. "Report of the global conference on the sustainable development of small island developing states" (A/CONF.167/9), Bridgetown, Barbados, 25 April–6 May 1994.

6

(Re)Imagining a Climate-Resilient Future
A Caribbean Approach

MICHAEL A. TAYLOR, TANNECIA S. STEPHENSON, FELICIA S. WHYTE, LE-ANNE ROPER,
RUTH POTOPSINGH, DONOVAN CAMPBELL, ABRAHAM ANTHONY CHEN, PETER CLARKE,
GEORGIANA GORDON-STRACHAN, ORVILLE GREY, TANNICE HALL, RANDY KOON KOON,
INDI McLYMONT-LAFAYETTE, ELECIA MYERS, HEATHER PINNOCK, ALLISON RANGOLAN,
DALE RANKINE, GREGORY ROBIN, IANTHE SMITH, ROSE-ANN SMITH, NEKEISHA SPENCER,
KIMBERLY STEPHENSON, AND JEREMY TAYLOR

CLIMATE VARIABILITY AND CHANGE, AND THE ASSOCIATED FAR-REACHING impacts, have become a distinguishing feature of an apparent new normal in the Caribbean that is characterized by heightened sensitivity, exposure and vulnerability across spatiotemporal scales. Climate, superimposed on other existing issues, internal and external to the region (including political instability, volatile markets and more recently, a global pandemic), is contributing to stymied economic development and a general erosion of the foundational pillars on which Caribbean life is premised (Pulwarty, Nurse, and Trotz 2010; ECLAC 2011).

An intensification of the climate threat in recent years has highlighted that the region in its present state is ill-equipped to handle recurrent heavy rainfall, prolonged drought events or the devastation associated with Category 5 hurricanes like Irma and Maria in 2017, or Dorian in 2019 (ECLAC 2018; Bello et al. 2020). Regional response has been constrained by factors including geography; demography; the small size and climate-dependent nature of the economies; human, technical and financial resource limitations; and by development plans and agendas that fail to adequately recognize and/or mainstream climate considerations (Bueno et al. 2008; Otker and Srinivasan 2020). Increasing awareness of the developmental challenge posed and the stoking of a regional "will to survive notwithstanding" are, however, driving a growing movement for the Caribbean to become the world's first climate-resilient zone (CCSA 2019).

This chapter asks the simple question: "What would a climate-resilient Caribbean look like?" The following section provides a brief present-day context as the starting point for the (re)imagination of a future resilient Caribbean followed by an explanation of how that picture will be developed. Section three looks at features of the (re)imagined resilient Caribbean society, premised on sixteen intervention points. Section four suggests six pillars on which the pathway to resilience will likely depend, inferred from the discussions of section three. Section five offers final thoughts.

THE CARIBBEAN CONTEXT

Caribbean climate is already changing and will continue to change (table 6.1). The observed changes suggest the emergence of a new and "unfamiliar" climate regime marked by its multi-hazard nature. By 2100, under a business-as-usual global emissions scenario, the magnitude of change will exceed that already seen (table 6.1).

The Caribbean, then, needs to cope with an already "unfamiliar" climate regime, while at the same time preparing for an "unprecedented" climate era to come. This regional climate context makes a strong case for the pursuit of a regional resilient state. In the Caribbean, key socioeconomic sectors (agriculture, tourism, health) are exceedingly climate-sensitive and the vulnerability of countries to climate variations is deeply embedded, due to age-old practices and models of development. Additionally, the majority of Caribbean cities and urban centres are in the coastal zone and approximately half of their population lives within 1.5 kilometres of the shoreline, indicating high vulnerability to sea level rise and tropical storms (Mycoo 2018).

In tandem with climate, unaccounted-for urbanization reinforces the need to examine pathways to regional resilience (see figure 6.1) (Mycoo and Bharath 2021). Densely populated coastal and low-lying capital cities

Table 6.1: Summary of climate trends and projections for the Caribbean, adapted from the State of the Caribbean Climate (CSGM 2020), Thomas et al. (2020) and IPCC (2019).

	Historical Trend[1]	Projection[2]
Rainfall	• In the long-term historical record (1900–2014), the Caribbean has not become wetter or drier (no significant observed linear trend). • The number of consecutive dry days is increasing, as well as the amount of rainfall during rainfall events.	• The Caribbean, as a whole, will gradually dry through to the end of the century. Drying is expected to be less in the far north Caribbean and more in the south and southeast. • Global climate models (GCMs) suggest that by the end of the century, the region may be up to 17% drier while regional climate model (RCM)-based projections suggest up to 25 and 35 per cent less rainfall by the end of the century. Subregional and seasonal variations are projected. • Small to large increases in consecutive dry days are projected across the region.
Air temperatures	• Caribbean air temperatures show a significant upward (linear) trend. • There is a positive linear trend in very warm days and nights for the Caribbean.	• The Caribbean, as a whole, will gradually warm through to the end of the century. • Minimum, maximum and mean temperatures increase irrespective of scenario through the end of the century. • The mean temperature increase (in °C) from GCMs will be 0.83–3.05°C by the end of the century with respect to a 1986–2005 baseline over all four representative concentration pathways (RCPs). • RCMs suggest higher magnitude increases for the downscaled grid boxes – up to 4°C by the end of the century. Regional variations in warming are evident in the RCM. • Projections based on statistical downscaling show an increase for both warm days and warm nights by the end of the century.
Sea surface temperatures	• More intense and extensive marine heat waves.	• Under a business-as-usual scenario, sea surface temperatures (SSTs) increase by 1.76 ± 0.39°C per century in the wider Caribbean. • The mean annual SST range (~ 3.3°C) currently observed in the Caribbean Sea is projected to contract to 2.9°C in the 2030s, and to 2.3°C in the 2090s. By the end of the century, years of coolest projected SSTs fall within the range of the warmest years in the present.

Table 6.1 continues

	Historical Trend[1]	Projection[2]
Sea levels	• There is a general increasing trend in the sea level of the Caribbean region: • A regional rate of increase of 1.8 ± 0.1 mm/year between 1950 and 2009. • Higher rate of increase in later years: 1.7 ± 1.3 mm/year between 1993 and 2010. • Larger sea level increases observed for post-2000 period, during which hurricane intensity and sea level interannual variability have both increased.	• For the Caribbean, the combined range for projected sea level rise (SLR) spans 0.26–0.82 metres by 2100 relative to 1986–2005 levels. The range is 0.17–0.38 for 2046–2065. Other recent studies suggest an upper limit for the Caribbean of up to 1.5 metres under RCP8.5. • Regional variation in SLR is small, with the north Caribbean tending to have slighter higher projected values than the southern Caribbean. By the end of the century, sea level rise is projected to reach or exceed 1 metre across the Caribbean.
Hurricanes	• Significant increase in frequency and duration of Atlantic hurricanes since 1995. • Increase in Category 4 and 5 hurricanes, rainfall intensity, associated peak wind intensities, mean rainfall for same period.	• No change or slight decrease in frequency of hurricanes. • Shift towards stronger storms by the end of the century as measured by maximum wind speed increases of +2 to +11%. • +20% to +30% increase in rainfall rates for the model hurricane's inner core. Smaller increase (~10%) at radii of 200 km or larger. • An 80% increase in the frequency of Saffir-Simpson Category 4 and 5 Atlantic hurricanes over the next 80 years using the A1B scenario.
Other variables	• Extreme wave heights have increased • Ocean acidification is increasing	• Extreme wave heights will continue to increase towards the end of the century. • Ocean acidification will continue to increase towards the end of the century.

Notes:

1. Historical trends are based on observations made over 1900–2014.
2. GCM-generated projections are relative to a 1986–2005 baseline, RCM-generated projections are relative to a 1961–1990 baseline.

have become the loci of economic, social and political activities, exacerbated by governments that have not supported a decentralized settlement strategy. Other urban centres have emerged because of the economic shift to tourism or industrial developments centred on mineral extraction; with cities offering better prospects for employment, higher education, health and social services, public utilities, and entertainment (Mycoo and Bharath 2021). It is estimated that by 2050, more than 80 per cent of the Caribbean's population will be living in urban areas (Donovan and Turner Jones 2017)

The unchecked pace of urbanization is challenging the sustainability of Caribbean societies by creating or expanding vulnerabilities (human, built and natural systems) on which climate preys, eroding the quality of life and stymying development. Primary cities are experiencing the greatest pressures, including high population density, inadequate housing, deteriorating road infrastructure, insufficient utilities and telecommunication provisions, and vehicular traffic disproportionate to

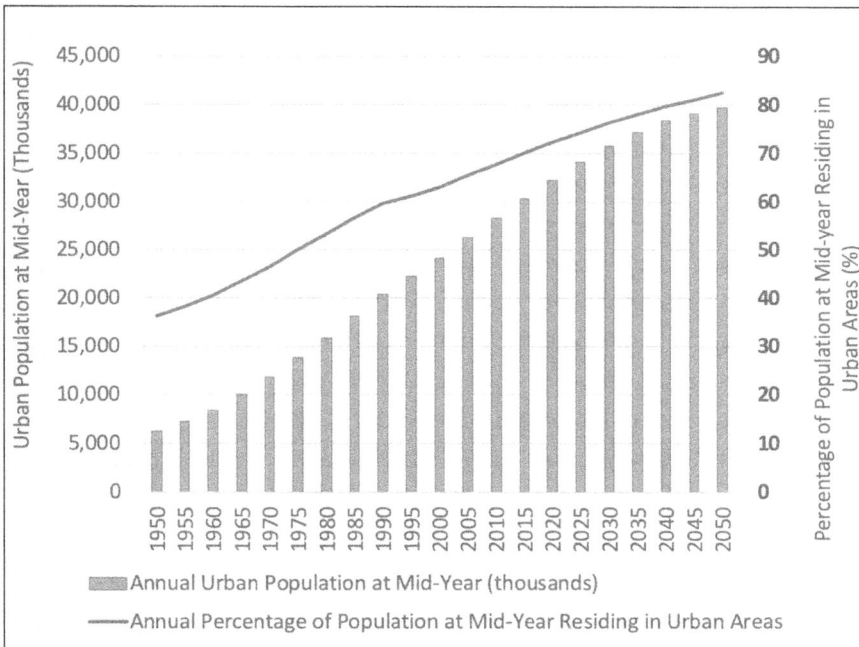

Figure 6.1: Urban population trends for the Caribbean for the period 1950–2050.
Source: World Urbanization Prospects: The 2018 Revision (United Nations, Department of Economic and Social Affairs, Population Division 2018).

the road infrastructure and traffic management systems (Mycoo and Bharath 2021). Urban form (street layout, building densities, and orientation) has largely been ignored, resulting in ad hoc settlements, mostly on the outskirts of major cities, unplanned and unregulated squatter communities, and densely packed inner-city communities. Consequently, urban sprawl, land and marine pollution, heat islands, air pollution, increased greenhouse gas emissions, the lack of green spaces, and greater demands on the natural resource base (for example, water) are becoming increasingly common regional issues. Not surprisingly, both the New Urban Agenda (2016) and the Paris Agreement (2016) suggest the attainment of Goal 11 of the Sustainable Development Goals (SDGs) as necessary for achieving climate resilience. Goal 11 identifies the development of sustainable cities and communities as important to a country achieving better quality of life for its citizens, ending poverty, protecting natural resources, creating a more just society, and ensuring peace and prosperity by 2030.

Climate resilience targets achievement of the latter ambitions, notwithstanding present and future climate threats. The present vulnerability of Caribbean countries should not be taken as an indication of a lack of willingness to accept risks or to act. In fact, over the last two decades, some Caribbean jurisdictions have increased their focus on establishing climate-smart or resilient states. For example, a Caribbean Climate-Smart Accelerator (CCSA) was established in 2018 with the aim of making the region the world's first "climate-smart zone" (CCSA 2019). That same year, following the passage of Hurricane Maria in 2017, Dominica set the goal of becoming the world's first climate-resilient nation (Commonwealth of Dominica 2018). Whereas climate-smart goals have largely focused on adaptation strategies to maintain and assure economic function and viability;[1] climate resilience further emphasizes ways to ensure that the "whole" Caribbean way of life continues to thrive (Robinson 2018). We suggest that a climate-resilient Caribbean is capable of anticipating, absorbing, accommodating and recovering from the effects of both slow onset and abrupt hazardous events in a timely and efficient manner, and in ways that enable assured economic security and a healthy environment; that can then be leveraged with robust social structures to improve standards of living, create vibrant societies and preserve Caribbean identity.

We further suggest that a resilient Caribbean society, so defined, prioritizes:

- preserving, restoring and improving the essential basic structures and functions of its cities, while limiting their contributions to the climate problem;
- implementing protections for the most climate-vulnerable (human and natural);
- using its abundant natural resources sustainably;
- creating, sustaining and expanding an environment for innovation, entrepreneurship, and economic diversification;
- embedding awareness of the scope of the climate challenge as a means of engendering action;
- safeguarding Caribbean identity, especially its indigenous aspects; and
- building a strong and unified Caribbean voice on common climate challenge issues.

So, what might such a society look like? Various regional and national reports catalogue measures and responses at all levels – community, national, regional and international – that should be targeted. For example, National Communications to the United Nations Framework Convention on Climate Change (UNFCCC)[2] highlight sectors considered most sensitive to climate change, and detail actions already being pursued or to be taken to build resilience. Using these reports as a guide and paying special attention to the priorities above, we (re)imagine a climate-resilient Caribbean where (a minimum of) sixteen key interventions have occurred. Twenty-three regional practitioners representing persons actively working in, researching on or with some knowledge about the area of focus, and who also have a knowledge of climate's general impact on the Caribbean, were approached to elaborate on each intervention. Most of the practitioners do not readily classify themselves as "climate experts", but all have a strong interest in how climate is impacting a particular area. No restrictions beyond a three-paragraph maximum limit were placed on their (re)imagining. The resulting picture of the resilient Caribbean society, through the eyes of Caribbean practitioners, is presented in the following section.

A RE-IMAGINED SOCIETY

STRONG SOCIAL PROTECTION PROGRAMMES AND A GENDER BIAS – D. CAMPBELL

A climate-resilient future Caribbean has invested in social protection policies and programmes, recognizing the multiple co-benefits and avoided costs that the built resilience engenders. A study of five Caribbean countries found that less than 3.2 per cent of their Gross Domestic Products (GDPs) was allocated per year for the decade 2008–2018 on social protection of the public sector (ECLAC 2019). Against a backdrop of high exposure and limited resources, comprehensive social protection initiatives protect and transform the poorest and the most vulnerable (children, women, the elderly and persons with disabilities), enabling them to absorb climate impacts and transform future response capacities.

Solórzano and Cárdenes (2019) identify public-works programmes, social transfers, climate risk insurance, early-warning systems, and forecast-based financing as avenues that can maximize the synergies between social protection, catastrophe risk reduction and climate change adaptation. Public-works social protection instruments provide important levers for climate-proofing critical infrastructure. Pension schemes and cash transfers are examples of social protection strategies to buffer shocks. Preventative social protection instruments, such as weather-indexed insurance and livelihood diversification reduce the use of depletive coping actions among weather-dependent livelihood groups. Transformative social protection instruments related to social justice attempt to redress the root causes of socio-political and structural imbalances that keep the poor and vulnerable in a cycle of poverty and hardship.

In a climate-resilient Caribbean, such programmes: (i) are guided by routine needs assessments; (ii) have a strong monitoring and evaluation component that, among other things, provides a feedback loop for improvements, including enhanced value creation; (iii) align with rights-based policies and targets (for example, those relating to gender equality) so as not to perpetuate inequities; and (iv) ensure equal access for those in informal sectors. In the Caribbean, women tend to mostly occupy low-skilled, service-oriented/informal jobs and are disproportionately impacted by climate change events compared to men (CSGM 2020). As such, gender-responsiveness is a critical cross-cutting feature of transformative social protection programmes.

RESILIENT LAND USE PLANNING AND INFRASTRUCTURE – H. PINNOCK

In the future climate-resilient Caribbean, infrastructure will be robust (able to absorb and withstand the threat); reliable (able to retain its function under threat); and restorable (able to be quickly recommissioned after an event). The pathway to achieving this is strongly premised on comprehensive and responsive planning for land and infrastructure due to the costs involved and the need for prudent use of limited resources (Mycoo and Donovan 2017). The framework, therefore, prioritizes upgrading and retrofitting existing infrastructure and ensuring new infrastructure is compliant with codes and standards that factor in climate and other environmental changes. The most vulnerable assets, including those needed to maintain societal functions, such as ports and hospitals as well as heritage sites, are targeted first, while designs for both upgraded and new infrastructure accommodate for and also maximize sustainable, independent technologies, such as renewable energy and water harvesting. Other priorities include: (i) establishing a programme for ongoing maintenance of existing infrastructure so that vulnerabilities are not due to avoidable structural weaknesses; (ii) implementing infrastructure specifically designed to protect against the climate threat, for example, sea walls or other engineered or nature-based solutions; and (iii) making available and affordable risk-transfer mechanisms to facilitate replacement or repair.

Improved land-use zoning and more attentive infrastructure developments are two complementary and necessary resilience-building activities. Their benefits include protection of existing assets and investments; preservation of ecosystems and the functions they provide (watersheds for water, mangroves for protections, and so on); reduced risks to human populations, for example, through no-build zones; enhancement of mitigation through the preservation of land and coastal forests, which remove greenhouse gas emissions; and serving as controls for some of the pressures that climate places on land use (such as urbanization, change in land use for livelihood options, and so on). Their success, however, depends on robust monitoring and enforcement mechanisms, as well as wide-scale public acceptance of their importance as the foundation of long-term sustainable and resilient development.

A CLIMATE-AWAKENED LEGISLATIVE FRAMEWORK – J. TAYLOR

Legal institutions and instruments play an increasingly important role in a future resilient Caribbean, given the need to successfully negotiate climate's several intertwined and compounding risks that straddle social, fiscal, environmental and political realms (McDonald and McCormack 2021). For example, the successful entrenchment of equitable response strategies will depend on the regulatory, standards-setting, enforcement and advocacy arms of law recognizing their growing role in addressing the social justice dimensions of climate. This includes facilitating reduced exposure or sensitivity to climate hazards through laws, policies, programmes and other governance instruments; protecting and preserving human rights from climate-induced threats (for example, rights to life, self-determination, development, food, health, water, sanitation and housing); establishing and overseeing accountability frameworks for adaptation decision-making, and assigning liability for climate impacts. Other emerging roles include establishing the legal architecture for emerging market mechanisms and funding arrangements governing emissions and adaptation costs; and supporting the negotiation of the Caribbean's position on the global stage.

In particular, the growth and development of the field of environmental law, appropriately nuanced for the Caribbean context, will be important (ECLAC and CCJ Academy of Law 2018). The future resilient society assigns rights to the environment – independent of the human being – to be healthy; productive; free from injury, damage (or the threat of) abuse and degradation. It also ensures enforcement of this provision by the authorities or the citizenry. In this context, reimagined features of a climate 'awakened' legislative framework are:

i.   A broadened concept of standing in law to allow citizens to take legal action on behalf of environmental objects or bring private prosecutions with the requisite legal aid provisions, or the creation of guardians or conservators for these environmental objects who can so act (for example, water resources authorities for rivers).

ii. A reworked approach to legislation that is not siloed but ensures that related legislation, particularly those with bearing on the environment, are reviewed and reformed together.

iii. A more serious treatment of environmental crime through the imposition of more severe penalties.

iv. The enactment of "user pays" and "precautionary principle" provisions throughout the breadth of environmental legislation.

v.   The greater use of certain evidential presumptions and negative averments without the need to prove *mens rea* or the guilty intention, to remove hurdles in enforcing environmental protections.

vi. The creation of an environmental tribunal/court to deal with hearings and appeals, and the removal of the power of the government minister to hear appeals from decisions of the authority.

HEIGHTENED RECOGNITION OF THE ROLE OF TERRESTRIAL AND OCEAN BIODIVERSITY – K. STEPHENSON AND T. HALL

The future resilient Caribbean neither sees ecosystems as expendable in the development agenda nor always adaptable to stresses applied because of that agenda. Rather there is recognition of the importance of biological ecosystems to the basic functioning and sustenance of all life, including their roles in regulating the climate; producing clean air, food, medicines, and other natural resources; and in supporting other ecosystem processes, such as pollination and nutrient cycling. Regional development is therefore cognizant of the sensitive nature of Caribbean ecosystems and seeks to maintain as much of the endemic biodiversity as possible. For example, regulation of human land use will consider conservation of natural ecosystems, and the redesign of agricultural systems, and the adjustment of human structures and activities will facilitate normal activities of organisms, such as dispersal (Tscharntke et al. 2012; Ouyang et al. 2016).

Research and data gathering will be of particular importance for addressing gaps in knowledge, including determining: the physiology, distribution, diversity and endemism of islands and surrounding waters; the tolerance of native species to the likely shifts in conditions, and the potential effect of invasive pests and pathogens on ecosystem structure and services. Biological conservation methods are prioritized in the reimagined, resilient future Caribbean. Ex-situ conservation, which is already being applied for many critically endangered species in the region, for example, the Jamaican iguana (Wilson et al. 2016), offers the advantage of temporarily relocating individuals of threatened species to captive locations until the threats to their habitats are addressed, or establishing gene banks or reservoir populations in case of disaster (IUCN/SSC 2014). In situ, conservation methods that protect the species within their habitats are also prioritized, and include laws and conventions aimed at preserving natural ecosystems and eliminating anthropogenic stressors that can exacerbate climate impacts. Conservation plans also include methods for prevention, monitoring and removal of invasive alien species that spread due to changes in climatic suitability.

RENEWABLES-BASED ENERGY SECURITY – R. KOON KOON AND A.A. CHEN

Solar, wind, hydropower and geothermal energy dominate the energy mix in the future climate-resilient Caribbean – in proportions dependent on availability of each source in each territory – through both large-scale projects and small-scale household integration of grid-tied and off-grid systems, and renewable powered electric transport options. Renewables account for significant future savings on avoided costs of fossil fuel importations and carbon dioxide emissions.

Because the integration of renewables adds complexity to the electricity grid, flexibility and frequency control need to be enhanced (Chen et al. 2020). Interventions such as large-scale storage, for example, Jamaica's 24.5 MW hybrid energy storage system, or small-scale integration at the household level, will assist in providing reliable power to the grid, especially in a post-disaster scenario. Smart grid platforms allow a two-way dialogue of electricity and information exchange (between the distributor and consumer) and the use of energy efficiency measures (for example, smart meters and sensors) - on both the electrical grid and at the consumer's point of usage – will also collectively enhance grid efficiency, reduce the time between power disturbances (Acharjee 2013), and reduce energy demand. Revised energy policies, for example, net metering and net billing to incentivize consumers to produce and sell energy, and a comprehensive and implementable regional energy conservation programme, will also be in place. Affordable government and private-sector, renewable energy-specific loans will also enable and attract more small and large-scale renewable energy solutions.

A reimagined energy scenario also sees an expansion in the energy options. Serious consideration is given to geothermal energy, especially for the eastern Caribbean where collectively, a minimum of 6280 MW of potential power exists (Ochs et al. 2015). Geothermal energy has a high-capacity factor of up to 90 per cent, is largely independent of climatic conditions, and offers the potential for inter-island grid connection, for example, the Dominica/Guadeloupe/Martinique or St Kitts and Nevis connection (Maynard-Date 2014). Given the region's large marine resources, ocean energy technologies are similarly explored. Large-scale innovative projects such as the 3MW LUCELEC Solar Farm in St Lucia (fifteen thousand panels); the 62.7MW Wigton Wind Farm in Jamaica (the largest wind power development in the English-speaking Caribbean), and the Megapower Electric Vehicle project in Barbados (three hundred-plus electric vehicles and eighty charging stations) are also encouraged and are prominent features of the future energy landscape.

FOOD SECURE – D. RANKINE AND G. ROBIN

Regional agricultural production (of crops and livestock) is dominated by small open field holdings sited primarily within low-lying coastal areas, or on steep slopes that are extremely climate-sensitive. Both slow onset and extreme events like droughts (leading to inadequate water supply), sea level rise (leading to loss of land or saline intrusion); floods and hurricanes (leading to crop loss and damage to agricultural and agricultural-related infrastructure), and high temperatures (leading to pest prevalence and heat stress on livestock) create inconsistent food production and supply. This, in turn, has cascading effects, including reduced availability of local produce, higher production costs, volatile consumer prices, greater importation of less nutritious substitutes, increased prevalence of chronic diseases due to poor diets; unreliability of the sector as a development pillar, and threatened livelihoods (Rhiney 2018).

The future resilient Caribbean society targets safeguarding and improving agricultural production systems as a means of achieving regional food security. Features of the resilient agricultural sector include: (i) production planning through crop suitability mapping, crop zoning and staggered systems of production to reduce reliance on imported food, decrease market oversupply and enhance production sustainability; (ii) greater investments in climate resilient crops, that are heat and drought tolerant, and targeted production of locally grown crops which are less exposed (including roots and tubers); (iii) increased support for applied research, such as crop modelling, and the development of seed and gene banks of climate-resilient crops; (iv) use of communication strategies and public-private partnerships (PPPs) to encourage greater consumption of locally produced, healthier food options; (v) the development and use of climate-smart agricultural approaches and technologies (greenhouses, water harvesting and recycling, renewable energy, nutrient supplementation for livestock to cope with heat stress); and (vi) enhanced inter-regional trade and cross-border investments that promote adoption of the CARICOM "basket of commodities" for food and nutrition security (CARICOM 2010; 2011), and facilitate regional production zones through country-specific crop production (CARICOM 2012).

WHERE EVERY DROP OF WATER COUNTS – P. CLARKE

A growing crisis looms for the already water-scarce Caribbean due to diminished total rainfall, and increased vulnerability of water resources and infrastructure in the harsher future environment (intense storms, heavier floods, higher levels of evaporation, and more incidents of saline intrusion). Indirectly, climate will also increase the pressure to deliver the resource, for example, from climate-induced urbanization, greater cooling requirements, the need to secure agriculture and to support other prioritized economic pursuits, such as tourism (Cashman 2014). The climate-resilient future Caribbean targets healthy ecosystems and their associated services as a first step toward water security. This involves embracing the symbiosis between natural and engineered solutions. So, services provided by nature are maintained, such as percolation, which replenishes aquifers, flood plains that manage floods or ponds that store freshwater; while engineered structures that are nature-based (that is, they mimic nature in order to assist it) are also emplaced to capture as much precipitation as possible and direct it towards aquifer recharge. Shoreline protection using replanted mangroves, coupled with breakwaters that are non-opposing to tidal flows, are also intuitive responses to sea-level rise and coastal erosion.

Thereafter, every policy, plan and investment regarding water resource sustainability tie into the strategy for adaptation of the natural structure as a means of creating a framework of resilience to climate. This framework is, of necessity, cross-cutting and straddles all other interacting goals, such as food security, waste management and poverty reduction. Critical in most instances will be proper water management using integrated water resource management principles, that is, considering social equity, economic efficiency and environmental sustainability when managing the resource (Cashman 2014). Equally important will be moving beyond pilot projects to large-scale implementation through household-level programmes and initiatives premised on tried and proven solutions. These include water harvesting, renewable-powered desalination plants that generate minimal unwanted by-products, and the widespread proliferation and use of conservation and recycling technologies.

HEALTHY PEOPLE – G. GORDON-STRACHAN

Robust healthcare facilities and health systems, capable of maintaining their functionality during extreme events, will help ensure a healthy future for Caribbean populations, equipped to enhance its economic and social potential, notwithstanding the climate (World Health Organization 2020). The aged and, in many instances, coastal health infrastructure of the Caribbean represents a present climate vulnerability. A comprehensive plan to retrofit and build new resilient health structures is therefore paramount. Deliberate complementary strategies and policies to reduce the sector's carbon footprint by utilizing renewable energy will also have important co-benefits, including reduced energy costs, improved air quality, and health systems resistant to extended power outages after extreme events.

Caribbean populations are presently susceptible to many climate-sensitive diseases, such as dengue, chikungunya, leptospirosis, ciguatera poisoning and gastroenteritis; and have a high prevalence of chronic diseases with demonstrated associations with climate, for example, cardiovascular events have been shown to increase during a warmer climate. The climate-resilient future health sector prioritizes research, with an emphasis on developing climate-disease models to predict future disease outbreaks and resource demands well in advance of the incident case. Additional features of the climate-resilient Caribbean health sector would be a proactive disease surveillance system complete with near and long-term future early warning and response systems; robust educational campaigns; greater use of technology for e-health and telemedicine; and integration with other sectors that monitor air quality, water quality, food security and the social determinants of health (PAHO 2019).

MANAGED WASTE – I. SMITH

Besides its role in environmental degradation, waste has a direct link to greenhouse gas emissions. The Caribbean region generates a significant amount of biodegradable, solid waste (approximately 50 per cent or more of all waste generated) which, for the most part, is taken to dump sites without the safeguards of sanitary landfills, where its decomposition without recapture releases methane, carbon dioxide and nitrous oxide into the air (Riquelme, Méndez, and Smith 2016). The treatment of wastewater that originates from industrial and agricultural effluents and sewage is a second source of greenhouse gases. Consumer goods manufacturing in the Caribbean (including the harnessing of raw materials such as water, fossil fuels, minerals, aggregates and wood) generally also uses fossil fuels. So even before goods become waste, significant amounts of greenhouse gases are released.

A climate-resilient Caribbean harnesses the mitigation potential of waste management, which includes waste minimization, reuse, recycling, recovery and disposal. Education is the best mitigation approach to generate less waste and produce several positive, mitigation-related impacts along the waste management value chain. These include less energy used in the manufacturing of consumer goods; less garbage to collect and less energy used in its collection; and less waste in disposal sites, resulting in less emissions. Government incentives and penalties promoting minimization are a feature of the resilient Caribbean, for example, those targeting reduced paper usage and the use of goods with some recycled content, which sends less biodegradable waste to disposal sites and minimizes the need for virgin material extraction. Other government strategies, such as improved zoning for developments and appropriately designed infrastructure, not only build resilience, but also reduce the amount of solid waste generated after a flood, landslide or hurricane.

The climate-resilient Caribbean prioritizes reuse and recycling as part of waste management. Composting biodegradable waste to reduce the need for inorganic fertilizers and implementing adaptation measures to offset the impact of a harsher environment on wastewater treatment plants and disposal sites are also pursued. The latter includes measures to minimize operational disruptions caused by flooding of wastewater plants or the overflow of wastewater treatment ponds; minimizing spontaneous fires caused by a greater frequency of dry hot spells; and preventing the transmission of leachate to land and water resources during extreme rainfall events.

A CLIMATE EDUCATED AND AWARE POPULACE – I. MCLYMONT-LAFAYETTE

Knowledge, attitude and practice surveys throughout the Caribbean indicate increasingly greater percentages of regional populations with climate change awareness (Kairi Consultants 2013). This is likely spurred on by more frequent and intense climate events, greater availability of regionally relevant climate material (Rankine, Maximay, and Gibbings 2021); greater infusion of climate change in the school curricula (Bekele and Ganpat 2015); and the emergence of country-level communication strategies and campaigns using a variety of media (Government of St Lucia 2018). In a climate-resilient future Caribbean, communication campaigns targeting all societal levels (from the ordinary man to high-level decision-makers) are key components of resilience-building efforts across all sectors.

Communication-based interventions move beyond merely sharing information and spreading awareness to engendering specific, feasible climate behavioural practices by: (i) highlighting practices at all levels that are harmful, or reduce and impede the ability to adapt to climate change, and (ii) highlighting positive and relatable instances of resilience building as examples of best practices. They also help to delineate responsibilities – individual and government – so that no one is absolved of acting, and support advocacy around resilience causes. In the reimagined communications landscape, formal and informal media entities and practitioners embrace the need to ensure their own understanding of the climate challenge, recognizing that climate change can be a complex issue and that they possess the skills and tools to communicate it. Given its critical role, communication capacity is prioritized and built across all sectors, especially the most climate-sensitive one, in a climate-resilient Caribbean, allowing for informed discussions and decision-making.

VALUES AND ATTITUDES – E. MYERS

Climate disproportionately impacts the most vulnerable populations and communities. Even when crafting and pursuing climate response strategies, care must be taken to not further disadvantage or create new disadvantaged groups, for example, through unequal access to the benefits to be gained. A climate-resilient future Caribbean recognizes the moral dimensions, and that values, beliefs and attitudes are important determinants of environmental behaviours (UNESCO 2018), and shape how that behaviour should look. Through a continuous, deliberate and consistent values-based campaign, it instils the idea that: (i) climate change is a social justice issue requiring ethical approaches, such as pro-social and values-based considerations and solutions; (ii) climate, like the rest of the environment, is a common good that all (including the future generation) should benefit from equally; and (iii) climate, as a part of the wider environment, has its own intrinsic worth. Therefore, the principles of stewardship, equitable and fair use of resources, and the common good become overarching guidelines when formulating individual and national responses to the climate challenge, and for governing behaviour and decision-making.

The climate-resilient Caribbean leverages the predominant worldviews of a largely faith-based region, with the support of faith-based institutions to encourage and foster responsible climate actions. Other key partners in promoting stewardship and values-based approaches to climate resilience include the regional educational frameworks, ministries with portfolio responsibility for the environment and climate change, non-governmental organizations, community-based organizations, local and regional integrity and action frameworks, and the political directorate.

INNOVATION AND ENTREPRENEURSHIP – F. WHYTE

Innovation and entrepreneurship, and the establishment of enabling frameworks and structures to support their entrenchment, are essential for a climate-resilient future Caribbean. A UNFCCC Policy Brief (2018) indicates that entrepreneurs are vital in "developing technologies, business models and services that society can use to achieve low-emission and climate-resilient sustainable development". It further suggests actions for encouraging individuals to become entrepreneurs, guiding their efforts towards addressing the multiplicity of climate threats, and continuously empowering and equipping them to address the challenges. The actions integrate capacity building (education, training, mentorship and sensitization), support policies (incentives) and structures (incubators and accelerators), and promote partnerships and enhanced collaborations, while giving due consideration to local realities and circumstances.

In a climate-resilient future Caribbean, the process of developing and institutionalizing the enabling framework requires building on lessons learned, replicating and scaling up good practices, and developing and executing innovative approaches. The process should be government-led (across ministries, departments and agencies), but will also require strong coordination and collaboration with the private sector to address several barriers and constraints facing entrepreneurs in the region, particularly in accessing low-cost and long-term financing. Other key stakeholder groups include the multilateral/international community,

NGOs, academia, and the wider populace from where innovators and entrepreneurs originate. Additional critical elements of the enabling framework include strong coherence and alignment with climate resilience plans, policies and programmes (so that the support offered to inventors, innovators and entrepreneurs will directly contribute to meeting Caribbean climate resilience targets), and ensuring equitable access to innovation and entrepreneurship opportunities, particularly for marginalized and underserved groups."

DIVERSIFICATION WITHIN AND ACROSS SECTORS – N. SPENCER

New income streams that can facilitate economic growth are important to the climate-resilient future Caribbean. In this paradigm, all economic sectors move toward greater resilience via diversification (Mycoo 2018). Diversification interventions employed on a sector level in support of climate resilience must be guided by a "no-worse-off" impact principle, that is, where the sectors, the environment and, by extension, the overall economic growth are not disadvantaged with an intervention. To abide by this principle, governments should, with continued private sector support, strengthen the ability of sectors to build climate resilience, while providing incentives and regulations to minimize environmental impacts.

In the climate-resilient future Caribbean, the tourism and agricultural sectors are among key sectors that benefit from diversification (others include energy, fisheries and forestry). For tourism, in addition to adaptation measures to protect coastal assets (beaches, infrastructure), the development of other tourist service areas, supported by government incentives, helps to protect the industry's income. Tourism niches include events, festivals and sports; remote work; people-to-people programmes; diasporic linkages; and medical procedures (Connell 2013). Similarly, diversification will support agricultural resilience. This includes (for example) changing planting patterns so that crops susceptible to wind damage do not mature in the peak of the hurricane season; and planting tubers and root crops, which are more resilient to hurricanes and flooding than those grown above ground (Spencer and Polachek 2015).

REGIONAL COOPERATION — O. GREY

Caribbean nations have long championed the climate change discourse, including the negotiations that led to the development of the UNFCCC. Under the umbrella of the Alliance of Small Island States, the region has also consistently advocated for global recognition for those countries particularly vulnerable to the adverse effects of a changing climate (Carruthers et al. 2020). The regional approach to advocacy and outreach has led to many successes, including the 2007 Bali Action Plan (a landmark breakthrough on adaptation), and the universally supported 2015 Paris Agreement. The "1.5°C to Stay Alive" sustained campaign is among one of the most visible and vocal calls for global action in response to existential climate threats to small islands (Carruthers et al. 2020).

In the climate-resilient future Caribbean, negotiations, advocacy and strength in numbers continue to be features of a region pursuing a coordinated and purposeful agenda on climate change. The future Caribbean is acutely aware of its climate-related challenges related to migration (including intra-regional voluntary or forced migration in search of better opportunities in the face of harsher environments), immigration, trade, loss of cultural identity, and the greater demand for inter and intra-regional approaches (strategies, agreements and institutions) to manage them. It also continues a coordinated push for greater global discussion on these issues in the context of "loss and damage" (see section 4).

A climate-resilient future Caribbean also has a renewed political and corporate vision, and viable partnerships capable of accessing new patterns of investment. Transformation to low-carbon and climate-resilient economies will require different advances in technology, policy changes and a greater ability to secure predictable and additional funds to address adaptation and mitigation targets. Programmes like the ECLAC-supported debt swap proposal for Caribbean economies to secure financing for adaptation and mitigation projects, while easing debt burdens (McLean et al. 2020), are therefore more widely pursued and undertaken. The resilient Caribbean maximizes opportunities and mechanisms that address economies of scale and coordinates to leverage further investments and retain key population groups necessary to sustain and drive local economies.

REDUCED RISK FROM DISASTERS – R-A. SMITH

Climate change is exacerbating disaster risk in the Caribbean; hence disaster risk reduction (DRR) is critical to achieving resilience and a sustainable future. Education, disaster risk financing and social protection represent important intervention points in DRR. In this context education further focuses on enhancing school curricula to include disaster management principles; capturing and disseminating traditional or indigenous knowledge that has proven successful in adaptation efforts across different sectors; and targeting enhanced knowledge and skills of vulnerable groups. These efforts will ensure the technical capacity of the region's human capital matches the demands imposed by disasters and climate change. Disaster risk financing eliminates the current practices of diverting funds from critical sectors to recovery and reconstruction after a disaster, or borrowing to mitigate the impacts and increasing fiscal debt.

In the climate-resilient future Caribbean, it is essential to create a budget line specific to DRR efforts; establish different financing instruments for transferring risk; and enhance social protection systems to protect the most vulnerable. Additionally, it is important to develop a supportive policy and legislative environment for reducing risk and enhancing resilience; to convert research into policy and practice; to enhance community governance and adaptive capacity; and to establish PPPs. These changes are ideally accompanied by greater coordination among actors and an enhancement of governance and infrastructural mechanisms, including critical facilities, housing and transport.

STRONG COMMUNITIES AND ACTIVE NGOS – A. RANGOLAN

Community groups and NGOs – through their work with and within communities – play important roles in building climate resilience (Bowen 2013). Community groups are very often the first responders after a disaster, especially in remote locations prone to isolation. Prior to events, they also participate in preparation and incorporation of DRR strategies, very often taking the lead in mapping vulnerabilities and defining appropriate disaster risk management plans specific to the locations. Even outside of an impending disaster, community groups and NGOs often represent a sustained on-the-ground partnering presence for (i) managing and safeguarding environmental resources located in the community; (ii) gathering and monitoring data in support of disaster management, for example, the location of the most vulnerable persons and a compilation of their needs; (iii) engaging community stakeholders, including delineating resilience building roles and responsibilities; (iv) disseminating information; and (v) implementing sustainable development projects.

There are numerous examples in the Caribbean of built capacity at the community level due to the joint effort of engaged community groups and the NGOs that very often offer their expertise in proposal development, project implementation and resource management. These are most often in the areas of food (greenhouses, aquaculture and hydroponics facilities), water (harvesting, storage and distribution systems) and energy security (solar, wind, biogas/biodiesel); as well as protection, using nature and ecosystem-based solutions (afforestation, mangrove replanting, vegetative barriers). The climate-resilient future Caribbean fosters strong community groupings; invests in strengthening community governance through all levels up to the local government level; opens communication channels between communities, NGOs and government, and makes a space for vibrant NGOs working in communities on resilience causes.

SIX PILLARS OF ACTION

An unmistakable theme emerging from the sixteen future visions is the need to deliberately adjust already defined development trajectories so that they are more systematic, inclusive and interdisciplinary in accounting for climate. That is, they all support a *systems-based approach* as the pathway to climate resilience, where considering the whole is integral to considering the individual elements. This makes sense as, while not discounting the value of action taken to date, under the present business-as-usual siloed approach to tackling climate, the risk is still increasing and countries are moving further away from their development aspirations.

The systems approach is inherent to the concept of sustainable development. Caribbean countries are among the 193 countries to have adopted the 2030 Agenda for Sustainable Development and the seventeen SDGs.[3] The SDGs, whether socially, ecologically/environmentally, or economically targeted, are meant to be seen as connected and harmonized. The systems approach of the SDGs involves trade-offs that are balanced and assigns priority to action accordingly (Barbier et al. 2014). The Climate Action SDG (#13) must therefore not be reduced to an environmental issue, as is often the case in the Caribbean, but be seen as a development issue that affects the whole.

Also strongly emerging from the reimagined pictures is that actions (plans, policies and other governance instruments) in response to the climate challenge must be entrenched in how risks are addressed at all societal levels and regionally. This will allow countries to continuously build on progress already made and be more responsive to the growing challenges.

We further pull out six interconnected pillars on which the resilient future relies, and which must be embedded in the systems approach. They are: a) risk assessment; b) adaptation and mitigation; c) research and data collection; d) collaboration and coherence; e) inclusivity across traditional and non-traditional sectors; and f) a culture of responsiveness. The extent to which progress is being achieved in each pillar – and to which each pillar reinforces and aligns with the others – offers an indication of whether Caribbean development trajectories are mainstreaming climate considerations and whether the region is on a pathway to the resilient future imagined. The systems approach also identifies an ideal sequencing of each pillar to achieve the desired outcome. Each pillar is briefly described below.

RISK ASSESSMENT

Making the region climate resilient begins with an appreciation of what the climate risks are. The reimagined visions of section 3 support increased investment in risk assessments (processes that scientifically estimate the risk whether quantitatively or qualitatively) and their use in designing response mechanisms. Several countries' National Communications qualitatively assess climate risks for priority and vulnerable sectors, for example, risks to water resources and agriculture because of drought, or to health from climate's impact on water and vector-borne diseases. At present, however, substantially more effort and resources are placed on understanding the effects of climate change compared with the economic impact through models, where minimal public funding is provided (Auffhammer 2018). A re-imagined approach corrects this imbalance by also prioritizing quantification of climate's impact on people, the economy and natural resources.

ADAPTATION AND MITIGATION

The Intergovernmental Panel on Climate Change (2018a) defines adaptation as "the process of adjustment to actual or expected climate and its effects, in order to moderate harm or exploit beneficial opportunities". The re-imagined futures all retain adaptation as the first line of defence for the region by acknowledging its necessity across all sectors and suggesting confronting the constraining factors in each. These include financing (including government expenditure), technical capacity (and resources), data/records, knowledge and understanding, and governance (including policies and legislation) (Robinson 2018). A systemic approach corrects the disproportionate consideration of adaptation across sectors as now exists which has resulted in some sectors being more advanced than others.

Mitigation, for example, the reduction in greenhouse gas emissions, has gotten much less regional consideration, even though the Caribbean will benefit significantly from any global collective effort that limits future global warming, including from reduced risk to life, natural ecosystems and economies, and lowered adaptation demands (IPCC 2019). Regional advocacy to limit global warming to no more than 1.5 °C above pre-industrial levels recognizes the importance and necessity of mitigation. Many of the re-imagined futures allow for both adaptation and mitigation measures, recognizing that there are co-benefits and synergies, such as increased energy sector resilience due to greater use of renewables. The pathway to resilience takes advantage of tools already being used for understanding the interactions of adaptation and mitigation such as National Adaptation Plans or Nationally Determined Contributions.

It bears noting that despite countries' best efforts, there are, however, limits to adaptation especially as options become fewer as temperatures increase. Caribbean countries are grappling with the effects of "loss and damage" which, according to the UNFCCC,[4] "includes, and in some cases involves more than, that which can be reduced by adaptation". The reimagined resilient Caribbean recognizes the limits of both adaptation and mitigation and proactively plans for them, for example, via risk transfer mechanisms, including insurance. Transferring risks *ex-ante* complements adaptation measures and lowers risks for loss and damage. Already, many Caribbean countries have purchased parametric insurance policies to support short-term recovery efforts.[5] A more diverse portfolio of options will however be needed inclusive of ex-ante and ex-post measures.

DATA AND RESEARCH

All the future pictures make a case for available and accessible data to track climate change, especially at the local level. Caribbean meteorological and hydrological services supported by regional technical bodies such as the Caribbean Institute for Meteorology and Hydrology have made significant advances with respect to climate data collection mechanisms. Climate data collection and monitoring also underpin the provision of climate services, including early warning systems, which are taking on even greater importance in the present era of unfamiliar climate (Mahon et al. 2018). The region must, however, continue to identify ways of reducing hurdles for and increasing investment in high-quality climate observational networks, state-of-the-art technology for storing, processing and communicating data and climate service delivery. Equal consideration must also be given to the routine collection and monitoring of socioeconomic and biodiversity-related data to support tracking of climate impacts. All sixteen intervention points need this as does the pursuit of the SDGs. In the re-imagined era, the depth and breadth of data collected and routinely monitored are expanded beyond climate variables, and capabilities strengthened to refine the quality of data already being collected e.g. by improving temporal or spatial representativeness.

It is research, however, that tells the story of the data more definitively and makes the climate connections across sectors and levels of society. When properly aligned with countries' needs and priorities, research clarifies, quantifies and validates the relationships of the systems approach. Research maximizes on the value of data collected to inform decisions in a sound, pragmatic manner. As seen, in the reimagined Caribbean, research is not optional but a targeted undergirding strategy for guiding national plans and positioning the region vis-à-vis its climate risks.

COLLABORATION AND COHERENCE

A systems approach by nature is built on relationships. Collaboration among stakeholders and coherence of the governance instruments and institutional frameworks are tenets for its success. The many policies and plans proposed in section three will rely on coordinating mechanisms to deliberately foster awareness and collaboration across sectors and ensure coherence of purpose and alignment of plans with overarching national climate goals and commitments. Some of these mechanisms are beginning to emerge in the region and include committees (some appointed by Cabinets) and focal point networks specifically focused on climate or more widely on the SDGs. Strengthening and expanding collaborative mechanisms are important to the reimagined approach since coherence (in policies) requires acknowledging feedback structures and causal relationships (Collste et al. 2017). The IPCC (2018b) notes that coherence is necessary in an enabling environment that includes, inter alia, multi-level governance. Collaboration and coherence are strengthened with interdisciplinary action and science-policy partnerships which, while difficult to maintain, facilitate sustained and rapid change (IPCC 2018b).

Interestingly, though limited financial resources are a major constraint to climate action in the region, it should also be a driving force for collaboration and coherence. As developing states, the efficient use of resources in a balanced and holistic manner is necessary. National public investment systems (SNIP) may represent a strategic opportunity to adequately build resilience into development planning. The SNIP of some Caribbean countries, however, require strengthening in areas of institutional frameworks, incorporating adaptation and disaster risk management in investment projects, and training and technical support (Inter-American Development Bank 2016). The absence of regulation regarding minimum parameters for considering climate change adaptation and disaster risk reduction limits the operationalization of these areas in public investment projects. There is also the need to use data to support compliance and monitoring (IDB 2016).

TRADITIONAL AND NON-TRADITIONAL SECTORS

The reimagined visions hint at the need for greater incorporation of non-traditional sectors in mainstreaming efforts. Some countries have begun to do this, but greater emphasis is required. We single out two overlooked sectors, namely education and finance because they are cross-cutting in their supportive roles to the more traditional sectors. Education, as noted by the IPCC (2018b), is able to accelerate wide-scale behaviour change for adaptation and mitigation action, thereby supporting effective governance. The education sector, including higher education institutions, can create strong linkages across sectors, build awareness and facilitate research. Finance, like education, is a key determinant of the vulnerability of the region. It is a part of multi-level governance that allows for the contribution of various actors, including the private sector. Innovative financing opportunities must be explored and adopted to complement traditional options, especially as digital technologies improve. Both education and finance typify the non-traditional sectors that the region must identify how best to incorporate as it advances climate action in the more traditional ones.

CULTURE OF RESPONSIVENESS

Climate variability and change are testing human and natural systems in novel ways. If response mechanisms are not sufficiently dynamic, the resilience being sought after is in peril. A culture of responsiveness recognizes that changes can and will always happen, but what is important is an evolution to meet the challenge (as opposed to malaise, indifference or kicking the can down the road). Effective governance is one of the fundamental ways to address this. Governance consists of public and private interactions that ultimately seek to solve societal ills and create opportunities (Munaretto et al. 2014). A necessary trait of governance is flexibility, which is the basis on which adaptive governance is conceptualized. This iterative process facilitates problem-solving on a continuous basis.

The data and research pillar also supports responsiveness. Greater value-added is derived when these feed into innovation, technology and entrepreneurship. With rapid digitalization and improvements in technology, there are numerous opportunities for entrepreneurs to solve many climate-related crises, be they artificial intelligence, blockchains or so much more (George et al. 2020). The right enabling environment – one that is supportive of innovation, technology and entrepreneurship – will foster a culture of responsiveness, allowing for the capitalization (safely) of these advancements to create a climate-resilient zone.

CONCLUSION

The feasibility of successfully achieving a climate-resilient Caribbean zone may be questioned, especially considering the region's diversity, its many challenges and constraints, associated costs, and the huge effort it will demand. The antithesis would, however, be unbearable, given the magnitude of the threats that the Caribbean has experienced, and the projections for an even worse reality in the future. The history of the Caribbean peoples is an epic centred on overcoming near-impossible odds to rise to prominence on the global stage. In this matter of a climate-resilient zone, the region is once again being called upon to work together, while leveraging its resources to achieve resilience for all Caribbean states.

In this chapter, we have (re)imagined the resilient Caribbean through the lens of sixteen intervention points which, we suggest, rest on six pillars. The intention is not to suggest that this is all that is required, but rather to point to some important features of a framework for resilience and the pursuit of it. The dynamism of the problem, and the dependence of the magnitude of the required solutions on levels, scales and extent of response within and external to the Caribbean, preclude making any claim of comprehensiveness and demand constant revision of both interventions and pillars. Notwithstanding, some things emerge from just attempting the reimagination, which is worth mentioning in closing. These include the following:

- There is an urgency associated with responding to the climate change challenge, given the pace at which the climate is changing. At the current rate of global emissions, the regionally advocated global target of no more than 1.5°C global warming will be achieved within fifteen years (Taylor et al. 2018), not leaving the Caribbean much time to respond to the changes even that temperature threshold will bring. The suggested interventions have different timescales for implementation. Nonetheless, there is a need to significantly ramp up and, in some areas, immediately commence response efforts, given how urgent the problem is.

- The reimagined resilience has to be driven by an internally driven reworking of political, economic and social structures, that is, instead of a reliance on external entities to drive the process due to, for example, resources they may provide. The region must be seized with the necessity to pursue a regionally defined resilience pathway, and then take on the challenge to do so, bearing in mind the Caribbean way of life that it is trying to preserve and protect. To do otherwise runs the risk of imposing ill-fitting solutions, whose parameters and bounds are defined by interests that do not necessarily align with that of the region, and which ultimately threaten Caribbean identity.

- In developing the future, we deliberately did not ask the practitioners to address financing the interventions explicitly, so as not to limit their visioning. Nonetheless, a range of options and approaches still emerged, including dedicated national DRR and adaptation funds; risk transfer mechanisms; multilateral and bilateral donor funds, to include the Adaptation Fund, and Global Environment Facility resources; debt-for-nature swaps; and private sector financing, including PPPs. We acknowledge that financing is a significant (and perhaps the biggest) constraint to achieving the future resilient Caribbean, and will require a range of options and its own separate chapter. However, having a picture of what the resilient state might look like, the necessary interventions, and the pillars on which it must rest, provides a useful framework for such a discussion and an opening to discuss the suitability of different options to match scale, level and purpose on the proposed responses.

Finally, the re-imagination interrogates leadership that will be required to achieve the future resilient Caribbean. Climate creates its own set of winners and losers, and as already seen, the most vulnerable fall into the latter category. Bold leadership at all levels will be needed to ensure equitable sharing of risks and gains. Visionary leadership will be needed since some resilience pathways are yet uncharted and untested, and the ability to see their transformational potential in advance will likely be the distinguishing and deciding factor governing which one is chosen. Integrative leadership that grasps the complexities of the interconnections and can guide the synergies and trade-offs will be needed. In the end, however, it will be inspired leadership that will keep the region's eyes firmly set on the resilience goal, notwithstanding the challenging path ahead to achieving it.

NOTES

1. The World Bank (2018) suggests a climate-smart zone is one with: (i) reduced vulnerability to a range of climate-related hazards and natural disaster risks by building resilient infrastructure; (ii) reduced greenhouse gas emissions from transportation and other pollutants; (iii) healthy ecosystems in the sea to support the Blue Economy and on land for food security; (iv) enhanced energy security via promotion of efficient use, renewables and use of low-carbon sources; and (vi) incorporation of one or more of the SDGs in all major projects sponsored by governments.

2. Countries are required to submit periodic reports to the United Nations Framework Convention on Climate Change (UNFCCC). Most Caribbean countries have submitted their first National Communication. Many are on their second or third. Reports can be viewed at https://unfccc.int/non-annex-I-NCs.

3. http://www.un.org.cn/info/6/620.html#:~:text=Countries%20officially%20adopted%20the%20historic,Sustainable%20Development%20Goals%20(SDGs).

4. https://unfccc.int/sites/default/files/resource/docs/2013/cop19/eng/10a01.pdf

5. https://www.ccrif.org/sites/default/files/publications/technical-materials/CCRIFSPC_Technical_Paper_Series_Volume4_October_2020_webversion.pdf

REFERENCES

Acharjee, P. 2013. "Strategy and Implementation of Smart Grids in India." *Energy Strategy Reviews* (special issue on "Future Energy Systems and Market Integration of Wind Power") 1 (3): 193–204. https://doi.org/10.1016/j.esr.2012.05.003.

Auffhammer, Maximilian. 2018. "Quantifying Economic Damages from Climate Change." *Journal of Economic Perspectives* 32 (4): 33–52. https://doi.org/10.1257/jep.32.4.33.

Barbier, Edward B., and Joanne C. Burgess. 2017. "The Sustainable Development Goals and the Systems Approach to Sustainability." *Economics – The Open-Access, Open-Assessment E-Journal* 11: 1–23.

Bekele, Isaac, and Wayne Ganpat. 2015. "Education, Extension, and Training for Climate Change." In *Impacts of Climate Change on Food Security in Small Island Developing States:* Hershey, PA: IGI Global. https://doi.org/10.4018/978-1-4666-6501-9.ch012.

Bello, Omar, Luciana Fonted de Meira, Candice Gonzales, Leda Peralta, Nyasha Skerette, Blaine Marcano, Machel Patin, et al. 2020. *Assessment of the Effects and Impacts of Hurricane Dorian in the Bahamas*. Washington, DC: Inter-American Development Bank. https://doi.org/10.18235/0002582.

Bowen, Glenn A. 2013. "Caribbean Civil Society: Development Role and Policy Implications." *Nonprofit Policy Forum* 4 (1): 81–97. https://doi.org/10.1515/npf-2012-0013.

Bueno, R., C. Herzfeld, E. Stanton, and F. Ackerman. 2008. "The Caribbean and Climate Change: The Costs of Inaction." http://frankackerman.com/publications/climatechange/CaribbeanAndClimateChange.pdf

Caribbean Community (CARICOM). 2010. *Regional Food and Nutrition Security Policy.* Georgetown: CARICOM Secretariat.

———. 2011. *Regional Food and Nutrition Security Action Plan (2012–2026).* CARICOM Secretariat, Georgetown, Guyana.

———. 2012. *CARICOM Agribusiness Development Strategy*. Report presented to the 40th Special Meeting of the Council for Trade and Economic Development (COTED), Dominica. 19 October 2012.

Carruthers, Pasha, Orville Grey, Clifford Mahlung, and Linda Siegele. 2020. "Alliance of Small Island States (AOSIS)." In *Negotiating Climate Change Adaptation: The Common Position of the Group of 77 and China*, edited by María del Pilar Bueno Rubial and Linda Siegele, 27–47. Springer Climate. Cham: Springer International Publishing. https://doi.org/10.1007/978-3-030-41021-6_4.

Cashman, Adrian. 2014. "Water Security and Services in the Caribbean." *Water* 6 (5): 1187–1203. https://doi.org/10.3390/w6051187.

CCSA (Caribbean Climate-Smart Accelerator). 2019. "Accelerating Climate Action in the Caribbean." Caribbean Climate-Smart Accelerator. https://www.carib-beanaccelerator.org/about.

Chen, A. Anthony, A.J. Stephens, R. Koon Koon, M. Ashtine, and K. Mohammed-Koon Koon. 2020. "Pathways to Climate Change Mitigation and Stable Energy by 100% Renewable for a Small Island: Jamaica as an Example." *Renewable and Sustainable Energy Reviews* 121 (April): 109671. https://doi.org/10.1016/j.rser.2019.109671.

Climate Studies Group Mona (CSGM). 2020. *State of the Caribbean Climate: Information for Resilience Building.* St Michael: Caribbean Development Bank.

Collste, David, Matteo Pedercini, and Sarah E. Cornell. 2017. "Policy Coherence to Achieve the SDGs: Using Integrated Simulation Models to Assess Effective Policies." *Sustainability Science* 12 (6): 921–31. https://doi.org/10.1007/s11625-017-0457-x.

Connell, John. 2013. "Medical Tourism in the Caribbean Islands: A Cure for Economies in Crisis?" *Island Studies Journal* 8 (1).

Donovan, Michael G., and Therese Turner-Jones. 2017. "Caribbean Housing Is Expensive and Scarce. Here's How to Change That." *Americas Quarterly,* 20 April. https://www.americasquarterly.org/article/caribbean-housing-is-expensive-and-scarce-heres-how-to-change-that/.

Economic Commission for Latin America and the Caribbean (ECLAC). 2011. *The Economics of Climate Change in the Caribbean – Summary Report 2011.* Port of Spain: ECLAC Subregional Headquarters for the Caribbean. https://www.cepal.org/en/publications/38620-economics-climate-change-caribbean.

———. 2018. "Irma and Maria by Numbers." *FOCUS Magazine of the Caribbean Development and Cooperation Committee (CDCC),* 1 March 2018.

———. 2019. "Caribbean expenditure on social protection of public sector, 2000–2018."

Santiago: ECLAC. https://observatoriosocial.cepal.org/inversion/en/indicator/expenditure-social-protection.

ECLAC and CCJ Academy of Law. 2018. *Ensuring Environmental Access Rights in the Caribbean: Analysis of Selected Case Law.* Santiago: ECLAC. https://repositorio.cepal.org/server/api/core/bitstreams/c2bd6840-f787-4cea-a3cc-5a3813979156/contentGeorge, Gerard, Ryan K. Merrill, and Simon J.D. Schillebeeckx. 2020. "Digital Sustainability and Entrepreneurship: How Digital Innovations Are Helping Tackle Climate Change and Sustainable Development." *Entrepreneurship Theory and Practice* 5 (5): 999–1027. https://doi.org/10.1177/1042258719899425.

Government of the Commonwealth of Dominica. 2018. *National Resilience Development Strategy Dominica 2030.* Roseau: Government of the Commonwealth of Dominica. https://observatorioplanificacion.cepal.org/sites/default/files/plan/files/Dominica%202030The%20National%20Resilience%20Development%20Strategy.pdf.

Government of St Lucia. 2018. "Saint Lucia's Climate Change Communications Strategy under the National Adaptation Planning Process." Department of Sustainable Development, Ministry of Education, Innovation, Gender Relations and Sustainable Development, Castries. https://www4.unfccc.int/sites/NAPC/Documents/Parties/Saint%20Lucia%20Climate%20Change%20Communications%20Strategy.pdf.

Inter-American Development Bank (IDB). 2016. *Status of Incorporation of Disaster Risk Management and Climate Change Adaptation in National Public Investment Systems: Results for The Bahamas, Guyana and Jamaica and Comparative Analysis for Five Caribbean Countries.* Technical Note No. IDB-TN-965. Washington, DC: IDB. https://publications.iadb.org/publications/english/document/Status-of-Incorporation-of-Disaster-Risk-Management-and-Climate-Change-Adaptation-in-National-Public-Investment-Systems-Results-for-The-Bahamas-G-uyana-and-Jamaica-and-Comparative-Analysis-for-Five-Caribbean-Countries.pdf.

Intergovernmental Panel on Climate Change (IPCC). 2018a. "Annex I: Glossary [Matthews, J.B.R. (Ed.)]." In *Global Warming of 1.5°C. An IPCC Special Report on the Impacts of Global Warming of 1.5°C above Pre-Industrial Levels and Related Global Greenhouse Gas Emission Pathways, in the Context of Strengthening the Global Response to the Threat of Climate Change, Sustainable Development, and Efforts to Eradicate Poverty,* edited by V. Masson-Delmotte, P. Zhai, H.O. Pörtner, D. Roberts, J. Skea, P.R. Shukla, A. Pirani, et al., 541–62. Cambridge and New York: Cambridge University Press. https://www.ipcc.ch/sr15/chapter/glossary/.

———. 2018b. "Summary for Policymakers." In *Global Warming of 1.5°C. An IPCC Special Report on the Impacts of Global Warming of 1.5°C above Pre-industrial Levels and Related Global Greenhouse Gas Emission Pathways, in the Context of Strengthening the Global Response to the Threat of Climate Change, Sustainable Development, and Efforts to Eradicate Poverty,* edited by V. Masson-Delmotte, P. Zhai, H.O. Pörtner, D. Roberts, J. Skea, P.R. Shukla, A. Pirani, 3–24. Cambridge and New York: Cambridge University Press.

———. 2019. *IPCC Special Report on the Ocean and Cryosphere in a Changing Climate.* [H.-O. Pörtner, D.C. Roberts, V. Masson-Delmotte, P. Zhai, M. Tignor, E. Poloczanska, K. Mintenbeck, A. Alegría, M. Nicolai, A. Okem, J. Petzold, B. Rama, N.M. Weyer (eds.)]. Cambridge and New York: Cambridge University Press.

International Union for Conservation of Nature/Species Survival Commission (IUCN/SSC). 2014. *Guidelines on the Use of Ex Situ Management for Species Conservation. Version 2.0."* Gland: IUCN Species Survival Commission.

Kairi Consultants. 2013. *Climate Change Knowledge, Attitudes and Behavioural Practices in the OECS: Report on the KAP Survey of Six Participating Member*

States. Castries: OECS Secretariat and USAID. https://climatefinance.gov.gd/wp-content/uploads/2019/10/Climate-Change-Knowledge-Attitudes-and-Behavioural-Practices-in-the-OECS.pdf.

Mahon, Roché, David Farrell, Shelly-Ann Cox, Adrian Trotman, Cedric Van Meerbeeck, and Garfield Barnwell. 2018. "Climate Services and Caribbean Resilience: A Historical Perspective." *Social and Economic Studies* 67 (2&3): 239–60.

Maynard-Date, Anelda. 2015. "The Eastern Caribbean Geothermal Energy Interconnection Grid Feasibility Study." Proceeding the World Geothermal Congress, Melbourne, 19–25 April 2015. https://pangea.stanford.edu/ERE/db/WGC/papers/WGC/2015/06047.pdf.

McDonald, Jan, and Phillipa C. McCormack. 2021. "Rethinking the Role of Law in Adapting to Climate Change." *WIREs Climate Change* 12(5): e726. https://doi.org/10.1002/wcc.726.

McLean, Sheldon, Hidenobu Tokuda, Nyasha Skerrette, and Machel Pantin. 2020. *Promoting Debt Sustainability to Facilitate Financing Sustainable Development in Selected Caribbean Countries: A Scenario Analysis of the ECLAC Debt for Climate Adaptation Swap Initiative*. Studies and Perspectives Series, ECLAC Subregional Headquarters for the Caribbean, No. 89. Santiago: ECLAC. https://repositorio.cepal.org/handle/11362/45108.

Mycoo, Michelle A. 2018. "Beyond 1.5 °C: Vulnerabilities and Adaptation Strategies for Caribbean Small Island Developing States." *Regional Environmental Change* 18 (8): 2341–53. https://doi.org/10.1007/s10113-017-1248-8.

Mycoo, Michelle A., and Keisha Bharath. 2021. "Sustainable Development Goal 11 and a New Urban Agenda for Caribbean Small Island Developing States: Policy, Practice, and Action." *Frontiers in Sustainable Cities* 3. https://doi.org/10.3389/frsc.2021.554377.

Mycoo, Michelle A., and Michael G. Donovan. 2017. *A Blue Urban Agenda: Adapting to Climate Change in the Coastal Cities of Caribbean and Pacific Small Island Developing States*. Washington, DC: IDB. https://publications.iadb.org/en/blue-urban-agenda-adapting-climate-change-coastal-cities-caribbean-and-pacific-small-island.

Ochs, Alexander, Mark Konold, Katie Auth, Evan Musolino, and Philip Killeen. 2015. *Caribbean Sustainable Energy Roadmap and Strategy (C-SERMS): Baseline Report and Assessment*. Washington, DC: Worldwatch Institute. https://doi.org/10.13140/RG.2.1.4351.1922.

Ötker, İnci, and Krishna Srinivasan. 2018. "Bracing for the Storm: For the Caribbean, Building Resilience Is a Matter of Survival." *Finance and Development* 55 (1): 49–51.

Ouyang, Zhiyun, Hua Zheng, Yi Xiao, Stephen Polasky, Jianguo Liu, Weihua Xu,

Qiao Wang, et al. 2016. "Improvements in Ecosystem Services from Investments in Natural Capital." *Science* 352 (6292): 1455–59. https://doi.org/10.1126/science.aaf2295.

Pan American Health Organization (PAHO). 2019. *Caribbean Action Plan on Health and Climate Change: Indicator Descriptors*. Washington, DC: PAHO. https://iris.paho.org/bitstream/handle/10665.2/38566/PAHOCDE19007_eng.pdf?sequence=19&isAllowed=y.

Pulwarty, Roger S., Leonard A. Nurse, and Ulric O. Trotz. 2010. "Caribbean Islands in a Changing Climate." *Environment: Science and Policy for Sustainable Development* 52 (6): 16–27. https://doi.org/10.1080/00139157.2010.522460.

Rankine, Dale, Steve Maximay, and Wesley Gibbings. 2020. *Reporting the Climate Crisis: A Handbook for Caribbean Journalists*. Port of Spain: Association of Caribbean Media Workers..

Riquelme, Rodrigo, Paola Méndez, and Ianthe Smith. 2016. *Solid Waste Management in the Caribbean: Proceedings from the Caribbean Solid Waste Conference*. Washington, DC: Inter-American Development Bank. https://publications.iadb.org/publications/english/document/Solid-Waste-Management-in-the-Caribbean-Proceedings-from-the-Caribbean-Solid-Waste-Conference.pdf.

Rhiney, Kevon. 2018. "Climate Change and the Future of Agriculture in the Caribbean: Prospects for South–South Cooperation." In *Routledge Handbook of South–South Relations*, edited by Elena Fiddian-Qasmiyeh and Patricia Daley. Abingdon and New York: Routledge.

Robinson, Stacy-Ann. 2018. "Adapting to Climate Change at the National Level in Caribbean Small Island Developing State." *Island Studies Journal* 13 (1): 79–100. https://doi.org/10.24043/isj.59.

Solórzano, Ana, and Iliana Cárdenes. 2019. *Social protection and climate change: WFP Regional Bureau for Latin America and the Caribbean's vision to advance climate change adaptation through social protection*. Rome: World Food Programme in collaboration with Oxford Policy Management.

Spencer, Nekeisha, and Solomon W. Polachek. 2015. "Hurricane Watch: Battening Down the Effects of the Storm on Local Crop Production." *Ecological Economics* 120: 234–40.

Taylor, Michael A., Leonardo A. Clarke, Abel Centella, Arnoldo Bezanilla, Tannecia S. Stephenson, Jhordanne J. Jones, Jayaka D. Campbell, Alejandro Vichot, and John Charlery. 2018. "Future Caribbean Climates in a World of Rising Temperatures: The 1.5 vs 2.0 Dilemma." *Journal of Climate* 31 (7): 2907–26. https://doi.org/10.1175/JCLI-D-17-0074.1.

Tscharntke, Teja, Yann Clough, Thomas C. Wanger, Louise Jackson, Iris Motzke, Ivette Perfecto, John Vandermeer, and Anthony Whitbread. 2012. "Global Food Security, Biodiversity Conservation and the Future of Agricultural

Intensification." *Biological Conservation* 151 (1): 53–59. https://doi.org/10.1016/j. biocon.2012.01.068.

United Nations Framework Convention on Climate Change (UNFCCC). 2018. "TEC Brief #12: Energizing Entrepreneurs to Tackle Climate Change". Bonn: UNFCCC secretariat.

United Nations Educational, Scientific and Cultural Organization (UNESCO). 2018. *Records of the General Conference, 39th Session, Paris, 30 October–14 November 2017, v. 1: Resolutions."* Paris: UNESCO. https://unesdoc.unesco.org/ark:/48223/ pf0000260889.page=127.

United Nations, Department of Economic and Social Affairs, Population Division. 2018. *World Urbanization Prospects: The 2018 Revision.* https://population.un.org/ wup/DataQuery/.

World Health Organization (WHO). 2020. *WHO Guidance for Climate Resilient and Environmentally Sustainable Health Care Facilities."* Geneva: WHO. https:// www.who.int/publications-detail-redirect/9789240012226.

Wilson, Byron, Tandora D. Grant, Rick Van Veen, Rick Hudson, Dawn Fleuchaus, Orlando Robinson, and Kimberly Stephenson. 2016. "The Jamaican iguana (*Cyclura collei*): A report on 25 years of conservation effort." *Herpetological Conservation and Biology* 11 (Monograph 6): 237–54.

World Bank. 2018. "Caribbean Aims to Become World's First Climate-Smart Zone." Press release, 9 August. https://www.worldbank.org/en/news/press-re-lease/2018/08/09/caribbean-aims-become-world-first-climate-smart-zone.

PART 3.

DIS/INTEGRATION MOVEMENTS IN THE CARIBBEAN – PREDICATE FOR A REGIONAL RESET

7

How the Eric Williams/Arthur Lewis Divergence Soured the Regional Integration Movement

HAMID GHANY

ACCORDING TO *THE REPORT OF THE JAMAICA INDEPENDENCE Conference, 1962*:

> Jamaica had been a member of the Federation of the West Indies since its inception in 1957. Having regard, however, to the growth of opposition in Jamaica to its continued participation in the Federation, and its desire to seek independence on its own, the Jamaican Government announced on the 31st May, 1960, that the electorate would be given an opportunity to determine the issue by way of referendum. The Government introduced the necessary legislation and the referendum which was held on the 19th September, 1961 resulted in a majority of 35,535 votes against Jamaica remaining in the Federation (Jamaica Independence Committee 1962, 5).

The actual question that was asked on the ballot paper was, "Should Jamaica remain in the Federation of the West Indies?" The number of persons who voted 'Yes' was 217,319. The number of persons who voted 'No' was 256,261. The turnout was 61.51 per cent. Jamaica was now poised to secede from the West Indian Federation on the basis of this outcome. The prospect of Jamaican secession from the federation caused a flurry of activity to take place between September 1961 and January 1962 between the Federal Government of the West Indies, the British government, the unit territories of the West Indian Federation, and the government of Trinidad and Tobago. This political outcome in Jamaica would come to haunt the Federation of the West Indies in 1961/62 as the Jamaican government, led by its premier,

Norman Manley, had exercised a right to self-determination to decide whether it should remain in the federation against the separatist view of the Leader of the Opposition, Alexander Bustamante. According to Robert Tignor: "British officials expected Manley to oppose Bustamante and his go-it-alone strategy with all of the legitimacy of his office and personality; instead, without even consulting the British, he agreed to hold a referendum on the question" (Tignor 2006, 230).

Manley's decision not to consult the British government about the holding of a referendum on the federal question was also a part of the act of self-determination for Jamaica. If Manley had consulted the British government about the issue, the matter may have been handled differently. When this is assessed against the following secret minute from the Secretary of State for the Colonies to the Prime Minister, it is apparent that even the British government misread the mood of the Jamaican public on the federal issue.

Manley's response to Bustamante's demand was a local political issue that had regional implications. The British government may have tried to talk Manley out of a referendum because they believed that there was majority support for Jamaica becoming part of an independent federation. For them, it was a matter of weighing the political risk involved in pursuing their interests to secure a federation. For Manley, it was apparently an important domestic matter that required a domestic answer that would have legitimized his determination to press forward with the federation.

The secret minute from the Secretary of State for the Colonies, Iain Macleod, to Prime Minister Harold Macmillan on 22 September 1961 read, in part, as follows:

1. The Jamaica referendum has resulted in a defeat for Manley on the Federation issue. We expected and hoped for a narrow but clear affirmative. The result is a narrow but clear negative.

2. This is a most grievous blow to the Federal ideal for which we and enlightened West Indian opinion have striven for so many years. It is certain that the Federation cannot continue in its present form and must be doubtful whether it can survive at all.

3. The decision of Jamaica to quit the Federation must be taken as final . . . (Macleod to Macmillan, 22d September 1961).

This internal decision by the Colonial Secretary that was communicated to Prime Minister Macmillan established the foundations of Colonial Office policy towards the federation and opened the door to Jamaica to proceed to its own independence.

The value of Jamaica to the regional movement is confirmed here insofar as the Colonial Office regarded their departure as a "grievous blow". The fact that the Colonial Secretary was already telegraphing the prime minister that it "must be doubtful" whether the federation could survive at all without Jamaica captures the essence of the severe uphill challenge that the regional movement would face minus the biggest island.

The other half of that policy matrix was what decision the British government would make about the future of the federation. The Federal Government was not going to enter into that debate without expert knowledge. Enter Arthur Lewis, principal of the University College of the West Indies (UCWI), who offered his services to the federal prime minister, Sir Grantley Adams, to try to salvage the federation with the remaining nine members, now that the secession of Jamaica was inevitable.

THE ENTRY OF ARTHUR LEWIS

In a secret telegram to the Secretary of State for the Colonies from the acting governor-general of the West Indies, John Mordecai, on 21 September 1961, which was labelled "Emergency, secret and personal", the following was revealed: "3. It is also relevant that Arthur Lewis who is now in Trinidad and has seen both Prime Minister and Premier has been formally accepted by the former as dollar a year representative to work here for the next three months to examine prospect of salvage proposals. It is a good sign that Williams while still non-committal personally welcomes this arrangement" (Mordecai to Macleod, 21 September 1961).

What was significant about this particular communication to the Colonial Office from Mordecai was that it revealed an arrangement between the federal prime minister, Sir Grantley Adams, and the principal of the UCWI, Arthur Lewis, even before the Federal Cabinet had been made aware of the decision to have Lewis hired as an expert to advise Adams.

At a meeting of the Federal Cabinet on Friday, 22 September 1961 at 2.30pm, the following matter was tabled for consideration:

> 579. With reference to Conclusions Nos. 574 and 575 of the Sixty-Fourth Meeting on 20th September, the Prime Minister informed the Cabinet of a timely offer, made by Professor Arthur Lewis, Principal of the U.C.W.I., to assist in any suitable capacity in the difficult situation created by the Jamaica Referendum results, and of his decision to appoint Professor Lewis immediately as his Special Adviser to undertake, in the first instance, a tour of the territories other than Jamaica to encourage them to continue in the Federation. It was understood that the arrangement would only entail provisions of office accommodation, secretarial assistance and a nominal payment of $1 per annum to Professor Lewis.
>
> 580. The Cabinet confirmed the actions taken by the Prime Minister (The West Indies, Cabinet, Sixty-Fifth Meeting, 22 September 1961).

These Cabinet minutes reveal that Lewis approached Adams, and not the other way around. This was also confirmed by Tignor (2006, 230): "At this juncture, when it was crucial to keep Trinidad and Barbados interested in federation, Lewis volunteered his services to Grantley Adams, the head of the prefederation government, as an emissary to salvage the project."

In a secret and personal letter from Mordecai to Ambler Thomas at the Colonial Office, dated 23 September 1961, Mordecai said, inter alia, the following:

> Dear Ambler,
>
> I take it that we need not for the moment meet the request in Douglas Williams' letter of 1st September for a report on the situation in the West Indies by the end of the month. That request was no doubt made in happier expectations of the Referendum, which we all shared; and the 'agonising re-appraisal' now proceeding in London and in the West Indies is indeed the first stage of a much larger exercise which may take many weary months . . . (Mordecai to Ambler Thomas, 23 September 1961).

Here one gets an inside look at how overconfident the federal government and the Colonial Office were about the referendum producing a favourable result to keep Jamaica in the federation. Back in those days, there were no opinion polls in the West Indies to gauge potential support for one side or the other in a referendum. There was just feeling and emotion, and clearly both the federal government and the Colonial Office were blindsided by the result, with Lord Hailes on vacation in Scotland and John Mordecai acting as governor-general of the West Indies. From time to time, Mordecai would consult Sir Solomon Hochoy, governor of Trinidad and Tobago, about the emerging situation.

In his secret minute to Prime Minister Macmillan on 22 September, Secretary of State for the Colonies, Iain Macleod, confirmed Lord Hailes' interruption of his vacation as follows: "9. I have asked for immediate assessments from the Acting Governor-General and Governors and Administrators. Hailes has broken his holiday in Scotland and I have held discussions with him . . ." (Macleod to Macmillan, 22 September 1961).

With both the British government and the federal government in the West Indies in total disarray over the Jamaican referendum result, Lewis' entry into the policy equation offered a measure of relief. This is best captured in the secret and personal letter from Mordecai to Thomas at the Colonial Office dated 23 September 1961, in which he stated:

> 7 . . .The entrance of Arthur Lewis into the picture brought further encouragement and his discussions with Williams inclined to a confirmation of impressions (which Hochoy and I had formed) that (a) there was a chance of Williams being gradually persuaded by a mounting and 'implied' appeal from the other units, to consider and work out a Federation of Nine based on his thesis of the Economics of Nationhood, and (b) that Williams, with an early election on his hands, if not needled by other events (e.g. a flare-up with the Americans), would not be in a hurry to declare for Trinidad's independence, however much some of his colleagues were known to be pressing him (Mordecai to Ambler Thomas, 23 September 1961).

Within days, a meeting was convened at the Colonial Office on Tuesday, 26 September 1961, and the secret minutes reveal the following:

> The SECRETARY OF STATE said that although nothing was legally or constitutionally changed by the result of the Referendum, we were in fact facing a completely new situation. It had to be accepted that Jamaica's decision was final and that the future of the Federation must be without her, though he hoped it would be possible to maintain regional services. Mr. Manley was coming to

London on the 2nd October and Sir Alexander Bustamante might be coming. The Jamaican leaders would ask for Her Majesty's Government's agreement that they should proceed to separate independence. The Cabinet had not yet taken any decision on this but for the purposes of the present discussion it could be assumed Her Majesty's Government would agree . . . (meeting at the Colonial Office, 26 September 1961).

The Colonial Secretary had set the table for the discussions that were about to take place with the following persons, who were listed as attendees:

United Kingdom	Federal Government
Secretary of State	Sir Grantley Adams
Lord Hailes	Dr La Corbiniere
Mr Fraser	Mr Bradshaw
Mr Mc Petrie	Professor Arthur Lewis
Mr Thomas	Mr Garnet Gordon
Mr D. Williams	Mr Da Costa
Mr Noakes	Mr F.D.C. Williams
Mr Jamieson	Mr Richardson

With the impending reality of Jamaican independence having been flagged by the Secretary of State, the meeting was pushed in the direction of considering what a federation of the remaining nine territories would look like. The minutes reveal that the proceedings were dominated by Lewis.

After this meeting between the Colonial Secretary and his delegation, and the Federal Government delegation, another was held between the Colonial Secretary and a Jamaican government delegation that ended on 5 October 1961. A press release was issued at the conclusion of those talks which read, in part, as follows: ". . . The Secretary of State informed the delegation that H.M.G. accepted the result of the Referendum as a final indication of Jamaica's wishes and would be prepared to introduce legislation as early as possible in the forthcoming session of Parliament to provide for Jamaica's withdrawal from the Federation. Every effort would be made to secure the passage of the legislation before the end of March 1962 . . ."

The policy position of the British government had now been publicly established on the future of the federation without Jamaica. Independence was coming to Jamaica on its own. Would there be a federation of nine territories that would include Trinidad and Tobago? Would they also seek to follow Jamaica and seek their own independence? These were the immediate challenges.

However, Adams had indicated at the meeting with Colonial Office officials over the period 26th–28 September 1961 that if Trinidad and Tobago were to withdraw from the federation, then the remaining eight would wish to remain associated.

Adams was trying to keep the federal idea alive if Williams were to make a move in the direction of independence for Trinidad and Tobago by seceding from the federation. Adams was seeing trouble ahead and realized that Williams was unlikely to commit to remaining in the federation.

THE RESPONSE FROM ERIC WILLIAMS

All eyes now turned to Dr Williams, premier of Trinidad and Tobago, who held a press conference on 8 October 1961, which was monitored by colonial government intelligence sources and reported to the Colonial Office. Some excerpts are as follows:

> Question from the *Guardian*: Has the Premier been asked to receive Professor Arthur Lewis? Does he propose to do so?
>
> *Dr Williams:* Well, the point is this, Professor Arthur Lewis is an old friend of the Premier, is not a professor and is not the Premier when they meet, and Arthur Lewis is free to meet the Premier at any time. In fact, he was asked by Professor Arthur Lewis to receive Professor Arthur Lewis and he did so before the Professor went to England. We met twice and I've met him again. Our relations are such that he is free to come in to see me at any time without notice to discuss any subject because when we discuss any subject at all we bear in mind that there are sometimes larger considerations than the immediate political considerations. We bear in mind that we are perhaps making history one way or the other.
>
> *Mr Espinet:* We are thinking in terms of his position as adviser to the PM.
>
> *Dr Williams:* I can't say anything. It doesn't cost Trinidad much, his advice he is a dollar a year man. I would like to get some dollar a year men for Trinidad. Trinidad only pays 38% of his salary, it costs us 38 cents. We don't mind that at

all. We don't tell the Federal Government whom they should appoint as advisers. What you want to know is whether he has discussed Federation with me. He has. He is an adviser on Federation so he would raise the point and you would want to know what I told him. I told him I wasn't free to discuss Federation, etc. But we made no effort to stop him (sic) discussions, any proposals that Professor Lewis makes to me or to the Government of Trinidad and Tobago is given careful consideration (excerpts from the Premier's Press Conference, 8 October 1961).

With this public confirmation from Williams that he and Lewis had met, it is clear that the latter was being given access to the premier in his new role as special adviser to the prime minister of the Federation. Williams' cryptic remarks were designed to show a sense of humour about the encounters with Lewis, but there was a warning signal of what was to come.

A NEW COLONIAL SECRETARY

On the following day, 9 October, Prime Minister Harold Macmillan reshuffled his Cabinet in the United Kingdom. Iain Macleod was moved from his position as Secretary of State for the Colonies and made Chancellor of the Duchy of Lancaster. Reginald Maudling was moved from his position as president of the Board of Trade and made Secretary of State for the Colonies.

This change came at a very delicate time in West Indian history. The British government was attempting to reformulate its own federal arrangements, while simultaneously dealing with the announcement of individual independence for Jamaica a few days before on October 5.

In a lengthy secret and personal letter from Mordecai to Ambler Thomas at the Colonial Office dated 11 October 1961, Mordecai assessed the current situation and said:

10. The more substantial danger as we see it – and this is an angle already identifiable in his war of nerves movements – is of Williams being able to avoid having to declare a position at all, on the argument that continuation of the present Federation after Jamaica's withdrawal is dissolved by Jamaica and H.M.G. between them. The psychological advantage of this approach is obvious. He has already said publicly that, by his mathematics, 'if you take away 1 from 10 you leave 0, not 9'. In his private discussions with Arthur Lewis, he has maintained

that, on the basis of his legal advice, the present Federation stands destroyed the moment Jamaica's secession is effected. He appears so firmly wedded to this view that in certain instances he acts almost as if it were already destroyed . . . (Mordecai to Ambler Thomas, 11 October 1961).

Mordecai's assessment was timely as it was copied to Lord Hailes, who was expected to return to duty a few days afterwards. This would have allowed Hailes to have a proper brief of the situation as he resumed duties after his interrupted vacation.

Thomas replied in a secret and personal letter on 16 October to Mordecai's lengthy assessment of the situation as follows:

> Thank you for your long letter of the 11th October. To say that we are grateful for it would be an understatement. It contains an analysis of the present situation and an indication of probabilities and possibilities, as well as advice and warnings about various courses, which cannot fail to be of the greatest possible use to all of us . . . In view of the great pressure from Jamaica, it was not unsatisfactory to have avoided commitment as to secession until not later than the end of March and to have left open an independence date during 1962 . . . (Ambler Thomas to Mordecai, 16 October 1961).

On his last day in office as acting governor-general of the West Indies, Mordecai sent out a confidential circular savingram, dated 16 October 1961 to federal governors and administrators, in which he said, inter alia:

> 2. The Prime Minister's Special Personal Adviser, Dr. Arthur Lewis, is now engaged in discussions in the Territories of the Eastern Caribbean, with a view to facilitating the formulation of proposals for the future that can, it is hoped, be welded into one common policy for presentation to Her Majesty's Government as early in 1962 as is feasible . . ." (Acting Governor-General to FEDER Governors & Administrators, excluding Jamaica, 16 October 1961. Repeated for information to Secretary of State and Governor, Jamaica).

LORD HAILES RETURNS TO OFFICE

On his first day back in office, Lord Hailes sent a secret letter to the new Colonial Secretary, Reginald Maudling, to advise him of the decision of the Federal Cabinet on the issue of Jamaica's secession from the federation and the communique issued by the Colonial Office on Jamaica's independence. He said, in part:

> 2. The Federal Government formally protests against the decision recorded in the above-mentioned communique that Her Majesty's Government would be prepared to introduce legislation as early as possible in the forthcoming session of Parliament to provide for Jamaica's withdrawal from the Federation, and that every effort would be made to secure the passage of this legislation before the end of March, 1962. The Federal Cabinet regards this decision as contrary to the spirit of the existing Federal Constitution, and considers that it would be highly impolitic for the act and timing of Jamaica's secession to be negotiated and decided solely between Her Majesty's Government and the Government of Jamaica, without consultation at all stages with the Federal Government and the Governments of the other Territories of the Federation . . . (Hailes to Maudling, 17 October 1961).

In this missive, Hailes was telegraphing the disagreement of the Federal Cabinet with the British government's decision to proceed with Jamaican secession and independence without reference to the Federal Government of the West Indies.

Already, the environment was being soured about the way forward on Jamaica's secession with the federal government refusing to accept the decision of the British government to deal directly with Jamaica about its independence.

In a personal letter from Hailes to Maudling dated 21 October 1961, Hailes said:

> . . . Later, I do trust you will be able to pay a visit. Hochoy feels this could hardly be until the Trinidad elections are over, but the fact remains, knowing Williams, that a real 'clearance' with him will not be possible until you have met. I hope I have not been laying down the law too much. I shall be writing to the office about general matters next week but there is little to add for the moment to Mordecai's excellent letter to Thomas of the 11th October."

(At this point, the full stop is changed to a comma and the sentence continues in handwriting): ". . . and I doubt if these will be until Arthur Lewis' return from his tour of the Territories at the beginning of November (Hailes to Maudling, 21 October 1961).

This continuation of the letter in his personal handwriting before he sent it off obviously eluded the typist and was effectively converted to a very personal note on what was becoming a very sensitive issue of political tactics surrounding the importance of Lewis' tour of the region. He also confirmed his discussions with Sir Solomon Hochoy.

Lewis completed his tour of the eight federation territories and in a secret and personal letter from Hailes to Thomas at the Colonial Office dated 4 November, he wrote:

> . . . Arthur Lewis has just returned from what seems to have been a very successful tour of the eight Territories. The long and short of what he tells me is that all these territories are anxious for a continuation of a Federation of nine, are prepared to make certain sacrifices of 'sovereignty', regard Trinidad as their natural leader and the seat of Federation; and in fact, seem to have generally accepted the principles of Williams' 'Economics of Nationhood'.
>
> So far, he has written a long and masterly report in the form of a letter on the subject to Williams (18 pages of foolscap with appendices), and during this weekend in Tobago will draft a Report for Adams, which will be an expurgated edition of his letter to Williams.
>
> Yesterday Williams asked Lewis to lunch and they discussed his 'letter'. Lewis spoke to me on the telephone afterwards on his way to Tobago and he will come and see me on Monday and give me a fuller report. However, it appears that Williams was not all bad on principles, i.e. he wants a Federation to continue if possible, he is quite against a Referendum on the subject in Trinidad, etc., but he made it quite clear that he is determined to smash this Federation first, and then start again, as he refuses to have any dealings or sit around a conference table with Adams or any of his 'bunch'. I fully expected this, but Lewis, who is not a politician, was very shocked by Williams' vehemence on this point . . . (Hailes to Thomas, 4 November 1961).

Lewis, having completed his tour, had gone to see Williams and then went off to Tobago to complete the writing of his report for Adams. There was obvious discomfort for Hailes in Lewis trusting Williams with the contents of what he was going to give to Adams. However, Hailes seemed impressed by the fact that Lewis had been able to convince all of the other chief ministers to adopt his plan for a future federation of nine, with Trinidad and Tobago being the dominant partner. Hailes confirmed his view that Lewis was politically naive as he (Lewis) could not understand why Williams was so vehement about smashing this federation first before he could agree to anything else in the future.

It would appear that Lewis had no idea what was in Williams' mind and what was coming in the future after the general election in Trinidad and Tobago on 4 December 1961. Williams was not using the general election as a virtual referendum on the future of the federation and he successfully kept the issue off the campaign trail. There was no self-determination approach to the federation in Trinidad and Tobago when compared to how the issue of Jamaica's secession from the federation was handled.

These were clues that were missed by Lewis in his interactions with Williams.

LEWIS SUBMITS HIS REPORT

In a secret and personal letter to the Secretary of State for the Colonies from Hailes, dated 10 November 1961, he wrote:

> Lewis who has now returned to Jamaica has produced his Report, and I enclose a copy. Yesterday he discussed it with the Federal Cabinet. Attached also is a note of his talks with Williams over the period 22nd September–8th November.
>
> Lewis' scheme was drawn up after he had visited the Leeward and Windward Islands and Barbados. He thinks that apart from Barbados, where attitudes are confused, it will be generally acceptable to Units. The scheme departs radically from anything previously put forward. In essence it suggests a unitary type of constitution – though to use this label would be little short of lethal as far as the small units are concerned – with a measure of devolution to local legislatures in a limited field of matters, chiefly Medical and Educational – both with heavy central subsidies – Agriculture and Social Services. Centralised services include Customs Excise and Inland Revenue, Post Offices, Ports, Police, Courts, Prisons, Broadcasting etc. The central Government would be financed from 70% of customs duties collected, and a 3/- in the £ company tax. It provides for a Customs Union with both a free trade area and a common external tariff, freedom of movement – possibly on a graduated basis – and representation in the Central Parliament based on the IGC formula. Territorial Governments and establishments are to be cut down, with the abolition of governorships and restrictions on the number of Ministers . . . (Hailes to Maudling, 10 November 1961).

Lewis met four times with Williams – on 22 September, 6 October, 3 November and 8 November (Hailes to Maudling, 10 November 1961, Enclosure, Secret and Personal Note by Dr. A. Lewis).

Lewis delivered his report to Adams on 9 November. It was attached to Hailes' secret and personal letter to Maudling the following day.

The last five paragraphs of Lewis' report read as follows:

> 41. I have had a number of talks with the Premier of Trinidad and Tobago, who has seen a draft of these proposals.
> 42. As he has stated publicly, he takes the position that the existing federation will come to an end when the British Parliament enacts the secession of Jamaica.
> 43. It is my impression that he desires that Trinidad and Tobago and the other islands should enter into a new association, rather than that Trinidad and Tobago should seek independence on its own. However, he is not prepared to enter into any commitment at this time.
> 44. I have reason to believe that he is willing to attend a conference to discuss the details of such an association, but I do not know whether the proposals made here will be acceptable to him.
> 45. The Premier is not at this time willing to name a date for a conference (Hailes to Maudling, 10 November 1961, Enclosure, Report to Sir Grantley Adams from W.A. Lewis, Special Adviser, dated 9 November 1961).

The Lewis report was vague on what Williams' intentions were and that should have been his first clue that the Trinidadian was intending to withdraw from the federation. He was facing a general election on 4 December and obviously was not in a position to make any commitments to Lewis at the time. Once Williams had jumped the hurdle of the general election, he would be prepared to make a more definitive statement. At that stage of their discussions on 8 November, there was nothing to suggest that Williams was going to commit to the Lewis proposals for a federation of nine.

In a secret and personal Letter to Hailes from Maudling, just prior to the latter's departure for Kenya, he had this to say, in part:

> . . . In the meantime, before I go I should like to give you my preliminary reactions to the many important questions raised in your letter of November 10th. It is plain that firm decisions about our tactics cannot be taken until the picture becomes a little clearer, and this is not likely to happen before the Trinidad elections on December 4th . . .

There is one point which seems to me to call for comment, and that is the handling of the Arthur Lewis report itself. As I understand it, circulation of the report has so far been confined to the Federal Cabinet, though unit Ministers have been made aware of his principal recommendations orally by Professor Lewis himself. You mentioned in one of your earlier letters that he might produce a special version of the document for Williams' benefit, and I wondered if the Federal Government had any plans for making his principal recommendations available to unit Governments in written form. I am at this stage merely asking this question for information and not suggesting that in my view something of this kind ought to be done. Clearly there would be advantage in giving the unit Governments some definite proposals, such as Arthur Lewis's (which at first sight appear eminently reasonable) to get their teeth into. On the other hand, for them to be circulated by the Federal Government might automatically prejudice consideration of them in some quarters, particularly in Trinidad. I should, however, like to know how they are being handled . . . (Maudling to Hailes, 20 November 1961).

The British government had not yet settled on its tactics for the future of the federation and were apparently awaiting the outcome of the general elections in Trinidad and Tobago. Meanwhile, the Colonial Secretary was preparing Hailes to consider a number of options and he was high in praise for the Lewis report, which he felt ought to be circulated, but not by the federal government.

In an immediate, secret and personal telegram on 29 November to Hailes, from Colonial Office Minister Hugh Fraser wrote:

Secretary of State (who is still in Africa) has now told us he will be able to pay visit of approximately 12 days. He will probably leave London on 15th January . . . but he would have to be back in London a reasonable time before opening of Jamaican Constitutional Conference which on present thinking cannot start before 31st January . . .

4. Regarding Williams our intention is that as soon as election result is declared Secretary of State should send him friendly message in which he would mention visit . . .

6. What Lewis told me was that he must in any case be in Trinidad in latter half of January on University business. There would be no need to whistle him up specially from Jamaica.

7. I take it we need not conceal from Adams that we have seen Lewis' report (it was circulated as Cabinet document and automatically sent to you). We pro-

pose to sound Adams gently while he is here as to what he thinks of it (Fraser to Hailes, 29 November 1961).

Fraser was making preparations for the visit by the Colonial Secretary to the West Indies in January 1962. At the same time, he was also handling the discussions on the Lewis report, which the Colonial Office proposed to have when Adams was in London. Lewis was planning to make himself available for meetings in January when the Colonial Secretary was in Trinidad, because he, too, had to be in Trinidad on university business. The end game was beginning to take shape and Lewis, Williams and the Colonial Secretary were going to be part of it.

WAS LEWIS NO LONGER DESIRABLE?

By 1 December, the desirability of having Lewis around in January when the Colonial Secretary was in Trinidad was beginning to wane. This is reflected in an immediate, secret and personal telegram to Fraser at the Colonial Office from Hailes, dated 1 December:

> 6. Your paragraph 6. Lewis' visit to Trinidad. The point of my remarks in paragraph 5 of my telegram Personal No. 257 was that while Lewis may be here on genuine university business his presence here could be misunderstood. Hochoy also writes 'whether Lewis is here or not makes no serious difference although I still hold that it would be better if he was not' (meaning until sent for). I agree.
> 7. Your paragraph 7. I consulted Adams before sending Lewis' report to you; no doubt Adams will say that he likes the report but I expect he may well regret having accepted Lewis' offer in the first place in view of its findings which will not suit his own designs for a so-called Federation of eight . . . (Hailes to Fraser, 1 December 1961, Repeated to Governor, Trinidad).

It was apparent that Hochoy was now lukewarm about the idea of Lewis coming to Trinidad when the Colonial Secretary was there, and this marked a turning point in the advance of the Lewis plan for a Federation of Nine that would have included Trinidad and Tobago.

Hochoy told Hailes that the presence of Lewis would make no difference and added that he would prefer that the advisor not be present. He apparently sold Hailes on the idea as he, too, was in agreement. The undercurrent of all of this was that Lewis had become persona non grata and was no longer desired politically. He had completed his task for the federal prime minister. Hochoy, as the governor of Trinidad and Tobago, would have been aware that Williams had no further use for Lewis and that what was likely to happen in January 1962 would render Lewis irrelevant to the outcome.

By 14 December, Fraser wrote to Lewis in a very diplomatic manner, which was reflective of what was happening between the Colonial Office in London and the Federal Governor-General's Office in Trinidad. The following excerpt captures this change of mood:

> When last we met I promised I would keep you informed of our thinking and that you could perhaps drop me a line on yours. I have not done so before as my Secretary of State has been in Africa.
>
> I told him of our talk which interested him greatly and we are just about to announce that he proposes to visit Trinidad about the 16th January to discuss the situation with Eric and other local leaders. At this distance it is very difficult to see precisely how the hand should be played but our thoughts – that is to say your thoughts and mine or mine, shall we say, as influenced by our meeting – remain the chief premise of our considerations. If, however, following your visit to Barbados and your reported visit with the new Premier to Eric, you have any new ideas I would be very happy to hear them.
>
> The Secretary of State plans to be in Port-of-Spain from around the 15th to the 27th January. You told me that you expected to be down there on university business about this time but if not, it would be most useful if you could hold yourself ready during that time to go to Port-of-Spain so that the Secretary of State could have the benefit of your advice . . . (Fraser to Lewis, 14 December 1961).

Fraser essentially tempers the original desire for Lewis to be present in Trinidad in mid-January 1962 into holding himself available to travel, if needed, when the Colonial Secretary was going to be there. This was an obvious shift. Lewis would have had enough experience to know that the game had changed now that Williams had been reelected.

One very significant item in Fraser's letter to Lewis was the mention of his visit with the new premier of Barbados to Williams. Such a visit indeed took place after the general election in Barbados, which was held on the same day as Trinidad and Tobago's – 4 December, but Lewis was not there.

One of Williams' ministers – Kamaluddin Mohammed – reported the effect of this meeting between Barrow and Williams to me when I was writing his (Mohammed's) biography. I wrote at the time:

> Shortly after the general elections of 4th December, 1961 in both Barbados and Trinidad and Tobago, Errol Barrow went to see Williams in Tobago to urge him to reconsider his position on the Federation. Williams felt that Barrow did not know what he was letting himself in for as he (Barrow) had not taken part in the federal negotiations before the Jamaican referendum. Williams refused to bend and this left Barrow very disappointed. It was to be an event that discoloured relations between these two Caribbean leaders for a long time to come and may have helped Williams to make up his own mind about what he should do. As to where the motivation for Barrow paying Williams a visit came from; it seems as though Arthur Lewis was instrumental in urging Barrow to do this (Ghany 1996, 150).

It was apparent that the meeting between Williams and Barrow in Tobago did not go very well. In 1966, when Barrow was addressing the Barbados House of Assembly on 4 January, to urge the British government to call a Barbados Independence Conference, he repeated a point of view expressed to him by Williams before the federation was dissolved: ". . . If I say that Dr Williams said that the proposal to have freedom of movement would create serious problems which Trinidad could not support and did not intend to support even after the end of ten years, is this supposed to be abuse of your neighbours?" (Haniff 1987, 71).

This was a clear reference to Lewis' proposal for freedom of movement in his report for Adams. Some five years later, it still seemed to rankle Barrow. The Williams-Lewis relationship had clearly been soured on the issue of freedom of movement. That issue remains a sore point in CARICOM more than fifty years later, as it is unresolved at the time of writing.

WILLIAMS CHANGES HIS APPROACH

There is no doubt that Williams' mood about a revised federation could now be revealed after he won re-election and subsequent to the visit by Barrow after the election victory. Hailes reported to the Colonial Secretary on a meeting he had with Williams and it was obvious that he (Williams) had other plans and this was clearly brewing in advance of the Colonial Secretary's visit. Hailes reported:

> After discussing with Hochoy, I saw Williams for an hour this morning, and made the points set out in paragraph 3 of your personal No. 385. He listened in silence, and then started on a monologue in which nearly everyone came in for castigation. I shall be sending you an account of this conversation in detail by the next bag, though most of it is not new. Meanwhile, this is simply to say that it is certainly not (repeat not) now necessary for you to send a special message to him. He said on parting that he had not replied to you, as it did not seem an answer was required . . . I did get over the point that you hoped that he would not feel it necessary to make public statements on matters affecting the future. He said that he would of course not be doing so, because matters of policy were decided by the party, and their Convention would not meet until 28th January (Hailes to Maudling, 16 December 1961).

Hailes had no idea that Williams had shifted the goal post by speaking about his party convention and that he would remain silent until that time. Williams had a plan and he was playing for time.

LEWIS CHANGES HIS VIEW OF WILLIAMS

In a secret letter to Hugh Fraser on 2 January 1962, written on a UCWI letterhead and signed by Lewis as principal in reply to Fraser's letter of 14 December instant, Lewis expressed his change of view on the revised federation as follows:

> Thank you for your letter of 14th December. I shall be in Trinidad from January 13 to 24. I shall see Bird and Barrow on my way down. I have not seen Dr. Williams since the beginning of November. However, from studying his speeches, and from what he said then, I conclude the following –
> (1) He would prefer 'association' with other territories to going it alone, but will go alone if he does not get his terms.
> (2) 'Association' does not mean federation. It means a unitary state, with other territories having the same status as Tobago.
> (3) He knows that this will not be acceptable to all the other territories. He would be content to have Grenada and St Vincent come in alone; St Lucia and Dominica too if they so desire.

(4) He will probably ask for a dowry as the price of taking any of the smaller islands into association; and will probably refuse if there is no dowry.
My reaction to this would be to let Trinidad go it alone, and establish the other islands as a federation centred on Barbados . . . (Lewis to Fraser, 2 January 1962).

Lewis had changed his view about Williams and there was an element of bitterness in his tone. One can only speculate about this *volte face* in relation to his more upbeat view about Williams leading up to the general election in Trinidad. Something happened after that election and there may be good reason to believe that it had something to do with Barrow's failed visit to Williams. In his letter to Fraser, Lewis had this to say about Barrow's visit to Williams: ". . . His attitude to Dr Williams was one of suspicion, and it took all my persuasive powers to get him to take the initiative in seeking an interview. I have not seen him since, and do not know what his attitude now is . . ." (Lewis to Fraser, 2 January 1962).

This part of Lewis' letter confirms the view of Kamaluddin Mohammed (above) that Lewis had influenced Barrow to visit Williams after their respective general election victories. It is clear now that Lewis had soured on Williams and he was quite prepared to recommend that Trinidad and Tobago be excluded from a future Federation of the West Indies.

WILLIAMS WITHDRAWS AND THE FEDERATION IS FINISHED

Having won the elections and formed a new government, Williams turned his party, the People's National Movement (PNM), to the task of considering its position on the future of the Federation of the West Indies. He timed a resolution that he had prepared for his party to be debated by its General Council on 14 January 1962, which coincided with Maudling's visit to Trinidad.

The resolution of withdrawal from the federation was accepted by the General Council of the PNM and Williams announced that Trinidad and Tobago would withdraw. The resolution read:

Be it therefore resolved that Trinidad and Tobago reject unequivocally any participation in the proposed Federation of the Eastern Caribbean and proceed forthwith to National Independence, without prejudice to the future association in a Unitary State of the people of Trinidad and Tobago with any Territory of the Eastern Caribbean whose people may so desire and on terms to be mutually agreed but in any case providing for the maximum possible degree of local government.

And be it further resolved that the P.N.M.'s Government in Trinidad and Tobago take the initiative in proposing the maximum possible measure of collaboration among the units of the disintegrated Federation in respect of such common services as the university and communications.

And be it further resolved that Trinidad and Tobago declare their willingness to associate with all the people of the Caribbean in a Caribbean Economic Community and to take such action as may be necessary for the achievement of this objective (PNM General Council Resolution, 14 January 1962).

Trinidad and Tobago had suddenly moved from a position of negotiating its independence as part of a revised Federation of the West Indies to seeking its own independence on the basis of a party resolution adopted by the General Council of the PNM.

According to Anthony Payne, who confirms the discord between Barrow and Williams as a result of their meeting in Tobago right after their respective election victories, Williams' attitude had created animosity:

When they heard the text of the resolution, the leaders of the eight remaining territories, who were all in Trinidad to consult with Maudling, agreed between themselves to form a new federation and (Gairy, the Premier of Grenada, briefly excepted) to ignore Trinidad's unitary state offer. Maudling appeared dubious, questioning the practicality of their plan, but was persuaded in the end that a merger with Trinidad – which in the view of the Colonial Office was the neatest solution – was indeed impossible. In his own talks with Maudling, Williams made no attempt to pursue the unitary state idea, whilst, for their part, the leaders of the other Eastern Caribbean islands privately made it clear that they had no intention of bowing to the terms offered by Trinidad, terms which they took to be the portent of a new local imperialism which would require their small island units to abandon their individuality and become wards of Trinidad after the example of Tobago. The new Premier of Barbados, Errol Barrow, who had flown to see Williams the previous December to offer his co-operation in building an Eastern Caribbean federation, articulated their views when some months later he referred to the PNM offer as 'the most gratuitous insult that could ever have been extended to any group of people' (Payne 1980, 33).

The federation was now over and only the final rites were left to be performed. Lewis had had a change of heart by the beginning of 1962 and Williams' political actions were consistent with his own feelings, as expressed in his letter to Fraser.

There would never be a Federation of the Little Eight for which Lewis had hoped if Trinidad and Tobago withdrew from the proposed revised Federation of Nine. The final rites were confirmed at a meeting of the British Cabinet on 6 February 1962:

> 3. The Colonial Secretary said that he would be expected to make an early statement in Parliament on his recent visit to the West Indies. His primary object had been to discuss with the leaders of the Governments in the Eastern Caribbean the situation arising from Jamaica's desire to leave the West Indies Federation. The main elements in the situation were that the Government had accepted the decision of Jamaica to withdraw from the Federation; that Trinidad and Tobago had decided not to participate in any federation of the Eastern Caribbean; and that the Ministers in the Leeward and Windward Islands, while advocating a new federation between their territories, were agreed that the present federation should be dissolved . . . (British Cabinet Conclusions, 6 February 1962).

It was Williams' machinations to outmanoeuvre Lewis, the Colonial Office, the federal government and the other Eastern Caribbean leaders politically that sounded the death knell for the federation.

The Lewis/Williams divergence on this issue led to disunity that soured the emergence of the regional movement, whose bitter taste rolled over into the early beginnings of further attempts at regional unity as captured by Payne (1980). Quite frankly, that disunity never went away and lives on today.

REFERENCES

Ghany, Hamid. 1996. *Kamal: A Lifetime of Politics, Religion and Culture*. St Augustine: Multimedia Production Centre, School of Education, the University of the West Indies.

Payne, A.J. 1980. *The Politics of the Caribbean Community 1961–1979: Regional Integration among New States* (Manchester: Manchester University Press, 1980), 299 pp.

Tignor, Robert. 2006. *W. Arthur Lewis and the Birth of Development Economics.* Princeton and Oxford: Princeton University Press.

OFFICIAL PUBLICATIONS

Archives of the Federation of the West Indies, The West Indies Cabinet, Sixty-Fifth Meeting, 22 September 1961, Mins. 579 and 580.

The Report of the Jamaica Independence Conference, 1962. Cmnd. 1638/1962 (London: Her Majesty's Stationery Office.

UK National Archives: CO 1031/3278, Macleod to Macmillan, Secret, P.M. [61] 73, 22 September 1961.

UK National Archives, CO 1031/3278, Mordecai to Macleod, Emergency, Secret and Personal, Personal No. 197, 21 September 1961.

UK National Archives, CO 1031/3278, Mordecai to Ambler Thomas, Secret and Personal, 23 September 1961.

UK National Archives, CO 1031/3278, Secret, Meeting at the Colonial Office on Tuesday, 26 September 1961.

UK National Archives, CO 1031/3278, Frank Williams to Mordecai, Secret No. 522, 27th September 1961.

UK National Archives, CO 1031/3278, Press Release issued after Meeting between Secretary of State and Federal Delegation, 28 September 1961.

UK National Archives, CO 1031/3278, Press Release issued after Meeting between Secretary of State and Jamaica Delegation, 5 October 1961.

UK National Archives, CO 1031/3278, Excerpts from the Premier's Press Conference, 8 October 1961.

UK National Archives, CO 1031/3278, Mordecai to Ambler Thomas, Secret and Personal, 11 October 1961.

UK National Archives, CO 1031/3278, Ambler Thomas to Mordecai, Secret and Personal, 16 October 1961.

UK National Archives, CO 1031/3278, Acting Governor-General (Ref. P.M. 12/016) to FEDER Governors & Administrators (excluding Jamaica), Confidential Circular Savingram No. W.I. 715/61, 16 October 1961. Repeated for information to Secretary of State (No. 626) and Governor, Jamaica (No. 2021).

UK National Archives, CO 1031/3278, Hailes to Maudling, Secret, 17 October 1961.

UK National Archives, CO 1031/3278, Hailes to Maudling, Personal, 21 October 1961.

UK National Archives, CO 1031/3278, Hailes to Thomas, Secret and Personal, 4 November 1961.

UK National Archives, CO 1031/3278, Hailes to Maudling, Secret and Personal, 10 November 1961.

UK National Archives, CO 1031/3278, Hailes to Maudling, Secret and Personal, 10 November 1961, Enclosure, Secret and Personal, Note by Dr A. Lewis.

UK National Archives, CO 1031/3278, Hailes to Maudling, Secret and Personal, 10 November 1961, Enclosure, Report to Sir Grantley Adams from W.A. Lewis, Special Adviser, dated 9 November 1961.

UK National Archives, CO 1031/3278, Maudling to Hailes, Secret and Personal, 20 November 1961.

UK National Archives, CO 1031/3278, Fraser to Hailes, Immediate, Secret and Personal, Personal No. 349, 20 November 1961.

UK National Archives, CO 1031/3278, Hailes to Fraser, Immediate, Secret and Personal, Personal No. 262, 1 December 1961. Repeated to Governor, Trinidad, Personal No. 14.

UK National Archives, CO 1031/3278, Fraser to Lewis, 14 December 1961.

UK National Archives, CO 1031/3278, Hailes to Maudling, Emergency, Secret and Personal, Personal No. 283, 16 December 1961.

UK National Archives, CO 1031/3278, Lewis to Fraser, Secret, 2 January 1962.

People's National Movement, General Council Resolution, 14 January 1962.

UK National Archives, British Cabinet Conclusions, CC (62) 11th Conclusions, 6 February 1962.

8

Dutch Disease in a Small Petroleum Exporting Country
Evidence from Trinidad and Tobago

ROGER HOSEIN, REGAN DEONANAN AND CARLTON THOMAS

WHILE THE DISCOVERY OF VALUABLE NATURAL RESOURCES SHOULD ideally be a blessing to an economy, research has shown that it can often lead to undesirable consequences. Corden and Neary (1982) and Kamas (1986), for example, found that it often leads to an appreciation of the real-effective exchange rate (REER) and a crowding out of other potential export sectors.

Trinidad and Tobago was a major beneficiary of the commodity boom in the 2002–2014 period.[1] Data from the World Bank indicates that the minerals export sector makes up the largest component of its export profile, which also expanded its share over the period of the commodity boom. Trinidad and Tobago's hydrocarbons sector, which includes oil, natural gas and petrochemicals, made up on average 83 per cent of exports over the 2000–2019 period.

Many studies have highlighted the country's experience and concluded that Dutch disease symptoms persisted over the last few decades (Gelb 1988; Hosein and Tewarie 2004; Moya, Mohammed, and Sookram 2010; Artana et al. 2007; Hilaire, Henry, and Ramlochan 2012; and Auty 2016). These studies, however, did not involve the use of empirical regression tools and, as such, none of the literature has explicitly identified the determinants of Dutch disease in Trinidad and Tobago, nor the relationships among the variables.

As such, the main purpose of this chapter is to firstly test whether the symptoms of the Dutch disease exist in Trinidad and Tobago. In doing so, it contributes to the literature by employing econometric methodology in examining the extent to which the real oil price has an impact on the real effective exchange rate (REER) over the 1980–2018 period.[2] Second, this chapter seeks to identify what factors contribute to the appreciation in the REER in Trinidad and Tobago, as well as the direction and magnitude of the relationship among the determinants and the REER. Third, the results from this chapter and the experiences of Trinidad and Tobago are used as the basis for providing some critical policy advice for countries that experience a natural resource boom, like neighbouring Guyana.

This is timely as ExxonMobil, over the period May 2015 to May 2021, has found more than nine billion barrels of recoverable oil resources in Guyana.[3] In December 2020, Guyana began commercial oil production at the Liza-1 development, which was designed to produce up to one hundred and twenty thousand barrels of oil daily. In fact, following its nineteenth discovery in December 2018, ExxonMobil (2021) noted that the find reinforces the potential for "at least six projects online by 2027" and up to ten floating storage, production and offloading vessels to develop the current resources.[4]

The rest of this paper proceeds as follows: section two outlines a review of the experience of Trinidad and Tobago. Section three provides a brief review of the major theoretical and empirical work on the topic. Section four outlines the regression model and methodology employed, and the results. Section five highlights other symptoms of Dutch disease that existed in Trinidad and Tobago. Section six then provides some policy recommendations and concluding remarks.

ANALYSIS OF THE TRINIDAD AND TOBAGO EXPERIENCE

The twin-island republic experienced a prior commodity boom over the 1973–1982 period and then adjustments from 1983 to 1993, so it has first-hand experience of the impact of improper management of windfalls on an economy. While Auty (2012) found "patchy evidence of policy learning in Trinidad and Tobago" during the 2004–2008 boom period, some researchers claimed that symptoms of the Dutch disease still existed.[5] The following highlights some of the areas where Trinidad and Tobago may have deviated from prudent policy advice in dealing with an energy boom.

First, on account of the energy boom, the state expanded spending on employment assistance schemes or 'make work' programmes like CEPEP.[6] Statistics during the boom period showed that unemployment levels were low and towards the latter half, near full employment levels,[7] with significant spare capacity in the manufacturing sector.[8] The provision of a social safety net is important to maintain for the most vulnerable in society, as the COVID-19 pandemic has highlighted, and may also be considered politically rational. However, the labour market intervention served to exacerbate any existing symptoms of the Dutch disease, as evidenced by the decline in manufacturing and agricultural employment in Trinidad and Tobago, together with a 41.2 per cent expansion in employment in the community, social and personal services (CSPS) group.[9]

Second, weak fiscal rules did not amply sterilize rents, but allowed them to be open to political manipulation in order to maximize allocation to budgetary spending over deposits to the Heritage and Stabilisation Fund.[10] Table 8.1 shows that while the net contribution to the HSF over the 2000–2020 fiscal period amounted to TT$12.3 billion,[11] this was equivalent to only 3.7 per cent of the energy revenues collected over the same period. This can imply that the HSF's current regulatory framework is not adequate to prevent the government from spending the rents.[12]

Fourth, like many other resource-exporting countries, windfall revenues motivated the state to expand its ownership of enterprises.[13] What often transpired was poor investment decision-making as most of the commercially oriented state-owned enterprises were loss making. Table 8.1 also shows that gross public-sector debt expanded significantly over the period.

Lastly, institutional quality deteriorated as energy rents were collected. Over the 2001–2018 period, Trinidad and Tobago witnessed the erosion of its social fabric, as murders spiralled upwards from 151 in 2001 to 536 by 2019, according to data from the Trinidad and Tobago Police Service. Additionally, our international rankings on the Corruption Perception Index worsened from thirty-one in 2001 to eighty-five by 2019. The relative ranking on the World Bank's Ease of Doing Business index also worsened to

Table 8.1: Central government energy revenues and increasing debt balance (TT$M)

Fiscal year	Total debt out-standing	Gross public-sector debt	Energy revenue	Expenditure on transfers and subsidies	Transfers and sub-sidies as percent of energy revenue	Non-energy fiscal balance	Heritage & Stabilization Fund: Gov't injections (US$)
1999–2000	22,097	28,346	3,689	3,980	108%	-3,929	0
2003–2004	24,940	38,730	7,642	7,911	104%	-6,419	2,593
2007–2008	41,692	60,412	32,463	20,114	62%	-18,172	0
2011–2012	63,134	87,928	26,626	27,206	102%	-28,779	272
2015–2016	88,449	119,709	6,644	27,856	419%	-14,617	-2,498
2017–2018	90,405	118,912	11,031	25,391	230%	-16,728	0
2018–2019	91,123	121,021	15,874	26,378	166%	-19,903	0
2019–2020	100,072	134,640	7,853	27,322	348%	24,625	-6644

Source: Central Bank of Trinidad and Tobago

an all-time low position of 105 out of 190 countries in 2019. Overall, Trinidad and Tobago not only quickly expended the energy rents it collected over the decades, but the rapid flow exacerbated fractures within its institutions, which deteriorated as focus shifted to the distribution of rents.

LITERATURE REVIEW

The resource curse posits that countries rich in natural resources tend to grow more slowly than those that are not.[14] In a repeat of the tests carried out by Sachs and Warner (1995),[15] Oomes and Kalcheva (2007), and Frankel (2012) found that the same negative relationship between natural resource exports and economic growth remained. Schmid et al. (2017), however, concluded that within the Caribbean region, commodity exporters performed much better and benefitted more than the group of commodity importers who faced higher prices over the 2000–2016 period. This was due to the unprecedented growth in the Chinese economy and its demand for natural resources, which motivated what has been referred to as a commodity pricing "super cycle" during the 2000s (see Erten and Ocampo 2013).[16]

The wider literature offers different schools of thought as explanations for the resource curse. Leite and Weidmann (1999), Sala-i-Martin and Subramanian (2003), Gylfason (2004), and Isham et al. (2005) provide evidence that poor institutional quality is responsible for the resource curse. Like the abovementioned studies, Acemoglu et al. (2005) claim that this poor institutional quality manifests itself in the display of rent-seeking behaviour and corruption. Another major explanation is that resource rents tend to be volatile, and that this volatility is not conducive to growth (Gylfason 2004; Van der Ploeg and Poelhekke 2009; and Cavalcanti et al. 2011). This chapter focuses on a third explanation of the resource curse – Dutch disease. Highlighted by Corden and Neary (1982), Kamas (1986) and Auty (1991), the hypothesis is, if a country experiences an exogenous boom in its exported natural resources, it leads to an appreciation of its real exchange rate and a crowding-out of its traditional export sector.

The account of the Dutch disease model underlying much of the literature is based on the work of Corden and Neary (1982). A major tenet of the work is their distinction between a resource movement effect and a spending effect on account of a natural resource boom. In their theoretical framework, an increase in the price of the booming tradable – holding incomes constant – will motivate the movement of labour from the sectors of the economy that are not experiencing an export boom – the non-booming and the domestic (non-tradable) sectors – into the booming tradable sector to facilitate expansion. This is the resource movement effect. The competition to attract labour in the rest of the economy manifests itself in the form of increased wages. This increasing income level in the rest of the economy eventually leads to increases in demand and price in the non-tradable sector. This represents the spending effect. As far as evidence is concerned, the literature typically considers an appreciation of the REER and deindustrialization as satisfactory for concluding that symptoms of the phenomenon exist in an economy (Corden and Neary 1982; Oomes and Kalcheva 2007). The extent of the relationship between oil prices and the REER, and the significance of the results using other control variables, is therefore key to arrive at causal factors regarding the Dutch disease in Trinidad and Tobago.

The notion that the country experienced symptoms of the Dutch disease has been postulated by various authors over the last few decades. Gelb (1988) found that out of the six economies he analysed in the 1980s, Trinidad and Tobago and Nigeria were the most affected, and experienced appreciating real exchange rates in the 1974–1984 period. Hosein and Tewarie (2004) carried out diagnostic testing on the Trinidad and Tobago economy and found clear support for the phenomenon. Artana et al. (2007) concluded that the it is one of the reasons why the republic has had difficulty diversifying its economy and building its non-energy sector. Moya, Mohammed, and Sookram (2010) concluded that Dutch disease may have been a permanent phenomenon. Hilaire, Henry, and Ramlochan (2012) claimed that on account of the 1970s boom, Trinidad and Tobago presented a classic case of Dutch disease, and while the second boom was more tempered, evidence of symptoms persisted. Also, Auty (2016) concluded that the country "absorbed its rent too rapidly, which triggered Dutch disease effects that postponed the labour market turning point, thereby retarding competitive structural change, impeding self-reliant social capital formation and reversing political maturation".

However, the earlier studies did not delve into explicitly identifying the factors that led to appreciation in the REER, nor provide estimates of the extent of the relationships among the variables and the REER. As such, this study will employ regression analysis to provide evidence of the main factors that led to the appreciation in the REER and assess the relationships among the variables.

EVIDENCE OF DUTCH DISEASE USING REGRESSION ANALYSIS

ECONOMETRIC METHODOLOGY AND DATA

In assessing Dutch disease in Trinidad and Tobago, annual data was collected for the period 1980–2018 on the REER, real oil price (and the ratio of GDP per capita PPP ($ International) as a measure for the productivity differential[17] between Trinidad and Tobago and its major trading partners

(DIFF).[18] The choice of variables employed was based on papers by Oomes and Kalcheva (2007), Mironov and Petronevich (2015) on Russia, and Elwereflli and Benhin (2015) on Libya. Prior to analysis, all variables were also transformed into logs.

Table 8.2 (below) shows the results from unit root testing carried out via the Augmented Dickey-Fuller (ADF), Phillips-Perron (PP) and Kwiatkowski-Phillips-Schmidt-Shin (KPSS) test. Lag selection is based on the Akaike Information Criterion prior to unit root testing. Tests confirmed that the variables were either stationary at level or stationary at first difference. Further, unit root tests by Bai-Perron (2003) and Zivot-Andrews (1992) confirmed the presence of structural breaks and appropriate dummy variables were assigned for 2004 and 2014.

The Auto-Regressive Distributed Lag (ARDL) model[19] and test for cointegration via the Bounds test, as introduced by Pesaran, Smith, and Shin (2001), was chosen to test for the presence of a long-run relationship between the REER and its determining factors.[20] Justification of the methodology employed is based on papers by Mustapha and Masih (2016) on Nigeria; Amin and Murshed (2017) on Bangladesh; Gasmi and Laourari (2017) on Algeria; and Asmau, Agility, and Amina (2019) on Nigeria, where, in testing for evidence of Dutch disease, these researchers utilized the ARDL framework (see also Jahan-Parvar and Mohammadi 2011). This approach is also justifiable, given the small sample size as the coefficients derived are

Table 8.2: Stationarity testing results

Variable (constant specification)	Augmented Dickey-Fuller		Phillips Perron		Kwiatkowski–Phillips–Schmidt–Shin	
	Levels (P-Value)	1st Difference (P-Value)	Levels (P-Value)	1st Difference (P-Value)	Levels (LM-Stat)	1st Difference (LM-Stat)
Log (REER)	0.564	0.002*	0.74	0.003*	0.421*	0.147*
Log (ROP)	0.328	0.001*	0.315	0.000*	0.468	0.208*
Log (DIFF)**	0.078	0.200	0.485	0.050*	0.301*	0.232*

* Indicates significance at the 5 per cent level.

more reliable than under Johansen. Further, the ARDL model has been hailed in the literature for its simplicity, given its Ordinary Least Squares basis as well as the ability to test for cointegration among variables without establishing whether the series are I(0) or I(1).[21]

COINTEGRATION AND MODEL RESULTS

The base model is elaborated below.[22] This model[23] is sufficient since the major focus is to assess the impact of the real oil price on the appreciation of the REER, while ensuring that we account for the Balassa-Samuelson effect, since it can be a major influencer of the REER in developing economies. Habib and Kalamova (2007) also utilized this model in assessing whether the real oil price impacted the REER in Norway, Russia and Saudi Arabia. Following Pesaran, Smith, and Shin (2001), the ARDL model for LREER can be estimated as:

$$\Delta LREER_t = \alpha_0 + \alpha_1 LREER_{t-i} + \alpha_2 LROP_{t-i} + \alpha_3 LDIFF_{t-i} + \sum_{i=1}^{\kappa} a_i \Delta LREER_{t-i}$$
$$+ \sum_{i=1}^{k} b_i \Delta LROP_{t-i} + \sum_{i=1}^{k} c_i \Delta LDIFF_{t-i} + \varepsilon_t$$

where $\alpha_1, \alpha_2, \alpha_3$, represent the long-run estimates, a_i, b_i, c_i, are the short-run εt estimates, is the residual term at time t and Δ represents the difference operator.

We firstly utilized the Bounds test procedure as developed by Pesaran, Smith, and Shin (2001) to assess whether a long-run relationship among the variables exist.[24] Cointegration was confirmed at the 5 per cent level. Thus, we then sought to derive the long-run and short-run coefficients.

Cointegration among variables eliminates spurious regression and thus permits the use of an error correction model (ECM) to distinguish between the long-run and the short-run dynamics among the variables. After deriving the long-run coefficients, we then estimated an ECM to determine the short-run relationship among the variables. The negative and significant error correction term shows that deviations from the long-run equilibrium are corrected for during each period, reconfirming the results we found of the existence of a long-run cointegrating relationship among the variables. We present the results from the short-run and long-run analysis in Table 8.3.

Table 8.3: Estimated long-run and short-run results using the ARDL Approach

	Coefficient	P-value
Log Real Oil Price	0.26*	0.032
Log Productivity Differential	0.47*	0.049
Serial correlation		0.429
Heteroscedasticity		0.003
D (Log Real Oil Price)	0.11*	0.000
D (Log Productivity Differential)	0.45*	0.003
ECT (CointEq1)	-0.93*	0.000
Serial correlation		0.892
Heteroscedasticity		0.118

Note: * and ** denotes significance at the 5 percent level.
Source: Results from Eviews 10

In the model, real oil prices were found to have a positive and significant coefficient of 0.26 in the long run, implying that a 1 per cent increase in real oil prices results in a 0.26 per cent appreciation in the REER over the 1980–2018 period.[25] Thus, in line with Dutch disease theory, increasing real oil prices causes the REER to appreciate in Trinidad and Tobago. With the appreciation in the REER, competitiveness is reduced as non-energy exports become more expensive relative to other countries' exports.[26] The results also showed that the productivity differential had a larger impact on the REER than the oil price, in both the short and long run.[27]

Further, the positive and significant coefficient provides evidence to support the conclusion by Khadan and Ruprah (2016) that, for the Trinidad and Tobago economy, "there is a strong Balassa-Samuelson effect".[28] The results showed that a 1 per cent increase in the productivity differential on account of the energy boom led to in a 0.47 per cent and 0.45 per cent appreciation in the REER for the long run and short run respectively. The stronger Balassa-Samuelson[29] impact implies that the relatively stronger productivity gains are likely to influence prices, as wage pressures in the tradable sector eventually lead to inflationary pressures for tradables and non-tradables alike. Nevertheless, prior to policy prescriptions the causal relationships among these variables are assessed to confirm the internal dynamics.

TODA-YAMAMOTO NON-CAUSALITY TEST RESULTS

Many papers confirm a long-run, cointegrating relationship between real oil prices and the REER. However, the literature is not clear regarding the direction of causality among both variables (see Ahmed and Nazir 2016; Jiranyakul 2015; and Beckmann, Czudaj, and Arora 2017). The direction of causality is important to confirm since Dutch disease literature suggests that an appreciation in real oil prices will lead to an appreciation in the REER (Corden and Neary 1995; Oomes and Kalcheva 2007). Using results from multiple studies on oil prices and real exchange rate determinants, Rickne (2009) highlights that while some studies concluded that oil is a "petro-currency" (Oomes and Kalcheva 2007; Korhonen and Juurikkala 2009), others have found that the relationship between oil prices and the REER is either weak or insignificant (Akram 2004; Gauthier and Tessier 2002). In addition, some have even found a negative coefficient.[30] Therefore, as a further robustness check of the ARDL cointegration results, the Toda-Yamamoto[31] (1995) non-causality test was carried out. The empirical results in table 8.4 indicates that unidirectional causality from oil prices to the REER existed in Trinidad and Tobago over the 1980–2018 period. This makes economic sense since the long-run relationship was established above via the ARDL framework and supports the Dutch disease prognosis. The results also show unidirectional causality from real oil prices to the productivity differential.[32] Further, in line with expectations, the results from

Table 8.4: Causality results for Trinidad and Tobago – Model 1

Hypothesis	Chi-Square	Probability
No causality from LROP to LREER	6.940061	0.031*
No causality from LDIFF to LREER	3.128023	0.209
No causality from LREER to LROP	0.502569	0.778
No causality from LDIFF to LROP	0.061665	0.970
No causality from LREER to LDIFF	2.660388	0.264
No causality from LROP to LDIFF	4.756735	0.093**

Note: * and ** imply significance at the 5 per cent and 10 per cent levels respectively.

causality testing show that oil prices appear to be determined exogenously. Thus, the results confirm that an exogenous shock to oil prices leads to a unidirectional positive impact on the REER (evidence supporting the presence of Dutch disease).

The results do not directly confirm causality from the productivity differential to the REER, but this is somewhat expected since, according to the Balassa-Samuelson relationship, productivity gains in the tradable sector actually give rise to wage appreciation and subsequently this momentum spreads to the wider economy, eventually resulting in an appreciated REER. Thus, the significant result for causality from oil prices to the productivity differential provides supporting evidence of the presence of the Balassa-Samuelson relationship in Trinidad and Tobago.

OTHER SYMPTOMS OF DUTCH DISEASE

Table 8.5 (below) shows a decline in output for the agricultural sector, but an expansion in overall manufacturing output over the 1996–2016 period, in line with the booming energy and services sector, contrary to Dutch disease expectations.[33]

A review of export-oriented manufacturing data in figure 8.1, however, showed that while there has been expansion in manufacturing exports over the period, the rate of growth across each period has been on the decline, except for SITC 6, which captured metal products exports.[34]

Another major symptom of the Dutch disease, services sector expansion, can be seen from data on sectoral employment. Table 8.6 shows that service sector[35] employment expanded from 70.9 per cent share in 1991 to an 81.3 per cent share in 2004, and an 86.4 per cent share by Q2 2018.

Lastly, Central Bank data also showed general increases in wages across all sectors on account of the boom in oil and gas.[36] This is consistent with

Table 8.5: Output growth by sector, Trinidad and Tobago (1996–2016)

Date	Energy	Agriculture	Manufacturing	Services
1996–2016	5.7	-1.3	4.5	3.9

Source: Central Bank of Trinidad and Tobago

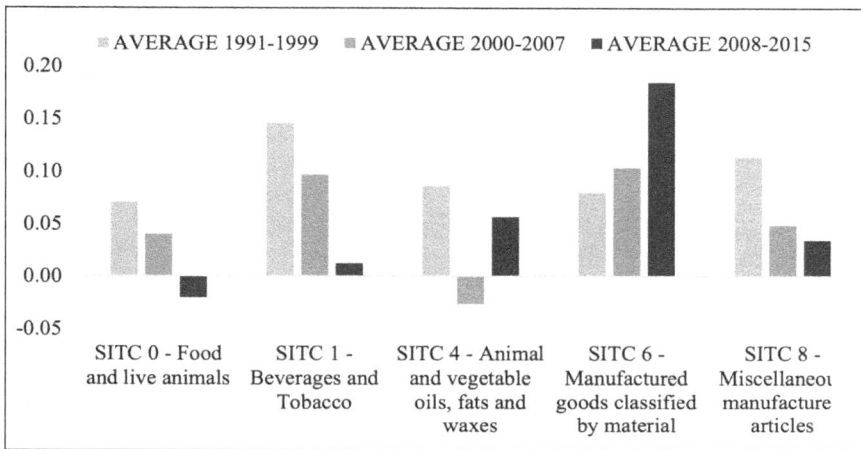

Figure 8.1: Average growth rates of manufacturing exports in Trinidad and Tobago (various years)
Source: World Bank's WITS Database

Table 8.6: Share of employment by sector, Trinidad and Tobago (various years)

	Agricultural	Manufacturing	Services	Oil and gas
1991	12.6%	11.7%	70.9%	4.8%
2004	4.6%	10.7%	81.3%	3.3%
2018Q2	3.5%	7.8%	86.4%	2.1%

Source: Central Bank of Trinidad and Tobago

Dutch disease theory, where spending and resource-movement effects of a hydrocarbon boom lead to higher wages throughout the Trinidad and Tobago economy. At work here also is the Balassa-Samuelson phenomenon, which was captured in the regression analysis earlier, confirming the strong, relative productivity gains and therefore wage appreciation throughout the economy. Table 8.7 shows that over the boom period wages expanded significantly in both the energy and manufacturing sectors, with the rate of wage growth moving closely with natural gas production.

However, it is difficult to clearly ascertain whether this growth in wages throughout the economy over the 1980–2018 period is attributed solely to Dutch disease or whether other factors can account for it. In fact, as the results showed earlier, the increase in real wages can be associated with increases in relative productivity in that sub-sector (Balassa-Samuelson 1959).

Table 8.7: Real wage growth index, Trinidad and Tobago (1980–2018, selected years)

Year	1980	1985	1990	1995	2000	2005	2010	2015	2016	2017	2018
Energy sector	46	84	87	93	100	131	157	146	144	145	151
Manufacturing sector	45	84	83	85	100	110	138	142	140	139	141

Source: Central Bank of Trinidad and Tobago

RECOMMENDATIONS AND CONCLUSION

This paper looked at data over the 1980–2018 period to ascertain if the symptoms outlined by Corden and Neary (1982) as attributes of the Dutch disease were present in the Trinidad and Tobago environment, and found clear evidence of an appreciated REER on account of a boom in oil prices. A major element of the results derived was a strong Balassa-Samuelson phenomenon at work, with a productivity differential coefficient of 0.47 in the long run and 0.45 in the short run. Therefore, the speed and mechanism by which energy rents enter an economy are critical, since while it can help governments expand the provision of goods and services, it can also place immense pressure on wages in the local economy. A critical recommendation for countries, therefore, is to ensure that a fiscal framework is utilized that will encourage or enforce an optimal windfall consumption pattern over the decades. Takizawa, Gardner, and Ueda (2004) found that while the balanced budget (Ricardo 1817; Smith 1937), or "hand-to-mouth" approach can lead to a rapid deterioration in the revenue stock, for capital-scarce economies like Guyana, they noted that it can improve welfare, "if government spending has positive externalities in production"[37] and is directed towards the growth-enhancing sectors.

However, while a larger share of revenue may need to be spent upfront in these economies, compared to a developed nation like Norway, legislation should be used to constrain any fiscal indiscipline by the government. The use of a sovereign wealth fund (SWF)[38] fiscal rules to prohibit the government from borrowing in periods when funds are deposited into a SWF is, therefore, also critical (International Monetary Fund 2019).

Additionally, Toda-Yamamoto causality results indicate evidence of unidirectional causality from real oil prices and the productivity differential to the REER, supporting earlier findings of their linkage in influencing an appreciation in the REER. An appreciated REER, as the evidence showed for Trinidad and Tobago, places significant pressure on other sectors of an economy to remain competitive. Multiple authors (Kaldor 1966, 1981; Al-Marhubi 2000; Agosin 2007; Lederman and Maloney 2007; and Damette and Seghir 2013) point to the benefits that can be derived from a diversified production and export base. Khadan and Ruprah (2015), however, noted that what is more important is to ensure that competitive advantages are also developed in other distinct sectors of the economy. Further, a review of economic data confirmed the presence of some relative deindustrialization in Trinidad and Tobago, and general wage rate increases. The intuition here is that an appreciating REER can erode competitiveness in non-booming export sectors and therefore countries that experience a natural resource boom should provide targeted support to ensure the survival of these sectors. Using Guyana as a continued example, husked brown rice and raw cane sugar represented its fourth and fifth- largest export products in 2018, worth US$208 million and represented 24 per cent of its non-gold exports. Guyana should, therefore, provide targeted support to ensure survival of the sector. Countries with similar sub-sectors who have initial built-up sectors should do the same.

Additionally, having a solid institutional framework is a major factor identified in the literature (Alesina et al. 2008; Noland and Pack 2003; Rodrik 2004; Acemoglu, Johnson, and Robinson 2002; Leite and Weidmann 1999) that can assist a country in reducing or overcoming the impacts of an energy boom. Wage appreciation, as seen in table 8.7, is only avoided if institutional checks and balances are strongly entrenched. Therefore, countries that experience a boom in a tradable good or service, as demonstrated by Botswana et al., can develop and maintain robust institutional frameworks so they can potentially inhibit rent-seeking activity and keep wage appreciation under control.

While other factors could have contributed to similar outcomes, tests confirm that the latest natural resource boom in Trinidad and Tobago resulted in the manifestation of most of the symptoms of the Dutch disease. Regardless, small countries that experience commodity booms should be cognizant of the decisions made by Trinidad and Tobago, and ensure that they implement some of the recommendations herein, to counter any deleterious impacts of any boom. Manufacturing in particular, because of the dynamism that it brings to an economy, should be protected. The COVID-19 pandemic, and the associated demand and price destruction that it brought to fore in commodity markets (World Bank 2020), points to a greater need for countries that receive large windfalls from energy rents to build up strong fiscal buffers to ensure resiliency against major disasters. However, nations who currently possess significant pockets of underdeveloped infrastructure should ideally spend a larger share of their income on improving infrastructure that will be vital for economic expansion and sustainability.

NOTES

1. Like most commodity exporters, Trinidad and Tobago experienced significant growth in revenues as oil prices and natural gas production expanded over the 2000–2016 period. Natural gas prices increased by 290 per cent over the 1999–2008 period, before declining to a 2016 average of US$2.52, while real oil prices over the 1999–2008 period increased from $27.83 to $111.57 per barrel, a 301 per cent increase. Over the 2000–2016 period combined oil and gas output increased by 170 per cent (World Bank 2018).

2. This period was chosen because it captures the latest commodity boom period, but was limited because of the availability of data for the respective variables chosen.

3. For ExxonMobil: Liza-1 in May 2015, Liza Deep in September 2016, Payara-1 in January 2017, Snoek in March 2017, Turbot-1 in October 2017, Ranger-1 in January 2018, Pacora-1 in February 2018, Longtail-1 in June 2018, Hammerhead-1 in August 2018, Pluma-1 in December 2018, Tilapia-1 and Haimara-1 in February 2019, Yellowtail- in April 2019, Tripletail-1 in September 2019, Mako-1 in December 2019, Uaru in January 2020, Yellowtail-2 in July 2020 Redtail-1 in September 2020 and Uaru-2 in April 2021. Further, Tullow has made three finds at Jethro-1, Joe-1 and Capara-1 wells in August 2019, September 2019 and January 2020 respectively. However, Tullow announced that with the first two wells the crude quality is poorer, and with Capara-1, the volumes are lower than expected.

4. In fact, Exxon is currently developing the Liza-2 and Payara fields, and is procuring infrastructure to produce a combined four hundred and forty thousand barrels of oil daily from the two projects by 2024. This, coupled with Liza-1's one hundred and twenty thousand barrels, is expected take maximum output to five hundred and fifty thousand barrels daily by 2024. Guyana anticipates that by 2027, production will be near one million barrels per day.

5. See Hilaire, Henry, and Ramlochan (2012); Moya, Mohammed, and Sookram (2010); and Auty (2016).

6. Community-Based Environmental Protection and Enhancement Programme (CEPEP)

7. Over the 2002–2014 period, the unemployment rate in Trinidad and Tobago averaged 6.29 per cent, reaching a low of 3.3 per cent in 2014, according to data from the Central Bank of Trinidad and Tobago.

8. See Ramlochan (2010) and *Central Bank Annual Economic Survey* 2018.

9. Data on the employment in manufacturing is available on the Central Bank of Trinidad and Tobago's website.

10. The existing rules require the state to save a minimum of 60 per cent of the total excess oil and gas production-derived revenues from what was budgeted in a financial year. What often transpires however is that the Minister of Finance – who also is the authority who must approve all withdrawals and deposits into the Fund – is able to set higher than expected budgetary figure and therefore guarantee that when there is a revenue surge, that the Government has full authority to spend it and is not constrained by fiscal rules regarding deposits into the HSF.

11. Further, as identified by the HSF 2020 Annual Report, for 2019/2020 there were "no deposits, however, four (4) withdrawals were made from the Fund during the 2019/20 financial year" equal to US$980 million (TT$6,644 million).

12. In fact, as many emerging economies have done, a sovereign wealth fund should ideally be coupled with robust fiscal responsibility legislation that will help curb the procyclical nature of discretionary fiscal policy and guarantee long-term debt sustainability.

13. Gelb and Grasmann (2004) cited a 2004 World Bank report which surmised that "at the turn of the century, public sector jobs represented around 80% of employment in the oil-rich countries of the Gulf." Hertog (2010) found that while state ownership appeared to be on the decline across the developing world, the opposite was true for a substantial number of resource rich countries who, motivated by windfall revenues, expanded participation in industries outside traditional utilities and natural monopolies. Further, Altunisik (2014) noted that for Arab countries, armed with natural resource revenues, the state is the major employer.

14. Earlier work by development economists, Prebish (1950) and Singer (1950) highlighted the "deteriorating terms of trade between primary products and manufactured goods."

15. In a cross-country study during the period 1970 to 1990, Sachs and Warner (1995, 2001) found a negative relationship existed between real GDP growth and the exportation of primary mineral resources.

16. See also Spatafora and Tytell (2008) and World Bank (2009).

17. The Balassa-Samuelson effect implies that a rise in productivity in the tradable sector will lead to an increase in wages in the tradable sector. The increased wages work its way throughout the economy, eventually leading to an increase in prices overall and thus an appreciation in the real effective exchange rate (REER). Thus, currency in a country that experiences a natural resource boom according to the Balassa-Samuelson effect is expected to lead to an appreciation in the real exchange rate.

18. The productivity differential was calculated using the top twelve trading partners of Trinidad and Tobago which included United States, United Kingdom, Brazil, Colombia, France, Germany, Barbados, China, Canada, Jamaica, Netherlands and Spain

19. Moreover, issues of endogeneity among the variables are avoided and the ARDL approach is more reliable than Johansen with smaller samples.

20. Further, diagnostic testing was also used to test for the presence of other symptoms of the Dutch Disease.

21. Belloumi (2014) and Menegaki (2019) hailed the superiority of the ARDL test in the presence of small and finite data sets. See Mustapha and Masih (2016) for a more detailed outline of the some of the limitations of other cointegration procedures like Engle and Granger (1987) and the Johansen procedure in the presence of small sample sizes.

22. Additional regressors like government expenditure were tried but the models did not behave well and therefore were excluded from final model.

23. Ramsey RESET Test does not show evidence of misspecification when model is run via Ordinary Least Squares (p-value of 0.39 so do not reject that excluded variables=0)

24. The model included two dummy variables for 2004 and 2014 and we confirmed the overall significance and robustness of the model.

25. Oomes and Kalcheva (2007) found that in the case of Russia, a 1% appreciation in the real oil price leads to a 0.50% appreciation in the REER. Mironov and Petronevich found a 0.25% positive relationship.

26. Similarly, booming gas production is expected to negatively impact export-manufacturing competitiveness because of the appreciating REER as both yield significant energy windfall revenues to an economy. Most studies that use oil and gas data, combine the influence of gas under the oil variable.

27. Habib and Kalamova (2007) found that the productivity differential variable is "particularly important for a transition country that has been subject to supply shocks" and that productivity growth would be larger in these economies as compared to an already advanced economy.

28. In a detailed study on the robustness of Balassa-Samuelson results from previous studies, Gulber and Sax (2016) found that confirmation of the Balassa-Samuelson effect is highly dependent on the model specification and dataset chosen.

29. Babatunde (2015) noted that this Balassa-Samuelson effect is important to consider since most productivity improvements would most likely be focused on the export-oriented sector and this sector will therefore also be vital for economic growth.

30. Fratzscher, Schneider and van Robays (2014); found that since the early 2000s, "causality between oil prices and exchange rates runs negative."

31. The Toda-Yamamoto causality test has been hailed in the literature for its superiority over Granger causality in the presence of non-stationary series since it avoids the potential biases and errors associated with Granger causality (See Mavrotas and Kelly 2001; and Wolde-Rufael 2005).

32. When the productivity differential (LDIFF) is the dependent variable, the resulting chi-square statistic (4.756735) is significant at the 10 per cent level, but when real oil prices (LROP) is the dependent variable, the causality result is insignificant – confirming unidirectional or one-way causality from oil prices to the productivity differential.

33. The intuition derived from the data is that the manufacturing sector in Trinidad and Tobago is highly dependent on growth in output from the oil and gas sector, probably manifested in the revenues that the state is able to spend via demand for goods and increased employment, thereby indirectly increasing demand for manufactured products.

34. Given Trinidad and Tobago's significant historical productive capacity in iron and steel, and given that metals prices are highly correlated with international oil prices, increasing oil prices would have led to an expansion in production and exports.

35. The services sector includes workers in retail, banking, insurance, education, government employees, construction, utilities, social services and communication sub-sectors.

36. Central Bank data further showed that over the period 1995–2017, wages in the refining and liquefaction of oil and LNG respectively increased the most – by 97 per cent, followed by the petrochemical sector (46 per cent).

37. For them, the critical factor that will ensure welfare gains from this fiscal approach is whether the economy is currently capital-scarce, and the quality

of government spending – or whether some portion of government spending is allocated towards GDP-growth enhancement areas. Nevertheless, as with all interventions, caution must be exercised. Sala-I-Martin, Doppelhofer, and Miller (2004) found that government spending is negatively correlated with long-run growth, and Maliszewski (2009) claimed that the hand-to-mouth approach can introduce volatility in government budgetary cycles from the commodity prices.

38. By reducing the rapid inflow of foreign exchange into the economy, a SWF can constrain any spending effect and avoid or slow the appreciation of real exchange rates.

REFERENCES

Acemoglu, Daron, Simon Johnson, and James A. Robinson. 2002. "An African Success Story: Botswana." CEPR Discussion Paper no. 3219. London: Centre for Economic Policy Research.

———. 2005. "Institutions as the Fundamental Cause of Long-Run Growth." In *Handbook of Economic Growth*, edited by Philippe Aghion and Steven Durlauf, Vol. 1A. Amsterdam: Elsevier.

Agosin, Manuel. 2007. "Export Diversification and Growth in Emerging Economies." Working Papers wp233, University of Chile, Department of Economics.

Ahmed, Shujaat S., and Sidra Nazir. 2016. "Oil Prices and REER with Impact of Regime Dummies." *Journal of Economics Bibliography*, KSP Journals 3 (1): 123–33.

Akram, Qaisar F. 2004. "Oil Wealth and Real Exchange Rates: The FEER for Norway." Norges Bank Working Paper 2004/16.

Al-Marhubi, Fahim. 2000. "Export diversification and growth: an empirical investigation." *Applied Economics Letters* 7 (9): 559–62.

Altunisik, Meliha B. 2014. "Rentier State Theory and the Arab Uprisings: An Appraisal." *Uluslararası İlişkiler/International Relations* 11 (42): 75–91.

Amin, Sakib, Muntasir Murshed, and Muntasir Murshed. 2017. "Remittance, Exchange Rate and Dutch Disease: The Case of Bangladesh." *International Review of Business Research Papers* 13 (2).

Artana, Daniel, Sebastián Auguste, Ramiro Moya, Sandra Sookram, and Patrick Watson. 2007. *Trinidad and Tobago: Economic Growth in a Dual Economy.* Washington, DC: Inter-American Development Bank.

Asmau, Yakubu J., Michael S. Agility, and Abarshi J. Amina. 2019. "Dutch Disease: Myth or Reality? An Analysis of the ARDL Model." *International Journal of Business, Economics and Management* 6 (3): 130–40.

Auty, Richard. 2016. "Natural Resources and Small Island Economies: Mauritius and Trinidad and Tobago." *Journal of Development Studies* 53 (2): 264–77.

———. 1991. "Resources-based industry in a boom, downswing and liberalization: Mexico." *Energy Policy* (January/February): 13.

———. 2012. "Is There a Policy Learning Curve? Trinidad and Tobago and the 2004–2008 Hydrocarbon Boom." In *Beyond the Resource Curse*, edited by Brenda Shaffer and Taleh Ziyadov, 84–109. Philadelphia: University of Pennsylvania Press.

Baffes, John, Donald Mitchell, Elliot (Mick) Riordan, William Shaw, Shane Streifel, Hans Timmer. 2009. *Global Economic Prospects 2009: Commodities at the Crossroads* (English). Washington, DC: World Bank. http://documents.world-bank.org/curated/en/586421468176682557/Global-economic-prospects-2009-commodities-at-the-crossroads.

Bai, Jushan, and Pierre Perron. 2003. "Critical values for multiple structural change tests." *Econometrics Journal* 6: 72–78.

Balassa, Bela. 1964. "The Purchasing Power Parity Doctrine: A Reappraisal." *Journal of Political Economy* 72 (6): 584–96.

Beckmann, Joscha, Robert L. Czudaj, and Vipin Arora. 2020. "The relationship between oil prices and exchange rates: Revisiting theory and evidence." *Energy Economics* 88 (C):104772. https://doi.org/10.1016/j.eneco.2020.104772.

Belloumi, Mounir, 2014. "The relationship between trade, FDI and economic growth in Tunisia: An application of the autoregressive distributed lag model." *Economic Systems* 38 (2): 269–87.

Cavalcanti, Tiago, Kamiar Mohaddes, and Mehdi Raissi. 2011. "Growth, Development and Natural Resources: New Evidence Using a Heterogeneous Panel Analysis." *Quarterly Review of Economics and Finance* 51 (4): 305–18. https://doi.org/10.1016/j.qref.2011.07.007.

Central Bank of Trinidad and Tobago. Online Statistical Data Centre. Accessed at: https://www.central-bank.org.tt/statistics/data-centre.

Central Statistical Office of Trinidad and Tobago. Ministry of Planning and Development. Accessed at: https://cso.gov.tt/.

Corden, Warner M., and James P. Neary. 1982. "Booming Sector and De-Industrialisation in a Small Open Economy." *The Economic Journal* 92 (368): 825–48. https://doi.org/10.2307/2232670.

Elwereflli, Ali, and James Benhin. 2015. "Is the Dutch disease ample evidence of a resource curse? The case of Libya." *International Journal of Management and Applied Science* 1 (9) Special Issue 2 (October): 66–69.

Engle, Robert, and Clive Granger. 1987. "Co-Integration and Error Correction: Representation, Estimation, and Testing." *Econometrica* 55 (2): 251–76. https://doi.org/10.2307/1913236.

Frankel, Jeffrey A. "The Natural Resource Curse: A Survey." 2012. In *Beyond the Resource Curse*, edited by Brenda Shaffer and Taleh Ziyadov, 17–57. Philadelphia: University of Pennsylvania Press.

Gasmi, Farid, and Imene Laourari. 2017. "Has Algeria Suffered from the Dutch Disease? Evidence from 1960–2016 Data." *Revue d'économie politique* 127: 1029–58. https://doi.org/10.3917/redp.276.1029.

Gauthier, Celine, and David Tessier. 2002. "Supply Shocks and Real Exchange Rate Dynamics: Canadian Evidence." Staff Working Papers 0231, Bank of Canada, Ottawa.

Gelb, Alan et al. 1988. *Oil Windfalls – Blessing or Curse? (A World Bank Research Publication)*. Oxford: Oxford University Press.

Gubler, Matthias, and Christoph Sax. 2019. "The Balassa-Samuelson effect reversed: New evidence from OECD countries." Swiss Journal of Economics Statistics 155 (3): 1–21. https://doi.org/10.1186/s41937-019-0029-3.

Gylfason, Thorvaldur. 2004. "Natural Resources and Economic Growth: From Dependence to Diversification." CEPR Discussion Paper no. 4804.

Habib, Maurizio M., and Margarita M. Kalamova. 2007. "Are there oil currencies? The real exchange rate of oil exporting countries." Working Paper no. 839, European Central Bank. http://doi.org/10.2139/ssrn.1032834.

Hertog, Steffen. 2010. "Defying the Resource Curse: Explaining Successful State-Owned Enterprises in Rentier States." *World Politics* 62 (2): 261–301. https://doi.org/10.1017/s0043887110000055.

Hilaire, Alvin, Angela Henry, and Krishendath Ramlochan. 2012. "Dutch Disease in Trinidad and Tobago: Then and Now." Port of Spain: Central Bank of Trinidad and Tobago.

Hosein, Roger, and Bhoendradatt Tewarie. 2004. "Dutch Disease and Deja Vu: Policy Advice for the Trinidad and Tobago Economy in the Wake of a Second Oil Boom." *West Indian Journal of Engineering* 26 (2) (January).

International Monetary Fund. 2019. "Guyana: 2019 Article IV Consultation-Press Release; Staff Report; and Statement by the Executive Director for Guyana. IMF Staff Country Reports 2019 (296). Washington, DC: IMF. https://doi.org/10.5089/9781513514093.002.

Jahan-Parvar, Mohammad R., and Hassan Mohammadi. 2011. "Oil Prices and Real Exchange Rates in Oil-Exporting Countries: A Bounds Testing Approach." *Journal of Developing Areas* 45: 309–18. https://doi.org/10.1353/jda.2011.0020.

Jiranyakul, Komain. 2015. "Oil Price Volatility and Real Effective Exchange Rate: The Case of Thailand." *International Journal of Energy Economics and Policy* 5 (2): 574–79. http://doi.org/10.2139/ssrn.2468946.

Kaldor, Nicholas. 1966. *Causes of the Slow Rate of Economic Growth of the United Kingdom: An Inaugural Lecture.* Cambridge and London: Cambridge University Press.

———. 1966. "The Role of Increasing Returns, Technical Progress and Cumulative Causation in the Theory of International Trade and Economic Growth." *Economie Appliquee* 34 (4): 593–617.

Kamas, Linda. 1986. "Dutch disease economics and the Colombian export boom." *World Development* 14 (9): 1177–98. https://doi.org/10.1016/0305-750X(86)90119-1.

Khadan, Jeetendra, and Inder J. Ruprah. 2016. "Diversification in Trinidad and Tobago: Waiting for Godot?" IDB Policy Brief 256. Washington, DC: Inter-American Development Bank.

Korhonen, I., and Tuuli Juurikkala. 2009. "Equilibrium exchange rates in oil-exporting countries." Journal of Economics and Finance 33 (1): 71–79. https://doi.org/10.1007/s12197-008-9067-x.

Lederman, Daniel, and William F. Maloney. 2007. *Natural Resources: Neither Curse nor Destiny.* Washington, DC: World Bank; Palo Alto: Stanford University Press. http://hdl.handle.net/10986/7183.

Leite, Carlos, and Jens Weidmann. 1999. "Does Mother Nature Corrupt? Natural Resources, Corruption and Economic Growth." IMF Working Paper no. 1999/085. Washington, DC: International Monetary Fund.

Maliszewski, Wojciech. 2009. "Fiscal Policy Rules for Oil-Producing Countries: A Welfare-Based Assessment." IMF Working Papers no. 2009/126. Washington, DC: International Monetary Fund. https://doi.org/10.5089/9781451872736.001.

Menegaki, Angeliki N. 2019. "The ARDL Method in the Energy-Growth Nexus Field: Best Implementation Strategies." *Economies* 7 (4): 1–16. https://doi.org/10.3390/economies7040105.

Mironov, Valeriy, and Anna Petronevich. 2015. "Discovering the Signs of Dutch Disease in Russia." BOFIT Discussion Paper no. 3/2015. http://doi.org/10.2139/ssrn.2558004

Moya, Ramiro, Anne-Marie Mohammed, and Sandra Sookram. 2010. "Productive Development Policies in Trinidad and Tobago: A Critical Review." IDB Working Paper Series no. IDB-WP-115. Washington, DC: Inter-American Development Bank.

Mustapha, Ishaq M., and Mansur Masih. 2016. "Dutch Disease or Nigerian Disease: A Prima Facie? New Evidence from ARDL Bound Test Analysis." MPRA Paper 69767, University Library of Munich.

Oomes, Nienke, and Katerina Kalcheva. 2007. "Diagnosing Dutch Disease: Does Russia Have the Symptoms?" BOFIT Discussion Papers 7/2007. Bank of Finland, Institute for Economies in Transition. http://dx.doi.org/10.2139/ssrn.1001659.

Pesaran, M. Hashem, Yongcheol Shin, and Richard J. Smith. 2001. "Bounds Testing Approaches to the Analysis of Level Relationships." *Journal of Applied Econometrics* 16 (3): 289–326. https://doi.org/10.1002/jae.616.

Prebisch, Raul. 1950. The economic development of Latin America and its principal problems. New York: United Nations.

Ramlochan, Krishendath. 2010. "Measuring Capacity Utilization in the Manufacturing Sector of Trinidad and Tobago." *Economic Bulletin* XII (2): 77–83.

Sachs, Jeffrey D., and Andrew M. Warner. 1995. "Natural Resource Abundance and Economic Growth." Working Paper 5398. Cambridge, MA: National Bureau of Economic Research. https://www.doi.org/10.3386/w5398.

———. 2001. "Natural resources and economic development: The curse of natural resources." *European Economic Review* 45: 827–38. http://doi.org/10.1016/S0014-2921(01)00125-8.

Sala-i-Martin, Xavier, and Arvind Subramanian. 2003. "Addressing the Natural Resource Curse: An Illustration from Nigeria." NBER Working Papers 9804. Cambridge, MA: National Bureau of Economic Research. https://doi.org/10.5089/9781451856064.001.

Sala-I-Martin, Xavier, Gernot Doppelhofer, and Ronald I. Miller. 2004. "Determinants of Long-Term Growth: A Bayesian Averaging of Classical Estimates (BACE) Approach." *American Economic Review* 94 (4): 813–35.

Samuelson, Paul. 1964. "Theoretical Notes on Trade Problems." *Review of Economics and Statistics* 46 (2): 145–54.

Schmid, Juan P., Allan Wright, Kimberly Waithe, Mark D. Wenner, Dillon Clarke, Jeetendra Khadan, and Juan Jose Pradelli. 2017. "Commodities in the Caribbean." *Caribbean Region Quarterly Bulletin* 6 (2).

Seghir, Majda, and Olivier Damette. 2013. "Natural resource curse: A non-linear approach in a panel of oil exporting countries." MPRA Paper 51604, University Library of Munich.

Spatafora, Nikola, and Irina Tytell. 2009. "Commodity Terms of Trade: The History of Booms and Busts." IMF Working Paper, 09/205. Washington, DC: International Monetary Fund. https://doi.org/10.5089/9781451873528.001.

Takizawa, Hajime, Edward Gardner, and Kenichi Ueda. 2004. "Are Developing Countries Better Off Spending Their Oil Wealth Upfront?" Working Paper WP/04/141. Washington, DC: International Monetary Fund. https://doi.org/10.5089/9781451856217.001.

Toda, Hiro Y., and Taku Yamamoto. 1995. "Statistical inference in vector auto regressions with possibly integrated processes." *Journal of Econometrics* 66: 225–50. http://doi.org/10.1016/0304-4076(94)01616-8.

Van Der Ploeg, Frederick, and Steven Poelhekke. 2009. "Volatility and the natural resource curse." *Oxford Economic Papers* 61 (2009): 727–60. http://doi.org/10.1093/oep/gpp027.

Wolde-Rufael, Yemane. 2005. "Energy demand and economic growth: The African experience." *Journal of Policy Modeling* 27 (8): 891–903. https://doi.org/10.1016/j.jpolmod.2005.06.003.

World Bank. 2020. "A Shock Like No Other: The Impact of COVID-19 on Commodity Markets." Commodity Markets Outlook, April. http://hdl.handle.net/10986/33624.

———. 2018. "World Development Indicators, 2018." Washington, DC: World Bank.

Zivot, Eric, and Donald Andrews. 1992. "Further evidence of great crash, the oil price shock and unit root hypothesis." *Journal of Business and Economic Statistics* 10: 251–70.

9

Policy Shifts and Analytics in the Caribbean Setting
Stress testing Growth Models in the COVID-19 Reset

WINSTON DOOKERAN AND PREEYA S. MOHAN

THE COVID-19 PANDEMIC IS FORCING A RETHINK IN macroeconomics and generating geo-strategic shifts in the world of diplomacy. In this context, small Caribbean states face complex challenges in the formulation of growth strategies in the loop-type shock cycles as the old paradigms are looking tired. At the same time, the liberal order upon which global institutions were premised is in flux and the changing geopolitics is opening up strategic shifts in areas of diplomacy, particularly for small states. This chapter examines aspects of the underlying logic of the Lewis model of growth, and points out some of the policy concepts – linearity and convergence, circular economy, frontier development and complexity analysis – to which growth models must respond as we face the negative growth challenges of COVID-19. The chapter ends by looking at Caribbean states' response to COVID-19 and the lessons from new growth models as the region strives to build a sustainable future.

THE LEWIS MODEL OF ECONOMIC GROWTH

The Lewis model of economic growth, rooted in classical analysis, has been credited as seminal to the theory of capital and growth in development economics. It is thus important to understand the logic and argument of the model, and locate it in the literature at the time. It is also important to look at the underlying assumption of linearity in models of development and the idea of convergence in the development strategy coming out of the Lewis model.[1] We must ask the question: Is it relevant to the situation today?

ARTHUR LEWIS' INTELLECTUAL HERITAGE

Lewis once said, "My interest was in the fundamental forces determining the rate of economic growth." It was the focus of his 1955 classic, *Theory of Economy Growth,* which, in the words of Gustav Ranis "revolutionized contemporary thinking on development . . . as he saw the development problem as focusing on a change in the basic rules of operation of an economic system" (Ranis 2004, 4). In Lewis' seminal article of 1954, "Economic Development with Unlimited Supplies of Labour", which generated extensive literature at the centre of development theory, and for which Lewis received the Nobel Prize, he adopted an analytical framework that depicts a two-sector world, and placed focus on organizational dualism and the reallocation process of surplus labour in phases towards modern economic growth. In applying his theory to the problems of the developing world, Lewis affirmed that, "This article is written in the classical tradition, making classical assumptions, and asking the classical question" (Lewis 1954, 1). His model became *the* basic model of development in extensive, scrutinizing literature that made economic development respectable in the world of scholarship.

Much of the commentary on Lewis' early work, however, was not about policy issues so much but rather the classical assumptions that underlined his analysis and the rigour of his argument, for example, the classical assumption that all profits are saved, and all wages are consumed. Ranis sums it up as follows, "The crux of the contemporary critique of the Lewis model is the rejection of an exogenous bargaining wage or consumption share, exceeding the marginal product of labor at any point of time" (Ranis 2004, 11).

Lewis' model was in line with Kuznets' structural analysis of income distribution and no wonder had "substantial influence on subsequent work on the relationship between growth and equity" (Ranis 2004, 8). Much effort was placed on the engine of economic growth, and in "The State of

Development Theory", Lewis expressed his views on the changing drivers of the engine of economic growth as follows: "Every school has offered its candidate for the driver of economic growth. The Physiocrats, agriculture; the Mercantilist, an export surplus; the Classicists, the free market; the Marxists, capital; the Neo-Classicists, entrepreneurship; the Fabians, Government; the Stalinists, industrialization; and the Chicago School, schooling" (Lewis 1984, 7). Nonetheless, as Lewis was aware, whatever the logic that propels the drivers of economic growth, the economy-wide terrain and global flows also significantly influence the outcome of the development process.

LEWIS AS A DEVELOPMENT ECONOMIC STRATEGIST

In *The State of Development Theory* Lewis critically asserted that "Growth occurs whenever there is a gap between capability and opportunity. Capability covers skills (domestic and foreign), government, savings, and technology. Opportunity can be of any kind, including markets, rainfall, access to licenses, and infrastructure. The engine may be at home or abroad, an innovation, a good site for a transportation center, or much else" (Lewis 1984, 8). He concluded that a model for the economy is rather complex. There is no one growth theory, but a set of complementary theories –including a theory of government, where the government would appear to be as much the problem as the solution. The analytical challenge is predictability, as one is bringing together the forces of history, the workings of institutions and the determinants of structure to yield "self-sustaining growth", using Rostow's phrase for development. Attuned to the "fundamental forces determining economic growth", Lewis' notions of dualism and unlimited supplies of labour were essentially thus tied to the frame of his growth theory of structural change.

Economic development ideas, however, still implicitly assumed a linear trajectory: stages of growth (Rostow 1960); the trade-off in growth and equality (Kuznets 1955); equilibrium and steady states (Harrod 1939) and (Domar 1946); and linkage and input-output flows (Leontief 1986). The corresponding strategies for economic development were mainly premised on linear processes, which were held to be underlining the basic rules of operation in the economic system. At times, feedback loops were inserted into the analysis, which introduced a dynamic element to a static logic that defined development pathways.

EXAMINING CONVERGENCE IN GROWTH MODELS – FROM THEORY TO PRACTICE

For example, the economic convergence hypothesis, which emerges out of the linear theory of economic growth, leads to a policy imperative of integration. This ostensive flow concept of convergence is now one of the more discussed fields in economics. Several approaches to the convergence of economies – real, nominal and structural – have been studied as an addition to the primary integration literature. Robert Solow, in his 1956 article, "A Contribution to the Theory of Economic Growth", connected growth models' behaviour to the definition of convergence. He argued that conditional convergence could be observed due to diminishing returns to capital, a logic of the Lewis model as well.

Economic growth and convergence in the neoclassical growth models look at factors affecting long-run growth, which determines the welfare of countries. Attila Gasper distinguishes between real convergence (GDP per capita); nominal convergence (interest rates); and structural convergence (labour and competitiveness). The implication for development policy is that growth and convergence spell out a need for a catching-up process, and growth sustainability feeds on a wider economic space. The resultant quest for, and emerging dynamics of, convergence is, however, also a response to the limitations of the orthodox integration model, the quest for resilience and self-sustaining growth (Dookeran 2013). As such, the economic logic of convergence is not just about the enlargement of markets and trade; it is about creating new economic space that is inwardly resilient, globally competitive and able to capture opportunities in the future. New vulnerabilities emerging out of the structure and size of economies which affect growth have furthermore given rise to concerns with institutional factors in the study of the subject. This brings to the fore theories of institutional change that could shape the outcome of development in society. Coccia (2018, 1) defines institutions "as rules and expectations that govern human interaction and paths of development in society". He argues that understanding deinstitutionalization – the process by which institutions weaken and disappear – is critical to institutional change that brings new ideas, beliefs and practices. Institutions are resistant to change "which can threaten existing patterns of status, wealth and power" (Coccia 2018, 1). In some cases, institutional change will only take place if the operating space expands to accommodate the changing dynamics of the growth model and new rules are adopted.

INTEGRATING INSTITUTIONS AND GROWTH MODELS INTO A FRONTIER ANALYSIS

Manfred (2021) thus crafted a frontier development framework that skilfully aligns the economic notions of shocks, vulnerability and resilience in a governance map that includes the role of the state in development and identifies strategic variables in policy analysis. The key strategic focus is on the catalytic role of the state, transforming the growth culture, and integrating the informal economy and aligning institutions for performance. Out of this framework analysis, Manfred concluded that the development challenge ahead will call for a reconceptualization of the orthodox growth theory, and relatedly World Bank/International Monetary Fund neoliberal programmes of structural adjustment and stabilization in order to reset the policy imperatives for equitable and sustainable development.

THE CIRCULAR ECONOMY

In addition, for today's discourse on development strategy, the assumption of linearity in the economic development path is being tested by the notion of the circular economy. With the linearity notion, the operating system of the economy is based on the-end-of-life concept, while with circularity, reusing, recycling and recovering materials in the production, distribution and consumption processes are the core of drivers of change in resource efficiency. According to MacArthur et al. 2015, 1), "A number of factors indicate that the linear model is increasingly being challenged by the very context within which it operates and that a deeper change of the operating system of our economy is necessary." It raises the dimension of structural waste, as the current economy is surprisingly wasteful in its model of value creation. MacArthur et al. spell out this vision and provide the circular perspective in rethinking value creation in economic systems.

In this vein, a workshop was held at the University of Alberta in Edmonton, Canada, titled, "The Guyana Project: A New Approach to Sustainable Development in Guyana: Towards a Circular Economy and Resilience in Businesses". Among the project ideas that came out of the workshop was a follow-up on CARICOM Circular Economy Package for Sustainable Development. In 2017, the Platform for Accelerating the Circular Economy (PACE), a public-private sector collaboration was set up, hosted and facilitated by the World Economic Forum (WEF). This platform is to encourage developing countries to adopt strategies – finance and growth – that will accelerate action in circular economy initiatives. The Economic and Social Council of the United Nations held a plenary session on the application of the principles of the circular economy. In 2008, China, based on the 3R Framework – Reduce, Reuse and Recycle – outlined a Circular Economy Promotion Law of the People's Republic of China and subsequently signed a technical cooperation agreement with the European Union. The overall aim is to accomplish sustainable development by simultaneously creating environmental quality, economic prosperity and social equity.

COMPLEXITY ANALYSIS – A NON-LINEAR DESIGN FOR DEVELOPMENT

Linear thinking has been the logic frame in the design of growth models from Rostow's stages of economic growth to Smith and Ricardo's laws of economics and Marx's deterministic laws of capitalist development. While these linear mathematical models allowed for predictability, history has shown that "the world does not work that way" (Bryne 1998, 19). Rihani and Geyer (2001) drew attention to nonlinear systems – a complex adaptive system – as a more appropriate framework for the study of development. They argue that social behaviour is based on "order, chaos and self-organized complexity", and that development studies focus on understanding the connectivity of the network, where "a complex system has to adapt in response to changing conditions and survive long enough for the next cycle of adaptation to begin" (Rihani and Geyer 2001, 240). This is the genesis of the nonlinear paradigm as a framework for development.

Later, this would lead to designing tools to measure complexity, as an indicator of productive potential and knowledge intensity of the economy. These metrics for measuring complexity in economic structure are gaining much attention. Hausmann et al. (2013) drew the "atlas of complexity" for countries around the world as a tool to study the productive structure and its potential for change – the diversification process – that may lead to sustainable development. Such studies aim to measure the future growth potential of an economy by focusing on the production structure and its evolution. Recently, measures of economic complexity are being used to quantify a country's productive structure and has revived interest in the macroeconomic role of structural transformation. These measures are seen as useful as they are highly predictive of future economic growth and potentially social welfare, given that economic growth and income levels are linked to poverty levels and social wellbeing.

For example, Servedio et al. (2018) offer a new approach to the construction of macroeconomics metrics that quantify the "fitness of countries, the quality of their industrial system, and the complexity of commodities by indirectly inferring the technological requirements needed to produce them". In their analysis, the key idea is to consider international trade of countries as a proxy of their internal production system. In defining the precise strategies to improve countries' economies, they introduced the notion of convergence, making a distinction between rank and absolute convergence to ascertain a country's fitness and product complexity. In their analytics the leading part of fitness is given by diversification, and they concluded that there is a power-law dependence between inefficiency and the diversification of the country. As such, the new metrics – fitness index, index of complexity, and the diversification and inefficiency link – add new ways to measure production structures of economies.

How may macro management then influence the production structures of an economy? This topic was taken up by Brito et al. (2018,1), using the classical Mundell-Fleming model for open economies. The paper shows that "investment to real exchange rate movements varies depending on the production structure of the economy" (Brito et al. 2018). Where there is a high degree of structural economic complexity, the logic of the Mundell Fleming model holds – investment is positively associated with a real exchange rate depreciation. However, where the degree of complexity is low, the positive impact of a real exchange rate depreciation on price competitiveness tends to outweigh the negative impact associated with increased cost of imported capital goods (Brito et al. 2018). The distinguishing feature of how investment responds to exchange rate moves relies not so much on whether it is an advanced or emerging economy, but more so on the degree of complexity in the economy. The missing link between macro management and structural transformation is a key factor limiting the integration process in the region.

Diversification, in response to the issues of expanding economic space or addressing inefficiencies, is thus a huge challenge for the region. What drives economic diversification in Caribbean Community (CARICOM) economies and how is it linked to the degree of complexity in small economies? These analytics are basic to the design strategies that will populate the cells in Leontief's input-output models, showing how changes in one economic sector affect other sectors. As a strong advocate against relying too much on theoretical assumptions and non-observed facts, Leontief felt that "too many economists were reluctant to get their hands dirty" in the actual metrics in the calculus of development. Relatedly, in moving beyond models and theory, towards specifying the calculus of development, the actual political setting sets the ceiling, particularly for risk analysis and resource mobilization. This was made palpably evident in the context of the responses to the COVID-19 crises, to which we now turn in order to illuminate this crucial political variable, by way of brief examination of the CARICOM response to this unprecedented global shock.

CARICOM STATES AND COVID-19

For Caribbean states, CARICOM represents the dominant structure for regional cooperation for economic, political, health and disaster response; the states themselves had limited resources to respond nationally to the COVID-19 crisis. On 1 March 2020, the first confirmed case of COVID-19 in the Caribbean was reported in the Dominican Republic. On 11 March, the World Health Organization declared a global pandemic as the virus had spread to every region of the world. From January CARICOM heads of government had started their engagement when regional interest in

COVID-19 first began to develop, and by March CARICOM was actively developing a regional public health response to the pandemic (CARICOM Today 2020). Ministers of Health began a series of emergency meetings in February, from which emerged a regional protocol establishing minimum standards for dealing with the virus. This work was guided by the CARICOM Secretariat, the community's institutions and their international partners, including the Caribbean Public Health Agency (CARPHA), the CARICOM Implementing Agency for Crime and Security (IMPACS), the Regional Security System (RSS) and the Caribbean Disaster Emergency Management Agency (CDEMA). The Pan American Health Organization (PAHO) was also a major partner.

The number of positive cases in CARICOM was kept relatively low and member states were ranked among the best in the world in their response to the pandemic in many global assessments. CARICOM has attributed this success to the politically coordinated regional approach across its twenty-member group; the swift and deliberate actions taken by its leadership; and the expert guidance and support from its specialized community institutions (CARICOM Today 2020). The following positive actions were taken:

- As Ministries of Health built up their own testing capacity, the RSS facilitated the transportation of samples to CARPHA's testing facilities in Trinidad.
- Daily surveillance and modelling from the George Alleyne Chronic Disease Research Centre at The University of the West Indies, which worked closely with CARPHA.
- Special emergency meetings of CARICOM heads of government and health ministers through the Council for Human and Social Development (COHSOD).
- CDEMA, through its Regional Response Mechanism, coordinated the logistical arrangements for critical COVID-19 supplies.
- CARPHA and IMPACS trained front-line security officers on measures to protect themselves in the line of duty.
- IMPACS and the RSS teamed up to help member states prevent and mitigate the spread of the virus to prisons and correctional facilities.
- CARPHA, through its Tourism/Travellers and Health Programme, facilitated training sessions in the tourism sector, while also using the

programme to help restore visitor confidence in the region's tourism product.

Certainly, the core lesson of the COVID-19 pandemic is that complex global problems cannot be solved by internal efforts only. Indeed, alongside regional efforts, global coordination and diplomacy are needed to add new resources – technical, business and financial– to the solution matrix. The G20 countries began to talk, but much more is required to get a coordinated global economic response to the uphill tasks ahead. The Working Group of the Caribbean, established as a doorway to the G20, could be revived to provide a Caribbean voice to the global financial demands. In addition, the Special Drawing Rights window of the IMF must be redesigned for a fair share in the application of the immediate balance-of-payment resources. These and other initiatives require, too, an entrepreneurial approach to diplomacy as small states pivot for space and alternative pathways to sustainable wellbeing.

ANCHORING THE PRACTICE OF DIPLOMACY FOR SMALL STATES

Small states are often viewed as inconsequential to world politics, thus requiring innovative approaches in the practice of diplomacy. Baldacchino and Wivel (2020, 382) summed up the challenge: "Small states today remain restrained by limited capacity and capabilities in pursuing their domestic and international ambitions and are stuck as weak actors in asymmetric relationships, creating dependency and threatening their values and interests. However, they also benefit from being weak, since this allows them a bigger action space and success in pursuing coping strategies." Coping strategies in diplomacy for small states will indeed be tested in this era of geopolitical reset and reconfiguring quests for global solidarity, occurring alongside a period of tired paradigms and starting over again in the context of changing geo-strategic shifts.

For example, Klaus Schwab, executive chairman of the World Economic Forum, in a call for a new capitalism urged that "The great reset should seek to lend a voice to those who have been left behind, so that everyone who is willing to co-shape the future can do so . . . some of the pillars of the global system will need to be replaced, and others repaired or strengthened" (World Economic Forum 2020). Others, like *The Economist* (2020, 1), in calling for a rethink in macroeconomics in the post COVID-19 era, succinctly quipped, "What is clear is that the old economic paradigm is looking tired." Still, others are exploring global collective action and equitable approaches to COVID-19, as expressed in the T20 Task Force "COVID-19: Multidisciplinary Approaches Complex Problems" (Thomas et al. 2020).

These initiatives pose opportunities for and challenges to small states in forging a platform that is unique, capable of mitigating risks and mobilizing resources in a global policy setting. Will small nations find their wiggle space restricted or enhanced in a world order of ever-changing geo-strategic shifts adding complex challenges in the practice of diplomacy?

IS THE WORLD POLITICAL ORDER OF THE BRETTON WOODS VINTAGE NOW ON ITS KNEES?

Academics have argued that the world order moved from hegemons to multipolar, and even to a multiplex world. Now, it may better be described as flat– not G20, not G7, but rather a Go order: no hegemons, no multipolar, and no multiplex (Acharya). Global security alliances, emerging out of the Cold War, are now faced with new global challenges in cyber and information technologies, and populist politics at home. In this setting of transactional and real politic, different configurations of power relations are emerging, and we are beginning to see the following trends that may shape the future political order.

- The renewed focus on regionalism – resiliency versus efficiency – drives the global economy.
- The growing divide in inequality among and within nations.
- A changing direction in the flow of funds and shifts in the supply chain.
- Liberal democracies that are less liberal, with more authoritarian tendencies, but adhering to the fundamentals of democratic systems.
- A global order in which small nations and island nations will not have an automatic place.
- Hedging politics that will lead to floating coalitions, based on interest and realpolitik, not so much on power and ideology.

How will these trends affect global cooperation? Prime Minister of Singapore Hsien Loong (2020), concluded that the strategic choices that the United States and China make will shape the contours of the emerging global order. It is natural for big powers to compete. But it is their capacity for cooperation that is the true test of statecraft, and it will determine whether humanity makes progress on global problems such as climate change, nuclear proliferation and the spread of infectious diseases. Will the Caribbean region be ready for the geo-strategic shifts? In the quest for a stable, peaceful international order, while preserving our strategic autonomy, small states will be on a constant search for strategic opportunities. Perhaps the strategic logic of our times will see the advent of floating coalitions in response to countries hedging in this fluid geopolitical climate. Countries like ours in the Caribbean cannot afford to be bystanders, but must engage constructively in the present order of things. Drawing on the lessons of COVID-19, the Caribbean will face strategic choices in the practice of diplomacy, and concrete actions will depend on an assessment of the following:

- Focus on regional pandemic surveillance and public health coordination;
- Select bridges for communications with major countries and adopt new protocols for decision making;
- Negotiate an economic platform with international financial institutions with both short- and long-term perspectives;
- Work out flexible arrangements in health diplomacy and development finance, and be partners in floating coalitions of the present;
- Secure access to the benefits of global research in medical science.

The pandemic has shaken up the foundations of the world of public policy – in finance, in politics, in health and elsewhere, if it is treated as temporary, we would have lost forever the opportunities for making public policy changes that are critical to our times. In this sense, notwithstanding its huge 'life and livelihood' costs across the globe, the pandemic may well be a catalyst for geopolitical shifts in the world order of things.

COVID-19 AND THE IMPERATIVE FOR NEW GROWTH STRATEGIES

In fighting this public health crisis, steps to suppress the spread; enhance the health system; find resources for immediate treatment; and pursue the protocol for discovering a vaccine have engaged governments widely. But what was most telling was the economic fallout of this effort. Global economic activity dropped dramatically in an uncertain policy environment. Awareness of the full implications of this falling off the edge is growing as the impact becomes multifaceted in several spheres.

As the economy enters into a 'loop type' cycle of shocks – between demand and supply – old policy prescriptions for recessionary times may no longer work. The COVID-19 crisis has induced a supply shock – reducing wages and production – which in turn fuel a demand shock- fall in purchasing power. This becomes a 'loop type' cycle of shocks in growth models, and shock absorbers mitigate the effects on growth. But buffers and shock absorbers are weak in the Caribbean economy. Shocks are absorbed through adjustments in labour and austerity. But that will work, depending on the magnitude of the shocks. Already, it is argued that to prevent an immediate collapse, the size of the fiscal injection must be equivalent to the fall in the gross domestic product (GDP). This is a tall order in any circumstance, and has dire complications for debt, credit, income and poverty levels. It is beyond current financing modes used and the prospect of recovery in a loop-like cycle. We are in unchartered waters, and the choice between lives and livelihood is already a harsh reality.

Measures currently being adopted by both powerful and small countries are dubbed as stimulus packages. This may not be an appropriate description, as it implies a sustained growth element, when its focus is more on survival than sustainability. For small countries, rapid economic growth requires a new look at the role of the state in economic development. A shift towards a catalytic role for the state, where it will act primarily as a catalyst for economic development. There are examples where the state has been the major catalyst to sustained development, notwithstanding the obstacles to the growth process that lie in undue reliance on the outdated controls and systems of state-centric development. The market forces by themselves will not suffice to protect the public good, exposing the myth that the private sector could be the driver of economic growth. Perhaps at this time we should embrace the notion of a catalytic role for the state in economic development – one that causes change while adopting measures of sustainability. This will open a new calculus in the orthodox distinction between the private and public sectors.

Credible analytical leadership is called for, and universities must become truly rigorous and entrepreneurial. Changes in research priorities and teaching methods initiated in this 'non-normal' period will likely remain permanent as the economic metrics change. This will call for new systems and a switch to the digital world. International mobility of students as the middle class gets hit will put at risk the outreach programmes for higher education's reach into the global marketplace. These and other changes will spur entrepreneurial outcomes within the university system.

On the wider front, new drivers of industry change may arise, more use of digital transaction, innovations in public hygiene, changes in the way the travel and tourism sectors operate, security of production of food and medicine, wider corporate goals and a truly entrepreneurial university could be the changing imperatives of our times. New research agenda, priorities for institutional progress, infrastructure for teaching and learning, and governance systems will all shape the curve ahead of us. This will speak to the relevance of the university to society and the revitalization of development.

CONCLUSION

The COVID-19 pandemic is forcing a rethink in our academic understanding of macroeconomics and generating geo-strategic shifts in the world of diplomacy. The Lewis model of growth offers lessons for the Caribbean as the region seeks to build a sustainable post-COVID-19 future. This chapter pulls out underlying concepts from the Lewis growth model and explores the need to go beyond linear analysis, such as convergence thinking, to non-linear thinking as guided by new models such as the circular economy, frontier development and complexity analysis. We posited that these non-linear models offer useful paradigms in aiding thinking about how the Caribbean could overcome the negative growth challenges of COVID-19. Using this as a natural case study, the regional response and experiences were used to highlight the value of new thinking in economic theory, which emphasizes the importance of socio-cultural adjustments, public policy, and the role of the political in effective change, whether through diplomacy or reordered institutional settings and governance actions, as possibilities for building sustainable futures for more resilient Caribbean societies.

NOTE

1.   See Dookeran (2013) for further details.

REFERENCES

Baldacchino, Godfrey, and Anders Wivel. 2020. "Small states: concepts and theories." In *Handbook on the Politics of Small States*, 2–19. Cheltenham, UK: Edward Elgar Publishing. https://doi.org/10.4337/9781788112932.00007

Brito, Steve, Nicolas E. Magud, and Sebastian Sosa. 2018. "Real Exchange Rates, Economic Complexity, and Investment." IMF Working Paper No. 18/107. Washington, DC: International Monetary Fund.

Coccia, Mario. 2018. "An introduction to the theories of institutional change." *Journal of Economics Library* 5 (4): 337–44.

Colgan, Jeff D., and Robert O. Keohane. 2017. "The Liberal Order Is Rigged: Fix It Now or Watch It Wither." *Foreign Affairs* 96 (3): 36–44.

Domar, Evsey D. 1946. "Capital expansion, rate of growth, and employment." *Econometrica* 4 (2): 137–47.

Dookeran, Winston. 2013. "A New Frontier for Caribbean Convergence." *Caribbean Journal of International Relations and Diplomacy* 1 (2): 5–20.

———. 2015. *Crisis and Promise in the Caribbean: Politics and Convergence*. Farnham: Ashgate.

Dookeran, Winston, and Manfred D. Jantzen. 2012. *Power, Politics and Performance: A Partnership Approach for Development*. Kingston: Ian Randle Publishers.

The Economist. 2020. "The COVID-19 pandemic is forcing a rethink in macroeconomics." https://www.economist.com/briefing/2020/07/25/the-covid-19-pandemic-is-forcing-a-rethink-in-macroeconomics

Harrod, Roy F. 1939. "An Essay in Dynamic Theory." *Economic Journal* 49 (193): 14–33.

Hausmann, Ricardo, César A. Hidalgo, Sebastián Bustos, Michele Coscia, Alexander Simoes, and Muhammed A. Yıldırım. 2013. *Atlas of Complexity: Mapping Paths to Prosperity*. Cambridge, MA: MIT Press.

Kuznets, Simon. 1955. "Economic Growth and Income Inequality." *American Economic Review* 45 (1): 1–28.

Leontief, Wassily. 1986. *Input-output economics*. Oxford: Oxford University Press.

Lewis, W. Arthur. 1954. "Economic Development with Unlimited Supplies of Labour." *Manchester School* 22 (2): 139–91.

———. 1955. *Theory of Economic Growth*. Homewood, IL: Richard D. Irwin.

———. 1980. "Biographical note." *Social and Economic Studies* 29 (4).

———. 1984. "The State of Development Theory." *American Economic Review* 74 (1): 1–10.

MacArthur, Ellen. 2013. "Towards the circular economy." *Journal of Industrial Ecology*: 23–44.

MacArthur, Ellen, Klaus Zumwinkel, and Martin R. Stuchtey. 2015. "Growth Within. A Circular Economy Vision for a Competitive Europe." Ellen MacArthur Foundation.

Manfred, D. Jantzen. 2021. "Frontiers of Human Enterprise Progress on Spaceship Earth." Foundation for Politics and Leadership.

Ranis, Gustav, and John C.H. Fei. 1961. "A Theory of Economic Development." *American Economic Review* 51 (4): 533–65.

Rihani, Samir Rihani, and Robert Geyer. 2001. "Complexity: An Appropriate Framework for Development." *Progress in Development Studies* 1 (3): 237–45.

Rostow, Walt W. 1959. "The Stages of Economic Growth." *Economic History Review* 12 (1): 1–16.

Servedio, Vito D.P., Paolo Buttà, Dario Mazzilli, Andrea Tacchella, and Luciano Pietronero. 2018. "A New and Stable Estimation Method of Country Economic Fitness and Product Complexity." *Entropy* 20 (10): 783–98.

Solow, Robert M. 1956. "A Contribution to the Theory of Economic Growth." *Quarterly Journal of Economics* 70 (1): 65–94.

PART 4.

PEOPLE ON THE MOVE –
MOBILITY JUSTICE FOR
CHANGING WORLDS

10

'I Thought No One Would Care'
Identity, (Mis)Recognition and the Windrush Scandal

BRIAN WALKER

THE WINDRUSH GENERATION PRIMARILY COMPRISES ECONOMIC MIGRANTS WHO were energized by the prospects of better opportunities in the 'mother country'. According to the UK National Archives, on 22 June 1948, the *Empire Windrush* docked with 1,027 Caribbean nationals, who came to the United Kingdom to help ease the labour shortage created by the Second World War. For various reasons, their short-term plans turned into a lifetime and many migrants were eventually joined by their immediate family.

In April 2018, international media buzzed with stories that members of the Windrush generation and their offspring, who were unable to prove their status, had been wrongly deported, threatened with deportation, detained or blocked from accessing public services (Gentleman 2018a). The Windrush scandal, sparked by reports in *The Guardian,* along with activism by power players online and offline, resulted in international outrage and unprecedented political consequences.

The scandal is significant on many fronts. On one hand, there is the psychosocial and economic impact on affected citizens whose lives have been uprooted. On a symbolic level, the scandal reached its tipping point in April 2018, exactly fifty years after Enoch Powell, a Conservative member of Parliament and Shadow Defence Secretary, gave what has been widely condemned as the racist "Rivers of Blood" speech, in which he criticized mass immigration. Additionally, two months after the scandal reached fever pitch, the Caribbean community observed the seventieth anniversary of their arrival on the *Empire Windrush.*

This chapter examines how power players deeply connected to the issues and naturalized members of the Windrush generation experienced this major sociopolitical moment through media coverage. The chapter begins with a historical sketch of the Windrush story, an overview of the key issues at play related to the Windrush scandal, and sociopolitical issues that shape black life in the United Kingdom. By deploying a social psychological lens, it unpacks how citizens historically represented as "bad" immigrants in public discourse suddenly became "good" immigrants in an international media storm. Importantly, it delineates how the scandal has come to define the Windrush generation, with keen focus on the (mis)recognition of the black community.

At a broader level, migration has and continues to be a key driver of sustainable development. Tracy McFarlane (2017, 367) asserts, "In Caribbean migration, a philosophy of survival is put into action, but not without pain." The Windrush scandal is a contemporary and complicated exemplar. Agency is nested in the philosophy of survival. So, the reordering of Caribbean futures in the fires of global change hinges on the purposeful foregrounding of the strengths and uniqueness of Caribbean people on the move. This will provide opportunities for Caribbean migrants to disrupt problematic and stereotypical representations that may order their social worlds, as well as facilitate sustainable social change.

LITERATURE REVIEW

HISTORICAL SKETCH – HOW DID WE GET HERE?

The black presence in the United Kingdom predates 1948, but as Kennetta Hammond Perry (2015) points out, the arrival of the *Empire Windrush* was a watershed moment in the construction of multi-racial Britain. It was the first mass movement of Caribbean nationals outside the basin to the British metropole. Transcribed landing cards of the 1,027 Windrushers, who arrived on 22 June 1948, show that Jamaica was the most popular country of origin, with 599 passengers. Trinidad and Tobago had 194 passengers, followed by Bermuda and Mexico, with 168 and sixty-six, respectively (University of London 2019).

It is estimated that six hundred thousand Commonwealth citizens migrated to the United Kingdom between 1948 and 1973, and had the right to remain indefinitely (House of Commons 2019). The British Nationality Act of 1948 granted Windrush migrants the right to enter and settle in the United Kingdom as Commonwealth citizens. These migrants played a critical role in the reconstruction efforts following the Second World War, by filling roles in public transportation, the manufacturing sector and the National Health Service. Despite the contributions made by Windrushers, legislative amendments in the 1960s changed the terms of freedom of movement. These changes were set against the backdrop of a wider political discussion that mass immigration would result in white British citizens becoming strangers in their own country (Powell 1968).

"The (Commonwealth Immigrants) 1962 Act severely curtailed primary immigration . . . For the first time, the right of British subjects to enter the 'Mother Country' was restricted" (Consterdine 2017, 5). The Immigration Act of 1971, which came into effect in January 1973, further tightened border controls, and employment vouchers were replaced with work permits, resulting in short-term residency (National Archives 2021). Notably, the 1971 Act empowered the Home Secretary to make new immigration rules and to deport migrants. It also confirmed that migrants who were present in the United Kingdom prior to the activation of the Act in 1973 were entitled to remain indefinitely (Home Affairs Committee 2018).

THE WINDRUSH SCANDAL – WHAT WERE THE ISSUES AT PLAY?

Most Windrush migrants got themselves and their children naturalized as British citizens, in line with the framework set out by the British Nationality Act of 1981. However, some failed to do so for various reasons. The Migration Observatory at the University of Oxford states that approximately fifty thousand individuals born in the Commonwealth, who have been resident in the United Kingdom before 1971 may not have regularized their status (Gentleman 2018a). The inability to prove one's status became problematic when the hostile environment policy took effect, through amendments to the Immigration Act in 2014 and 2016. Theresa May, the then Home Secretary, wanted to reduce immigration numbers by targeting illegal migrants. This policy was designed to restrict their access to employment, healthcare, housing and social protection by essentially shifting the border and granting immigration powers to private citizens and other non-state actors (Griffiths and Yeo 2021).

In November 2017, *The Guardian* featured Paulette Wilson (now deceased), a Windrush migrant who worked at the House of Commons (Gentleman 2017). She was threatened with deportation to Jamaica, having spent fifty years in the United Kingdom. In subsequent months, there was coverage in international media led by Gentleman telling narratives like Wilson's, thereby highlighting a systemic problem (*Al Jazeera* 2018; *British Broadcasting Corporation* 2018; Bulman 2018). As more and more affected migrants shared their experiences of life at its lowest, the stories gained meaningful traction and developed into what has now been called the Windrush scandal. It reached a tipping point in April 2018, when Amber Rudd resigned as Home Secretary and the then prime minister, Theresa May, apologized to her Caribbean counterparts, who were in London for the Commonwealth Heads of Government Meeting (Walker and Gentleman 2018).

Langer and Gruber (2021) advance that the scandal demonstrates why legacy media (print, television and radio) still matter in political agenda setting. News coverage from traditional media houses complemented the confluence of online petitions, digital activism and engagement by political and diplomatic actors. They employ the definition of a media storm by Boydstun et al. (2014) that sets a minimum threshold of seven days of intense coverage and a 150 per cent increase in reporting over the period. Their analysis shows that the number of stories jumped from nineteen between 9 and 15 April to 445 between 16 and 22 April. This period had sixty-four front pages and opening TV headlines. So, these traditional media houses amplified the issue and sustained it in the public sphere.

The media storm moved the issue onto the political agenda as the Home Office rolled out the Windrush Scheme on 30 May 2018. This programme allows members of the Windrush generation and their children who were born in the United Kingdom and those who arrived as minors to apply for citizenship free of charge (Javid 2019). As at June 2019, the Home Office reported that eighty-three persons were wrongly deported. Additionally, as of March 2021, 13,213 individuals have either confirmed their status or citizenship (Home Office 2021). The top three countries represented in the applications include: Jamaica (24 per cent, 3,145), India (13 per cent, 1770) and Barbados (4 per cent, 551).

The Windrush Compensation Scheme was operationalized in 2019 and has paid out £14.3 million in compensation up to March 2021 to 633 citizens, out of the potential fifteen thousand applicants estimated by the government (National Audit Office 2021). It is important to note that £11.6 million has been paid since December 2020 and approximately sixty per cent of the payments between December 2020 and March 2021 are top-up awards on previous claims, as opposed to new pay-outs. Media stories have characterized the claims process as burdensome, bureaucratic and heavily legalistic (Gentleman 2020; White and Turnnidge 2020).

The National Audit Office (2021) asserts that the Home Office should improve its case management systems to ensure that members of the Windrush generation are fairly compensated. This takes on added significance within the context that as at 21 May 2021, twenty-one claimants had reportedly died without receiving compensation they were entitled to (Gentleman 2021). According to the "Windrush Lessons Learned" independent review, the problems caused by the scandal were avoidable and the Home Office should overhaul its operational ethos. "The Home Office must acknowledge the wrong which has been done; it must open itself up to greater external scrutiny; and it must change its culture to recognise that migration and the wider Home Office policy is about people and, whatever its objective, should be rooted in humanity (Williams 2020, 7).

THEORETICAL FRAMEWORKS

SOCIAL REPRESENTATIONS THEORY

In social psychology, social representations theory (SRT) allows people to understand their social worlds, and it provides codes for communication and social exchange (Moscovici 1973). This is the ideal framework to analyse media experiences, as it makes room for issues of identity, social interactions, collective memories, inter alia, which are critical to this study. SRT is similar to Stuart Hall's (1980) encoding/decoding theory, as it provides a framework to deconstruct how people make sense of media messages. Like encoding/decoding's dominant, negotiated and oppositional readings, SRT has three types of representations: hegemonic, emancipated and polemic (Moscovici 1988). A hegemonic representation is a widely held view across society. An emancipated representation offers a degree of divergence and is embraced by a subgroup. A polemic representation is in direct contrast to a hegemonic representation and this is usually based on conflict and is not shared by the public at large.

SRT is a sharper analytical lens than encoding/decoding as it gives clearer tools to unpack how people make sense of the unfamiliar in day-to-day (media) experiences and it has a stronger focus on the social processes at play. Within the SRT toolkit, anchoring and objectification are the two ways in which representations are mobilized communicatively (Moscovici 1984). Anchoring is a process of classification that allows people to deconstruct a phenomenon. In the same vein, objectification relates to how an idea or concept is translated into something tangible. For instance: human trafficking is anchored to the idea of modern-day slavery and objectification is done through social marketing campaigns that use images of people in shackles and chains. Höijer (2011), an audience reception scholar, has been extending SRT to explore how a phenomenon becomes attached to emotions.

REPRESENTATIONS OF BLACKNESS IN BRITAIN

Broadly speaking, most of the literature on representations of blackness in Britain came to the fore through cultural studies and sociological research (Gilroy 1987; Hall 1997, 2001). Historically, within the race-immigration prism, blackness was used to anchor and objectify what was wrong with British society. The representations of black citizens as socially dysfunctional permeated discourse in relation to the negative impact of these migrants on crime, housing and the welfare state (Solomos 2003).

In terms of crime, blackness was also represented as a threat to citizen security and this guided top-down approaches by state institutions. Gilroy's

(1987) path-breaking book, *There Ain't No Black in The Union Jack,* pays close attention to dominant imagery related to black youth and criminality. This intersects with Höijer's theorization of emotional anchoring and objectification within SRT. Gilroy posits that representations of black people in police and media reports objectify them as criminals and are anchored by the notion that criminality is fostered through cultural values (Gilroy 1987).

The black as criminal representation is still commonplace in discussions on knife crime and manifests itself in stop and search statistics. Government data for the fiscal year ending March 2020 reveal that 48.9 per cent of stop and searches done in England and Wales were conducted by the Metropolitan Police in London. There were 71.2 stop-and-searches for every thousand black people, in comparison to 17.6 for every thousand white people (Race Disparity Unit 2021).

Caroline Howarth has opened up an analytical space through SRT to explore blackness and racism at large in social psychology. She argues that the discipline should ferret out the new and ongoing ways in which marginalized groups unsettle and transform racist and stigmatizing representations and practices (Howarth 2006a). This form of resistance is similar to positive marginality, whereby members of minoritized groups embrace stigmatizing attributes as meaningful parts of their self-concept and push for social change (Unger 2000; McFarlane 2006).

IDENTITY AND RECOGNITION

Howarth (2002, 159) reasons that, "To theorise social identity…we need to highlight the dialectic between how we see ourselves and how others see us." This notion dovetails with the concept of recognition by Hopkins and Blackwood (2011) as the validation of one's identity by others, which has consequences for one's own self-concept. This aligns with and extends foundational work in political philosophy by Honneth (1992, 2007) and Taylor (1994). Misrecognition is presented as the use of racialized/ stereotypical/problematic assumptions to shape someone's identity and nonrecognition pertains to the complete erasure of someone's identity. Recognition and citizenship go hand in hand. Many social researchers have embraced Turner's (2001, 12) definition of citizenship as "the capacity to participate effectively, creatively and successfully within a national culture."

More and more qualitative studies have been using recognition theory to operationalize how people with seemingly incompatible identities negotiate their social worlds. Blackwood, Hopkins, and Reicher (2013) examine the misrecognition that emerges from interactions between Scottish Muslims and the police at airports in Scotland. The airport is a space of hyper surveillance for Muslims due to fears regarding extremism. Despite their Scottish nationality, their Muslim identity takes centre stage during airport exchanges and the social costs of misrecognition play out in humiliation and perceptions of criminality.

Amena Amer (2020) also unpacks how white British Muslims deploy performative strategies to mitigate instances of misrecognition that would trigger marginalization and harm. In some cases, deliberate acts are done to prompt misrecognition, in a push to challenge dominant norms. Seemingly incompatible social categories also extend to black British citizens. Within the Windrush context, many Caribbean migrants were British, based on colonial rule at the time and this was infused in their identity. However, they encountered a social reality that excluded and 'othered' them based on race once they moved to the United Kingdom.

The New Cross fire in 1981, Brixton riots of 1981 and 1995, and London riots of 2011 are key examples of the thorny interplay between blackness and injustice in the United Kingdom (Elliott-Cooper 2019; Hammond Perry 2015; Howarth 2002). The Macpherson Report into the handling of the 1993 racially driven murder of Stephen Lawrence, a black teenager, shifted the conversation around race and racism in terms of policy. The report stated that the investigation by the Metropolitan Police was "marred by a combination of professional incompetence, institutional racism and a failure of leadership by senior officers" (Macpherson 1999, 365).

This report helped to validate the realities of the black community, to some extent, from the state's perspective, as it ushered in a wave of policing reforms and racial equality measures (Phillips 2011). However, scholars continue to highlight that the ameliorative responses remain highly problematic. This is evidenced by the prevailing inequities in education, the criminal justice system, the creative and cultural industries, among others (Bhopal 2018; Nwonka and Malik 2018; Phillips 2011).

Media content shapes and is shaped by social representations. More critically, social representations are important because of what they *do*. Howarth (2006b) reasons that social representations not only describe phenomena, but demonstrate how the social order is reified, contested or disrupted. Challenges emerge when representations are monolithic and stigmatizing. These representations feed into the institutional practices of differentiation and discrimination.

According to Sarita Malik (2002, 79), ". . . It becomes particularly important when, how and, where Black people are and are not seen and empowered". Over the years, blackness in the United Kingdom has been essentialized, resulting in the community being defined by its worst expressions: criminality and social deviance. In recent years, there has been very little exploration of how Windrush migrants or the black British community at large experience news media coverage. This chapter helps to fill that gap by examining how naturalized members of the Windrush generation and power players experienced the political scandal through media coverage. There is also keen focus on the implications for identity and recognition within the black Caribbean community.

METHODOLOGY

Based on the research question and SRT as a framework rooted in social constructivism, a qualitative approach was deployed to deconstruct a mixture of subjectivities, as opposed to generating generalizable data. Fifteen semi-structured interviews were conducted with ten Windrush migrants over seventy years of age and five power players. The Windrush migrants are all naturalized British citizens, who migrated from Jamaica between 1948 and 1971. The focus on Jamaican Windrush migrant interviewees for this chapter is based on the island being the country of origin for most of the affected citizens.

I have conceptualized power players as individuals who helped to drive public discourse on issues related to the scandal, and they were selected purposively based on the insights they could offer. The five power players include: Seth George Ramocan, the then Jamaican high commissioner to the United Kingdom; Reverend Dr Joe Aldred, chair of the Windrush 70th

Anniversary Church Service Committee; Jacqueline McKenzie, immigration and human rights attorney; Kimberly McIntosh, then senior policy officer – Runnymede Trust (a racial equality think tank); and Amelia Gentleman, a reporter with *The Guardian*.

Windrush migrants were recruited through convenience and snowball sampling methods.[1] Interestingly, while recruiting Windrush migrants for interviews, once I mentioned the focus, the initial reaction from participants was to distance themselves from the scandal and those impacted. Meaning, they made it clear that they were naturalized UK citizens and their knowledge was restricted to media stories. After explaining that they were the interviewees I was looking for, they agreed to participate. This took care of the potential ethical dilemma that would have arisen if I had selected individuals who were swept up in the crisis or had relatives in that position.

Interviews were conducted between May and July 2019 and ran on average for thirty-five minutes. Data collection ended after fifteen interviews, as saturation in terms of not only codes, but meanings had been attained. The responses from the power players were not anonymized because these individuals featured prominently in the debacle. Moreover, the convention of anonymity transcends simply using pseudonyms and, in this instance, would include omitting or changing many other identifiers. For this chapter, the conceptual strategy of gaining the views of power players would be reduced in value and richness with anonymity. More importantly, the power players gave written consent for their data to be public. The Windrush migrants also gave written consent, but unlike the power players, they were given pseudonyms. Ethical approval was granted by the research ethics committee in the Department of Psychological and Behavioural Science at the London School of Economics and Political Science.

As a Jamaica-born researcher, I was able to activate an insider status and build rapport based on shared nationality with the Windrush migrants and power players (except Amelia Gentleman). However, age and the disparity between the experience of blackness in the United Kingdom versus Jamaica showcased divergent realities, which provided rich insights. Additionally, going into the interview with Gentleman, I was attentive to the social dynamics of a black male graduate student interviewing a white woman journalist about an issue that affected the black British community.

I was guided by Burford May's (2014) concept of "insider moments" – shared experiences/interests that build rapport between a researcher and participants, and transcend race, ethnicity and gender, among other variables. With this in mind, I ensured the topic guide had open-ended questions and I also tried to convey a dispassionate tone throughout the interview.

Thematic analysis was selected as the analytical grid because it provides a useful framework to distil responses from participants and then analyse patterns of meanings (Clarke and Braun 2017). Responses were then classified using Attride-Stirling's (2001) network of global, organizing and basic themes. After transcription, I did multiple readings before conducting the analysis. I deployed an inductive approach, which allowed the data to guide the interpretation. I also coded by hand, in a push to become fully immersed in the data (Bowling 2009). Codes and themes were discussed with two colleagues.

FINDINGS

TENSION BETWEEN RECOGNITION AND NON-RECOGNITION OF WINDRUSH MIGRANTS

The dominant representation that surfaced from the interviews was that the affected migrants were dealt an injustice by way of the hostile environment policy. Across the board with Windrush interviewees, there was consensus that although affected citizens did not become naturalized years ago, the immigration cases were handled poorly by the government.

Edna (London, May 2019): "To know that they came here, they did work, they worked hard – the pay, I'm sure they were getting less than their White counterparts. But they managed and they built a life. They had their families. . . . I was angry, really angry, even now, I am talking about it and I'm still angry, because there's no way they should have been treated like that."

Jennifer (London, May 2019): "Many of them are pensioners. What are you going to send them off to do? Why are you going to send these people home – not because they didn't opt to have the British passport or citizenship?

Why you want to do that? They should get it naturally without having to go through all that."

There is a tension between the recognition by interviewees and the media of the affected citizens as upstanding members of British society versus nonrecognition by the government due to their inability to produce documentation. The aforementioned representation for these interviewees is swept up in collective memories of how they all got to the United Kingdom and their experiences as part of the Windrush generation. The taxonomy of the "good" immigrant versus the "bad" immigrant is at the base of their representations and collective memories.

The positioning of impacted Windrushers as meaningful contributors to British society was evident in the emotional anchoring that came shining through in the interviews with the migrants. Objectification emerged as the cases related to Paulette Wilson and Albert Thompson (pseudonym used for media stories) were key reference points for the interviewees, especially Thompson's case. He was struggling to survive as he was denied cancer treatment through the National Health Service, which struck a chord with many interviewees (Gentleman 2018b).

All Windrush respondents were over seventy and most had retired. From a developmental psychological perspective, they are at the final phase of Erikson's (1950) theory of psychosocial development: ego integrity and despair, whereby, they are actively reflecting on life. So, these stories of affected Windrush migrants, who are in a similar age-group as them, would connect at a deeper level.

Gentleman explained that Thompson's story was what changed the game politically in the construction of the scandal. It moved from a story of mild interest as other media houses started digging – then, it entered the parliamentary sphere. From a journalistic perspective, Gentleman spent a lot of time ensuring that her stories were airtight in terms of accuracy, based on the complex nature of the issue and the socio-political matrix.

Gentleman (London, May 2019): "If you've been classified as an illegal immigrant, you often don't talk to your family about it, you don't talk to your friend about it and you absolutely don't want to have your picture in the newspaper beneath the headline that suggests that you're here illegally. Because the debate in the UK around immigration is so toxic and stigmatized . . ."

A noteworthy observation made by Windrush interviewees was that this scandal was a point of departure from other historical moments of injustice in the black community. This was based on the absence of violent protest and there has been some movement towards a resolution.

Researcher: "Were you surprised that this escalated? Have you ever seen a scandal of this nature with black people?"

Jennifer: "No, only away from when they have a riot. When they do things to black people and they don't like it, they make a riot and burn down Brixton!"

Richard (London, May 2019): "New Cross fire, people lost their lives there, people got burnt up there and nothing came of it – that affected me as well. And they were all black people. Brixton riot, they were fighting for recognition, to be seen as a human being, like anybody else and that wasn't happening."

These quotes from Richard and Jennifer speak to a lingering hegemonic representation – black as criminal, which is anchored to the theme of hooliganism and objectified through images of looting and streets set ablaze. Although, these forms of criminal conduct were in resistance to racialized forms of state oppression and violence, the black as criminal representation blurred the narrative and made justification of the protests more complex. However, Kimberly McIntosh postulates that if one juxtaposes the riots with the Windrush scandal, the latter is less complicated to explain and that was evidenced by media coverage.

McIntosh (London, May 2019):

> I would say the coverage of the Windrush scandal was extremely positive. But I think that's also easier to do . . . it'd be so difficult to try and blame the victims of the scandal . . . I mean, some people did try, I'm not saying no one did – "Oh, they should've sorted out their papers, you know, that kind of thing." But it is quite hard to not be on side. . . . So, if you're covering the Tottenham riots, it's easier for people to make the link between, "Oh, well, of course, black people would be rioting, that's what they do. Oh, look at them looting." Rather than having to understand cuts to youth services, interactions with the police and the history of that.

MISRECOGNITION – LOW-HANGING FRUITS FOR THE HOME OFFICE

For Jacqueline McKenzie and McIntosh, who interacted with impacted citizens and government stakeholders on the issues at play, misrecognition formed the centre of gravity of how they made sense of and experienced news coverage.

McKenzie (London, May 2019): "So, the scandal came about because they (the government) viewed, I mean, in fact, in one of their own reports, they referred to this cohort of people as 'low hanging fruits'. So, they viewed this group as a kind of docile, not highly-mobile, not highly educated group of people. They didn't really expect the response that they got."

McIntosh: ". . . But for a group of working-class, black Caribbean people to evoke public sympathy on a mass scale, in right-wing tabloid media, surprised me. I thought no one would care, to be frank. And people really did."

These examples of misrecognition underscore the ways in which social representations from a top-down, governmental perspective can become institutionalized and inform practice (Howarth 2006b). At the same time, this misrecognition from the government brought definition to the scandal and gave it momentum, which surprised McIntosh. For McKenzie, misrecognition by the government prompted her to reflect on the politics of recognition, set against the backdrop of the Windrush generation's presence in the United Kingdom, beyond the scope of the scandal.

McKenzie: ". . . We've been here seventy years. We've been one of the oldest migrant groups. But what have we got to show for those seventy years? So, I completely forgot about the fact that we've been here for seventy years and whether the government had been complicit in treating the Windrushers the way they were. I was really focused on where is our own response to this? Where's our own response to this scandal?"

The crux of McKenzie's statement relates to her view that the black community in the United Kingdom is splintered, with no leadership akin to Malcolm X or Martin Luther King. So, the lack of an organizing force in the community inhibits a strong bottom-up movement of resistance that can stand on its own without overreliance on allies. She wants the black community to be able to command attention on its own from those in power.

WINDRUSH SCANDAL AS A DEFINER OF THE GENERATION

Ambiguity in relation to the scale of the immigration problem produced a representation that the entire Windrush generation was affected by the crisis. This concern was raised by Seth Ramocan, then Jamaica's High Commissioner to the United Kingdom.

Ramocan (London, May 2019): "Yes, it is a perception that had to be addressed. Because some people thought it was all of the community that fell into this situation. When it was not. So gradually, as the issue played out, it showed that there were a few thousand persons that were involved."

Furthermore, Rev Dr Joe Aldred found this example of misrecognition deeply troubling based on what it means for the group's collective identity. Aldred (London, June 2019):

> I'm shouting to my TV screen, saying, "For God's sake, stop it!" You know, we haven't all sat here for seventy years on our hands and not sorted out (our documents). That's not the Windrush generation I know. . . . It was a problem. But I think quite early on, it would have been helpful not to so categorize an entire people as vulnerable. That sense of vulnerability plays into a stereotype of weakness, of exclusion, of being outsiders, of being not in charge of your own destiny, being in the hands of other people. So, they invite you, you come, then they kick you out and you go, you are the victim.

This extract demonstrates that Rev Aldred has an emancipated representation of blackness in regards to the Windrush scandal. While he agrees with the dominant view that the hostile environment policy is brutal and needs to be addressed, he breaks away by denouncing the ambiguous classification of the scope of the problem, which he believes has damaged the Windrush brand. His representation was influenced by his own work within the church community in which there were campaigns to get people naturalized during the 1980s. Additionally, his representation of the Windrush generation as a resilient and progressive people was being challenged through the emergence of the hegemonic representation of victimhood in the media. This chasm coincides with what Hall (1997) argues is the manner in which representations can affect identities and the struggles that ensue.

There have been ongoing efforts to bolster recognition of the Windrush generation through self-definition. Patrick Vernon, a social justice activist, played an instrumental role in having 22 June declared as Windrush Day by the government. The announcement in 2018 coincided with the seventieth anniversary of the *Empire Windrush*'s arrival and was complemented by the introduction of an annual grant of up to £500,000 for charities and community groups to host commemorative and educational events (Ministry of Housing, Communities and Local Government 2018; Vernon 2018). While the Windrush interviewees were not engaged with the anniversary celebrations, most power players felt the milestone was not overshadowed by the scandal. One of the major events was the official church service, which was held at Westminster Abbey. Power player interviewees assert that the service provided a space for heightened recognition of the Windrush generation. Ramocan: "I think there's a positive side to it, in that maybe if those celebrations were taking place at a time when people did not know what was Windrush and so on, we would've had to go through the pains of trying to tell them what Windrush is."

Aldred: "I suppose the real effect was our decision not to have any politician involved (in the church service), where there could have been politicians, if that was not the background. So, essentially, we screened it out and marked the event by recognising the contribution of Black people to Britain."

DISCUSSION

Media coverage was a double-edged sword as it simultaneously facilitated recognition and misrecognition. It is clear that there was a critical point of departure in the social representation of blackness in the British public sphere. Historically, the hegemonic representations of blackness have been linked to criminality, social deviance, animality and other problematic tendencies (Gilroy 1987; Hall 1997; Howarth 2006a). An important point in relation to black citizens moving from "bad" to "good" immigrants, is that those affected by the crisis are not a threat to British society and values, as articulated in the 1960s and 1970s. Most of them are at a pensionable age, which helped to evoke sympathy for their plight. Therefore, media coverage moved the needle from misrecognition to recognition, by presenting the migrants as "good" and "deserving" citizens, which created a spectacle and gave the issue political momentum.

Despite the sympathy and outrage in the public sphere, and the departure from historical notions of blackness, the scandal shows that the black body is still a perennial site for stigmatizing representations. Moreover, it is problematic that the increased visibility and respect for the Windrush generation at large and their contributions to British life hinged on the adverse experiences of the small subset of individuals, who were not naturalized. Höijer's (2011) framework on emotional anchoring and objectification was particularly useful in exploring how people experienced the scandal. Through this trajectory, the interplay between their emotions and objectification made the issues even more accessible in their minds, in terms of recalling what they felt as the scandal unfolded.

At the same time, the lack of clarity regarding the scale of the crisis (which was based on the nature of the issue) produced a widescale representation of victimhood for the entire Windrush generation. This form of misrecognition has done some damage to the group's collective identity. For instance, an important observation was made during the recruitment phase of this project and in the interviews with Windrush migrants. The initial reaction of these interviewees was to distance themselves from the scandal, noting that they are naturalized and in good standing.

The interviewees engaged in ma(r)king a boundary between themselves and impacted citizens. This highlights that there is a stigma attached to those migrants and they have become blemished, to some extent, within the community (Goffman 1968; Howarth 2006a). The mounting of that boundary could also be seen as a default response by Windrush interviewees to affirm their identity and citizenship, while mitigating the social costs of misrecognition generated by the news coverage.

The Windrush seventieth anniversary church service is a strong example of how hegemonic and stigmatizing representations can be resisted. The prime minister, Home Secretary and other politicians were present, but the organizers restricted their participation. In the world of protocol, this would be deemed a major subversive move by the organizers to shift the focus from the political scandal, in a drive to amplify positive representations of the Windrush generation.

The decision by Anthony Bryan, Albert Thompson, Paulette Wilson and other affected citizens to step forward and share their stories in the media should not be discounted. Their actions represent powerful expressions of agency and resistance, which in turn, help to problematize notions of victimhood. This is nested within Dietrich Jones' (2013, 59) conceptualization of ". . . migrants as *strategic actors* with the capacity to undertake goal-oriented and intentional actions and decisions, in response to border structures . . ." For this reason, they are not referred to as victims in the chapter. Such a classification would have to be based on their own assessment of their experiences and the implications for self-identification on the victim-survivor continuum. More importantly, their ability to cope and craft routes of action does not mean that they ought to shoulder the burden of solving problems that are inherently structural.

LIMITATIONS AND FUTURE RESEARCH

This chapter has a retrospective dimension. For Halbwachs (1952; 1992), memory is acquired in and through society, while Olick (2007) argues that memories oscillate between the past and the present, which invariably leads to reconstruction of some form. Furthermore, the interplay between the interviewee and interviewer as co-constructors of memories is an important dynamic to consider in the process of remembering (Gemignani 2014).

So, for this study, it is possible that certain details were omitted or opinions were refined based on new information regarding the scandal. There is also the possibility, especially in relation to the Windrush interviewees, that they responded in keeping with the prevailing view on the scandal. This would have been influenced by how they probably felt I expected them to respond as members of the Windrush generation and based on our shared nationality.

Looking to the future, other studies can explore the perspectives of Windrush migrants from other Caribbean islands. Interviewees could also include affected migrants and their relatives, but it would be prudent for this to be done once matters related to the Windrush Compensation Scheme are settled. These interviews would offer illuminating insights into how media shape and are shaped by experiences of (in)justice. This could be explored through themes of identity, citizenship, recognition, representation and solidarity. However, the research process would have to be tailored to minimize (re)traumatization.

CONCLUSION

The Windrush scandal underscores social representations as a product and process that can lead to "extremely concrete and real consequences" (Jovchelovitch 2001, 177). For decades, black citizens have been misrecognized in the United Kingdom based on representations that positioned them as social problems. These representations shaped public discourse, policies and legislation that led to the curtailment of mass immigration.

Importantly, this chapter demonstrates how those impacted and the Windrush generation at large moved from the margins and became part of the collective 'we'. The belated embrace of the Windrush generation as upstanding citizens prompted an unprecedented level of visibility and 'respect'. However, the widescale framing of victimhood added another layer to stigmatizing representations of blackness, leading to further misrecognition of the black community and complex responses. The research adds value to the literature, having taken a dialogical approach to recognition theory, by interrogating what representations of the 'other' mean for personal and group identities.

Critical moments in the international public sphere, like the Windrush scandal and the 2020 killing of George Floyd in the United States, play important roles in connecting historical and contemporary issues of racial (in)equality and (in)justice. "The effects of agenda setting are considerable, not just because it allows news to set the grounds for discussion, but also because it defines when it is time for narrative closure or exposure" (Malik 2002, 84). Therefore, the salience and shift in representations of black Britons that emerged during media coverage of the Windrush scandal will not last without structural change.

Going forward, migration will continue to be central to Caribbean life. Therefore, the reordering of Caribbean futures within the context of migration requires Caribbean migrants to play a more active role in defining who they are within and across varying social contexts. This will help to bolster their resilience and create avenues for sustainable social change.

NOTE

1. I am grateful to my interviewees whose experiences, insights and thoughts made this work possible. I would also like to thank Cathy Nicholson, who supervised this research as a dissertation project as well as Natalie Dietrich Jones, Tracy McFarlane, and two anonymous reviewers for feedback on an earlier draft of the chapter.

REFERENCES

Al Jazeera. 2018. "The UK's Windrush Generation: What's the Scandal About?" *Al Jazeera*, 18 April. https://www.aljazeera.com/news/2018/4/18/the-uks-windrush-generation-whats-the-scandal-about.

Amer, Amena. 2020. "Between Recognition and Mis/Nonrecognition: Strategies of Negotiating and Performing Identities among White Muslims in the United Kingdom." *Political Psychology* 41 (3): 533–48.

Attride-Stirling, Jennifer. 2001. "Thematic Networks: An Analytic Tool for Qualitative Research." *Qualitative Research* 1 (3): 385–405.

Bhopal, Kalwant. 2018. *White Privilege: The Myth of a Post-Racial Society.* Bristol: Policy Press.

Blackwood, Leda, Nick Hopkins, and Stephen Reicher. 2013. "'I Know Who I Am, but Who Do They Think I Am?' Muslim Perspectives on Encounters with Airport Authorities." *Ethnic and Racial Studies* 36 (6): 1090–108.

Bowling, Ann. 2009. *Research Methods in Health.* Berkshire: Open University Press.

Boydstun, Amber E, Anne Hardy, and Stefaan Walgrave. 2014. "Two Faces of Media Attention: Media Storm Versus Non-Storm Coverage." *Political Communication* 31 (4): 509–31.

British Broadcasting Corporation. 2018. "Windrush Row: I Was Denied NHS Cancer Treatment." *BBC*, London, 18 April. https://www.bbc.com/news/av/uk-43818671.

Bulman, May. 2018. "Daughter of Windrush Immigrant Facing Imminent Deportation Despite Dying Mother and Young Grandchildren in UK." *Independent*, 25 April. https://www.independent.co.uk/news/uk/home-news/windrush-scandal-yvonne-williams-immigrants-migration-theresa-may-uk-government-a8320401.html.

Burford May, Reuben A. 2014. "When the Methodological Shoe is on the Other Foot: African American Interviewer and White Interviewees." *Qualitative Sociology* 37 (1): 117–36.

Clarke, Victoria, and Victoria Braun. 2017. "Thematic Analysis." *Journal of Positive Psychology* 12 (3): 297–98.

Consterdine, Erica. 2017. "Community versus Commonwealth: Reappraising the 1971 Immigration Act." *Immigrants and Minorities* 35 (1): 1–20. University of London. 2019. "Windrush: Arrival 1948 Passenger List." Department of History, Goldsmiths, University of London, 19 June. https://www.gold.ac.uk/windrush/passenger-list/.

Dietrich Jones, Natalie. 2013. "The Ma(r)king of Complex Border Geographies and Their Negotiation by Undocumented Migrants: The Case of Barbados." PhD thesis, University of Manchester. https://www.research.manchester.ac.uk/portal/files/54548900/FULL_TEXT.PDF.

Elliott-Cooper, Adam. 2019. "'Our Life is a Struggle': Respectable Gender Norms and Black Resistance to Policing." *Antipode* 51 (2): 539–57.

Erikson, Eric. 1950. *Childhood and Society*. New York: Norton.

Gemignani, Marco. 2014. "Memory, Remembering, and Oblivion in Active Narrative Interviewing." *Qualitative Inquiry* 20 (2): 127–35.

Gentleman, Amelia. 2017. "I Can't Eat or Sleep: The Woman Threatened with Deportation after 50 Years in Britain." *Guardian*, 28 November. https://www.theguardian.com/uk-news/2017/nov/28/i-cant-eat-or-sleep-the-grandmother-threatened-with-deportation-after-50-years-in-britain.

———. 2018a. "Caribbean Nations Demand Solution to 'Illegal Immigrants' Anomaly." *Guardian*, 12 April. https://www.theguardian.com/uk-news/2018/apr/12/caribbean-nations-demand-solution-to-illegal-immigrants-anomaly.

———. 2018b. "Windrush Scandal: Albert Thompson Gets Cancer Treatment Date." *Guardian*, 24 April. https://www.theguardian.com/uk-news/2018/apr/24/windrush-scandal-albert-thompson-gets-cancer-treatment-date.

———. 2020. "Windrush Pay Out Scheme Not Fit for Purpose, Say Lawyers." *The Guardian,* 27 August. https://www.theguardian.com/uk-news/2020/aug/27/windrush-payout-scheme-not-fit-for-purpose-say-lawyers#:~:text=The%20Windrush%20compensation%20scheme%20is,firms%20to%20the%20home%20secretary.

———. 2021. "Windrush Scandal: 21 People Have Died Before Receiving Compensation." *Guardian*, 21 May. https://www.theguardian.com/uk-news/2021/may/19/windrush-scandal-21-people-have-died-before-receiving-compensation.

Gilroy, Paul. 1987. *There Ain't No Black in the Union Jack*. London: Hutchinson.

Goffman, Erving. 1968. *Stigma: Notes on the Management of Spoiled Identity*. Harmondsworth: Penguin.

Griffiths, Melanie, and Colin Yeo. 2021. "The UK's Hostile Environment: Deputising Immigration Control." *Critical Social Policy* 41 (4): 1–24.

Halbwachs, Maurice. 1992. *On Collective Memory*. Chicago: University of Chicago Press.

Hall, Stuart. 1980. "Encoding/Decoding." In *Culture, Media, Language: Working*

Papers in Cultural Studies, edited by Centre for Contemporary Cultural Studies, 1971–1979. London: Hutchinson.

———. 1997. "Racist Ideologies and the Media." In *Media Studies: A Reader*, edited by Paul Marris and Sue Thornham, 271–82. Edinburgh: Edinburgh University Press.

———. 2001. "The Multicultural Question." *Pavis Papers in Social and Cultural Research*. Milton Keynes: Open University Press.

Hammond Perry, Kennetta. 2015. *London is the Place for Me: Black Britons, Citizenship and the Politics of Race*. Oxford: Oxford University Press.

Höijer, Birgitta. 2011. "Emotional Anchoring and Objectification in Media Reporting on Climate Change." *Public Understanding of Science* 19 (6): 717–31.

Home Affairs Committee. 2018. "Oral Evidence: Windrush Children." UK Parliament, 3 July. https://publications.parliament.uk/pa/cm201719/cmselect/cmhaff/990/99004.htm.

Home Office. 2021. "Windrush Task Force Data: Q1." UK Home Office, 27 May 2021. https://www.gov.uk/government/publications/windrush-task-force-data-q1-2021.

Honneth, Axel. 1992. "Integrity and Disrespect." *Political Theory* 20 (2): 187–201.

———. 2007. *Disrespect: The Normative Foundations of Critical Theory*. Cambridge: Polity Press.

Hopkins, Nick, and Leda Blackwood. 2011. "Everyday Citizenship: Identity and Recognition." *Journal of Community & Applied Social Psychology* 21 (3): 215–27.

House of Commons. 2019. "Windrush Generation and the Home Office." UK Parliament, 27 February 2019. https://publications.parliament.uk/pa/cm201719/cmselect/cmpubacc/1518/1518.pdf.

Howarth, Caroline. 2002. "Identity in Whose Eyes? The Role of Representations in Identity Construction." *Journal for the Theory of Social Behaviour* 32 (2): 145–62.

———. 2006a. "Race as Stigma: Positioning the Stigmatized as Agents, Not Objects." *Journal of Community and Applied Social Psychology* 16 (6): 442–51.

———. March 2006b. "A Social Representation is Not a Quiet Thing: Exploring the Critical Potential of Social Representations Theory." *British Journal of Social Psychology* 45 (1): 65–86.

Javid, Sajid. 2019. "Update to the Home Affairs Committee on Windrush." UK Government, 10 June. https://www.gov.uk/government/publications/update-to-the-hasc-on-windrush-10-june-2019/update-to-the-hasc-on-windrush-10-june-2019.

Jovchelovitch, Sandra. 2001. "Social Representations, Public Life and Social Construction." In *Social Representations: Bridging Theoretical Traditions*, edited by Kay Deaux and Gina Philogene, 165–82. Oxford: Blackwell Publishers.

Langer, Ana, and Johannes Gruber. 2021. "Political Agenda Setting in the Hybrid Media System: Why Legacy Media Still Matter a Great Deal." *International Journal of Press/Politics* 26 (2): 313–40.

Macpherson, William. 1999. *The Stephen Lawrence Inquiry*. London: Home Office.

Malik, Sarita. 2002. *Representing Black Britain: A History of Black and Asian Images*. London and Thousand Oaks: SAGE Publications.

McFarlane, Tracy. 2006. "The Intersection of Race, Gender, and Class in Social Transitions: Caribbean Immigrant Women Negotiating US Higher Education." PhD thesis, City University of New York. https://search.proquest.com/openview/872cfac529cc6aa004f62e2204139be8/1?pq-origsite=gscholar&cbl=18750&diss=y.

———. 2017. "Poetry as Data: Art for the Social Psychological Study of Migration." In *The Caribbean Writer*, 361–69. Kingshill: University of the Virgin Islands.

Ministry of Housing, Communities and Local Government. "Annual Day of Celebrations for the Windrush Generation." UK Government, 18 June 2018. https://www.gov.uk/government/news/annual-day-of-celebrations-for-the-windrush-generation.

Moscovici, Serge. 1973. "Foreword." In *Health and Illness: A Social Psychological Analysis*, edited by Claudine Herzlich, 10–14. London: Academic Press.

———. 1984. "The Phenomenon of Social Representations." In *Social Representations*, edited by Robert M. Farr and Serge Moscovici, 3–69. Cambridge: Cambridge University Press.

———. 1988. "Notes Towards a Description of Social Representations." *European Journal of Social Psychology* 18 (3): 211–50.

National Archives. 2021. "Commonwealth Immigration Control and Legislation." UK National Archives, 1 February 2021. https://www.nationalarchives.gov.uk/cabinetpapers/.

National Audit Office. 2021. "Investigation into the Windrush Compensation Scheme." UK National Audit Office, 21 May. https://www.nao.org.uk/report/investigation-into-the-windrush-compensation-scheme/.

Nwonka, Clive James, and Sarita Malik. 2018. "Cultural Discourses and Practices of Institutionalised Diversity in the UK Film Sector: 'Just Get Something Black Made'." *Sociological Review* 66 (6): 1111–27.

Olick, Jeffrey K. 2007. "From Usable Pasts to the Return of the Repressed." *Hedgehog Review* 9 (2) :19–31.

Phillips, Coretta. 2011. "Institutional Racism and Ethnic Inequalities: An Expanded Multilevel Framework." *Journal of Social Policy* 40 (1): 173–92.

Powell, Enoch. 1968. "Speech at Birmingham." https://www.enochpowell.net/the-birmingham-speech.html.

Race Disparity Unit. 2021. "Stop and Search Data and the Effect of Geographical Differences.". UK Government, 31 March. https://www.gov.uk/government/publications/stop-and-search-data-and-the-effect-of-geographical-differences/stop-and-search-interpreting-and-describing-statistics#stop-and-search-latest-facts-and-figures.

Solomos, John. 2003. *Race and Racism in Britain*. Basingstoke: Palgrave Macmillan.

Taylor, Charles. 1994. "The Politics of Recognition." In *Multiculturalism: Examining the Politics of Recognition*, edited by Amy Gutmann, 25–73. Princeton: Princeton University Press.

Turner, Bryan. 2001. "Outline of a General Theory of Cultural Citizenship." In *Cultural Citizenship*, edited by Nick Stevenson, 11–32. London: Sage.

Unger, Rhoda. 2000. "Outsiders Inside: Positive Marginality and Social Change." *Journal of Social Issues* 56 (1): 163–79.

Vernon, Patrick. 2018. "The Windrush Shaped Britain. Why Not Recognise That?" *Guardian*, 9 May. https://www.theguardian.com/commentisfree/2018/may/09/windrush-shaped-britain-70-years-immigration-national-holiday.

Walker, Peter, and Amelia Gentleman. 2018. "Theresa May apologises for treatment of Windrush citizens." *Guardian*, 17 April. https://www.theguardian.com/uk-news/2018/apr/17/uk-still-uncertain-about-windrush-era-deportations.

White, Nadine, and Sara Turnnidge. 2020. "The Government's Windrush Compensation Scheme is Traumatising Victims All Over Again." Huff Post UK, 23 April. https://www.huffingtonpost.co.uk/entry/windrush-day-victims-and-families-await-compensation-two-years-later_uk_5eeb3013c5b62b2cae2785f-d?guccounter=1.

Williams, Wendy. 2020. "Windrush Lessons Learned Review." UK Home Office, 31 March. https://www.gov.uk/government/publications/windrush-les-sons-learned-review.

11

The Canada-Caribbean Seasonal Agricultural Worker Program (SAWP) in and Beyond COVID-19

Involuntary Mobilities, Liberalized Food Systems and Multiple Inequities

KRISTIN LOZANSKI, TALIA ESNARD AND TOMASO FERRANDO

EACH YEAR, THOUSANDS OF CARIBBEAN AND MEXICAN WORKERS travel to Canada to participate in the Seasonal Agricultural Workers Program (SAWP), a temporary work venture in which workers are assigned to agricultural employers for up to eight months at a time (Government of Canada 2020a). SAWP has become a mainstay of labour for Canadian agricultural employers and also for the Mexican and Commonwealth Caribbean governments as a source of foreign remittances. Though it has been in operation since 1966, it was put at risk in March 2020, when the Canadian government closed its borders to all but essential travel in response to the COVID-19 pandemic. An immediate intervention from the Canadian agricultural lobby resulted in the Canadian government designating migrant agricultural workers[1] as essential workers and reopening the border to these transnational labourers (Ramsaroop 2023).

The media coverage of the border closure and reopening to migrant agricultural workers brought widespread public attention to the critical labour provided by these men and women. To protect the Jamaican government from liability and medical expenses, SAWP applicants were required to sign an "Instrument of Release and Discharge" exempting regional governments from costs or losses associated with the pandemic (Mojtehedzadeh 2020). As many researchers and worker advocates foresaw, migrant agricultural workers experienced significant COVID-19 outbreaks (Venkatesh et al. 2023). In Ontario, for instance, the province with the greatest number of SAWP workers, saw outbreaks at Greenhill Produce (103 workers, Pedro 2020); Scotlynn Farms (199 workers, Mojtehedzadeh 2020); and Pioneer Flower Farms (60 workers, LaFleche 2020), along with smaller outbreaks at other agricultural workplaces (for example, Ontario Plant Propagation, according to De Bono and Bieman 2020) in the early summer. Through the season, approximately eighteen hundred migrant agricultural workers were infected with COVID-19. Three of those workers – Juan López Chapparo, Rogelio Muñoz Santos, and Bonifacio Eugenio Romero – died from the virus which they contracted on their farms (Baum and Grant 2020).

The coverage of these outbreaks and deaths began to shift attention in both Canada and the Caribbean towards the structural elements of the SAWP, which exacerbated workers' susceptibility to COVID-19 and rendered migrant agricultural workers the second most vulnerable group in Canada. This visibility has helped to direct attention to the experiences and aspirations of migrant agricultural workers who participate in such bilateral work programmes, an underexplored area in Caribbean scholarship (Beckford 2016). Even less attention has been directed at the micro and macro implications of a work programme that provides cheap labour to one of the granaries of the world, while reproducing uneven social and economic conditions within Canada, and between Canada and the Caribbean. In this chapter, we situate the SAWP in the context of COVID-19. We seek to leverage this unique moment to propose a people-centred, systemic and critical reflection on the desirability – or not – of programmes like the SAWP for the future of the Caribbean region.

METHODS

Methodologically, this project is informed by critical race theory and the need to engage research methods that are consistent with the tenets of CRT, including knowledge generated by people of colour – in this case, the SAWP workers. The use of the narrative inquiry and counter narrative as a method aligns with objectives of critical race theory (Delgado and Stefancic 2001; Reynolds and Mayweather 2017), and enables researchers to "deliberately see the world and its corresponding realities from the position of the subjugated" (Moore Mensah 2019, 1413). This project is oriented towards "a process that is thorough and reflective in its understanding of the expressed concerns of communities experiencing and resisting White supremacy" (Stovall 2018, 80).

This analysis of agricultural labour in Niagara-on-the-Lake (NOTL) is a specific intervention within an ongoing yet larger ethnographic research project that explores the relationships with English-speaking SAWP workers from Jamaica. For this narrative inquiry project, however, researchers employed semi-structured interviews with six workers in NOTL, which took place in October 2020. In the debriefing process, workers understood that the intention of learning about their experiences – both in the ongoing research and in the specific inquiry about COVID-19 – is to help others understand the living and working conditions that underpin local food production, within a clearly articulated critique of their experiences as SAWP workers and the impact of these experiences not just for themselves, but for their families as well. Given the nature of farm work and the limited access to farms, interviews remained informal with several conducted face to face, via telephone and WhatsApp. During these conversations, short prompts were written openly by hand and drafted into detailed field notes as soon as possible afterwards. Only face-to-face interviews were recorded.

In this analysis, we situate those reflections and shared stories alongside formally documented and anecdotal responses to COVID-19 by employers and governments in both Canada and the Commonwealth Caribbean. Interviews were subsequently thematically analysed with attention to COVID-19 and the SAWP experience, structured risk associated with farm work in Canada, and implications for future mobilities. Through the integration of SAWP workers' stories, these responses, and consideration of the historical and economic context of SAWP, we reveal the ways that the precarity structured into the programme is a metonym for the precarity that organizes the relationship between Canada and the Commonwealth Caribbean. This research has been approved by the Research Ethics Review Committee at King's University

College (Ontario, Canada), but is also situated within an understanding of ethical research conduct that exceeds institutional review processes and instead engages ethics as ongoing practice and commitment towards participants (Roger and Mignone 2018; Stovall 2018).

HISTORY OF THE SAWP

Subsequent to the globalization of food systems, the SAWP was introduced to ensure Canadian food security, and the financial viability of Canadian agribusiness (Preibisch 2007; McKarney 2013), which were reliant upon temporary workers (Preibisch and Binford 2007; Glassco 2012). In the 1960s, Canadian agricultural employers, lobbyists and private investors advanced a call for a formalized programme of seasonal labour as a means to provide a more sustained – and compliant – supply of agricultural workers (Reid-Musson 2014; Preibisch and Binford 2007; McLaughlin 2010; Glassco 2012). As a migrant labour scheme, the SAWP (originally called the Federal-Provincial Agricultural Manpower Program) met the seasonal requirements of production and also offered lower wage labour for employers and social welfare savings for the Canadian state.

In the context of economic depression and de-industrialization experienced by the Caribbean region in the 1970s and 1980s, the SAWP offered a promising opportunity for those who faced employment challenges amidst an economic downturn (Weis 2006). In Jamaica, social and economic hardship – alongside civil unrest; the reduced recruitment of Jamaicans under the US H2 programme; and the introduction of the British Commonwealth Immigrants Act (1962), which ended the automatic right to settle in the United Kingdom – pushed the government to agree to a formal migrant labour scheme that would provide employment and remittances for its citizens (Braun 2012). For participants, the SAWP offered an alternative option for employment and economic mobility (although one without access to permanent residency in the Global North.) For Caribbean sending countries, the SAWP inferred the introduction of new farming knowledge and technologies acquired in Canada, alongside remittances and financial support for families and communities experiencing unemployment and economic hardship.

This bilateral agreement between the Canadian government and the Caribbean region began with 264 Jamaican workers as part of a pilot scheme in 1966 (Beckford 2016; E. Thomas 2020). This programme extended to workers from Barbados, and Trinidad and Tobago (1967), and subsequently to workers from the Organization of Eastern Caribbean States (1976). Mexican workers, who now make up the majority of SAWP workers, were included in the programme in 1974 in a deliberate effort to limit the negotiating power of Caribbean states (Satzewich 2008).

STRUCTURAL PROBLEMS AND DRAWBACKS

Canada's SAWP has been often depicted as an international best practice model (see Hennebry and Preibisch 2010; Vosko 2018) that benefits workers, Canadian employers, and the involved states (Headley and Henry 2015). However, the SAWP reproduces micro and macro asymmetries between individuals, countries, economies and food systems. The programme's negative impacts are disproportionately borne by individual participants who experience precarious work that is situated within gendered and racialized discrimination. While abroad, SAWP workers have limited access to basic necessities and are exposed to occupational hazards and stressors, as well as threats to their reproductive, physical and mental health (Preibisch and Otero 2014; McLaughlin, Hennebry, and Haines 2014). In Canada, SAWP workers endure poor living and working conditions (Headley and Henry 2015; Beckford 2016), and constrained mobility (Reid-Musson 2017; Smith 2005). They are "permanently temporary" (McLaughlin 2010), with no formal path to permanent status. They can also be repatriated for "noncompliance, refusal to work, or any other sufficient reason", as determined by their employer (Employment and Social Development Canada 2020, 11; Vosko 2018; Wells et al. 2014).

GENDER DISCRIMINATION

While women have been encouraged to participate since 1989, their numbers have been consistently and substantially lower compared to men (Beckford 2016) comprising less than 5 per cent of total participants over the fifty years of the programme's existence (see Gabriel and Macdonald 2019) due, in part, to their maternal responsibilities or other seasonal employment in their home country. The inability of family members to travel with SAWP workers is often seen as a guarantee that women, in particular, will return to their home country. Despite this expectation of familial obligations as a form of mobility discipline (Mannon et al. 2011), men continue to be preferred as a direct result of the gender stereotypes around agricultural labour and the "essentialized masculine attribute [that is] mapped on to their racialized, gendered, and classed bodies" (McDowell cited in E. Thomas 2020, 3). Once within employer-provided bunkhouses, Perry (2018) contends that the dormitory system produces intensified worker self-discipline, hyper-normative notions of gender, with the ultimate result of a hyper-productive transnational workforce (see also Binford 2009).

RACIALIZED SUBJECTIVITIES

Like other temporary labour programmes, the SAWP depends on and reiterates the racialized subjectivities of workers. Smith (2015a) notes that the racialized representations of migrant agricultural workers within the media and stereotypes within the local community sustain the SAWP. The subject positions of Caribbean SAWP workers – most often brown and black men with low socioeconomic status – do not align with that of worthy migrants, so their inclusion in Canada is "permanently temporary" (Hennebry 2012), and instrumentalized as their work (Sharma 2006). These discourses support a "racist immigration policy that denied [and continues to deny] temporary visas or permanent residence to people of colour" (Preibisch and Binford 2007, 9). Yet within these exclusionary spaces, SAWP workers struggle to support their families and communities: agricultural spaces become dual sites of exploitation and of actualization, as they negotiate neoliberal subjectivities that command individual endurance to transform their lives and the lives of others.

COVID-19 AND THE SAWP

The biological threat posed by COVID-19 and the subsequent surveillance apparatus targeted towards migrant agricultural workers amplified the existing discursive, symbolic and material violence experienced by SAWP workers, while simultaneously intensifying their precariousness and disposability. Yet, the conversations we had with SAWP workers, alongside the political mobilization of migrant agricultural workers across the country and increasing public awareness in Canada of the conditions of agricultural production, signalled the potential for tangible reforms of the programme, and food production systems overall.

In order to manage the push by employers to designate migrant agricultural workers as essential workers and reopen the border to them, the Canadian government introduced a mandatory fourteen-day quarantine period for arriving SAWP workers in late March 2020, when there were nineteen confirmed cases of COVID-19 in Jamaica (Tufton 2020) and over one thousand cases in Canada, including 318 confirmed cases in Ontario (Canadian Press 2020). On arrival in Canada, the majority of SAWP workers were confined to bunkhouses for fourteen days. During their confinement, many SAWP workers reported violations of essential rights, including their right to food, despite a federal provision of $1500 per worker to agricultural employers to offset costs associated with workers' confinement (Government of Canada 2020b). These funds were intended to support payment of wages (thirty hours per week at $14.25/hour) and any other expenses incurred by the employer. Yet one community organizer reported that an employer provided workers with two slices of bread and one egg each for the first forty-eight hours they were in Canada (Interview with Niagara resident 2020; see also Haley et al. 2020). At another farm, workers were required to sign a contract committing to repay the employer the cost of food purchased on their behalf, food that included more expensive items (such as premium cuts of meat) purchased at a more expensive grocery store than agricultural workers would usually shop at.

SAWP workers also encountered widespread restrictions of essential liberties. A report by the Migrant Workers Alliance for Change (2020, 22) includes examples of workers being forced to sign agreements indicating they "would not leave the bunkhouse – not even for essential items like food and personal supplies". Many employers banned visitors to the farms, including community members dropping off food and other necessary items for workers who were effectively confined (Nash 2020). Multiple accounts exist of the strict enforcement of isolation and severe discipline for minimum deviations from this rule. One news report highlights the case of two Mexican SAWP workers who were repatriated for speaking to a Canadian who was dropping off food and warm clothing, which the workers had been unable to procure themselves due to restrictions on their mobility (M. Thomas 2020). The mandatory quarantine – without testing – not only impacted workers' ability to obtain essential goods for themselves, but it also meant that they were unable to send money to support their families. One worker was frustrated that "[we] even have to ask to go on the road to send money. Have to ask permission to send money. I [don't] think all these are right" (KB, St James).

The mandatory isolation of workers arriving in Canada from countries with lower infection rates, the absence of any testing on arrival, and the quarantining of many workers together in bunkhouses (rather than individually, per 2021 quarantine standards) indicate that workers were identified as a *source of risk,* rather than themselves being *at risk.* This narrative of SAWP workers as a source of infection builds upon historical, racialized stereotypes of black men as a source of embodied risk that must be controlled and disciplined (Keegan 2023). Even prior to the global pandemic, SAWP workers were subjected to surveillance and controls over their mobility within Canada. Indeed, such "immobilities are . . . systemic to SAWP and the power to control workers' mobilities is invaluable to the labor control that family farm operations harness through Canada's labor migration programmes" (Reid-Musson 2014, 717). Notably, similar restrictions did not apply to Canadian workers on the same farms: according to CB (St James), "some people who work with we [sic] and they go where they want and we use the same tools in the morning." In this way, Jamaican SAWP workers had their mobility policed in the name of limiting COVID-19 transmission, while others with whom they worked closely did not experience the same restrictions.[2]

WORKER IMMOBILITY

Even for SAWP workers not in quarantine, the intensification of employer control over mobility, and the limitation of their rights in the name of "health and safety", was so widespread that the Canadian government issued a letter to employers that stated:

> The Government of Canada has received allegations that some employers are requiring TFWs [temporary foreign workers] to remain on the property where they live (and work, in some cases) when not at work outside of mandatory quarantine or self-isolation periods. [...]
>
> – The TFW Program does not provide employers with the right to limit the free movement of workers, such as movement off the property where TFWs live and/or work. Like all workers, TFWs are free to run errands, access services, and enjoy their time off work when not in quarantine, self-isolating, or otherwise restricted from doing so as per government laws and orders.
>
> – Limiting a TFW's movement may be considered abuse under the Immigration and Refugee Protection Regulations and a violation of the TFW Program's conditions. (Massé 2020, original emphasis).

As one SAWP worker in Niagara-on-the-Lake suggested, "This year is the worst year [. . .] The problem I find with my work now, you see, you come from work, you have a shower, have something [to] eat, probably a smoke or a drink, a drink of beer and you relax and then you go to your bed and then you go back to work" (S.D., St Mary).

Another SAWP worker also reflected on the psychological consequences of not being able to gather socially: "You remember, we are people" (T.P., St Andrew).

In all provinces outside of British Columbia, the SAWP contract requires that the employer "provide clean, adequate living accommodations" (Employment and Social Development Canada 2020, Section II A1). While this provision reduces the participation costs for workers, it means that many SAWP workers live in close proximity to their employers, who – as the owners or lessees of the residence – have access to workers' non-working spaces (Smith 2015b). Even pre-COVID, many employers required that all guests to the bunkhouses be approved in advance, even though no such provision appears in the bi-laterally approved contract. Due to lack of public transportation in rural areas, migrant agricultural workers' primary form of autonomous transportation is by bicycle (see Reid-Musson 2018) and, as such, it is difficult for workers to get away from these spaces. During COVID-19, some employers withheld workers' access to their bicycles as a means of restricting their independent mobility. Even in public spaces, the surveillance of migrant agricultural workers increased during COVID-19 (Ramsaroop 2023): anticipating scrutiny of their presence in public spaces like the bank and grocery stores, several employers provided their workers with letters confirming their completion of quarantine, apparently as a form of protection.

STRUCTURED RISK FOR MIGRANT WORKERS

While increased controls and surveillance were imposed upon migrant agricultural workers to reduce transmission of COVID-19, the very structure of the SAWP renders its workers at high risk of contracting the virus. As Binford notes in his analysis of Mexican participants, "In order to have the opportunity to earn an income that moves the Mexico- [and Caribbean-] based members of the household unit out of economic poverty, SAWP participants must themselves live in poverty, Canadian-style, during their time in the destination country" (Binford 2013, 144).

Workers' accommodation and living arrangements are deeply problematic, and often their living conditions are antithetical to the public health measures that limit the spread of COVID-19 (Haley et al. 2020). Housing is inspected by municipal inspectors who may follow Schedule F of the Housing Inspection Report, which provides housing guidelines (not requirements) for migrant agricultural workers. These guidelines fall far short of dignified and safe living conditions and are inconsistent with pandemic public health protocols. For instance, the schedule calls for workers' beds to be eighteen inches apart "for comfortable movement" (Employment and Social Development Canada 2018, 5). Another guideline states that "[t]o prevent poor air quality, adequate ventilation by either natural means (windows) or artificial means (ceiling fans) is required" (ESDC 2018, 3), and that there should be at least one toilet and shower for every ten workers. These guidelines have not yet been revised to account for public health responses to COVID-19. Bunkhouses with poor ventilation and insufficient space for physical distancing substantially increase the risk for SAWP workers. Even the long hours of work over a period of months with insufficient rest (Otero and Preibisch 2010; Haley et al. 2020), the limited time to prepare and consume nutritious food (Weiler, McLaughlin and Cole 2017), and challenges for mental health due to isolation and separation from family (Hennebry and McLaughlin 2011) contribute to SAWP workers' susceptibility to COVID-19.

Despite often problematic conditions, employer-provided accommodations were subject to less rigorous inspection during COVID-19, as inspections could be "conducted in a virtual manner" (Government of Canada 2020c). The suitability – and safety – of SAWP workers' living conditions were assessed via phone interviews, video conference or the submission of photos. Notably, there was no requirement to provide evidence of the conditions inside the bunkhouses: "When providing photos of accommodations during quarantine, Service Canada does not advocate or expect employers to enter the space occupied by the workers in quarantine. *Photos can be taken from outside the structure* (our emphasis) or by workers" (Government of Canada 2020c #14).

These living conditions and workers' limited access to medical care (even prior to COVID – see Barnes 2013) have contributed to their health-related vulnerabilities. COVID-19 has amplified the structural inequities between those who possess privilege and those whose lives are most precarious (Smith and Judd 2020). Yet, these same structural inequities drive many SAWP workers to choose to participate in the programme. C.C. (St Thomas) described the very difficult decision to participate in the SAWP under pandemic conditions.

KL: So, were you nervous to come here for COVID?

CC: Very nervous. Very, very nervous. Yea, yea. I came on the second call [. . .] I went home because they gave us a piece of paper saying we're coming at our own risk so I think not to come. And my family, they didn't want me to come [but] when I look at the aspect of my kids, they're the ones that really motivated me to come because I don't have a job at home, so I really want to come here to like make money for them to like go to school and have clothes on their backs and food to eat. So that's when I really decided I'm coming.

The possibility of contracting COVID-19 weighed heavily on several workers – many opted not to participate – especially regarding the potential impact on their families. S.D. (St Mary) was concerned about how his family would be supported should he contract the virus and be unable to work: "Who gonna take care of our family back home in Jamaica for that period of time that we cannot work, for all that time that we cannot work? Because if we get sick by the virus, the boss will close [the farm for] a month, two month, or whatever until [they] say, 'It clear now, you can go back to work'. And for all those two month you are sitting down here, nothing."

The SAWP not only made participants more vulnerable to COVID-19 infection, but also their home communities because, in contrast to their arrival to Canada, workers *returning* to their home countries had to quarantine in their homes, putting their families and communities at risk. While COVID-19 testing was widely available in Canada prior to their departure, they were not tested before returning home. To enter Jamaica, tourists from high-risk countries staying within the "resilient corridor" required a negative COVID-19 test within five days of departure to obtain travel authorization (Visit Jamaica 2020). There was no similar requirement for SAWP workers returning to their communities. As one worker reflected, "[If I will infect my family] is the biggest question. We should get tested before we go home" (T.P., St Andrew).

While workers were unsure about how they might quarantine away from their families, they recognized the ways that the Jamaican government was actively off-loading risk onto the workers, particularly through the required COVID-19 waiver. "So, what they tell us back home in Jamaica, if we went here, we are [at] our own risk if we should catch COVID-19 because they're not going to respond to us. So, they make [us] sign back home at the Ministry of Labour, that's what they make us do […] They [don't] respond [to] us. We're [at] our own risk coming here" (S.D., St Mary). Fortunately, there were no documented cases of returning SAWP workers introducing COVID-19 into their communities.

At the same time that the Jamaican government individualized the risks of COVID-19, it continued to benefit from SAWP workers' remittances and the foreign goods they brought back in barrels and crates. T.P. (St Andrew) observed, "We don't get support. The[y] should recognize us more. Even

Jamaican government. We get COVID, they aren't respon[ding] [to]us. We come up and work and build their economy. That's why this year I did not] ship [anything]."

Despite their (labour) contributions to Canada and their (remittance) contributions to their home countries, SAWP workers are keenly aware of their ongoing disposability as workers. One explained the disposability of his labour in a vivid way, suggesting that a SAWP worker sent home early (due to injury or discipline) would breathe the breath of the person coming to replace him as they passed each other in the airport. The lives and labour of precarious, interchangeable workers serve the capitalist needs of a foreign country as they work towards the economic survival of their own families. One worker understood this replaceability to operate even through death, which he felt would not be recognized as a loss of his government: "If I should go out there tomorrow morning in the field, and I die, the only thing that they do, call the paramed, 'One die.' They bag you up, probably get a casket, put you in, the Ministry or whatever put $10,000 on your stomach, 'Another one in Canada.' One gone, one come, one gone, one come and your family just sacrifice[d] your life" (S.D., St Mary).

While COVID-19 has exacerbated the poor living and working conditions of some SAWP workers, it is noteworthy that not all identified the pandemic as the primary source of their difficulties. For those who work on larger-scale farms in more remote communities, the isolation was not significantly different than usual , as they have very little capacity to travel the relatively long distances between farms or to public places (Reid-Musson 2017); and may not even know where they are. Beyond geography, the living and working conditions of SAWP workers are dependent upon the extent to which their employer prioritizes their dignity and well-being (Wells et al. 2020). As he was about to transfer to a remote apple farm, C.B. (St James) was grateful to leave his first farm, despite colder working conditions and possible COVID-19 exposure (due to workers from multiple farms transferring in without the requirement for testing or quarantine) because harvesting apples meant "likkle more space, likkle more peace of mind. Boss treat[s] we like normal people." Similarly, N.F. (Manchester) explained his particularly challenging season outside of COVID-19: "COVID didn't change anything. It's all the boss." Thus, while the pandemic intensified the biological risk and surveillance that they faced, the underlying living and work conditions did not necessarily change, but was only revealed.

FUTURE MOBILITIES

As a transnational labour regime, the SAWP draws from countries with poor employment opportunities and more willing participants than there are spaces. This global supply guarantees the continuous provision of labour for Canada, the fifth-largest food trader in the world. The production of food for transnational distribution relies upon transnational mobilities. As such, the SAWP institutionalizes the involuntary mobilities of those who live precarious lives in the Caribbean (and Mexico). The men and women who participate in SAWP and other similar cyclical migration programmes rely on the sale of their labour abroad as a way to cover housing, food and clothing expenses; support their children's education; cover medical expenses; and repay debts (Budworth, Rose, and Mann 2017; Wells et al. 2014). Similar prospects are not available in their home country or region.

While Caribbean SAWP workers shoulder a disproportionate burden of risk, their willingness to accept it through involuntary mobility has been taken for granted by those who benefit the most – agricultural employers in Canada, the Canadian state, and Caribbean states. The employers don't have to invest in local training, the creation of long-term relationships with the local workforce, or changes to agricultural working conditions, including paying more than the minimum wage. As Sharma (2006, 98) notes, this labour shortage is a qualitative one, not a quantitative one, which is tied to the poor working conditions rejected by those with permanent status. In 2010, Canadian horticultural producers exported more than $3 billion in fruit, vegetables and floriculture products (Government of Canada 2011). These exports are, in turn, dependent upon the taken-for-granted 'import' (temporary and cyclical) of SAWP workers, who are not entitled to the same social welfare benefits as Canadians. Though SAWP workers must pay into Canadian social programmes via income tax deductions, employment insurance premiums and Canada Pension Plan contributions, their capacity to access such benefits is extremely limited. For instance, in 2014, SAWP workers' contributions to these three programmes were more than $90 million (see UFCW 2014). These direct financial contributions must not be overlooked.

Caribbean governments have come to rely upon the continuous flow of capital that supports the housing and small business formation of workers and their families, and enables the privatization of public goods, such as education and healthcare in the context of shrinking social programmes, which have introduced a new form of North-South dependence. According to a World Bank study, remittance flows into Latin America and the Caribbean are continuous and growing, reaching a total of $88 billion in 2018 (World Bank 2018). Even more troubling is the proportion of remittances as a percentage of GDP in individual countries: with 33.6 per cent of the Haitian GDP in 2018 composed of remittances; 21.1 per cent in El Salvador; 15.9 per cent in Jamaica and Guatemala; while Nicaragua and Dominica received 12.1 and 9.6 per cent respectively (World Bank 2019). As a stimulus to these flows, the SAWP plays a crucial role in filling gaps in the welfare state and in deferring moments of political and economic transformation that may reshape the future of the region.

From the point of view of economic urgency, we recognize the merits of the SAWP in providing economic relief to families and governments. In this short-term framing, there is a need for a decisive improvement of working conditions and working status. However, from a long-term and systemic perspective, the SAWP reiterates the transnational asymmetries that underpinned not only colonial plantations, but also the modern policies that have transformed the Caribbean into a hub for tourists. In this context, any so-called improvements to the SAWP are effectively counter to those required for a just and sustainable response to both COVID-19 and the climate crisis. With the intensification of climate change and COVID-19's interruption of just-on-time trade, people and the planet do not need more involuntary mobility or more food obtained through monoculture and long value chains. They need a radical transformation of the food system that is based on local, stable, reliable and agroecological practices, so that small-scale landholders are empowered and able to access local and regional markets for the sale of their healthy and fresh products (Weis 2006). In this sense, the Canadian permanent status for Caribbean seasonal agricultural workers is a step of dignity, solidarity and respect of human rights that must be taken. However, this status would crystallize a vulnerable and unsustainable food system. The true political revolution would thus consist in the re-politicization of the ongoing "people and food" trade (im)balance of the Caribbean, and in the adoption of systemic land and food system reforms that would put small-holders, agricultural workers, eaters, and the regeneration of the planet at the centre; eradicate the root causes of hunger and climate change; and free the region from a future of dependency, uncertainty and food insecurity.

CONCLUSION

The COVID-19 pandemic increased the visibility of the poor living and working conditions of SAWP workers and generated political momentum for change. From the "ghettos" of Borgo Mezzanone in southern Italy to British Columbia, migrants, advocacy groups and unions are asking for regularization (in the case of migrants who are not part of any scheme) and permanent residency as key instruments to improve living conditions, increase workers' bargaining power, and guarantee access to justice and the full respect of their human rights. Permanent status undermines the conditions of economic disposability and political invisibility and reduces the fear of retaliation. While permanent residency will guarantee more bargaining power to workers and unions, it may be counterproductive if still subordinated to the fluctuations of the international market for food commodities. Canadian employers depend on trading food-as-commodity internationally and to maintain their market share and competitive advantage, labour is often seen as the one cost that can be squeezed to produce cheaper goods. When labour standards increase, costs are commensurate.

The fight for permanent residency through the SAWP cannot be dissociated from the fight to solve the structural problems underpinning the Caribbean economy and its food system. Access to permanent residency for SAWP workers would not disrupt the region's dependence on remittances. A further risk is that the fight for permanent residency would be dissociated from the fight against the global liberalization that is producing unemployment and low wages in both the Caribbean and

Canada, while also dissipating the political and organizing energies that are critical to establishing a strong, regional food system. An increase in remittances and the deepening of the uneven ties with economies in the Global North should not be seen as success if they are contrary to the achievement of collective economic and food self-reliance in the Caribbean.

For these reasons, visions for the future of mobility should not be disentangled from visions for the future of food systems. Caribbean states not only export labour and depend on remittances, they also import a significant share of the food that they consume: their food security is closely tied to production that happens elsewhere, primarily in North America. According to the Food and Agriculture Organization, the combined food import of the fourteen CARICOM member countries increased by 50 per cent between 2000 and 2018, reaching $4.75 billion in 2018 (cited in Ewing-Chow 2019). This total is expected to reach $8–$10 billion by 2020. These figures indicate that, for almost all CARICOM members, more than 60 per cent of the food consumed is imported, with half of them importing more than 80 per cent of the food they consume.

We cannot overlook the fact that the same trade and liberalization policies that have resulted in Canada's status as a world leader in food export have simultaneously rendered the Caribbean a source of cheap labour that enables Canadian economic success. While COVID-19 has revealed many of the deeply problematic living and working conditions that enable the SAWP's viability as a migrant agricultural work programme (Haley et al. 2020), these conditions reveal the unsustainability of the contemporary Canadian model of agriculture. Rather that re-organizing a system based on legacies of colonialism, or exclusively advocating for the permanent status for agricultural workers in Canada (who continue to be embedded in a food and trade system that is impoverishing and starving the Caribbean region), we are calling for a reorientation of the post-COVID-19 political impetus and of the renewed consciousness towards the establishment of self-reliant food systems in the whole Caribbean region. This vision is based on principles of food and land sovereignty, and addresses, as its core mission, the financial and food poverty that drives the SAWP's migratory labour patterns.

NOTES

1. The term migrant agricultural worker is used to refer to both SAWP workers and other migrants who are in Canada as part of the agricultural stream of the Temporary Foreign Worker Program.
2. These workers are typically Mexican Mennonites, (white) Mennonites with Canadian citizenship who migrate between Canada and Mexico, and hold higher status jobs on farms, while also being marginal in Canadian society.

REFERENCES

Barnes, Nielan. 2013. "Is Health a Labour, Citizenship or Human right? Mexican Seasonal Agricultural Workers in Leamington, Canada." *Global Public Health* 8 (6): 654–69.

Baum, Kathryn Blaze, and Tavia Grant. 2020. "Third Migrant Farm Worker Dies as Canada Reaches Deal with Mexico." *Globe and Mail,* 21 June 2020. https://www.theglobeandmail.com/canada/article-third-migrant-farm-worker-dies-as-canada-reaches-deal-with-mexico/.

Beckford, Clinton. 2016. "The Experiences of Caribbean Migrant Farmworkers in Ontario, Canada." *Social & Economic Studies* 65 (1): 153–88.

Binford, Leigh. 2009. "From Fields of Power to Fields of Sweat: The Dual Process of Constructing Temporary Migrant Labour in Mexico and Canada." *Third World Quarterly* 30 (3): 503–17.

———. 2013. *Tomorrow We're All Going to the Harvest: Temporary Foreign Worker Programs and Neoliberal Political Economy.* Austin: University of Texas Press.

Braun, James. 2012. "Respectable Subjects: The Commonwealth Caribbean Seasonal Agricultural Workers Program in Postcolonial Context." MA thesis, Carleton University.

Budworth, Marie-Hélène, Andrew Rose, and Sara Mann. 2017. *Report on the Seasonal Agricultural Worker Program.* Ottawa: Inter-American Institute for Cooperation on Agriculture Delegation. https://drive.google.com/drive/folders/0BoJfN-QODk2eob2cyLUN4VnZnXzg.

Campbell, Taylor. 2020. "Shared Bunkhouse Triggers 17 New COVID-19 Cases at Kingsville Farm." *Windsor Star,* 9 October 2020. https://windsorstar.com/news/local-news/shared-bunkhouse-triggers-17-new-covid-19-cases-at-kingsville-farm.

Canadian Press. 2020. "The Latest Numbers of COVID-19 Cases in Canada." *National Post,* 20 March, 2020. https://nationalpost.com/pmn/news-pmn/canada-news-pmn/the-latest-numbers-of-covid-19-cases-in-canada-as-of-march-20-2020.

De Bono, Norman, and Jennifer Bieman. 2020. "COVID-19 Outbreak at Greenhouse Grows with 19 Migrant Workers now Sick." *London Free Press*, 30 May. https://lfpress.com/news/local-news/covid-19-outbreak-at-greenhouse-grows-with-19-migrant-workers-now-sick.

Delgado, Richard, and Jean Stefancic. 2001. *Critical Race Theory: An Introduction*. New York: New York University Press.

Dubinski, Kate. 2020. "Canada Lifts Restrictions on Foreign Workers, including Migrant Farm Workers." CBC News, 21 March 2020. https://www.cbc.ca/news/canada/london/canada-lifts-travel-restrictions-for-foreign-workers-1.5505579.

Employment and Social Development Canada. 2018. "Schedule F: Housing Inspection Report Seasonal Agricultural Worker Program and Agricultural Stream." https://catalogue.servicecanada.gc.ca/content/EForms/en/CallForm.html?Lang=en&PDF=ESDC-EMP5598.pdf.

———. 2020. "Contract for the Employment in Canada of Commonwealth Caribbean Seasonal Agricultural Workers." https://www.canada.ca/content/dam/canada/employment-social-development/migration/documents/assets/portfolio/docs/en/foreign_workers/hire/seasonal_agricultural/documents/sawpcc2020.pdf.

Ewing-Chow, Daphne. 2019. "Five Overlooked Facts about Caribbean Food Security." *Forbes,* 20 February 2019. https://www.forbes.com/sites/daphneewing-chow/2019/02/20/five-facts-about-caribbean-food-security/?sh=4c037bb25016.

Gabriel, Christina, and Laura Macdonald. 2019. "Contesting Gender Discrimination in the Canadian Seasonal Agricultural Worker Program." *Canadian Ethnic Studies* 51 (3): 17–34.

Glassco, Clare. 2012. "Harvesting Power and Subjugation: Canada's Seasonal Agricultural Workers Program in Historical Context." MA thesis, Trent University.

Government of Canada. 2020a. "Hire a Temporary Worker through the Seasonal Agricultural Worker Program: Overview." https://www.canada.ca/en/employment-social-development/services/foreign-workers/agricultural/seasonal-agricultural.html.

———. 2020b. "Mandatory Isolation Support for Temporary Foreign Workers Program." https://www.agr.gc.ca/eng/agricultural-programs-and-services/mandatory-isolation-support-for-temporary-foreign-workers-program/?id=1588186409721.

———. 2020c. "Frequently Asked Questions: Changes to the Temporary Foreign Worker Program Regarding COVID-19." https://www.canada.ca/en/employment-social-development/services/foreign-workers/employer-compliance/covid-faq.html.

———. 2011. "Statistical Overview of Canadian Horticulture, 2009–2010." https://cnla.ca/uploads/pdf/Statistical-Overview-of-Canadian-Horticulture-2009-2010.pdf

Habib, Rima R., and Fadi A. Fathallah. 2012. "Migrant Women Farmworkers in the Occupational Health Literature." *Work* 41: 4356–62.

Haley, Ella, Susana Caxaj, Glynis George, Jenna Hennebry, Eliseo Martell, and Janet McLaughlin. 2020. "Migrant Farmworkers Face Heightened Vulnerabilities during COVID-19." *Journal of Agriculture, Food Systems, and Community Development* 9 (3): 1–5.

Headley, Bernard, and Kay Ann Henry. 2015. "Temporary Migration Work Programmes in the Caribbean (Jamaica and Trinidad and Tobago)." In *Migration and Development: Perspectives from Small States*, edited by Wonderful Hope Khonje, 33–59. London: Commonwealth Secretariat.

Hennebry, Jenna. 2012. "Permanently Temporary? Agricultural Migrant Workers and Their Integration in Canada." *Institute for Research on Public Policy* 26: 1–39. https://irpp.org/research-studies/permanently-temporary/.

Hennebry, Jenna, and Janet McLaughlin. 2011. "Key Issues and Recommendations for Canada's Temporary Foreign Worker Program: Reducing Vulnerabilities & Protecting Rights." *IMRC Policy Points* no. 2 (1 March). https://scholars.wlu.ca/imrc/14/.

Hennebry, Jenna, and Kerry Preibisch. 2010. "A Model for Managed Migration? Re-examining Best Practices in Canada's Seasonal Agricultural Worker Program." *International Migration* 50 (s1): 19–40.

Keegan, Caroline. 2023. "Essential agriculture, sacrificial labor, and the COVID-19 pandemic in the US South." *Journal of Agrarian Change*, 23(3), 611–21.

LaFleche, Grant. 2020. "COVID-19 Sickens 60 Pioneer Flower Farms Workers." *St Catharines Standard*, 3 June. https://www.stcatharinesstandard.ca/news/niagara-region/2020/06/03/covid-19-sickens-60-pioneer-flower-farms-workers.html.

Mannon, Susan E., Peggy Petrzelka, Christy M. Glass, and Claudia Radel. 2011. "Keeping Them in Their Place: Migrant Women Workers in Spain's Strawberry Industry." *International Journal of Sociology of Agriculture and Food* 19 (10): 83–101.

Massé, Philippe. 2020. "Notice Regarding Temporary Foreign Workers' Freedom of Movement." 30 August 2020. https://migrantworkerhub.ca/wp-content/uploads/2020/06/reminderfreedomofmovementTFW_english-version.pdf.

McKarney, Matthew. 2013. "In Defense of a Livelihood: Ontario Growers and the Seasonal Agriculture Agricultural Workers Program Debate." MA thesis, Western University.

McLaughlin, Janet, Jenna Hennebry, and Ted Haines. 2014. "Paper versus Practice: Occupational Health and Safety Protections and Realities for Temporary Foreign Agricultural Workers in Ontario." *Pistes: Interdisciplinary Journal of Work and Health* 16 (2): 2–17.

McLaughlin, Janet. 2010. "Classifying the Ideal Migrant Worker: Mexican and Jamaican Transnational Farmworkers in Canada." *Focaal – Journal of Global and Historical Anthropology* 57: 79–94.

Migrant Workers Alliance for Change. 2020. "Unheeded Warnings: COVID-19 & Migrant Workers in Canada." June 2020. https://migrantworkersalliance.org/wp-content/uploads/2020/06/Unheeded-Warnings-COVID19-and-Migrant-Workers.pdf.

Mojtehedzadeh, Sara. 2020. "Migrant Farm Workers from Jamaica are Being Forced to Sign COVID-19 Waivers." *The Star,* 13 April 2020. https://www.thestar.com/business/2020/04/13/migrant-farm-workers-fear-exposure-to-covid-19.html?rf.

Moore Mensah, Felicia. 2019. "Finding Voice and Passion: Critical Race Theory Methodology in Science Teacher Education." *American Educational Research Journal* 56 (4): 1412–56.

Nash, Chelsea. 2020. "Migrant Agricultural Workers Experiencing a Food Crisis." Rabble.ca. 23 July 2020. https://rabble.ca/news/2020/07/migrant-agricultural-workers-experiencing-food-crisis.

Otero, Gerardo, and Kerry Preibisch. 2010. "Farmworker Health and Safety: Challenges for British Columbia." WorkSafeBC. https://www.worksafebc.com/en/resources/about-us/research/farmworker-health-safety-challenges-for-bc?lang=en.

Pedro, Paul. 2020. "Greenhill Produce COVID-19 Outbreak Officially Over. *Blackburn News,* 17 June 2020. https://blackburnnews.com/chatham/chatham-news/2020/06/17/greenhill-produce-covid-19-outbreak-officially/.

Perry, J. Adam. 2018. "Play-making with Migrant Farm Workers in Ontario, Canada: A Kinaesthetic and Embodied Approach to Qualitative Research." *International Review of Qualitative Research* 18 (6): 591–603.

Preibisch, Kerry, and Gerardo Otero. 2014. "Does Citizenship Status Matter in Canadian Agriculture? Workplace Health and Safety for Migrant and Immigrant Laborers." *Rural Sociology* 79 (2): 174–99.

Preibisch, Kerry. 2007. "Local Produce, Foreign Labor: Labor Mobility Programs and Global Trade Competitiveness in Canada." *Rural Sociology* 72 (3): 418–49.

Preibisch, Kerry, and Leigh Binford. 2007. "Interrogating Racialized Global Labour Supply: An Exploration of the Racial/National Replacement of Foreign Agricultural Workers in Canada." *Canadian Review of Sociology* 44 (1): 5–36.

Ramsaroop, Chris. 2023. "Discipline and resistance in southwestern Ontario: Securitization of migrant workers and their acts of defiance." *Journal of Agrarian Change,* 23(3), 600–10.

Reid-Musson, Emily. 2014. "Historicizing Precarity: A Labour Geography of 'transient' migrant workers in Ontario tobacco." *Geoforum* 56: 161–71.

———. 2017. "Grown Close to HomeTM: Migrant Farmworker (Im)Mobilities and

Unfreedom on Canadian Family Farms." *Annals of the American Association of Geographers* 107 (3): 716–30.

———. 2018. "Shadow Mobilities: Regulating Migrant Bicyclists in Rural Ontario, Canada." *Mobilities* 13 (3): 308–24.

Reynolds, Rema, and Darquillius Mayweather. 2017. "Recounting Racism, Resistance, and Repression: Examining the Experiences and #Hashtag Activism of College Students with Critical Race Theory and Counternarratives." *Journal of Negro Education* 86 (3): 283–304.

Roger, Kerstin, and Javier Mignone. 2018. "Living Your Ethics: 'It's Not Just a Dusty Document." In *The Craft of Qualitative Research: A Handbook*, edited by Steven W. Kleinecht, Lisa-Jo K. van den Scott, and Carrie B. Sanders, 46–52. Toronto: Canadian Scholars Press.

Satzewich, Vic. 2008. "Business or Bureaucratic Dominance in Immigration in Canada: Why was Mexico Included in the Caribbean Seasonal Agricultural Workers Program in 1974?" *Journal of International Migration and Integration* 8 (3): 255–75.

Sharma, Nandita. 2006. *Home Economics: Nationalism and the Making of 'Migrant Workers' in Canada.* Toronto: University of Toronto Press.

Smith, Adrian. 2005. "Legal Consciousness and Resistance in Caribbean Seasonal Agricultural Workers." *Canadian Journal of Law and Society* 20: 95–122.

———. 2015a. "Troubling 'Project Canada': The Caribbean and the Making of 'Unfree Migrant Labor.'" *Canadian Journal of Latin American and Caribbean Studies* 40 (2): 274–93.

———. 2015b. "The Bunk House Rules: Housing Migrant Labour in Ontario." *Osgoode Hall Law Journal* 52 (3): 863–904.

Smith, James A., and Jenni Judd. 2020. "COVID-19: Vulnerability and the Power of Privilege in a Pandemic." *Health Promotion Journal of Australia* 31 (2):158.

Stovall, David. 2018. "The Commitment to Break Rules: Critical Race Theory, Jazz Methodology and the Struggle for Justice in Education." In *Understanding Critical Race Research Methods and Methodologies: Lessons from the Field*, edited by Jessica T. DeCuir-Gunby, Thandeka K. Chapman, and Paul A. Schutz, 76–85. New York: Routledge.

Thomas, Edward. 2020. "'Forgetting' to Survive: Black Jamaican Masculinities in Canada's Seasonal Agricultural Worker Program." *Gender, Place & Culture* 27 (12): 1785–1805.

Thomas, Molly. 2020. "Fields of Wrath: Tough Times for Canada's Invisible Migrant Workforce." *W5.* CTV Online, 27 September 2020. https://www.youtube.com/watch?v=oyhKWBlXmzs.

Tufton, Chris. 2020. "Jamaica now has a total of 19 confirmed cases of COVID-19. 5 of which are from local cases." Twitter (@christufton), 20 March 2020. https://twitter.com/christufton/status/1241131170139533312.

UFCW. 2014. "The Great Canadian Rip-Off! An Economic Case for Restoring Full EI Special Benefits Access to SAWP workers." http://www.ufcw.ca/templates/ ufcwcanada/images/directions14/march/1420/The-Great-Canadian-Rip-Off-An-Economic-Case-for-Restoring-Full-EI-Special-Benefits-Access-to-SAWP-Workers.pdf.

Venkatesh, Vasanthi, Talia Esnard, Vladimir Bogoeski and Tomaso Ferrando. 2023. "Migrant farmworkers: Resisting and organising before, during and after COVID-19." *Journal of Agrarian Change*, 23(3), 568–78. Visit Jamaica. 2020. "Travel Authorization." https://www.visitjamaica.com/travelauthorization/ (accessed 6 October 2020).

Vosko, Leah. 2018. "Legal but Deportable: Institutionalized Deportability and the Limits of Collective Bargaining among Participants in Canada's Seasonal Agricultural Workers Program." *ILR Review* 71 (4): 807–22.

Weiler, Annaliese, Janet McLaughlin, and Donald Cole. 2017. "Food Security at Whose Expense? A Critique of the Canadian Temporary Farm Labour Migration Regime and Proposals for Change." *International Migration* 55 (4): 48–63.

Weis, Tony. 2006. "The Rise, Fall and Future of the Jamaican Peasantry." *Journal of Peasant Studies* 33 (1): 61–88.

Wells, Don, Janet McLaughlin, André Lyn, and Aaraón Díaz Mendiburo. 2014. "Sustaining Precarious Transnational Families: The Significance of Remittances from Canada's Seasonal Agricultural Program." *Just Labour* 22: 144–67.

World Bank. 2018. *Migration and Remittances. Recent Development and Outlook.* Washington, DC: World Bank. https://documents.worldbank.org/en/publication/ documents-reports/documentdetail/907921534404019026/migration-and-re-mittances-recent-developments-and-outlook-transit-migration.

12

Hauntings of Islands' Sovereignties
An Examination of the Responses by Curaçao and Trinidad and Tobago to the Venezuelan Migration Crisis

NATALIE DIETRICH JONES AND SHIVA S. MOHAN

CURAÇAO AND THE REPUBLIC OF TRINIDAD AND TOBAGO are ruins of empire. As is the case elsewhere in the Caribbean region, the legacies of colonialism are evident in these islands' social relations, economy and government. This article focuses on the complexities surrounding the exercise of sovereignty in Curaçao and Trinidad and Tobago in a contemporary moment decidedly shaped by their geo-historical contingencies and specificities. In the wake of an ongoing crisis in Venezuela, both countries have seen an increase in arrivals of vulnerable migrants and asylum seekers since 2014. What have been the policy responses of these two countries to this unanticipated and unprecedented large-scale migration flow? How has sovereignty impacted their execution of immigration policy in relation to this migration crisis? What lessons are to be learned by other countries in the Southern Caribbean with similar geo-historical experiences?

It is of course important to highlight early in the discussion that Curaçao and Trinidad and Tobago are governed quite differently, a feature of their colonial experiences and trajectories. Only a decade has passed since Curaçao became an autonomous country within the Kingdom of the Netherlands in 2010. However, this former Dutch dependency faces limitations with respect to its exercise of autonomy over foreign affairs and defence issues, responsibility for which are held by the government of the Kingdom of the

Netherlands. On the other hand, Trinidad and Tobago has exercised policy autonomy in these two areas as an independent state since 1962. However, its engagement with the United States (US), as well as Venezuela, reflect fraught neo-colonial relationships. While both islands are classified as sub-national island jurisdictions (Baldacchino and Milne 2006), we have opted to utilize the terms independent and non-independent countries (see Corbin 2012) to distinguish between the structures of government which are found in the two jurisdictions. We also eschew the label non-sovereign (contra Veenendaal and Oostindie 2018), to avoid conceptual confusion especially in reference to non-independent Curaçao.

Despite these political differences, their responses to the management of the Venezuelan migration crisis have parallels. Both applied restrictive migration and border control measures, resulting in censure from the international community due to possible breaches of migrants' human rights. Many developments have taken place since mid-2019 most notably deportations of Venezuelans from Trinidad and Tobago (Ramdass 2020), and Curaçao (*Curaçao Chronicle* 2020b).[1] With these deportations, the respective governments have been attempting to project full control over the management of the crisis. However, these 'wins' for sovereignty, unfortunately, have negative implications for migrant rights and underscore our later argument that sovereignty may take the shape of resistance against the demands of human rights actors. In addition, Curaçao held elections in March 2021, before which the incumbent government announced – three days prior to polls – that Venezuelans in good standing would be granted temporary residence permits (*Curaçao Chronicle* 2021). However, the new administration did not implement a temporary permit scheme and the visa regime introduced in 2020 remains in place (*Curaçao Chronicle* 2020c; Yayboke and Zúñiga 2023). Finally, the COVID-19 pandemic resulted in border closures, limiting mobility and heightening migrant precarity in these two jurisdictions (*Curaçao Chronicle* 2020b; UN News 2021).

In the section which immediately follows, we present our methodological framework. We then ground our discussion in the productive conceptual pairing of 'haunting' and 'ruination' to illustrate the varied ways that colonial jurisdictions mobilize sovereignty in contemporary and urgent moments. Thereafter, we discuss the implications for migration policy and conclude with observations for other small island developing states (SIDS) in the Caribbean.

METHODOLOGY

This chapter draws on research undertaken independently by each author on the respective case studies. We each sought to examine the responses of national governments to increasing arrivals of Venezuelan migrants: Dietrich Jones in a multi-sited project examining destinations in the southern Caribbean (Aruba, Curaçao, Guyana, and Trinidad and Tobago), and Mohan focusing on Trinidad and Tobago. Notwithstanding differences in scale and disciplinary approaches, we faced similar challenges while conducting research, for example, limited or no access to government officials who work in migration management (see Dietrich Jones 2020b; Mohan and Dietrich Jones 2023 for a reflection on the fieldwork experience). As a result of this constraint, we relied on secondary data, including newspaper articles, institutional reports, legislative and policy documents, employing critical discourse analysis. This chapter represents a synthesis of our analyses.

We are concerned with tangible manifestations of migration policy – new initiatives implemented to regulate and control entry and residence in Curaçao and Trinidad and Tobago, that is, policy change; government inaction (retention of policy status quo); as well as speech acts about the migration issue in question (cf. Mitchell 1989; Freeman 1995 on the definition of migration policy), or related discussions concerning the border. This enables us to capture "the ordinary and routine points of connection between state imaginaries and state performances" (Coddington 2011, 761), an important element of our 'haunting(s)' analytic.

As migration policy is an intermestic issue, we examined actions and speech acts in the domestic and foreign policy spheres. It should be noted, however, that isolating the factors that influence migration policy utilizing a single methodological framework is challenging (Boswell 2007). We therefore adopt an approach that draws on several theoretical frameworks and varied disciplines, in particular international relations and political geography. Our research connects three fields of study, which scholars indicate rarely intersect – island studies, migration studies and post-colonial studies (Adamson and Tsourapas 2019; Vezzoli and Flauhaux 2017).

This chapter contributes to the emerging scholarship on Venezuelan migration in the Caribbean context (see, for example, van Marwijk 2019; Mohan 2019; Dietrich Jones 2019). While comparatively the numbers travelling to the Caribbean are significantly lower than other regions, such as South America, they are no less significant. Indeed "the consequences of immigration on [small island developing states] tend to be exaggerated" (UNECLAC 1998, iii). The scale of the islands under study, and the concomitant development concerns associated with unanticipated arrivals, raise questions of vulnerability and viability, which we theorize using the lens of sovereignty.

THE VENEZUELAN MIGRATION CRISIS AND THE SOUTHERN CARIBBEAN

It is well-documented that there is currently a multi-dimensional crisis in Venezuela. The significant increase in immigration from Venezuela is in response to humanitarian issues, such as political repression, hyperinflation, rising poverty and lack of access to food and public goods and services (Legler, Serbin, and Garelli-Ríos 2018; Ceriani Cernadas 2023). Since 2014, approximately 7.7 million Venezuelans have emigrated (International Organization for Migration 2023). Although most have fled to South America, many have also migrated to the Dominican Republic in the northern Caribbean and four countries in the southern Caribbean – Aruba, Curaçao, Guyana, and Trinidad and Tobago. This most recent migratory movement is distinctive in scale, composition and acuteness of flow (Vargas 2018). Most notable is the number of vulnerable migrants and those seeking asylum. As at August 2023, an estimated two hundred and thirteen thousand Venezuelans were in the Caribbean region (R4V Platform 2023). The scale of the migrant in-flow currently being experienced by both Curaçao and Trinidad and Tobago have been influenced by the closeness to Venezuela and the porosity of their borders. Cultural ties and historical patterns of migration have also contributed to the movements (Dietrich Jones 2019; 2020a). In 2018, the UNHCR regional representative for United States and the Caribbean depicted the crisis as on "the scale of Syria". This description highlights the vulnerabilities of SIDS in the southern Caribbean in relation to the increasing number of migrant arrivals (Welsh 2018).

According to Human Rights Watch (2018), Trinidad and Tobago has received the largest number of Venezuelan migrants in the southern Caribbean. The two islands have received estimates ranging from forty to sixty thousand people (UNHCR 2019; Vice News 2019), equating to approximately 3 to 5 per cent of the country's population. Migrant stock data has been in contention. In May 2019, through its Migrant Registration Framework, the Trinidad and Tobago government claimed to have registered (only) 16,532 Venezuelans (Senate Debate 2019).

Aruba and Curaçao are most impacted by the Venezuelan migration crisis among the Dutch Caribbean islands. As at August 2023, fourteen thousand Venezuelans are resident in Curaçao (R4V Platform 2023); in 2018, it was estimated that the population of undocumented persons was six thousand (*Curaçao Chronicle* 2018a). These estimates indicate that roughly 10 per cent of the Curaçaoan population are Venezuelans. Unlike Trinidad and Tobago, the island has not undertaken a formal registration process. However, in early 2020, undocumented migrants were encouraged to register to become eligible for food packages. Seventeen hundred Venezuelans registered during this process (*Curaçao Chronicle* 2020a). Between 2014 and 2018 (the height of the crisis), more than fourteen thousand persons submitted claims for asylum in Trinidad and Tobago, and approximately three hundred in Curaçao (R4V Platform 2020). In both cases, these represent exponential increases, as well as a change in the demographic composition of asylum seekers.

In the sections which follow, we discuss the significance of the reported increase in numbers of Venezuelan arrivals in each country. We also acknowledge that geo-political factors must be understood against the background of intervening socio-economic issues, which shaped the response of the Curaçaoan and Trinbagonian governments. These two SIDS face constraints of limited geographic size and financial resources. Curaçao has been in recession since 2016, with high unemployment, in particular among the youth population (International Monetary Fund 2019). Trinidad and Tobago, like Venezuela, was also impacted by the fall in global oil prices, which precipitated a steep decline in the economy (IMF 2018). The depressed economy impacted multiple state sectors, primarily affecting provision of public goods, that reverberated throughout the country at all levels. Within an already troubled economic landscape, increased media reporting on migrant discrimination suggests a prevailing anti-immigrant sentiment among the local populations.

SOVEREIGNTY A 'ZOMBIE' CATEGORY

Although at times ill-defined, sovereignty is a key concept in literature on migration management. In the realist tradition, which relies on a Westphalian concept of sovereignty, power resides in the ability to defend territory from external threats and (thus) protect and secure national interest through the regulation of entry and exit at the border (Hollifield 1992). With the emergence of discourse on a borderless world, some have questioned the efficacy of the state in this respect. Others, too, have argued that for states to adequately manage their borders there must be collaboration or 'pooled' sovereignty (Deleixhe and Duez 2019). Other discourse examines the dispersal of sovereign power beyond state borders, as evidenced by the extra-territorialization of border management (See Mountz 2011; Loyd et al. 2016).

While we offer a critique of the traditional (realist) concept of sovereignty, we nonetheless assume the respective governments of each of the case studies are unitary actors. We should note that this is problematic for empirical and theoretical reasons. In the case of the latter, neo-institutionalists have shown the impact of domestic institutions on the formulation of migration policy (see Boswell 2007 for a critique of this and the political economy schools). Secondly, the unitary rational actor model is more appropriate for countries "with functioning policymaking and bureaucratic apparatuses, clearly defined national borders and a coherent sense of national identity" (Adamson and Tsourapas 2019, 860). It is therefore not a suitable fit for countries which "suffer from low levels of state capacity, ongoing internal conflict or compromised sovereignty".

Both Trinidad and Tobago and Curaçao face problems with public administration. For Curaçao a two-tiered political structure – the local government and the Dutch government – is embedded in the *Statuut*.[2] Despite its *status aparte*, Curaçao is heavily dependent on the Kingdom of the Netherlands, which has intervened in local political affairs in the interest of the kingdom (see Woldendorp 2014 on the historical origins of this mode of engagement). For Trinidad and Tobago, its racialized political system has produced societal tensions over the distribution of public goods and offices (Ramcharitar 2020).

Notwithstanding lack of clarity regarding its meaning, 'sovereignty' continues to have relevance to our understanding of social phenomena. This qualifies it as a 'zombie category' according to Everuss (2020, 116 citing Beck and Beck-Gernsheim 2002). This understanding of sovereignty is particularly relevant in the context of the Caribbean, where sovereignty takes on many layers due to degrees of autonomy, issues of territorial integrity arising from border disputes, challenges of border management related to islandness or scarce resources, as well as countries' positionality in relation to (neo-)colonial powers.

As islands faced with several issues related to (il)licit transnational flows, sovereign power, or lack thereof, is a defining element of (post-) colonial national identity. In a discussion on a US-led initiative designed to manage one such transnational flow – narco-trafficking – Watson (2003) makes some key observations regarding sovereignty. He applies a distinct ontology of sovereignty that is rooted in the Caribbean's interaction with (global capitalist) social relations. For him, sovereignty is not an "outcome of decolonization", but rather a part of the process of reshaping of nations within the (contradictory) processes of global restructuring (Watson 2003, 256). This historical materialist approach is not central to our methodology; however, we adopt the position that it is the social relations of colonization that continues to shape the exercise of sovereignty in the Caribbean, in this instance, in respect of migration management. As explained by Boyce Davies and Jardine (2003, 163–64), "The state is the peculiarly long intersection of European and American power, and the peculiar apparatus of domination existing formally or acted out locally at the institutional level (sic)." This argument alludes to, but does not name, the analytic of haunting, which we discuss below.

Finally, we are concerned with the exercise of sovereign power during times of exception (Werner and De Wilde 2001). The variegated jurisdictional arrangements of islands present limitations in direct and indirect ways, which are made more pronounced in acute moments. The Venezuelan migration crisis has placed pressures on governments to respond, in the face of an already complex regional migration landscape. Berta Fernández-Alfaro and Gerard Pascua's (2006) work, from the outcomes of International Organization for Migration and Caribbean governments' dialogues, for example, underscore the realities and complexities of mixed migration flows. The authors, against the backdrop of the understanding of the limited physical capacities of islands, indicate that there is no ready-made migration management model, given the uniqueness of circumstance for each island. The deficiencies in accommodating different types and categories of migratory flows are quite visible in islands' migration policies. Public policy and legislative positions on island migration management, particularly when dealing with mixed flows of movement, cannot be considered in abstraction. The haunting of islands' histories, and geo-political and economic configurations weigh on certain decisions being made in the locality, as we show in our discussion of Curaçao and Trinidad and Tobago.

HAUNTING AND RUINATION IN (POST)COLONIAL SITES

The Caribbean region, as a product of colonial and imperialistic experiences, has retained fragility, constraints and structural vestiges, which are continually manifested in islands' modern-day political, economic and social systems. These vestiges in socio-historical terms can be represented through the processual analytics of 'haunting' and 'ruination'. "Hauntings," Scholz (2020, 515) argues, "grasp[s] the ongoing presence of the colonial past after the formal end of empire". While Gordon (2008, xvi) uses "haunting" as a verb to reflect the functions in daily life where oppressive forces are assumed to be historically "over-and-done-with", but which are effectively operating in the historical present. Specific to migration management, Mountz (2011) in her discussion of offshore border enforcement, uses "haunting" as an analytic to explain the mobility of sovereign power in spaces where the state may appear absent, but manifests on islands as strategic sites of detention. This collective body of work has presented "haunting" as an ethereal and pervasive expression that configures sovereign action.

Drawing a more tactile perspective, Stoler (2008; 2013) identifies "ruins" or debris left behind, as being manifested in the present in material, discursive and embodied ways. She suggests that the process of ruination, "weighs on the future and shapes the present" (Stoler 2008, 194). In similar imagining, Loyd et al. (2016) engages "ruination" to connect histories of US territorial control to contemporary humanitarian militarization through military bases on islands. Here, "ruination" is launched as a material process-driven manifestation. The interconnectivities between these two engagements illustrate how past structures and experiences follow mobile bodies and are reproduced on island sites in the present.

Building on these conceptual strands, we launch the functioning of these two processes, in tandem, as a critical lens to analyse the active, ongoing processes of sovereignty. We suggest that migration governance in postcolonial territories is mediated through pervasive historical notions of sovereignty that have inherently configured the capacity and latitude of interventions in the contemporary moment. In acute situations like the Venezuelan migration crisis, the spectres of coloniality are brought to relief, and through processes of ruination, are manifested in constrained public policy and other interventions. In the (post-) colonial settings of Curaçao and Trinidad and Tobago, therefore, understandings of sovereignty are deeply entrenched in the "debris of empire" or "ghosts of colonialism" (Tuck and Rees 2003), transcending spatio-temporal scales. This has significantly impacted and informed the articulation of government policy and their legislative ambitions. This approach links not only the region's colonial experience but its later (neo)imperialist interventions, to the Caribbean's present, as observed through its modern-day structurations and geo-political consciousness.

CURAÇAO: AN AUTONOMOUS COUNTRY IN THE KINGDOM OF THE NETHERLANDS

In October 2020, Curaçao marked ten years of its status as an autonomous country in the Kingdom of the Netherlands, which is also constituted by the Netherlands in Europe, and its Caribbean counterparts, Aruba and Sint Maarten. Scholars writing on the process of independence in the Dutch Caribbean emphasize two key issues. The first is that decolonization was not, as initially conceived, intended for the Dutch Caribbean. The decolonial project was directed at the Dutch East Indies (Indonesia), which eventually wrested independence violently from the metropole (Oostindie 2009; Oostindie and Klinkers 2003). The second is that while the Dutch wished to shed the burden of colonies, it did not believe the islands were capable of managing their affairs independently (Woldendorp 2014). Thus, although Curaçao is autonomous over its internal affairs, its role in matters defined as "Kingdom affairs" by the *Statuut* is proscribed. These include foreign relations, defence, citizenship, and admittance and expulsion of foreigners. In this vein, Curaçao occupies a space of semi-autonomy and therefore operates in a dependency periphery (Corbin 2009).

In addition to its governance structure, it is important to highlight additional characteristics of Curaçao, which are salient to this discussion. Although the largest of the Dutch Caribbean islands, Curaçao is only 444 square kilometres. It therefore has a high population density, with a population of approximately one hundred and sixty thousand (World Bank 2020). Secondly, although Curaçao is considered a small island tourism economy, it remains dependent on the petroleum sector. This has had implications for its relationship with Venezuela, which until 2019 had a lease of the Isla Refinery based in Curaçao (Venezuela Analysis 2019). Third, prior to the increase in arrivals of Venezuelans after 2014, Curaçao had limited experience with refugees. It had processed claims for asylum from other Latin American countries, including Cuba and Colombia (CUW_3_28.03.2018).[3] However, its proximity – the Venezuelan state of Falçon is roughly 40 kilometres away – meant that it has traditionally been a destination for Venezuelan migrants and tourists. This is a complicated bond; for while Venezuelans have contributed significantly to the labour market and economy of Curaçao, concerns have been raised over the years about their involvement in various forms of transnational crime, including piracy, human trafficking and drug-trafficking (de Jong 2009). As explained further below, this established migratory pattern as well as several geo-political factors in Venezuela have encouraged emigration from Venezuela to Curaçao.

THE REPUBLIC OF TRINIDAD AND TOBAGO

As its name suggests, the nation of Trinidad and Tobago comprises two islands – Trinidad being the larger island, with its sister isle totalling a mere three hundred square kilometres. The Republic is the southernmost territory of the Caribbean archipelago and sits just eight miles off the north-east coast of Venezuela. Fostered on the colonial plantation model, both islands exchanged hands among several European powers, eventually culminating in a merged British crown colony in 1889 (MacDonald 1986; Carmichael 1961). Trinidad and Tobago achieved independence from the British in 1962 and was proclaimed a republic in 1976. Its post-independence political system functions within the framework of a unitary state, with a parliamentary system modelled after that of the United Kingdom of Great Britain and Northern Ireland, that is, the Westminster model.

In Trinidad and Tobago, contemporary migrations from Venezuela are tied to a long history of politico-economic inspired movements that follow from the earlier migrations. The Venezuela-Trinidad and Tobago migration corridor has been characterized by extensive reciprocal mobilities and movements (Dietrich Jones 2019). Contemporary inter-territorial mobilities are primarily structured through highly formalized and regulated energy arrangements, given common maritime geology (see Braveboy-Wagner 2010 on the contentious relationship between Venezuela and Trinidad and Tobago due to petro-diplomacy in the region). However, the trade of goods and services, human migration and smuggling between both nations are historically routed/rooted.

THE CRISIS IN THE DUTCH CARIBBEAN

There is broad consensus that a crisis faces Curaçao, both with respect to the number of arrivals, as well as the small size of the country. In 2016, the Red Cross had indicated, "If things continue this way, we can expect that maybe people will try to flee their country and they will come our way. *Of course we don't have the capacity to help them all*,"[4] (*Curaçao Chronicle* 2016). Later in 2018, Lesley Fer, the Risk Management & Disaster Policy Director in Curaçao, warned that a "destabilizing situation is created if we go over our capacity and cannot return illegal Venezuelans" (*Curaçao Chronicle* 2018d). While we cannot address in extensive detail here how rhetoric was utilized by the government to justify an overly restrictive, and in some instances inhumane, border regime (Coddington et al. 2012), we wish to note that the increasing number of arrivals, and the country's limited technical, financial and administrative resources, resulted in the framing of Venezuelans as a threat. Correspondingly, a plan was devised through collaboration between various agencies of government to contain the crisis (*Curaçao Chronicle* 2018d).

An important dimension of political rhetoric was the tension between the Curaçaoan and Dutch governments concerning responsibility for management of the crisis (see Dietrich Jones 2020a). The statement by the Minister of Justice that "We cannot solve the [Venezuelan] problem" was therefore a reflection of Curaçao's limited capacity, as well as the expectation regarding support from the Dutch government for assistance. This was emphasized in commentary regarding the (estimated) proportion of undocumented migrants in Curaçao, in contrast to the comparatively lower number of migrants in the Netherlands, as unsustainable (*Curaçao Chronicle* 2018e).

In addition to the challenges to sovereignty noted above, there are legal dimensions to Curaçao's response to the crisis. Curaçao has not ratified the 1951 Convention Relating to the Status of Refugees nor the 1967 Protocol Relating to the Status of Refugees. It should be noted that among the Dutch Caribbean islands, Curaçao is distinct in this regard.[5] Aruba seceded to the Protocol when it obtained *status aparte* in 1986. The Protocol also applies to the three Caribbean non-sovereign jurisdictions of the Netherlands – Bonaire, Saba and Sint Eustasius – by territorial application (Advisory Committee on Migration Affairs 2019).[6] Curaçao's limited capacity was cited as an impediment to its ratification of the 1951 Convention on Refugees, and its Protocol (*Curaçao Chronicle* 2018b). Its non-ratification, coupled with a deficient refugee protection framework, created a hostile environment for Venezuelan migrants. The weak protection space was the result of the dismantling by the Curaçaoan government of a system it previously had in place for the processing of claims, which was coordinated by the local Red Cross in collaboration with the United Nations High Commission for Refugees (UNHCR). Facing an increase in arrival of Venezuelans, the government suspended this process, assuming control from the local Red Cross in 2017. It has been reported there is currently a backlog of applications and that since the change in process there have been no awards of refugee status (Amnesty International 2018a). As a result of the above, ratification of the Convention became a leitmotif in recommendations from international organizations.

Also of note is the 2019 agreement (between the Dutch government, the United States and the Venezuelan opposition) that Curaçao serve as a hub for humanitarian aid to Venezuela. This move so angered Venezuelan officials, who in a "sovereign decision" closed their nation's borders with the Aruba, Bonaire and Curaçao (Casey 2019). The closure heightened tensions between Venezuela and the Dutch Caribbean islands, later providing opportunity for further displays of sovereignty when Aruba opted not to reopen its borders to persons travelling from Venezuela (Aruba Gobierno 2019). In Curaçao the government continued its practice of detention and deportation (Dietrich Jones 2021), a feature of its response to the migratory pressures, which drew intense criticism from the international community (Amnesty International 2018a; Leghtas and Thea 2019).

THE CRISIS IN TRINIDAD AND TOBAGO

The Trinidad and Tobago government's strategic and intermittent actions in its domestic context to the Venezuelan crisis, and its migration outcomes, have consistently run counter to hemispheric political opinion, developments, shifts and provocations. This kind of individualistic and defiant response has been evidenced by the country's efforts to maintain a cordial relationship with Venezuela in its foreign and geo-economic policies, compounded by its amplified restrictive immigration policies and enforcement actions.

In May 2016, Venezuela made "historic" deals with T&T (Boothroyd 2016) in the supply of manufactured goods and natural gas. After a myriad of diplomatic skirmishes, in February 2020, this highly publicized gas agreement with Venezuela was rescinded. This was as a consequence of the imposed US sanctions on Venezuela's PDVSA, which impeded the country's ability to operate with certain external stakeholders. Trinidad and Tobago was obliquely impacted by this US sanction on its Venezuelan neighbour. In the latter part of 2023, however, the gas project was finally given the green light, with US concessions after much lobbying by the Trinidad and Tobago government.

In addition to its continued geo-economic arrangements with Venezuela, Trinidad and Tobago's enduring relationship with the Maduro government is reflected in its engagements at the Organization of American States. Trinidad and Tobago's record of abstaining on any resolutions pertaining to Venezuela has been consistent (Johnson 2019). From the very outset, the prime minister, Keith Rowley, declared very strong objections to OAS Secretary General Luis Almagro's handling of the Venezuelan matter, and called for his removal (Hassanali 2017).

In addition to the unfolding events on the international scene, burgeoning issues and agitations at home also impacted the response. The government's interventions have been incremental, and culminated with the deportation of Venezuelans, followed by the implementation of a temporary work-exempt permit programme – abdicating efforts at refugee protectionism – and ultimately, the installation of a visa regime specific to Venezuelan immigrants. Throughout these developments, Trinidad and Tobago's coast guard officers were mandated to increase patrols along the island's western peninsula, while at the same time, police and immigration officials would undertake raids or searches in specific places inland. The government's policy in practice continues to be exclusionary and restrictive.

The deportation of a plane full of Venezuelans in 2018 brought the twin-island into world focus. Major contentions surrounded the circumstances of their repatriation. The government stated that the eighty-two individuals volunteered to be sent back to Venezuela. Deportees' relatives, on the other hand, contended that the deportees were forced to sign documents that they did not fully understand. The UNHCR stated that the actions by Trinidad and Tobago, being signatory to the 1951 Convention, went against the principles of non-refoulement and asylum-seekers' confidentiality. The prime minister subsequently wrote to the United Nations and publicly stated that the country "will not allow without protest any international agency to misrepresent our circumstance to the world and stay in TT"

(Bridglal 2018). His statements caused the fraught news headline, articulating the country's position: "TT Not Refugee Camp" (Bridglal 2018). Rowley invoked the island's physical geography: ". . . bearing in mind we are not China, Russia or America. We are a little island. We have limited space – 1.3 million people. Therefore, we cannot and will not allow UN spokespersons to convert us into a refugee camp" (Bridglal 2018).

In 2019, the government initiated a one-year work-permit exempt scheme to all Venezuelans in the island. This "Migrant Registration Framework" (Office of the Prime Minister 2019) effectively placed all Venezuelans in the neat and manageable category of "economic migrant". The Minister of National Security claimed that ". . . we do not have refugees here, we are dealing with migrants" (Senate debate 2019). This programme ascribes a degree of temporariness to the situation, to which the state has a limited commitment. Critical readings of this governmental action suggest that this short-term measure serves as a rudimentary counting and surveillance mechanism, and was an attempt to appease international and domestic agitations, while maintaining political expedience (Mohan 2019).

RUINATION AND THE POLICY RESPONSE FROM CURAÇAO
AND TRINIDAD AND TOBAGO

Curaçao has, through its requests to the Kingdom's government for assistance, underscored its continued dependence on the metropole, and thus its limited autonomy over the management of the Venezuelan migration crisis. While these requests are in keeping with the principles of the Kingdom Charter, it underscores the sovereignty dilemma faced by Curaçao. Its dependence on the Kingdom's government for a sustainable solution thus demonstrates the permanence of its colonial ties. This dilemma is especially palpable considering the claim by the Dutch government that the management of migration is a local issue (*Curaçao Chronicle* 2018c).

Curaçao is also haunted by the legacy of its transition to autonomous country status, which has implications for its ratification of international laws for the governance of migration. Only the Netherlands has international legal personality, and thus can conclude, accede to or ratify international treaties on behalf of its constituent members (Ministry of Foreign Affairs,

Kingdom of the Netherlands 2015). It is moot, therefore, whether in this area of migration governance Curaçao has been able to exercise policy autonomy through its non-accession, since it would also require involvement of the the Kingdom government in the treaty ratification process (see Dietrich Jones forthcoming). In addition, it is a reservation by the Dutch that limits the geographical coverage of the Convention to the European part of the kingdom (See Depositary Notification C.N.20U.1968.TREATIES-14).

In this regard, Curaçao is also distinct from Trinidad and Tobago, which acceded to both the Convention and the Protocol in 2000, well after its independence.[7] The Republic is an interesting case, since the state has made pronouncements to suggest that it has no responsibility to adhere to the obligations of these treaties. These statements, however, have been refuted. For example, Amnesty International (2018b) correctly opined that with its accession, Trinidad and Tobago signalled its commitment to the Convention and that its actions ought to be in keeping with its principles (see also Dietrich Jones 2020a). However, with the implementation of the Migrant Registration Framework, Trinidad and Tobago has completely absconded from its political commitment to refugee protectionism in favour of short-term migrant management that features frequent deportations.

Although it is an independent nation, in contrast to Curaçao, the country's responses to the migration crisis also demonstrate that sovereignty and its capacity to act autonomously are constrained by hauntings of (neo)colonial histories of interventionism and exploitation. In these terms, as evidenced by government statements regarding asylum for Venezuelans in Trinidad and Tobago, acceding to external requests from larger geopolitical players or global agencies like the UNHCR could potentially usurp the island's sovereignty, thus reproducing historical manipulations and exploitations. Although its principal argument focuses on the limitations of the nation's physical and economic capacity to treat with the in-flow of migrants, we can read ruination here, as a tangible manifestation, through the government's (re)articulation of the island's restrictive and repressive migration policies.

These moves are undergirded by hauntings of the orthodox notion of sovereignty, which serves to preserve its independence. We see, however, that while Trinidad and Tobago attempts to resist external instruction or dictates, it has, in fact, relented to these very agitations, which have yielded inadequate migration schemes, as explained above. These initiatives followed intense criticism from the international community regarding the restrictiveness of its policy approach. In Curaçao, however, no changes were made to the refugee policy framework. However, the actions of a local non-governmental organization and a small boutique law firm in the private sector highlighted the country's obligations under Article 3 of the European Convention on Human Rights. These underscore tensions within the state and institutional bargaining that must take place in migration policy practice.

Finally, the haunting of colonialism is also evident in these islands' attempts to manage the decline of the oil industry, which was developed with the expansion of industrial capitalism in the region, by US and European interests. The deterioration in this sector in both Trinidad and Tobago and Curaçao has caused a severe contraction in the labour market. The restrictive policy regime in these countries, in particular, the active deportation agenda which continues, and was even amplified during COVID-19, could therefore be read not merely as an attempt to deal with the constraints of small size, but also the challenges of a "dying colonialism" (Boyce Davies and Jardine 2003).

CONCLUSION

We have demonstrated that 'imperial debris' have produced complex articulations and embodiments of sovereignty in Curaçao and Trinidad and Tobago. Both territories are not new to the process of refugee status determination; they are, however, unaccustomed to large inflows of migrants over a sustained period. Their weak institutional mechanisms, as well as cultural attitudes regarding who is an acceptable migrant, have significantly shaped the responses in these two SIDS. Despite distinct governance arrangements, both jurisdictions struggle with designing just migration management regimes, which are responsive to migrants' needs. Indeed, one of the implications of being 'haunted' is colonial countries' mirroring of migration practices employed in metropoles (Vezzoli and Flauhaux 2017). Restrictive management that dominates the global mobilities regime in the contemporary landscape is thus reflected in these peripheral countries.

This is particularly relevant for Curaçao, which is a European frontier and thus serves as a gateway to that continent.

The responses by both countries to the Venezuelan migration crisis reinforces the fallacy of the idea of sovereignty. While the case of Curaçao illustrates semi-direct control (mainly) by its metropole, control in the case of Trinidad and Tobago manifests discursively through external dictates, condemnations and agitations, and the nation's resistances to same. Within perceived constraints, both countries mobilize their autonomous selves to preserve and protect their territoriality and capacity to self-determine, which ultimately generate less than favourable outcomes for the constituency of mobile persons that states have a responsibility to protect. Both countries' slow but inevitable capitulations to external provocations were masked as their self-determined actions. However, their responses, in fact, worked to reaffirm the unevenness and limitations of a colonial dynamic that was consistently invoked through haunting and ruination in the contemporary moment. The approaches of both islands are problematic as the region is the product of a highly mobile colonial and capitalist enterprise.

Are there any lessons to be learned by other states similarly impacted by the crisis? The experiences of Curaçao and Trinidad and Tobago indicate that Caribbean SIDS are not solitary actors, but rather part of larger, complex geo-political systems. There are therefore direct and indirect consequences of these geopolitics, which will have bearings on the way they respond to the migration crisis. Guyana, for example, should therefore be cognizant of possible intersections related to the unfolding development of its oil and gas sector, and its response to the increasing arrivals of Venezuelan migrants. Evidence of this can be observed in the escalation in volatile relations between both territories through the rehashing of the age-old Venezuela-Guyana border dispute.

In addition, while countries may prefer non-interference, partnerships and collaborations will become essential in the management of the crisis. The limited availability of resources suggests that this is inevitable. It is also required, since the crisis, if mismanaged, is bound to have ripple effects throughout the region. This necessarily entails ceding one's sovereignty to a more collaborative approach. In this regard, also of import is the adoption of a human-rights based approach, rather than a securitized approach that typifies pooled sovereignty in other jurisdictions. This point is especially salient considering the weak refugee protection space evident in both countries. Notwithstanding political views regarding asylum, international customary law requires protection of refugees and other vulnerable migrant categories. In this instance, sovereignty must be surrendered if these countries are to be respectable members of the international community. Refoulement, including through the practice of (pre-emptive) deportation, is thus a response that should be discouraged throughout the subregion.

Finally, resisting the edicts of external actors can prove counter-productive in the short and medium term. These skirmishes merely shed light on the deficiencies of the refugee protection space within the region, which requires significant improvement to yield just results for migrants. It is therefore a much more worthwhile investment of time to work with regional and global agencies to build institutional and human resource capacity.

NOTES

1. This chapter builds on a conference paper, "An Analysis of Forced Migration in the Caribbean Basin: The Case of Venezuelan Migration to the Dutch and Anglophone Caribbean", presented by Dietrich Jones at the SALISES Annual Conference on 25 April 2018, as well as fieldwork conducted independently by both authors between 2018 and 2019. Where possible, attempts have been made to update the paper to align the arguments with more recent developments.

2. The *Statuut* is the constitutional arrangement governing the affairs of the Kingdom of the Netherlands, of which Curaçao is a constituent country.

3. Anonymized interview from fieldwork

4. Author's emphasis

5. The position of Sint Maarten is less clear, though it appears that it is in a similar position to Curaçao.

6. The Netherlands acceded to the Protocol in 1968, but only for its European region. After June 2011, the Protocol applied to the Caribbean part of the Netherlands. See Endnote 10 of the Status of the Protocol regarding territorial application for the Netherlands of the Protocol. https://treaties.un.org/pages/ViewDetails.aspx?src=TREATY&mtdsg_no=V-5&chapter=5&clang=_en

7. The United Kingdom did not include Trinidad and Tobago in its reservations regarding territorial application of the treaty.

REFERENCES

Adamson, F., and G. Tsourapas. 2019. "The migration state in the Global South: Nationalizing, Developmental, and Neoliberal Models of Migration Management." International Migration Review 54 (3).

Adviescommissie voor Vreemdelingenzaken/Advisory Committee on Migration Affairs. 2019. Notification: "The Kingdom of the Netherlands and the International Protection of (Asylum) Migrants." Adviescommissie voor Vreemdelingenzaken/Advisory Committee on Migration Affairs, The Hague.

Amnesty International. 2018a. Detained and deported: Venezuelans denied protection in Curacao." London: Amnesty International. https://www.amnestyusa.org/wp-content/uploads/2018/09/AMN_18_45_rapport-Curacao.pdf.

———. 2018b. "Trinidad and Tobago: Authorities have no justification for failure to respect international obligations over asylum." Press release, 21 November. https://www.amnesty.org/en/latest/news/2018/11/trinidad-and-tobago-authorities-have-no-justification-for-failure-to-respect-international-obligations-over-asylum/.

Aruba Gobierno. 2019. "Aruba extends border closure with three more months." https://www.government.aw/news/news_47033/item/aruba-extends-border-closure-with-three-more-months_44602.html.

Boswell, C. 2007. "Theorizing migration policy: Is there a Third Way?" International Migration Review 41 (1): 75–100. https://www.jstor.org/stable/27645653?seq=1#metadata_info_tab_contents.

Boyce Davies, C., and M. Jardine. 2003. "Imperial geographies and Caribbean Nationalisms: At the Border Between 'a Dying Colonialism' and US Hegemony." CR: The New Centennial Review 3 (3): 151–74.

Braveboy-Wagner, J. 2010. "Opportunities and limitations of the exercise of foreign policy power by a very small state: the case of Trinidad and Tobago." Cambridge Review of International Affairs 23 (3): 407–27.

Ceriani Cernadas, Pablo, Raísa Cetra, Elizabeth Chacko, Natalie Dietrich Jones, Michael Espinel, Luciana Gandini, Berti Olinto, Gladys Prada, Marie Price, Gloriana Sojo, Álvaro Botero Navarro. 2023. Reception and Integration of Migrants and Refugees in Cities Across the Americas, prepared for the Organization of American States, Pan American Development Foundation, International Organization for Migration and UNHCR https://www.padf.org/wp%20content/uploads/2023/04/Report_OAS_PADF_IOM_UNHCR.pdf

Casey, N. 2019. "Venezuela closes border to 3 Caribbean islands ahead of aid showdown." New York Times, 2019. https://www.nytimes.com/2019/02/20/world/americas/venezuela-borders-aid.html.

Coddington, K. 2011. "Spectral geographies: haunting and everyday state practices in colonial and present-day Alaska." *Social & Cultural Geography* 12 (7): 743–56. https://doi.org/doi/abs/10.1080/14649365.2011.609411.

Coddington, K., T. Catania, J. Loyd, E. Mitchell-Eaton, and A. Mountz. 2012. "Embodied possibilities, sovereign geographies and island detention: Negotiating the 'right to have rights' on Guam, Lampedusa and Christmas Island." *International Journal of Research into Island Cultures* 6 (2): 27–48.

Corbin, C. 2009. "Dependency governance and future development in the non-independent Caribbean." In *The diplomacies of small states: Between vulnerability and resilience*, edited by A. Cooper and T. Shaw, 81–95. London: Palgrave MacMillan.

———. 2012. "Self-governance deficits in Caribbean non-independent countries." In *Non-independent territories of the Caribbean and Pacific*, edited by P. Clegg and D. Killingray. London: Institute of Commonwealth Studies.

Curaçao Chronicle. 2016. "Red Cross: Curaçao is ready for possible Venezuelan refugees." *Curaçao Chronicle*. https://curacaochronicle.com/politics/red-cross-curacao-is-ready-for-possible-venezuelan-refugees/.

———. 2018a. "10% of the Population Is Venezuelan." *Curaçao Chronicle*. http://curacaochronicle.com/local/10-of-the-population-is-venezuelan/.

———. 2018b. "Minister of Justice: 'Curaçao does not violate human rights." Curaçao Chronicle, 2018b. http://curacaochronicle.com/politics/minister-of-justice-curacao-does-not-violate-human-rights/.

———. 2018c. "No financial assistance for Curacao to give asylum to refugees." Curaçao Chronicle. http://curacaochronicle.com/politics/no-financial-assistance-for-curacao-to-give-asylum-to-venezuelan-refugees/.

———. 2018d. "Crisis plan for refugee flow." Curaçao Chronicle, 2018a. https://curacaochronicle.com/politics/crisis-plan-for-refugee-flow/.

———. 2018e. "Kingdom Must Assist In Curaçao With The Issue Of Venezuelan Refugees." Curaçao Chronicle, 2018b. https://curacaochronicle.com/politics/kingdom-must-assist-in-curacao-with-the-issue-of-venezuelan-refugees/.

———. 2020a. "Curaçao starts registering migrants via food packages." Curaçao Chronicle. https://www.curacaochronicle.com/post/local/curacao-starts-registering-migrants-via-food-packages/#:~:text=WILLEMSTAD%20%2D%20Venezuelans%20without%20papers%20are,Cura%C3%A7ao%20actively%20registers%20undocumented%20migrants.

———. 2020b. "Illegal Venezuelans are still not tolerated, even during corona crisis." Curaçao Chronicle. https://www.curacaochronicle.com/post/local/illegal-venezuelans-are-still-not-tolerated-even-during-corona-crisis/.

———. 2020c. "Visa requirement for Venezuelans." Curaçao Chronicle. https://www.curacaochronicle.com/post/main/visa-requirement-for-venezuelans/.

———. 2021. "Venezuelans can stay on Curaçao under certain conditions." Curaçao Chronicle, 2021. https://www.curacaochronicle.com/post/main/venezuelans-can-stay-on-curacao-under-certain-conditions/.

de Jong, L. 2009. "The implosion of the Netherlands Antilles." In *Governance in the non-independent Caribbean: Challenges and opportunities in the twenty-first century*, edited by P. Clegg and Pantojas-García. E., 24–44. Kingston: Ian Randle Publishers.

Deleixhe, M., and D. Duez. 2019. "The New European Border and Coast Guard Agency: Pooling Sovereignty or Giving it up?" *Journal of European Integration* 41 (7): 921–36.

Dietrich Jones, N. 2019. "Trinidad and Tobago-Venezuela Migration Corridor." In *Routledge Handbook of Migration and Development*, edited by T. Bastia and R. Skeldon, 492–500. London: Routledge.

———. 2020a. "Between a 'Kingdom' and a hard place: the Dutch Caribbean and the Venezuelan Migration Crisis." Migration and Development.

———. 2020b. "Critical reflections on the process of undertaking qualitative research on forced migration in small island developing states." Emerging Scholars and Practitioners on Migration Issues (ESPMI) *Refugee Review IV* (Spring): 32–52.

———. 2021. "A Welcome Reception? Interdiction, Detention and Deportation in the Dutch Caribbean." 18 January 2021. https://www.law.ox.ac.uk/research-subject-groups/centre-criminology/centreborder-criminologies/blog/2021/01/welcome-reception.

Dietrich Jones, Natalie. Forthcoming. "'Disharmony' in the Kingdom of the Netherlands: (De)colonialization and Non-Accession in Aruba and Curaçao" in *Non-signatory states in International Refugee Law*, edited by Maja Janmyr, Arjumand Bano Kazmi and Özlem Gürakar-Skribeland. Leiden: Brill

Economic Commission for Latin American and the Caribbean (ECLAC). 1998. *The impact of immigration on Caribbean micro-states*. Port of Spain: ECLAC.

Everuss, L. 2020. "Westphalian sovereignty as a zombie category in Australia." Borderlands 19 (1). https://doi.org/10.21307/borderlands-2020-006.

Freeman, G. 1995. "Modes of immigration politics in Liberal Democratic States." International Migration Review 29 (4): 881–902.

Hollifield, J. 1992. "Migration and International Relations: Cooperation and Control in the European Union Community." *International Migration Review* 26 (2): 568–95. https://www.jstor.org/stable/2547072.

International Monetary Fund. 2019. Kingdom of the Netherlands –Curacao and Sint Maarten 2018 Article IV Consultation discussions – Press release and staff report. Washington, DC: IMF.

International Organization for Migration. 2023. "About the Regional Venezuela Situation" https://respuestavenezolanos.iom.int/en/about-regional-venezuela-situation#:~:text=As%20of%20August%202023%2C%20more,largest%20displacement%20in%20the%20world.

Leghtas, I., and J. Thea. 2019. Hidden and afraid: Venezuelans without status or protection on the Dutch Caribbean island of Curacao. Refugees International (Washington, DC). https://www.refugeesinternational.org/reports/2019/4/10/hidden-and-afraidvenezuelans-without-status-or-protection-on-the-dutch-caribbean-island-of-curaao.

Legler, T., Andrei Serbin, and O. Garelli-Ríos. 2018. "Introducción: La naturaleza compleja y multidimensional de la crisis venezolana." *Pensamiento Propio* 47 (23): 9–12.

Ministry of Foreign Affairs, Kingdom of the Netherlands. 2015. One Kingdom – Four Countries: European and Caribbean. Ministry of Foreign Affairs, Kingdom of the Netherlands (The Hague).

Mitchell, C. 1989. "International migration, international relations and foreign policy." *International Migration Review* 23 (3) Special Silver Anniversary: 681–708.

Mohan, S.S. 2019. "A 'Migrant registration framework': Counting Venezuelan immigrants in Trinidad and Tobago." *Oxford Monitor of Forced Migration* 8 (1).

Mohan, S.S., and Dietrich Jones, N. 2023. "Navigating Data Silence (r) s": Researching Migration in the Caribbean." In *The Routledge Companion to Applied Qualitative Research in the Caribbean*, 241–59). London: Routledge.

Oostindie, G. 2009. "Migration paradoxes of non-sovereignty: A comparative perspective on the Dutch Caribbean." In *Governance in the non-independent Caribbean*, edited by P. Clegg and E. Pantojas-García, 163–81. Kingston, Jamaica: Ian Randle.

Oostindie, G., and I. Klinkers. 2003. *Decolonising the Caribbean: Dutch policies in a comparative perspective.* Amsterdam: Amsterdam University Press.

Organization of American States. 2021. *Venezuelan Migration and Refugee Crisis.* Washington, DC: OAS. http://www.oas.org/fpdb/press/Crisis-Overview-ENG.pdf.

Ramcharitar, R. 2020. "Ethnic anxiety and competing citizenships in Trinidad and Tobago." *Journal of Ethnic and Migration Studies.* https://doi.org/doi/full/10.10 80/1369183X.2020.1774116.

Ramdass, Rickie. 2020. "160 Venezuelans deported." *Trinidad Express*, 2020. trinidadexpress.com/newsextra/160-veneuelans-deported/article_243ce37c-31df-11eb-93ff-870a155c2b4e.html.

Response for Venezuelans Coordination Platform for Refugees and Migrants from Venezuela. 2020. "Refugees and Migrants from Venezuela." https://data2.unhcr.org/en/situations/platform/location/7493.

Regional Inter-Agency Coordination Platform for Refugees and Migrants from Venezuela (R4V). 2023. Refugee and Migrant Needs Analysis. https://rmrp.r4v.info/rmna2023/.

Scholz, N. 2020. "Ghosts and Miracles: The Volkswagen as Imperial Debris in Postwar West Germany." *Comparative Studies in Society and History* 62 (3): 487–519.

Senate debate. 2019. 35th Sitting, 4th Session, 11th Trinidad & Tobago Parliament, 25 June. https://www.ttparliament.org/wp-content/uploads/2022/01/hs20190625.pdf

UN News. 2021. "Deadly shipwreck off Venezuela underscores need for safe migration pathways, protection." news.un.org/en/story/2021/04/1090582.

van Marwijk, J. 2019. "Stuck in a Caribbean deadlock: The entrapment of Venezuelans refugees in the Kingdom of the Netherlands." Masters in Human Geography, Nijmegen School of Management, Radboud University.

Vargas, Claudia Ribas. 2018. "La migración en Venezuela como dimensión de la crisis " *Pensamiento Propio* Enero/Junio (Año 23): 91–128.

Veenendaal, W., and G. Oostindie. 2018. "Head versus heart: The ambiguities of non-sovereignty in the Dutch Caribbean." *Regional and Federal Studies* 28 (1): 25–45.

Venezuela Analysis. 2019. "Venezuela's PDVSA Secures Temporary Lease Extension for Curacao Refinery ". https://venezuelanalysis.com/news/14736.

Vezzoli, S., and M-L. Flauhaux. 2017. "How do post-colonial ties and migration regimes shape travel visa requirements? The case of Caribbean nationals." *Journal of Ethnic and Migration Studies* 43 (7): 1141–63. https://doi.org/doi/full/10.1080/1369183X.2016.1228446.

Watson, H. 2003. "The 'Shiprider Solution' and Post-Cold War Imperialism: Beyond Ontologies of State Sovereignty in the Caribbean." In *Living at the borderlines: Issues in Caribbean Sovereignty and Development*, edited by C. Barrow-Giles and D. Marshall, 226–74. Kingston: Ian Randle Publishers.

Welsh, T. 2018. "Venezuelan crisis is 'on the scale of Syria' UNHCR says." Devex, 2018. https://www.devex.com/news/venezuela-crisis-is-on-the-scale-of-syria-un-hcr-says-93465#:~:text=Venezuela%20crisis%20'on%20the%20scale%20of%20Syria%2C'%20UNHCR%20says&text=WASHINGTON%20%E2%80%94%20The%20Venezuelan%20exodus%20into,Refugee%20Agency%20official%20said%20Tuesday.

Werner, W., and J. De Wilde. 2001. "The Endurance of Sovereignty." *European Journal of International Relations* 7 (3): 283–313.

Woldendorp, J. 2014. "Good governance and local autonomy in the Kingdom of the Netherlands in Europe and the Caribbean: An uneasy relationship." *The Tocqueville Review/La Revue Tocqueville* XXXV (2): 11–24.

Yayboke, E. and Á. Zúñiga. 2023. *Forgotten Frontlines: Aruba, Curacao and the Venezuelans Displacement Crisis.* Centre for Strategic and International Studies.

13

Implications of Environmental Change for Migration and Sustainable Futures of Caribbean States

ELIZABETH THOMAS-HOPE

CLIMATE-RELATED ENVIRONMENTAL CHANGE IN THE CARIBBEAN AND THE potential for migration in response has long-term implications for the region. Climate-induced hazardous events, and also tectonic activity, namely volcanic eruptions and earthquakes, have had devastating consequences for some Caribbean states.[1] Whereas such events will recur intermittently and with little or no prior warning, the impacts of climate change on the environment will continue as predicted, until or unless global carbon emission is significantly reduced.[2]

Climate-induced extreme events are already impacting millions of individuals both in the Global North and South. As a consequence, new trajectories of migration are expected to emerge across the globe and the Caribbean is predicted to be among the earliest and most severely affected over the course of this century (Pulwarty et al. 2010; Trotz and Lindo 2013, cited in Rhiney et al. 2017). Understanding the potential for migration in response to increasingly hazardous environmental change is critical. Only on that basis can appropriate policies and governance structures be developed proactively to enhance the resilience of those parts of the region most vulnerable to the climate-related risks, thereby supporting their viability and sustainability.

The nature of exposure to climate-related environmental change is summarized below, followed by the extent of vulnerability to climate-induced risks for the Caribbean. Understanding migration as a component of this unfolding scenario is then addressed, as well as the implications for governance.

EXPOSURE TO CLIMATE-INDUCED HAZARDOUS ENVIRONMENTS IN THE CARIBBEAN

The predicted climatic changes as they relate to the Caribbean are based on global and regional models of temperatures, rainfall regimes, hurricanes and sea-level rise.

TEMPERATURES WILL BE MUCH WARMER

Temperatures will increase by 1°C–3.5°C by the end of the twenty-first century (Taylor et al. 2017). The higher temperatures will occur across the entire Caribbean region over water and land, but with the greater magnitude warming over land, especially the larger islands, Cuba, Hispaniola and Jamaica (Karmalkar et al. 2013; Campbell et al. 2010, cited in Taylor and Stephenson 2017).

THERE WILL BE LESS RAINFALL

Models predict that the Caribbean will receive up to 20 per cent less rainfall by the end of the current century, as compared with 2021 (Karmalkar et al. 2013; Campbell et al. 2010, cited in Taylor and Stephenson 2017). The drier conditions will affect the whole Caribbean, but more so the southeastern parts. The region accounts for seven of the world's top thirty-six water-stressed countries, with Barbados in the top ten. The Food and Agriculture Organization (FAO) defines countries like Barbados, Antigua and Barbuda, and St Kitts and Nevis as water-scarce, with less than 1,000m3 of freshwater resources per capita.

HURRICANES WILL BE MORE INTENSE AND MORE FREQUENT

It is suggested that rainfall related to tropical cyclones will increase under conditions of elevated surface air temperatures (Intergovernmental Panel on Climate Change 2012, cited in Taylor and Stephenson 2017). Rainfall rates near to and wind speeds in the hurricane's inner core are predicted to become much higher (IPCC 2012). These conditions increase the occurrence of Category 4 and 5 hurricanes. For example, Hurricane Irma that hit Barbuda and the Virgin Islands as a Category 5 storm in September 2017 was followed twelve days later by an even more powerful Category 5 Hurricane Maria, the tenth most intense Atlantic hurricane on record. Again, in 2019, Dorian, which pounded the Bahamas as a Category 5 hurricane, was one of the strongest Atlantic hurricanes on record.

SEA LEVELS WILL BE HIGHER

The estimated levels could be up to 1.5 metres for the Caribbean Sea by the end of the twenty-first century. In the case of Guyana, it was noted that a mean relative sea level rise of 10.2 mm per annum is expected (United Nations Framework Convention on Climate Change 2002). This is estimated to be about five times the global average. The global circulation models indicate average rises of 2–4 mm per year in the first half of the twenty-first century and of 3–6 mm per year in the latter half (Johnson-Bhola 2017).

VULNERABILITY IN RELATION TO CLIMATE-INDUCED HAZARDOUS ENVIRONMENTS

The region's vulnerability to climate-related hazards is manifested in loss of life, and annual economic and financial costs that result from strong winds, flooding and drought. Between 1970 and 2000, the Caribbean region suffered direct and indirect losses estimated between US$700 million and US$3.3 billion due to disasters associated with weather and climate events (FAO 2016).

Vulnerability is manifest in a variety of situations and conditions. Aspects of vulnerability to which populations fall victim relate to locations and livelihoods that are susceptible to the effects of sudden shocks (such as hurricanes or floods), or gradual deterioration caused by unpredictable weather patterns, prolonged drought or sea level rise (Thomas-Hope 2017, 5–8). Usually, a combination of factors relates to the extent of exposure to the risk: location relative to recurrent hurricane paths; or the extent of concentration of economic and other activity in low-lying areas relative to average sea levels; or the lack of the physical, economic, social or political resilience to protect lives and livelihoods. Livelihood can be defined as the combination of assets, abilities and activities that enable a person, household or community to survive. These include physical assets, such as dwellings and infrastructure of all types; financial assets, such as available money, savings, pensions, access to credit and insurance; environmental assets, such as natural resources; social assets, which are based on the cohesiveness of communities and societies; and human assets, which depend on education, knowledge, skills and capabilities. These assets, in combination, generate resilience that reduces the impacts of hazardous conditions.

In the face of climate-induced environmental change, the geographic distribution of those places and populations most vulnerable to the risk of hazardous situations need to be identified and the basis of vulnerability addressed. It is not only farmers, fishers and herders who are vulnerable, but also poor or low-income households in cities – in both developed and developing countries. Their sources of livelihood are at risk from the impact of extreme weather events, and they lack adequate insurance coverage. Rising sea levels and increasing incidence of extreme events pose new risks for the assets of people living in affected zones, threatening livelihoods. Besides, such changes could result in a periodic geographic redistribution of vulnerability at regional and national levels – prospects that need to be considered in the formulation of adaptation strategies for people who are currently vulnerable or could become so within the foreseeable future, given the new conditions predicted.

Vulnerability in the face of the negative effects of climate change on the livelihoods of human populations and status of ecological systems is reflected in the physical, economic, social and political characteristics of the Caribbean.

PHYSICAL VULNERABILITY

The topography of much of the Caribbean region, with its very high percentage of coastal area in relation to overall size, contributes significantly to the physical vulnerability of each country in terms of exposure to the effects of climate change. In the case of the islands and also the continental countries of Belize, Guyana, Suriname and French Guiana, the concentration of infrastructure and economic activities on the coast leads to an inescapable exposure to hazardous events such as hurricanes, storms, and related storm surges and flooding with ever-increasing average sea levels. For example, in Jamaica, 25 per cent of the population lives in a coastal area, and 90 per cent of the country's total income is produced within those areas. The low coastal plain of Guyana, where approximately 60 per cent of the population (seventy thousand) and infrastructure are located, and where most of the fertile farmlands occur, lies 1–3 metres below the mean spring tide level, protected by a sea wall. Sea level is projected to rise by about 40–60 cm by the end of the twenty-first century, and could result in breaching and overtopping the sea defences (Guyana Sugar Corporation 2009, cited in Johnson-Bhola 2017). Another scenario is presented by the small coral atoll islands, as for example, the Turks and Caicos Islands, where the predicted rise in mean sea level could have disastrous consequences for sustaining the economy and society due to submergence of parts, or even entire islands.

ECONOMIC VULNERABILITY

A general aspect of regional and national vulnerability is the heavy reliance on one or two economic sectors –namely, tourism and agriculture – both of which are dependent on climatic stability and predictability. Tourism and agriculture together employ approximately 30 and 13 per cent respectively of the Caribbean regional labour force (Pulwarty et al. cited in Taylor 2017). The overall effects could therefore be in the region of 34 per cent reduction in GDP from 2025 to 2100. Decline in either of these sectors would have significant implications for national and regional macro-economic performance and, at the micro-level, for household livelihoods and food security, especially of the poor. For example, monetary losses from Hurricane Maria were estimated at upwards of US$91.61 billion (2017), mostly in Puerto Rico, ranking it as the third-costliest tropical storm on record.[3] In Dominica, the losses were equivalent to 226 per cent of the GDP (Government of the Commonwealth of Dominica 2017). Then in 2019, Hurricane Dorian caused about $3.4 billion in damages in the Bahamas, the equivalent of a quarter of its GDP (Inter-American Development Bank 2019).

Dependence on tourism is greater in some parts of the region than others. For example, in the British Virgin Islands, Antigua and Barbuda, and Anguilla, up to recent years tourism constituted over 70 per cent of GDP, while in other islands, such as Aruba, Barbados and the Bahamas, around half of GDP is generated through tourism and related receipts (World Travel and Tourism Council 2010). Hurricanes alone have considerable negative impacts on tourism-dependent Caribbean economies. It has been estimated that the impact of the average hurricane in the Caribbean translates into a two per cent loss in monthly tourist arrivals while, in contrast, the largest hurricane events caused up to a 20 per cent reduction in tourism (Granvorka and Strobl). In 2004, Hurricane Ivan is believed to have caused damage in Grenada of some US$1.1 billion, resulting in a dramatic reduction in tourism. Hurricane Irma completely wiped out the economic base of the island of Barbuda by destroying tourism, which contributed 60 per cent to GDP. When tourism is negatively impacted, this affects the livelihoods of persons across the range of engagement in the industry – owners of hotels and associated facilities, employees in a variety of capacities, and large numbers engaged in the informal sector.

Agriculture also plays an important role in the economic and sociocultural landscape of much of the Caribbean. In Jamaica, for example, agriculture contributes 7 per cent of the GDP and employs 17 per cent of all economically active employees (FAO 2014). Climate change impacts are already being observed in the Jamaican agricultural sector, resulting in lower yields (Caribsave 2012).

Temperature changes directly affect crop growth rates, increase the incidence of pests, and reduce water supplies in soils and reservoirs placing crops under drought-stress. For example, cocoa is a high-value perennial crop being affected by reduced rainfall in combination with progressively warmer temperatures. Similarly, coffee – an export crop – has also been affected by increased temperatures as well as extended droughts, affecting the livelihoods of small farming communities (Birthwright 2017).

Although hurricanes, when they occur, have a devastating effect on agriculture and consequences for poor recovery levels, reduced rainfall and changed rainfall regimes have even more enduring negative effects on the sector (Planning Institute of Jamaica 2015). Drought is expected to be an increasingly significant factor in livelihood vulnerability in many parts of the region. The longest drought conditions are feared for Barbados, southern Belize, the eastern part of Cuba, the southern area of the Dominican Republic, southwestern Haiti, the northern Leeward Islands, Martinique, coastal French Guiana, Aruba, Bonaire and Curaçao. But other parts of the region will also be negatively affected. The results from a study conducted in Jamaica and Trinidad and Tobago indicated that there would be an overall reduction in area of land suitable for growing most crops as the region's climate becomes progressively warmer and drier. The largest reduction in suitability is expected in low-lying areas, particularly affecting Trinidad's and Jamaica's southwestern regions, and the Rupununi Savannah of Guyana (Rhiney et al. 2017; Johnson-Bhola 2017).

SOCIAL VULNERABILITY

Despite continued overall improvements in living standards in the Caribbean, according to World Bank data, poverty rates average 30 per cent of the population.[4] The percentage of the population below the poverty line varies widely, with Barbados, Dominica, Grenada and the Bahamas at 0 per cent (based on calculations for 2023). Poverty levels remained relatively high in other countries, such as the Dominican Republic, where it was calculated as 23.2 per cent (in 2021), and in Trinidad and Tobago and Jamaica as just over 29 per cent in 2023. More serious situations, with an excess of 50 per cent of the population reported to be below the poverty line, occurred in Belize, Guyana, Suriname and Haiti, for which no detailed data is available for recent years. The high incidence of poverty is associated with a general lack of financial, social and personal assets, and a limited capacity to adopt new technology. This means that, at the local level, implications of climate change will be wide-ranging and potentially severe, especially for the most resource-poor urban and rural communities. The IPCC (2012) concluded that the effects of climate change in Guyana, for example, are virtually certain to be overwhelmingly negative, most importantly as a result of the limited ability to respond and adapt. The inadequacy of government structures and the relevant resources to respond effectively to the new challenges of environmental change are major aspects of vulnerability that are also evident in other parts of the Caribbean, as in the case of desertification in Haiti.

Food security is affected by climate change through its impacts on all components of global, national and local food systems (FAO 2008), but its consequences will continue to be most severe as part of the syndrome of poverty. For example, agriculture-dependent parishes in Jamaica have the highest incidence of poverty in the country (FAO 2013). Furthermore, within countries, the urban poor are particularly challenged by food price increases associated with drought (Kinlock et al. 2019; Heslop-Thomas et al. 2015). Women are disproportionately represented among the poor and are usually in weaker positions regarding access to credit and resources. Yet they bear the greatest responsibility for food production as well as for ensuring the nutrition and food safety of their household (UNFCC 2011, cited in Constable 2017).

People's perceptions of challenging environmental changes, including those related to extreme climatic events, represent the first step towards planning a rational coping strategy to reduce their vulnerability. A number of short-term coping mechanisms have been employed at community level across the Caribbean, such as harvesting rainwater and generating home-made compost and fertilizer by small farmers (Constable 2017). Reports also suggest that there has been exposure to training among farmers in various adaptive strategies to combat the effects of new and unpredictable weather patterns. These are all commendable efforts, but longer-term strategic responses may require resources and government support which are, so far, conspicuously absent.

MIGRATION IN THE CONTEXT OF CLIMATE-INDUCED ENVIRONMENTAL CHANGE IN THE CARIBBEAN

Black et al. (2011, 53) remind us that, "The natural environment is more than simply a backdrop to the social world." Ecosystem services, hazards and deep human-environment relations affect every important social and cultural phenomenon – from the location of settlements to people's emotional attachment to a place. Yet most theoretical approaches and explanations of migration as an important social phenomenon do not incorporate environmental aspects (and environmental differentials or variations) in a meaningful manner. At the same time, academic discussions on environmental change have been, until recently, almost completely silent on the role of migration (Black et al. 2011).

First, it must be emphasized that displacement and migration are not the same and that different forms of environmentally induced migration occur (Warner et al. 2009). Displacement is movement associated with discrete events that challenge safety. The average duration of environmental displacement between 2013 and 2018 was estimated at twelve days (Zuñiga and Garrido 2020, cited in Francis 2021). In this scenario, the dispersal or evacuation is a form of 'forced' population movement to save lives. Caribbean islands experience extremely high levels of environmental displacement risk per capita. The ten countries and territories with the highest average annual displacement risk relative to population size due to sudden-onset hazards are all small island developing states (SIDS), the top six of which are located in the Caribbean (UNFCCC 2018, cited in Francis 2021). Environmental mobility also occurs in the context of urbanization, and the Caribbean is among the most urbanized subregions in the developing world.

Displacement at the time of a disaster does not necessarily determine the extent to which migration will follow. In contrast to displacement, migration is broadly interpreted as a voluntary and proactive move for reasons of improving livelihoods, economic or educational opportunities, or social – including family – arrangements. Migration is typically purposeful, being based on assessments and decisions, and to some extent is planned. Nevertheless, although a distinction is drawn between displacement and migration, it is recognized that these can be on a spectrum of mobility responses to environmental change (Warner and Laczko 2008), where displacement may be followed by migration.

In the context of extensive exposure to increasingly more degraded and hazardous environmental conditions across the region, the options are that people: (1) will stay at their location either because they cannot or do not wish to move, and accept the worsening situation with a lower quality of life; (2) try to adapt to the new conditions so as to mitigate the worst effects, thereby building resilience at the household, community and national level; or (3) migrate elsewhere. How this third option – whether short-term cyclical or long-term permanent –is taken up is more complex than sometimes envisaged. The relationship between hazardous environmental conditions and migration cannot be accurately conceptualized as a linear causal relationship based on simplistic assumptions of hazards as drivers of migration or push factors. As has been stated: "It is far from clear that there is any consensus on what the 'drivers of migration' are, with some recent work critiquing whether a comprehensive theory of migration is even possible given, for example, different disciplinary perspectives on the issue" (Portes and De Wind 2007, cited in Black et al. S5). This reflects what has been termed an 'impasse' in migration theory consequent on the complex relationship between causal explanations that relate to structures on the one hand, and agency on the other (Black et al. 2011; Bakewell 2011).

Environmental change has the potential to affect the hazardousness of places, and thereby affects migration indirectly, in particular through its influence on ongoing economic conditions and impacts on livelihoods. This implies that migration decisions will be induced by environmental change in so far as it influences other factors – namely economic, social and political variables. Therefore, environmental change has a multiplier effect on other explanations for migration (Afifi and Warner 2008) and indicates why quantifying numbers of 'environmental migrants' is problematic. What this explanation does not include is the strength of the propensity for migration, and the historical structural factors that have contributed to building the current migration culture and its role in the region's wider lived experience.

PROPENSITY FOR MIGRATION

The propensity for migration is related, in the first instance, to the perception of migration and its benefits and risks (Thomas-Hope 1992; 2002). Over time, migration became deeply embedded in the Caribbean psyche, relied upon as the means of expanding small-island and otherwise limited horizons and environments. Not only did migration become a significant part of life and livelihood, but it also became embedded in official thinking (Thomas-Hope,

1998). With the exception of post-1960 Cuba, migration has been facilitated by governments, and this continues to be the case. The wide array of private agents recruiting migrants or otherwise promoting and assisting migration in various ways has been officially tolerated or encouraged. Furthermore, contracts on a seasonal basis, negotiated and managed bilaterally between governments of Caribbean states for agricultural work in the 1970s and 1980s, later shifted to the United States and Canada. These arrangements currently involve the movement of thousands of persons annually to work in agriculture and the hospitality industry (Thomas-Hope 2018). The official rationale expressed for supporting large-scale migration in past decades was that it provided a "safety valve" in the face of economic and social pressures of the time (Senior and Manley 1955). However, the dependence on migration to fill the shortfall in employment opportunities at home continues, suggesting that the effects of environmental change in future years could reinforce the already existing reliance on migration.

PROPENSITY FOR MIGRATION AND THE ACTUAL MOVE

Whatever the underlying explanations for a high propensity for migration, this may or may not be followed by actual moves. The role of agency in effecting migration is important and decisions vary with the individual's access to information, as well as personal networks that provide social capital and reduce the costs of migration. Family and friends who have previously migrated provide the reservoir of social capital elsewhere – whether within the same country or internationally. Additionally, migrants need finance and personal assets in the form of relevant educational and skill sets to fit national, urban-based work and residence, or international transfers. Where international migration is the choice, immigration regulations at potential destinations are even more important than assets in determining volume and direction of movement. This highlights the fact that environmental change influences migration in the context of prevailing socio-economic and political conditions at both source and prospective destination.

International migration opportunities for Caribbean populations have always been a reflection of labour requirements or political forces at prospective destinations. These are articulated in immigration legislation and visa requirements in countries external to the region, or by CARICOM with respect to intra-regional movements. Since 2002, intra-regional migration has been permitted within the context of the free movement of CARICOM nationals within the Caribbean Single Market and Economy (CSME).[5] Assuming that intra-regional migrations would increase under the conditions associated with climate-induced environmental change, then the direction of net migration would predictably be from the most vulnerable to the most economically robust and resilient states.

THE IMPLICATIONS OF ENVIRONMENT-INDUCED MIGRATION

The potential consequences of migration for the viability of the places of origin and destination need to be assessed to evaluate the implications if it should occur in response to the effects of climate change. Therefore, there is a need to understand the connections between environmental processes and the broader societal transformations of which migration is a part.

SOCIO-ECOSYSTEMS AND MIGRATION NEXUS

The concept of socio-ecological systems provides a theoretical framework for an analysis of environmental processes and migration, and is defined as a complex system characterized by multiple, stochastic or non-linear interactions between elements of the system (Gallopın 2006, cited in Warner 2010). Central to this is the idea that human action and ecological structures are linked and dependent upon each other; so, if one collapses, the other collapses also. The threshold of vulnerability and resilience determines sustainability of the overall system. This is an important consideration, not only to increase the explanatory power of the underlying theoretical constructs, but also to influence current debates at the interface of global environmental governance.

This conceptualization of the socio-ecosystem and migration nexus considers environmentally induced migration to be part of complex human-environmental systems (Barnett and Jones 2002; Berkes et al. 2003; Young et al. 2008). Ecosystems are shaped by human activities, but they also impose constraints on human activities by affecting ecosystem services (cyclical restoration of water, soil and air), thus conditioning economic activities and societal livelihoods. Migration can represent a response to changing environmental conditions, such as a farmer's choice to migrate due to unpredictable weather conditions or deteriorating ecosystems that cause crops to fail and make livelihood prospects insecure. Tourism is also dependent on predictable weather, as well as the natural functioning of ecosystem services, such as the absorption of waste and sequestration of carbon dioxide (see Thomas-Hope and Jardine-Comrie 2006). Serious degradation of the required amenities or environmental services would lead to eventual collapse of the industry if the process went unchecked.

Successive waves of large-scale migration have consequences for reduced socio-ecosystem resilience and ultimately decline or even total degradation of livelihood activities in places from which migrants leave. Once the people who are the economically and socially active have left, the previously weak socio-ecosystem will eventually collapse, thus increasing the propensity for further migration. This trend was found in Jamaica in communities where land was left idle and later became ruinate following the migration of the farmer (Thomas-Hope 1993). Therefore, it is important that proactive policies and adaptive mechanisms are put in place to build resilience in vulnerable localities in anticipation of such possible collapse before the threshold is reached or even dangerously approached.

MIGRATION AS ADAPTATION TO ENVIRONMENTAL CHANGE AND HAZARDS

An evaluation of migration as part of the adaptive response to environmental change involves addressing the question of whether migration can relieve the environmentally induced hazardous situation without impairing the sustainability of the locality or island from which people leave. This also raises questions about the impact of such migration on the destinations.

IMPLICATIONS FOR PLACES OF ORIGIN

Taking a pragmatic approach to evaluating migration as a means of advancing sustainability in the socio-ecological system, a pertinent question is whether the poorest communities and households would be the most likely to migrate from the most vulnerable localities of a country or region. Past evidence indicates that the short answer is no: the poorer cohorts with least assets living in difficult or degraded environments do not migrate as freely and in numbers as do the richer in less hostile environmental situations. Furthermore, migration flows are dominated by the young, educated and economically active cohorts of the population. It has been found in other parts of the Global South that the poor and the elderly remain 'trapped' in the villages and continue to rely on agriculture as their main source of income, despite deteriorating conditions (Burke and Moench 2000). This has been supported by research in different Caribbean states, which showed that whereas the propensity for migration was highest in the poorest and least accessible locations, the actual migrations chiefly occurred from the urban areas and the better financially resourced households (Thomas-Hope 1992; 2002). So, in the event of large-scale, unmanaged migration, the poorest and least accessible will be left in places negatively affected by climate-induced environmental change, with limited resources. Both people and place will be relegated to conditions of reduced viability and, commensurately, increased vulnerability to risk.

An alternative view is based on an assessment by some organizations and academics who point out the role that migration may play in helping communities adapt, using the resources from migrant remittances (International Organization for Migration 2007; Barnett and Jones 2002). Remittances are highly valuable at the national level as a source of revenue and as foreign exchange. The contribution of remittances to GDP (2022) in the Caribbean ranged from more than 22 per cent in the case of Haiti and Jamaica, to between 7 and 10 per cent in the Dominican Republic (9 per cent), Dominica (8.5 per cent), and St Vincent and the Grenadines (7.3 per cent), to as low as 1.5 per cent in Barbados.[6] Although Constable (1917) found that 100 per cent of the women in her study in rural Jamaica used remittances for supporting their farming as well as for their household needs, the greatest proportion of the remittances to Jamaica, overall, does not go to the rural areas. In 2015, only 24 per cent of total remittances went to rural households, while 76 per cent went to urban centres. Furthermore, the higher proportion of remittances (55 per cent) went to the richest population sectors and 40 per cent to the poorest, with the rest to the middle-income cohorts (STATIN 2015, cited in Thomas-Hope 2018). Although remittances to the poor provide critical inputs for meeting the recipients' needs, and significant support for households facing the aftermath of disasters such as hurricane damage, they are typically irregularly received and in very small amounts, hence cannot be relied upon to promote sustainability at the community level in the long term.

Return of previous emigrants has also been cited as a positive aspect of migration for the home location. The problem is that generally, those who return are the elderly who have retired, and to rural locations. As a consequence, their impact in stimulating sustainable economic growth at such locations, other than house constructions, is variable and often minimal. An exception to this occurs with respect to seasonal labour migration for employment in farmwork or hospitality, mentioned above. This type of short-term migration has encouraged the return of financial capital to rural areas, where employment opportunities are limited (Thomas-Hope and Jardine-Comrie 2011a; 2011b). Strategic investment of these financial and human resources should be made to support adaptation to changing environmental conditions, thus building resilience. Should these resources be managed to focus on mitigating hazardous environmental trends in the most vulnerable areas, short-term cyclical migration could be geared to building the resilience of such communities and localities. For this to materialize, intentional policies and projects would be required.

IMPLICATIONS FOR MIGRATION DESTINATIONS

The view has been expressed that migration is a maladaptive response to negative environmental trends because it may trigger increased risk for the migrants themselves, as well as for the centres in which they settle (Oliver-Smith 2009). At destinations of large migrations, existing social and economic stressors could be exacerbated, whether within the same country or at international and intra-regional destinations. This has the potential for negatively affecting livelihoods at the destinations and diminishing the agency of the migrants themselves. It could also engender political or social upheaval, and generate other negative consequences for the migrants' culture and security (Bunce et al. 2010, cited in Revi and Satterwaite et al. 2013).

These challenges highlight the need for formal structures to manage the settlement of incomers effectively to avoid negative consequences, including the emergence of xenophobia and social unrest.

IMPLICATIONS FOR GOVERNANCE: ENVIRONMENTAL CHANGE, MIGRATION AND SUSTAINABILITY GOALS

With environmental changes taking place at previously unprecedented levels, there is urgency in generating plans guided by current predictions of the timing for climatic conditions to move outside the range of historical variability (Taylor and Stephenson 2017). The extent and ways in which migration should be seen as a component of such planning gains relevance in light of the inclusion of migration and displacement in the UNFCCC climate negotiations in mid-2008, and for consideration within the context of a post-2012 adaptation framework.

In the Caribbean, emphasis has been on mitigation of risk of disaster, with negligible attention paid to long-term adaptation and assessment of the potential implications. As a consequence, no serious consideration has been given to the effects of the ad hoc, spontaneous long-term migration which could occur with deteriorating environmental conditions.

MITIGATION OF RISK OF CLIMATE-INDUCED ENVIRONMENTAL CHANGE IMPACTS

Three frameworks have been developed for disaster risk reduction (DRR) in the region: the Comprehensive Disaster Management Strategic Framework; the CARICOM Regional Framework for Achieving Development Resilient to Climate Change, 2011–2021; and the Jagdeo Initiative. In addition, the Caribbean Drought and Precipitation Monitoring Network was established in 2009 after a prolonged drought that year.

Regional frameworks are a first step in building the necessary resilience to be sure, but the most pressing need is for countries to develop strong national initiatives as well. National Climate Change Policy Frameworks to integrate both disaster risk reduction and adaptation have been developed for Jamaica and St Lucia (Government of Jamaica 2015; Government of St Lucia 2015). Some other countries have developed mechanisms to attempt to monitor climate change, such as the Climate Change Focal Point Networks in Trinidad and Tobago, and Jamaica (Government of Trinidad and Tobago 2015; Government of Jamaica 2015). In the case of Dominica, there is awareness of the need for an integrated approach to climate change, but no relevant policy has been developed (Government of the Commonwealth of Dominica 2015). In St Vincent and the Grenadines, a Pilot Programme for Climate Resilience to include data collection, modelling and analysis lacked the funding to proceed (Government of St Vincent and the Grenadines 2015).

Barbados, which is physically water deficient, is reported to manage its water provision relatively effectively, principally as part of a sectoral approach to integrate water management with tourism (Burke and Moench 2000, cited in Wolfe and Brooks; Government of Barbados 2015). However, it is estimated that across the Caribbean, some 85 per cent of wastewater is piped directly into the ocean untreated, producing harmful algal blooms and killing coral reefs, thus harming the all-important tourism industry. Expensive, desalinated water resources are becoming more important, accounting for as much as 70 per cent of the water in Antigua and Barbuda. Yet, the adoption of less expensive, decentralized wastewater treatment operated by alternative energy sources such as the sun, wind or waves could produce a supply of water for uses such as agricultural irrigation, thus protecting limited supplies of potable water (Fluence News Team 2019).

The emphasis throughout the region in terms of DRR has been in responding to floods and storms. Policy and planning to deal effectively with drought are hindered by weak governance, lack of finance and poorly coordinated land management (FAO 2013). Although there would be high costs involved to adequately strengthen capacities, these could be overcome by strong political will that encourages the participation in policy and planning processes of all stakeholders. Such measures are essential for enabling the sustainability of water supplies to face the forthcoming and worsening climate-induced challenges.

ROLE OF MIGRATION AS PART OF THE ADAPTIVE STRATEGY IN POLICY AND PLANNING

Migration is generally absent from policies and plans for adaptation to climate-induced change in the Caribbean. Population mobility has only been conceptualized, and legal frameworks developed, in terms of dispersal in the event of sudden-onset disaster (Francis 2021). The absence of migration in deliberations is a significant omission, given the high propensity for it in many parts of the region. Moreover, studies have found that it is often a proactive risk-diversification strategy for households facing environmental stressors amidst a range of other risks that must be managed at the same time (Berkes et al. 2003). The critical issue is that while this may provide a solution for specific households, at the wider community or national level a number of negative outcomes could result from ad hoc migration, increasing the vulnerability of the locality abandoned and of the migrants themselves. Alternatively, proactively planned migration can reduce vulnerability by including possibilities for diversifying livelihoods, thus minimizing the extent of net outflow.

Reports that focus on SIDS globally have described climate pressures, in particular the lack of fresh water and loss of land as sea levels rise as primary drivers of migration. Some SIDS in the Pacific have already begun planning for future mass migrations of their citizens as an adaptive measure to mitigate the effects of the worsening conditions (Gheuens et al. 2019). In general, however, governments have not widely viewed migration as an adaptive strategy, and very few National Adaptation Programmes of Action mention migration or relocation options as a solution to environmental degradation (Martin 2009, cited in Warner et al. 2010).

The United Nations University Institute for Water, Environment and Health (UNU-INWEH) 2020 report examined global agreements, institutions and policies on migration to provide an exaggerated outlook as to how international and inter-agency cooperation agreements and policies either reflected or were missing climate crises as direct or indirect triggers of migration. This was the concern behind the new directives related to migration governance in the New York Declaration and the Global Compact for Migration (Nagabhatla et al. 2020). The report recommends an enhanced focus on migration arguing that, as an adaptive strategy, migration would maximize the interconnectedness with the Sustainable Development Goals 5, 6, 13 and 16 that aim to strengthen capacities related to water, gender, climate and institutions. But this approach does not take into account the consideration that any large migration relative to population size could have negative socio-psychological effects on the community left behind. It could also have the effect of depressing the local economy because of reduced activity and less money in circulation. The size of the place (including some islands) and extent of vulnerability of the specific community, as well as of the general resilience of the state, are critical in determining the threshold of collapse. This largely depends on the numbers relative to population that migrate and, importantly, the demographics of those who leave and those who remain.

In summary, although relocation of both temporarily displaced persons and long-term migrants from SIDS has been highlighted in the international arena, no concrete measures are in place to address concerns about the future sustainability of the places from which migrations occur or those to which they would go. The narratives so far discussed point to the fragmented nature of existing governance mechanisms and their current unpreparedness to proactively manage the links between migration and socio-ecosystems in promoting sustainability.

CONCLUSION

The Caribbean is not a major contributor to climate change, but a major victim of its effects. Therefore, the need for adaptive strategies to address the climate-induced impacts is unquestionable, and multiple approaches are clearly required.

As indicated in an earlier section, vulnerabilities are embedded in the existing locations of settlement and infrastructures, and economic dependency on fragile sectors that require climatic reliability. Additionally, vulnerability is inherent in widespread poverty manifested in limited financial and social assets – in particular, education and skill-based capabilities. Mitigating the effects of climatic conditions and hazardous events on infrastructure, settlements and economic sectors have to move along in tandem with addressing the issue of reducing poverty. Further, given the region's existing high propensity for internal and international migration, the source locations, volumes and directions of spontaneous, large-scale migrations under the predicted conditions of environmental change should be taken into account. These measures are critical aspects of adaptation to future environmental conditions in order to avoid the negative effects of population movement, and promote conditions that would have positive implications for viability and sustainability of places affected. To date, not only are the processes relating to environmentally induced migration unclear but also, conceptualization of the consequences of such migration for the places of origin and destination is lacking.

One could argue no single solution exists to this complex issue with so many ecological and human ramifications. A major challenge is to determine the ways and sequence in which the various approaches to reducing vulnerability and enhancing resilience should be included in an overall adaptive strategy. In order to optimize the benefits, those decisions have to be guided by the objective of enhancing the prospects of sustainable futures for individual states, and also for the region as a whole.

NOTES

1. For example, on 8 April 2021 and the days following, the La Soufriere volcano in St Vincent erupted – the first time since 1979, and the most dangerous since 1902. Roughly sixteen thousand people who lived in communities close to the volcano were evacuated under government orders the previous day. On the smaller island of Montserrat, after three hundred and fifty years of being dormant, the volcanic Soufriere hills became active in 1995. The eruption was associated with powerful explosions and large pyroclastic flows from dome collapse. A large part of the island was destroyed, including the capital, Plymouth, and the population of some fifteen thousand persons were evacuated to the northern part of the island. http//:www.VolcanoDiscovery. com montserrat.html). Thereafter, two thirds of the population migrated to neighbouring Caribbean countries and the United Kingdom. In 2010, Haiti experienced an earthquake (measuring 7 on the Richter Scale) which caused the deaths of around three hundred and sixteen thousand people, and damage amounting to about 125 per cent of Haiti's GDP (http://www. learnodo-newtonic.com/2010-haiti-earthquake-facts).

2. The Paris Agreement goal is to limit global warming this century to well below 2°C, and pursuing 1.5°C. However, government pledges under the agreement, known as Nationally Determined Contributions, are still woefully inadequate. Predicted emissions in 2030 leave the world on the path

to a 3.2°C increase this century, even if all unconditional contributions are fully implemented (*Emissions Gap Report*, UNEP, 2020).

3.   https://en.wikipedia.org/wiki/Hurricane_Maria

4.   Poverty headcount ratio at US$5.50 a day is the percentage of the population living on less than $5.50 a day at 2011 international prices. As a result of revisions in PPP exchange rates, poverty rates for individual countries cannot be compared with poverty rates reported in earlier editions. ("poverty in the Caribbean statistics" – search on bing.com).

5.   The Revised Treaty of Chaguaramas establishing the Caribbean Community, including the CARICOM Single Market and Economy (CSME), was signed in 2001. This economic union is comprised of the following twelve states – Antigua and Barbuda, Barbados, Belize, Dominica, Grenada, Guyana, Jamaica, Suriname, St Kitts and Nevis, St Lucia, St Vincent and the Grenadines, and Trinidad and Tobago. The CSME permits the free movement of nationals without a work permit – including wage earners and the self-employed at the time of settlement. Individuals that qualify for free movement within CSME include university graduates of recognized universities, artists, musicians, media workers, athletes, nurses, teachers, artisans with Caribbean Vocational Qualifications and holders of associate degrees or comparable qualifications.

6.   World Bank data: https://www.economicsonline.co.uk/Global_economics/Remittances.html.

REFERENCES

Afifi, T., and K. Warner. 2008. "The impact of environmental degradation on migration flows across countries." Working Paper No. 5/2008, UNU-EHS, Working Paper Series. Bonn: United Nations University, Institute for Environment and Human Security. http://www.ehs.unu.edu/article:476?menu=94.

Bakewell, O. 2011. "Some reflections on structure and agency in migration theory." *Journal of Ethnic and Migration Studies* 36 (10): 1689–708.

Barnett, J., and R. Jones. 2002. "Forced migration: The influence of environmental security." *Global Change* 7 (4): 3.

Berkes, F., J. Colding, and C. Folke, eds. 2003. *Navigating Social-Ecological Systems: Building Resilience for Complexity and Change.* Cambridge: Cambridge University Press.

Birthwright, A. 2017. "Liquid Gold or Poverty in a Cup? The Vulnerability of High Mountain and Blue Mountain Coffee Farmers to the Effects of Climate Change." In *Climate Change and Food Security: Africa and the Caribbean,* edited by Elizabeth Thomas-Hope, 70–83. London: Routledge.

Black. R., W. Neil, B. Adger, W. Nigel, C. Arnell, S. Dercond, A. Geddes, S. David, and J. Thomas. 2011. "The effect of environmental change on human migration." *Global Environmental Change* 21S: S3–S11.

Bunce, M., S. Rosendo, and K. Brown. 2010. "Perceptions of climate change, multiple stressors and livelihoods on marginal African coasts." *Environment, Development and Sustainability,* 12 (3): 407–40.

Burke, J., and M. Moench. 2000. *Groundwater and Society: Resources, Tensions, Opportunities.* Sales no. E.99.II.A.1. New York: United Nations.

Campbell, J.D., et al. 2010. "Future climate of the Caribbean from a regional climate model." *International Journal of Climatology* 31 (12): 1866–78. http://doi.wiley. com/10.1002/joc.2200.

Constable, A. 2017. "Climate change perceptions and attitudes: Strategies for food security among female farmers in Sherwood Content, Trelawny." In *Climate Change and Food Security: Africa and the Caribbean,* edited by Elizabeth Thomas-Hope, 115–27. London: Routledge.

Fluence News Team. 2019. Drought Hits the Caribbean. https://www.fluencecorp. com/drought hits the Caribbean.

Food and Agricultural Organization. 2013. "Climate Change and Agriculture in Jamaica: Agriculture Support Analysis." http://www.fao.org/3/a-i3417e.pdf.

———. 2014. *Statistical Yearbook 2014: Latin American and the Caribbean: Food and Agriculture.* Santiago, Chile: FAO.

———. 2016. "The Caribbean must prepare for increased drought due to climate change." FAO News, 21 June 2016, Barbados. http://www.fao.org/americas/ noticias/ver/en/c/419202.

Francis, A.R. 2021. *Global Governance of Environmental Mobility: Regional Paper Latin America & the Caribbean.* Zolberg Institute on Migration and Mobility.

Gallopı́n, G.C. 2006. "Linkages between vulnerability, resilience, and adaptive capacity." *Global Environmental Change* 16: 293–303.

Gheuens, J., N. Nagabhatla, and E.D.P. Perera. 2019. "Disaster-risk, water security challenges and strategies in small island developing states (SIDS)." *Water* 11 (4): 637. https://doi.org/10.3390/w11040637.

Government of Barbados. 2015. Intended Nationally Determined Contribution, UNFCCC. Bridgetown.

Government of the Commonwealth of Dominica. 2015. Intended Nationally Determined Contribution, UNFCCC.

Government of the Commonwealth of Dominica, 2017. Post-Disaster Needs Assessment Hurricane Maria, 18 September 2017. https://resilientcaribbean.car-icom.org/wp-content/uploads/2017/11/DOMINICA-EXECUTIVE-SUMMARY. pdf.

Government of Jamaica. 2015. Intended Nationally Determined Contribution, UNFCCC.

Government of St Lucia. 2015. Intended Nationally Determined Contribution, UNFCCC.

Government of St Vincent and the Grenadines. 2015. Intended Nationally Determined Contribution, UNFCCC.

Government of Trinidad and Tobago. 2015. Intended Nationally Determined Contribution, UNFCCC.

Granvorka, C., and E. Strobl. (n.d.). "The impact of hurricanes strikes on the tourism in the Caribbean." Université des Antilles et de la Guyane (CEREGMIA), Ecole Polytechnique and the Sir Arthur Lewis Institute of Social and Economic Studies. https://sta.uwi.edu/conferences/09/salises/documents/C Granvorka.pdf.

Guyana Sugar Corporation. 2009. "Vulnerability and capacity assessment: impacts of climate change on Guyana's Agriculture Sector." Belmopan: Caribbean Community Climate Change Centre.

Heslop-Thomas, C., P. Fuller, R. Chambers, E. Galbraith, T.K. Jeffrey-Biggs, J. Francis, A. Thomas, and C. Brett. 2015. "The Impact of Drought on 2014 Prices of Select Food Items in Jamaica." Paper presented to the conference on Climate Change, Resilience and Food Security, Kingston, Jamaica, April 2015.

Inter-American Development Bank. 2019. IDB news releases, 15 November. https://www.iadb.org/en/news/damages-and-other-impacts-bahamas-hurricane-dorian.

Intergovernmental Panel on Climate Change. 2012. "Managing the Risks of Extreme Events and Disasters to Advance Climate Change Adaptation. A Special Report of Working Groups I and II of the Intergovernmental Panel on Climate Change." [Field, C.B., V. Barros, T.F. Stocker, D. Qin, D.J. Dokken, K.L. Ebi, M.D. Mastrandrea et al., eds. Cambridge, London and New York: Cambridge University Press.

Johnson-Bhola, L. 2017. "Smallholder adaptation to climate change." In *Climate Change and Food Security: Africa and the Caribbean*, edited by Elizabeth Thomas-Hope, 94–104. London: Routledge.

Karmalkar, A.V., M. New, M.A. Taylor, J. Campbell, and T. Stephenson. 2013. "A review of observed and projected changes in climate for the islands in the Caribbean." *Atmosfera* 26 (2): 283–309.

Kinlock, R., E. Thomas-Hope, A. Jardine-Comrie, B. Timmers, T. Ferguson, and C. McCordic. 2019. *The State of Household Food Security in Kingston, Jamaica*. Hungry Cities Report No. 15. Centre for African Cities, University of Cape Town, South Africa & the Balsillie School of International Affairs, Waterloo, Canada: The Hungry Cities Partnership.

Martin, S.F. 2009. "Managing environmental migration." In *Migration, Environment and Climate Change: Assessing the Evidence,* edited by Frank Laczko and C. Aghazarm. Geneva: International Organization for Migration.

Nagabhatla, N., P. Pouramin, R. Brahmbhatt, C. Fioret, T. Glickman, B. Newbold, and V. Smakhtin. 2020. *Water and Migration: A Global Overview.* United Nations University Institute for Water, Environment and Health (UNU-INWEH).

Oliver-Smith, A. 2009. *Nature, Society, and Population Displacement: Toward an Understanding of Environmental Migration and Social Vulnerability.* InterSecTions No. 8, UNU-EHS, Bonn.

Planning Institute of Jamaica. 2015. *Economic and Social Survey of Jamaica 2014.* Kingston: PIOJ.

Portes, A., and J. De Wind. 2007. *Rethinking Migration: New Theoretical and Empirical Perspectives.* Oxford: Berghahn.

Pulwarty, R.S., L.A. Nurse, and U.O. Trotz. 2010. "Caribbean islands in a changing climate: Issues and trends." *Geography Compass* 9 (3): 97–114.

Revi, A., D. Satterthwaite, F. Aragón-Durand, J. Corfee-Morlot, B.R. Kiunsi, M. Pelling, D. Roberts, and W. Solecki. 2013. "Anthropogenic and Natural Radiative Forcing." In *AR5 Climate Change 2013: The Physical Science Basis.* Contributing authors: J. da Silva, D. Dodman, A. Maskrey, S.P. Gajjar, and R. Tuts. Geneva: Intergovernmental Panel on Climate Change (IPCC).

Rhiney, K., A. Eitzinger, A. Farrell, and M. Taylor. 2017. "Assessing the vulnerability of Caribbean farmers to climate change impacts: A comparative study of cocoa farmers in Jamaica and Trinidad." In *Climate Change and Food Security: Africa and the Caribbean,* edited by Elizabeth Thomas-Hope, 19–69. London: Routledge.

Senior, C. and D. Manley. 1955. *A Report of Jamaican Migration to Great Britain.* Kingston: Government Printing Office.

Simpson, M.C., J.F. Clarke, D.J. Scott, M. New, A. Karmalkar, O.J. Day, M. Taylor, S. Gossling, M. Wilson, D. Chadee, et al. 2012. *CARIBSAVE Climate Change Risk Atlas (CCCRA) – Jamaica.* DFID, AusAID and The CARIBSAVE Partnership, St Michael, Barbados.

Statistical Institute of Jamaica. 2015. *Jamaica Survey of Living Conditions 2015.* Kingston: Planning Institute of Jamaica and STATIN.

Taylor, M., J. Jones, and T. Stephenson. 2017. "Climate Change and the Caribbean: Trends and Implications." In *Climate Change and Food Security: Africa and the Caribbean,* Elizabeth Thomas-Hope, 31–56. London: Routledge.

Thomas-Hope, E. 1992. *Explanation in Caribbean Migration.* London: Macmillan.

———. 1993. "Population mobility and land assets in hill farming areas of Jamaica." *Caribbean Geography* 4 (1): 49–63.

———. 1998. "Globalization and the development of a Caribbean migration culture." In *Globalized Identities,* edited by Mary Chamberlain, 188–200. London, Routledge.

———. 2002. *Caribbean Migration.* Kingston: University of the West Indies Press.

———, ed. 2017. *Climate Change and Food Security: Africa and the Caribbean.* London: Routledge.

———. 2018. *Migration and Development: A Jamaica Country Profile*. Geneva: International Organization for Migration.

Thomas-Hope, Elizabeth, and A. Jardine-Comrie. 2006. "Valuation of environmental resources for tourism in small island developing states: Implications for planning in Jamaica." *International Development Planning Review* 29: 93–112.

———. 2011a. *Maximizing the Benefits of Migration for Sustainable Development and Food Security: Jamaica*. Rome: Food and Agricultural Organization of the United Nations.

———. 2011b. *Maximizing the Benefits of Migration for Sustainable Development and Food Security: St. Vincent and the Grenadines*. Rome: Food and Agricultural Organization of the United Nations.

Trotz, U., and S. Lindo. 2013. "Vulnerability and resilience building in CARICOM countries." *Small Island Digest* 2: 25–39.

United Nations Development Programme. n.d. "Climate Change Adaptation: Latin America and the Caribbean." UNDP Climate Change Adaptation. https://www.adaptation-undp.org/explore/caribbean.

United Nations Framework Convention on Climate Change. 2002. *Report of the Conference of the Parties on its Seventh Session*. http://unfccc.int/resource/docs/cop7/13a01.pdf.

———. 2011. "Fact sheet: Climate change science – the status of climate change science today." UNFCCC.

———. 2018. "UNFCCC WIM Task Force on Displacement Activities III. 1–3: Report for Final Review" (Warsaw International Mechanism Task Force on Displacement). Internal Displacement Monitoring Centre, Geneva. https://unfccc.int/sites/default/files/resource/WIM%20TFD%20III_1-3%20IDMC.pdf.

Warner, K., and F. Laczko. 2008. "Migration, environment and development: New directions for research." In *International Migration and Development, Continuing the Dialogue: Legal and Policy Perspectives*, edited by J. Chamie and L. Dall'Oglio. New York and Geneva: International Organization for Migration and Center for Migration Studies.

K. Warner, M. Stal, O. Dun, and T. Afifi. 2009. "Researching Environmental Change and Migration: Evaluation of EACH-FOR Methodology and Application in 23 Case Studies. Worldwide." In *Migration, Environment and Climate Change: Assessing the Evidence*, edited by Frank Laczko and C. Aghazarm, 197–244. Geneva: International Organization for Migration.

K. Warner, M. Hamza, A. Oliver-Smith, F. Renaud, and A. Julca. 2010. "Climate change, environmental degradation and migration." *Natural Hazards* 55: 689–715.

Wolfe, S., and D.B. Brooks. 2003. "Water scarcity: An alternative view and its implications for policy and capacity building." *Natural Resources Forum* 27: 99–107.

World Travel and Tourism Council. 2016. "Travel & Tourism Economic Impact 2016: Caribbean." Available at: http://www.wttc.org/-media/files/reports/economic%20impact %20research/ regions%202016/caribbean2016.pdf.

Young, O.R., L.A. King, and L.A. Schroeder, eds. 2008. *Institutions and Environmental Change: Principal Findings, Applications, and Research Frontiers*. Boston: The MIT Press.

Zuñiga, R.A., and J. Garrido. 2020. "Internal displacement due to disasters in Latin America and the Caribbean." In *Change, Hazards and Adaptation Options: Handling the impacts of a changing climate*, Chapter 21, 1st ed. https://doi.org/10.1007/978-3-030-37425-9.

Appendices

APPENDIX 1

Embassies of China and the United States and Overseas Offices of Taiwan in the Caribbean and Central America (September 2020)

Country	Embassy of China	Overseas Office of Taiwan	Embassy of the United States
Antigua & Barbuda	X		
The Bahamas	X		X
Barbados	X		X
Belize		X	X
Cuba	X		X
Dominica	X		
Dominican Republic	X		X
Guyana	X		X
Grenada	X		
Haiti		X	X
Jamaica	X		X
St Kitts & Nevis		X	
St Lucia		X	
St Vincent		X	
Suriname	X		X
Trinidad & Tobago	X		X
Costa Rica	X		X
El Salvador	X		X
Guatemala		X	X
Honduras		X	X
Nicaragua	X		X
Panama	X		X

APPENDIX 2

Table 4.8: Select macro-economic and fiscal indicators in Caribbean countries, 2020–2022

Countries	Real GDP growth %			Government primary balance % GDP			Gross government debt % GDP		
	2020	2021	2022	2020	2021	2022	2020	2021	2022
Antigua	(17.5)	6.6	8.5	(3.7)	(2.3)	(1.2)	98.2	96.3	86.2
Aruba	(24.0)	27.6	10.5	(11.1)	(4.8)	3.4	112.3	101.8	90.1
Bahamas	(23.5)	17.0	14.4	(4.4)	(9.0)	(1.3)	75.3	100.0	88.9
Barbados	(13.3)	(0.2)	9.8	(1.0)	(0.9)	2.5	148.8	135.1	122.5
Belize	(13.4)	15.2	12.7	(6.7)	(1.8)	0.9	101.4	80.1	63.4
Dominica	(16.6)	6.9	5.7	(5.6)	(6.2)	(0.4)	113.1	107.2	98.5
Grenada	(13.8)	4.7	6.4	(2.6)	2.1	2.2	71.4	69.9	63.6
Jamaica	(9.9)	4.6	5.2	3.5	6.8	5.8	109.7	94.2	77.1
St Kitts-Nevis	(14.6)	(0.9)	8.8	(1.7)	6.8	(2.0)	68.0	69.1	61.1
St Lucia	(23.6)	11.3	15.7	(7.7)	(2.2)	1.5	94.2	82.9	74.2
St Vincent	(3.7)	0.8	5.5	(2.9)	(5.0)	(7.2)	79.5	90.0	87.9
Caribbean: Tourism dependent	(14.6)	9.1	9.0	(1.9)	(0.4)	2.2	100.6	98.6	85.5
Guyana	43.5	20.1	62.3	(7.3)	(6.8)	(4.9)	51.1	43.2	26.0
Suriname	(15.9)	(2.7)	1.0	(8.4)	(0.6)	1.1	147.8	119.6	120.1
Trinidad and Tobago	(9.1)	(1.0)	1.5	(8.6)	(5.4)	2.7	62.3	61.6	51.0
Caribbean: Commodity exporters	3.0	4.8	25.4	(8.3)	(5.3)	0.2	68.6	62.5	48.4
Haiti	(3.3)	(1.8)	(1.7)	(2.2)	(2.2)	(1.7)	22.0	25.6	23.9
Caribbean: Non-tourism dependent	0.7	2.5	17.1	(6.3)	(4.1)	(0.4)	53.2	48.3	40.9

Source: International Monetary Fund. *Regional Economic Outlook: Western Hemisphere –Securing Low Inflation and Nurturing Potential Growth.*" Washington, DC (October 2023).
Data extracted from Appendix Table 1. Western Hemisphere – Main Economic Indicators (p.31) and Appendix Table 2. Western Hemisphere –Main Fiscal Indicators (p.32)
(Regional aggregates in bold asterisks for GDP growth are PPP/GDP weighted averages.
Regional aggregates for fiscal indicators (Government primary balance and gross debt) are Fiscal Year US$ nominal GDP weighted averages).

APPENDIX 3

Table 8.1: Details on chosen variables

Variable	Name	Source	Frequency	Description
Real effective exchange rate	REER	IFS	Annual	CPI-based index, 1995=100.
Real oil prices	ROP	FRED	Annual	WTI Oil Prices – real US$ per barrel
Productivity differential	DIFF	WDI, ILO	Annual	The trade-weighted GDP per capita PPP (International $) differential

Contributors

DILLON ALLEYNE, PhD, is Professor of Applied Economics and Honorary Research Fellow, Sir Arthur Lewis Institute of Social and Economic Studies, UWI, Mona. Interim Director of the Fiscal Research Centre (FRC), UWI, Mona. He focuses on public finance issues.

RICHARD L. BERNAL, PhD, former Ambassador to the USA and Organization of American States and Professor of Practice at the Sir Arthur Lewis Institute of Social and Economic Studies, as well as former Pro Vice-Chancellor, Global Affairs at The University of the West Indies. Recent publications include *Dragon in the Caribbean. China's Global Re-Positioning. Challenges and Opportunities for the Caribbean* (2016).

DONOVAN CAMPBELL is Professor of Geography and former Head of the Department of Geography and Geology at The UWI, Mona. He specializes in the use of place-based research techniques to explore climate impacts and adaptation strategies in farming and fishing communities across the Caribbean.

ABRAHAM ANTHONY CHEN is Professor Emeritus in the Department of Physics at The UWI, Mona. He was a lead author for the IPCC's Fourth Assessment Report, when it shared the 2007 Nobel Peace Prize with Vice President Al Gore.

PETER CLARKE is a professional engineer and the Managing Director of the Water Resources Authority, Jamaica. His training includes Water & Environmental Management, Waterworks Engineering, Construction Engineering, Project Management, Natural Resource Management, and Water Sustainability & Climate.

NATALIE DIETRICH JONES is Research Fellow at the Sir Arthur Lewis Institute of Social and Economic Studies, The University of the West Indies (Mona). Her research interests include geographies of the border, managed migration, and intra-regional migration in the Caribbean.

REGAN DEONANAN, PhD, is a Lecturer of Economics at The U.W.I., St. Augustine. His research specialty is International Finance and Development. He lectures undergraduate and postgraduate courses, and supervises MSc and PhD-level students.

WINSTON DOOKERAN, a graduate of The London School of Economics and a visiting scholar at Harvard University He recently completed his tenure as Professor of Practice at The University of the West Indies. He has written widely on Caribbean development and diplomacy. His book, *The Caribbean on the Edge*, published by The University of Toronto press is his latest publication, launched at The University of Manitoba, Canada and in Trinidad.

ELECIA EDWARDS-MYERS is a PhD candidate doing research on Theocentrism and the Church in fostering Pro-environmental values. She specializes in environmental stewardship research, policy development and implementation, and sustainable development planning. She engages in environmental stewardship programmes in faith-based communities

TALIA ESNARD, PhD, is a Sociologist and Senior Lecturer in the Department Head-Behavioural Sciences, Faculty of Social Sciences, The University of the West Indies (UWI), St. Augustine campus, Trinidad and Tobago. She specialises in areas of social equity and justice.

TOMASO FERRANDO, PhD, is an Associate Research Professor at the Faculty of Law and IOB, University of Antwerp. His action research works mostly concerns the legal construction of food systems, law in global value chains and the financialization of the green transition.

ORVILLE GREY holds a PhD in Environmental Biology from The UWI, Mona and is Head of Secretariat for the NAP Global Network at the International Institute for Sustainable Development. Orville's work focuses on climate change adaptation and climate finance.

HAMID GHANY is Professor of Constitutional Affairs and Parliamentary Studies and former SALISES Director, St. Augustine. He published *Constitutional Development in the Commonwealth Caribbean* (2018) and guest-edited the 2023 Social and Economic Studies edition on *"Republicanism in the Commonwealth Caribbean"*.

GEORGIANA GORDON-STRACHAN, PhD, is the Director of the Tropical Metabolism Research Unit, CAIHR, UWI. She is also Executive Director of the Lancet

Countdown's Regional Centre for Small Island Developing States on Health and Climate Change.

TANNICE A. HALL holds a PhD in Zoology and is a Lecturer in the Department of Life Sciences, UWI, Mona. Her research focus is on entomology, especially species diversity, ecology and host-plant relationships.

ROGER HOSEIN, PhD, is a senior lecturer and coordinator of the Trade and Economic Development Unit at the Department of Economics, The University of the West Indies, St Augustine. His specialty is in international trade, public spending, budgeting, fiscal responsibility and immigration economics.

RANDY KOON KOON, BSC, PhD, AFHEA, is a Lecturer in Renewable Energy at Coventry University, UK. His research interests are resource assessment and site suitability analysis for geothermal, solar PV, wind, hydropower, green hydrogen and energy storage design and exploration.

ROBERT CLIVE LANDIS, BSc, MSc, PhD, is Pro Vice Chancellor and Principal, The University of the West Indies, (The UWI), Cave Hill Campus, and Professor of Cardiovascular Research. Recent research interests have focused on emerging viruses and public health responses in a pandemic. Professor Landis served as chair of The UWI's Zika Task Force, and COVID-19 Task Force.

ALTHEA DIANNE LA FOUCADE, PhD, is Director of the Centre for Health Economics and a Senior Lecturer, Department of Economics at The University of the West Indies, St. Augustine, Trinidad and Tobago. Her research and publications focus on health economics, poverty, equity and social security.

STANLEY LALTA, PhD, is a Health Economist with substantial experience in policy research, teaching and consulting on Caribbean health matters. He is Advisor at HEU/Centre for Health Economics, UWI, Trinidad and Tobago with special interests in universal health, health financing and pharmaco-economics.

KRISTIN LOZANSKI, PhD, is Professor in the Department of Sociology at King's University College in London, Ontario, Canada. The findings from her extensive ethnographic research with Jamaican migrant workers in Niagara-on-the-Lake, Canada appear in *Tourism Geographies*, *ACME*, and *Social Inclusion*.

DON MARSHALL, PhD, is a Professor of International Political Economy and University Director of the Sir Arthur Lewis Institute of Social and Economic Studies at The University of the West Indies, Cave Hill. His current research projects focus on China, Globalisation, Offshore Financial Centres and Democracy in the Eastern Caribbean.

INDI McLYMONT-LAFAYETTE is a multi-award winning Journalist and Communications Specialist with her own company, CHANGE Communications Limited. She holds a BA in Media and Communications and an MA in Counselling Psychology. Her expertise includes communications for development focusing on climate change and gender.

PREEYA MOHAN is a Senior Research Fellow at The University of the West Indies, St. Augustine. She has conducted research on and is widely published in a range of topics focused around Caribbean growth and development.

SHIVA S. MOHAN, PhD, is a Research Fellow in the Canada Excellence Research Chair (CERC) in Migration & Integration program at Toronto Metropolitan University. He is a human geographer with research interests in irregular migration, critical geopolitics, and islands' mobilities.

ALICIA D. NICHOLLS, BSc, MSc, LL.B, is an international trade and development specialist. She is a Junior Research Fellow (Trade) and an adjunct lecturer at The University of the West Indies, Cave Hill, Barbados.

PATRICIA NORTHOVER, PhD, is a development economist and Senior Fellow at the Sir Arthur Lewis Institute of Social and Economic Studies, The University of the West Indies, Mona. (SALISES, UWI). She specializes in the philosophy of economics and critical development studies.

MACHEL PANTIN is an Associate Statistician at the Economic Commission for Latin America (ECLAC) subregional headquarters in Mexico. He previously worked as an economist at ECLAC Caribbean; his main research interests were the economics of tourism and sovereign debt sustainability.

HEATHER PINNOCK is a built environment specialist leading her own boutique development company, LUCEA Caribbean, which focuses on sustainable development, climate resilience and conscious living for tropical regions. She holds a BA in Architecture and an MSc in Development and Planning.

RUTH POTOPSINGH is an Energy and Environment specialist who holds a PhD in Sustainable Development. A leader in driving Jamaica's energy ambitions, her experience in government, academia and the private sector is complemented by sound business management and strategic thinking.

ALLISON RANGOLAN, former Chief Technical Director of the Environmental Foundation of Jamaica, has represented Jamaica at regional and international conservation financing and project management events. She is a director of the GraceKennedy Foundation, Chair of its Environment Committee and serves on several public boards in Jamaica.

DALE RANKINE is an agro-meteorologist who holds a PhD in Applied Physics. He is a member of the Climate Studies Group Mona researching climate and crop simulation modelling. Dale has conducted climate change impact assessments for the Caribbean Agriculture sector.

GREGORY ROBIN is a root and fruit crop agronomist. He worked with the Caribbean Agricultural Research and Development Institute (CARDI) for 39 years as their Representative in Jamaica, St. Vincent and the Grenadines, Antigua and Barbuda, and Dominica. He has a PhD in Molecular Pathology and extensive experience in Farming Systems.

LE-ANNE ROPER is an avid environmentalist and author of the book, "Rock-Solid Resilience to Natural Hazards: The Church Edition". Her contribution in this edited volume reflects her personal interest in Caribbean climate issues.

MIMI SHELLER, PhD, is Inaugural Dean of The Global School at Worcester Polytechnic Institute. Her recent books include *Island Futures: Caribbean Survival in the Anthropocene* (2020), *Mobility Justice* (2018), *Aluminum Dreams* (2014), and *Citizenship from Below* (2012).

IANTHE SMITH is the Principal Consultant/ Director at Environmental & Engineering Managers Ltd. Her wide expertise includes Environmental Impact Assessments, Indoor Air Quality Assessments, Water and Wastewater Engineering, Solid Waste Management, and Planning and Controlling Construction. She has a Master of Engineering in Environmental Engineering.

ROSE ANN SMITH, PhD, is a Lecturer and environmental researcher at the Department of Geography and Geology at The UWI, Mona. Her research focuses on climate justice, disaster risk management, political ecology and sustainable livelihoods, exploring the socio-political dimensions of environmental challenges.

NEKEISHA SPENCER, PhD, is a Senior Lecturer in the Department of Economics at The UWI, Mona. With a keen focus on environmental and climate economics, her research sheds light on pressing issues facing Caribbean economies, influencing both academic discourse and real-world applications.

TANNECIA S. STEPHENSON is Professor of Climate Science, Co-Director of the Climate Studies Group Mona and Deputy Dean of the Faculty of Science and Technology, The UWI, Mona. She is a lead author for the IPCC Sixth Assessment Report.

KIMBERLY STEPHENSON has researched Caribbean climate change for over 10 years through her association with the Climate Studies Group, Mona. She has contributed to UNFCCC and IPCC reports and assisted in recovery efforts for the critically endangered Jamaican Iguana.

MICHAEL TAYLOR is Professor of Climate Science, Co-Director of the Climate Studies Group Mona and Dean of the Faculty of Science and Technology, The UWI, Mona. He is a coordinating lead author for the IPCC's special report on *1.5 degrees.*

JEREMY TAYLOR, Kings Counsel, is the Senior Deputy Director of Public Prosecutions, Jamaica. He is a graduate of The UWI and the Norman Manley School of Law and has held several positions in Jamaica's judicial system.

KARL THEODORE, PROFESSOR EMERITUS is the former Director of the HEU, Health Economics Unit, Centre for Health Economics at The UWI. As professor of economics, he taught Public Sector Economics and Fiscal Policy and Development as well as Health Economics.

ELIZABETH THOMAS-HOPE, D.Phil. (Oxon), FRGS, CD, was the first James Seivright Moss-Solomon (Snr.) Professor of Environmental Management at UWI and is currently Professor Emerita in SALISES (Mona). Her research interests are in the fields of ecological justice, food security and Caribbean migration

CARLTON THOMAS JR is currently an MPhil student at The University of the West Indies, St Augustine. His current research interest includes industrial economics and the macroeconomic implications of decarbonisation in oil-rich countries.

BRIAN WALKER is a PhD Candidate at the University of Cambridge. His research explores how news coverage shapes and is shaped by experiences of (in)justice. He sits on the Global Alumni Board of the London School of Economics and Political Science.

FELICIA WHYTE has 15 years' experience as a climate and energy professional. She has an MPhil in Physics from The UWI, Mona and an MSc in Electrical Engineering and Sustainable Development from the University of Lille.

Index

A denotes appendix; *f* denotes figure; *n* denotes endnote; *t* denotes table

www.ingramcontent.com/pod-product-compliance
Lightning Source LLC
Chambersburg PA
CBHW022130020426
42334CB00015B/835